Arthur Symons
Poet, Critic, Vagabond

LEGENDA

LEGENDA is the Modern Humanities Research Association's book imprint for new research in the Humanities. Founded in 1995 by Malcolm Bowie and others within the University of Oxford, Legenda has always been a collaborative publishing enterprise, directly governed by scholars. The Modern Humanities Research Association (MHRA) joined this collaboration in 1998, became half-owner in 2004, in partnership with Maney Publishing and then Routledge, and has since 2016 been sole owner. Titles range from medieval texts to contemporary cinema and form a widely comparative view of the modern humanities, including works on Arabic, Catalan, English, French, German, Greek, Italian, Portuguese, Russian, Spanish, and Yiddish literature. Editorial boards and committees of more than 60 leading academic specialists work in collaboration with bodies such as the Society for French Studies, the British Comparative Literature Association and the Association of Hispanists of Great Britain & Ireland.

The MHRA encourages and promotes advanced study and research in the field of the modern humanities, especially modern European languages and literature, including English, and also cinema. It aims to break down the barriers between scholars working in different disciplines and to maintain the unity of humanistic scholarship. The Association fulfils this purpose through the publication of journals, bibliographies, monographs, critical editions, and the MHRA Style Guide, and by making grants in support of research. Membership is open to all who work in the Humanities, whether independent or in a University post, and the participation of younger colleagues entering the field is especially welcomed.

ALSO PUBLISHED BY THE ASSOCIATION

Critical Texts
Tudor and Stuart Translations • *New Translations* • *European Translations*
MHRA Library of Medieval Welsh Literature

MHRA Bibliographies
Publications of the Modern Humanities Research Association

The Annual Bibliography of English Language & Literature
Austrian Studies
Modern Language Review
Portuguese Studies
The Slavonic and East European Review
Working Papers in the Humanities
The Yearbook of English Studies

www.mhra.org.uk
www.legendabooks.com

STUDIES IN COMPARATIVE LITERATURE

Editorial Committee
Dr Duncan Large, British Centre for Literary Translation,
University of East Anglia (Chair)
Dr Emily Finer, University of St Andrews
Dr Dorota Goluch, Cardiff University
Dr Priyamvada Gopal, Churchill College Cambridge
Professor Timothy Mathews, University College London
Professor Wen-chin Ouyang, SOAS, London
Professor Elinor Shaffer, School of Advanced Study, London

Studies in Comparative Literature are produced in close collaboration with the British Comparative Literature Association, and range widely across comparative and theoretical topics in literary and translation studies, accommodating research at the interface between different artistic media and between the humanities and the sciences.

ALSO PUBLISHED IN THIS SERIES

20. *Aestheticism and the Philosophy of Death: Walter Pater and Post-Hegelianism*, by Giles Whiteley
21. *Blake, Lavater and Physiognomy*, by Sibylle Erle
22. *Rethinking the Concept of the Grotesque: Crashaw, Baudelaire, Magritte*, by Shun-Liang Chao
23. *The Art of Comparison: How Novels and Critics Compare*, by Catherine Brown
24. *Borges and Joyce: An Infinite Conversation*, by Patricia Novillo-Corvalán
25. *Prometheus in the Nineteenth Century: From Myth to Symbol*, by Caroline Corbeau-Parsons
26. *Architecture, Travellers and Writers: Constructing Histories of Perception*, by Anne Hultzsch
27. *Comparative Literature in Britain: National Identities, Transnational Dynamics 1800-2000*, by Joep Leerssen with Elinor Shaffer
28. *The Realist Author and Sympathetic Imagination*, by Sotirios Paraschas
29. *Iris Murdoch and Elias Canetti: Intellectual Allies*, by Elaine Morley
30. *Likenesses: Translation, Illustration, Interpretation*, by Matthew Reynolds
31. *Exile and Nomadism in French and Hispanic Women's Writing*, by Kate Averis
32. *Samuel Butler against the Professionals: Rethinking Lamarckism 1860–1900*, by David Gillott
33. *Byron, Shelley, and Goethe's Faust: An Epic Connection*, by Ben Hewitt
34. *Leopardi and Shelley: Discovery, Translation and Reception*, by Daniela Cerimonia
35. *Oscar Wilde and the Simulacrum: The Truth of Masks*, by Giles Whiteley
36. *The Modern Culture of Reginald Farrer: Landscape, Literature and Buddhism*, by Michael Charlesworth
37. *Translating Myth*, edited by Ben Pestell, Pietra Palazzolo and Leon Burnett
38. *Encounters with Albion: Britain and the British in Texts by Jewish Refugees from Nazism*, by Anthony Grenville
39. *The Rhetoric of Exile: Duress and the Imagining of Force*, by Vladimir Zorić
40. *From Puppet to Cyborg: Pinocchio's Posthuman Journey*, by Georgia Panteli
41. *Utopian Identities: A Cognitive Approach to Literary Competitions*, by Clementina Osti
43. *Sublime Conclusions: Last Man Narratives from Apocalypse to Death of God*, by Robert K. Weninger
44. *Arthur Symons: Poet, Critic, Vagabond*, edited by Elisa Bizzotto and Stefano Evangelista
45. *Scenographies of Perception: Sensuousness in Hegel, Novalis, Rilke, and Proust*, by Christian Jany
46. *Reflections in the Library: Selected Literary Essays 1926–1944*, by Antal Szerb
47. *Depicting the Divine: Mikhail Bulgakov and Thomas Mann*, by Olga G. Voronina
48. *Samuel Butler and the Evolutionary Debate: Science, Literature and Unconscious Memory*, by Cristiano Turbil
49. *Death Sentences: Literature and State Killing*, edited by Birte Christ and Ève Morisi
50. *Words Like Fire: Prophecy and Apocalypse in Apollinaire, Marinetti and Pound*, by James P. Leveque

Arthur Symons

Poet, Critic, Vagabond

Edited by
Elisa Bizzotto and Stefano Evangelista

Studies in Comparative Literature 44
Modern Humanities Research Association
2018

*Published by Legenda
an imprint of the Modern Humanities Research Association
Salisbury House, Station Road, Cambridge* CB1 2LA

*ISBN 978-1-78188-497-3 (HB)
ISBN 978-1-78188-498-0 (PB)*

First published 2018

All rights reserved. No part of this publication may be reproduced or disseminated or transmitted in any form or by any means, electronic, mechanical, photocopying, recording or otherwise, or stored in any retrieval system, or otherwise used in any manner whatsoever without written permission of the copyright owner, except in accordance with the provisions of the Copyright, Designs and Patents Act 1988, or under the terms of a licence permitting restricted copying issued in the UK by the Copyright Licensing Agency Ltd, Saffron House, 6–10 Kirby Street, London EC1N 8TS, *England, or in the USA by the Copyright Clearance Center, 222 Rosewood Drive, Danvers MA 01923. Application for the written permission of the copyright owner to reproduce any part of this publication must be made by email to legenda@mhra.org.uk.*

Disclaimer: Statements of fact and opinion contained in this book are those of the author and not of the editors or the Modern Humanities Research Association. The publisher makes no representation, express or implied, in respect of the accuracy of the material in this book and cannot accept any legal responsibility or liability for any errors or omissions that may be made.

Trademark notice: Product or corporate names may be trademarks or registered trademarks, and are used only for identification and explanation without intent to infringe.

© *Modern Humanities Research Association 2018*

Copy-Editor: Charlotte Brown

CONTENTS

❖

	Acknowledgements	ix
	List of Illustrations	x
	Introduction STEFANO EVANGELISTA AND ELISA BIZZOTTO	1
	PART I: ARTISTIC CONNECTIONS	
1	The Rhythms of Life and Art: Symons and the Interrelationship between Rodin's Sculpture and Modern Dance at the *Fin de Siècle* LENE ØSTERMARK-JOHANSEN	12
2	Symons, Beardsley, and the 'Minims and Crotchets' of Art JANE DESMARAIS	30
3	'A New Art of the Stage': Edward Gordon Craig and the Seven Arts of Arthur Symons JOHN STOKES	42
	PART II: INTERNATIONAL MEDIATIONS	
4	Symons and D'Annunzio: Decadence in Translation STEFANO EVANGELISTA	54
5	The Sinister Guest: Arthur Symons, Villiers de l'Isle-Adam, and Post-Victorian Decadence MATTHEW CREASY	69
6	Arthur Symons, a Mediator of Belgian Symbolist Writers CLÉMENT DESSY	84
7	Arthur Symons in France: Transnational Journalism and the French Reception BÉNÉDICTE COSTE	103
	PART III: PLACES AND CONNECTIONS	
8	'They Keep Mad People There': Symons and Venice NICHOLAS FREEMAN	118
9	Symons on Italy and the Metamorphoses of Aesthetic Travel Writing ELISA BIZZOTTO	131
10	'Against Civilisation': Symons, the Gypsy Lore, and Politicised Aestheticism KATHARINA HEROLD	145

11 'Serious in the Reality of his Devotion to Art': The Genealogy of
   Symons's Assessment in *A Study of Oscar Wilde*   160
   LAURA GIOVANNELLI

Bibliography   172
Index   187

ACKNOWLEDGEMENTS

Arthur Symons: Poet, Critic, Vagabond originates in a symposium on Arthur Symons that the editors held at the Università Iuav di Venezia in September 2015. Our first thanks go to the colleagues and friends who were present there, and especially to Angelo Maggi and Catherine Maxwell. We are grateful to the Department of Design and Planning in Complex Environments of Università Iuav di Venezia for granting funds towards publication, and to the English Faculty of the University of Oxford for covering reproduction costs. Ushashi Dasgupta provided crucial help with the editing. The Tate Archives kindly gave us permission to reproduce the cover illustration. Our gratitude also goes to the Archivi del Vittoriale degli italiani (Gardone Riviera, Italy), and to their curators Alessandro Tonacci and Roberta Valbusa, for allowing access to the D'Annunzio-Symons correspondence and giving permission to cite from it; and to the Gypsy Lore Society Collections at the University of Liverpool, and especially to Katy Hooper, Special Collections Librarian at the University of Liverpool Library. Last, but not least, our thanks go to Graham Nelson for his help and support.

December 2017

LIST OF ILLUSTRATIONS

FIG. 1.1. Loïe Fuller rehearsing, <https://commons.wikimedia.org/wiki/File:Houghton_MS_Thr_415_-_La_Loie_Fuller_rehearsing.jpg>.

FIG. 1.2. Isadora Duncan at the Theatre of Dionysus, Athens, <https://commons.wikimedia.org/wiki/Category:Isadora_Duncan#/media/File:Isadora_Duncan_1903.jpg>.

FIG. 6.1. Félicien Rops, *La Tentation de Saint Antoine*, 1878, Royal Library of Belgium, Brussels.

FIG. 6.2. Félicien Rops, *Impudence*, c. 1878, Royal Mariemont Museum, Morlanwelz.

FIG. 6.3. Théo Van Rysselberghe, design for the cover of *Les Aubes* by Émile Verhaeren (Brussels: Edmond Deman, 1898).

FIG. 10.1. Photograph of Arthur Symons (second from right) posing with his Romani friends ('Snapshots of Arthur Symons, with wife Rhoda, & with Gs.', possibly in Dora Yates's hand), University of Liverpool, Gypsy Lore Society Archive, GLS C1/13 [19]. By courtesy of the University of Liverpool.

FIG. 10.2. Photograph of Arthur Symons (left) posing with his Romani friends ('Snapshots of Arthur Symons, with wife Rhoda, & with Gs.', possibly in Dora Yates's hand), University of Liverpool, Gypsy Lore Society Archive, GLS C1/13 [18]. By courtesy of the University of Liverpool.

FIG. 10.3. Alan Odle, frontispiece for *The Gypsy*, 1.1 (May 1915), Oxford, Bodleian Libraries, Per. 2705 d.316 (1/2(1915/1916)). By permission of The Marsh Agency Ltd on behalf of the Estate of Alan Odle and the Bodleian Library, Oxford.

INTRODUCTION

Elisa Bizzotto and Stefano Evangelista

In the autobiographical sketch 'A Prelude to Life' (1905), Arthur Symons excavates the origins of a feeling of rootlessness that had accompanied him since his childhood:

> If I have been a vagabond, and have never been able to root myself in any one place in the world, it is because I have no early memories of any one sky or soil. It has freed me from many prejudices in giving me its own unresting kind of freedom; but it has cut me off from whatever is stable, of long growth in the world.[1]

'A Prelude to Life' is a condensed portrait of the artist as a young man, in which the older self of the writer looks back on childhood and early adulthood to find the first gleanings of what he calls his 'passion for places' and his love of books, music, and foreign languages.[2] It concludes with the arrival of the protagonist in London, where he plunges into the appealing sensual overload of metropolitan life, haunting the busy streets like a sensation-hungry *flâneur*:

> If there ever was a religion of the eyes, I have devoutly practised that religion. I noted every face that passed me on the pavement; I looked into the omnibuses, the cabs, always with the same eager hope of seeing some beautiful or interesting person, some gracious movement, a delicate expression, which would be gone if I did not catch it as it went. This search without an aim grew to be almost a torture to me; my eyes ached with the effort, but I could not control them; I grasped at all these sights with the same futile energy as a dog that I once saw standing in an Irish stream, and snapping at the bubbles that ran continually past him on the water. Life ran past me continually, and I tried to make all its bubbles my own.[3]

The rootlessness that Symons portrays in 'A Prelude to Life' is inextricably bound with the creative and social freedom that is the core of his identity as poet and critic; but at the same time it produces a feeling of dislocation that amounts almost to an obsession or neurosis, and lends a precarious quality to his social relations. It is telling that, to describe his cultural mobility, Symons chooses the term 'vagabond' rather than the more respectable if anodyne 'cosmopolitan'. For the word 'vagabond' captures Symons's fascination with deracination, low life, and the demi-monde, as well as his constant attraction for people and places on the borders of culture and society: gypsies, bohemian artists, exotic dancers, prostitutes, and tramps, and venues such as music halls and seedy cafés, the East End of London, and the back streets of Paris and Venice. This is where Symons saw the most significant and appealing manifestations of modernity. He identified with outcasts because vagabondage was for him an ontological and emotional condition, providing at the same time a self-mythology that acted as a constant in his life and his *oeuvre*.

Symons was, to use a paradoxical expression, a crucial liminal figure in the British literary landscape of the turn of the twentieth century: his place is between two centuries, British and foreign cultures, literature and non-verbal art forms, sanity and illness. As a member of the Rhymers' Club and then editor of the avant-garde journal, *The Savoy* (1896), he was a key agent of English literary Decadence. His early poetry, with its fascination with urban life and frank portrayal of eroticism, left a mark on the 1890s, shocking or delighting his contemporaries. Walter Pater consecrated the young Symons as part of the poetic avant-garde in a review of his first poetic collection *Days and Nights* (1889), in which he hailed Symons as a worthy successor to Robert Browning and drew attention to the 'world of sickly gaslight and artificial flowers' (an unmistakable reference to Charles Baudelaire) conjured by his poems, which he praised for 'their substance, their dramatic hold on life, their fine scholarship'.[4] Symons himself was to make his countercultural and francophile stance explicit in the 'Preface' to the second edition (1897) of his third collection *London Nights* (1895), dedicated to Paul Verlaine and issued by the highly controversial publisher Leonard Smithers. Here, even in the midst of the reactionary and nationalistic backlash that followed the imprisonment of Oscar Wilde, he showed himself proud of the 'singular unanimity of abuse' that met his poetry in the British press, speaking out bravely against hypocrisy and censorship: 'I contend on behalf of the liberty of art, and I deny that morals have any right of jurisdiction over it. Art may be served by morality, it can never be its servant'.[5]

Although he has mostly been known as a Decadent poet, Symons was also the author of influential critical essays and volumes. The connection with Pater (Symons had reviewed Pater's *Imaginary Portraits* in 1887 and had in fact dedicated *Days and Nights* to him) developed into an important intellectual friendship. Symons often wrote in the shadow of the older critic, handing down the legacy of 'aesthetic criticism' and 'impressionistic criticism' to the new century, as T. S. Eliot recognised in 'The Perfect Critic' (of course, for the astringent Eliot, a 'perfect critic' was precisely what Symons was not).[6] Unlike Pater, though, Symons did not have a secure job, nor did he possess enough family money to be able to live without working; he therefore had to write for a living, and this resulted in an extensive journalistic production that, while it undeniably lacked the polish of Pater, exhibited a remarkable range of interests — from literature to music, the visual arts, theatre, and dance — and was much less afraid of taking risks, thriving on the ephemerality of the periodical medium. In this vast body of work perhaps even more than in his poetry and rare pieces of fiction, Symons served as a skilled cultural mediator who facilitated the transition from the *fin de siècle* to Modernism, highlighting the continuity between these two periods of literary history that are still too often viewed in isolation. His special contribution was an enthusiasm for French culture, which he first experienced first-hand in the early 1890s in the company of the critic and sexologist Havelock Ellis, and on which he became one of the foremost authorities in Britain. His book-length study *The Symbolist Movement in Literature* (1899), a much enlarged and reworked version of the important earlier article 'The Decadent Movement in Literature' (1893), was ground-breaking. The critic Edmund Gosse hailed it as 'the finest product of pure criticism which has been seen in England for years', adding in a letter to the author: 'I ask myself — if, now, you are not the best English critic since Pater, who is?'.[7] Even T. S. Eliot, in the same essay where he sniffed at Symons's impressionism, would describe this book as 'an introduction to wholly new feelings' and 'a revelation' for having brought French literary modernity to Anglophone readers.[8] This commitment to introducing foreign voices into English literary culture was a constant of Symons's work, and also took the form of a series of important translations of advanced and controversial literature, which included Émile Zola's *L'Assommoir* (1876, trans. 1894), Émile Verhaeren's *Les Aubes* (1989, trans. 1898), Pierre Louÿs's *La Femme et le pantin* (1898, trans. 1935), various works by Gabriele D'Annunzio, and poems by Baudelaire, Verlaine, and Stéphane Mallarmé.

The great turning point for Symons's career was his mental breakdown of 1908, which took place in Italy, with first unequivocal signs manifesting themselves in Venice and full symptoms in Ferrara, a city that had evocative personal associations with Browning, the subject of Symons's first critical monograph (1886). If Symons was once a leading and bold voice of literary modernity, his illness now triggered an irreversible artistic decline, which affected both his new productions and the reception of his previous output. In the euphemistic account that his close friend W. B. Yeats gave to actor and theatre director Allen Wade, the incident made of Symons 'a classic, overnight':[9] ironically, to readers in the early twentieth century he quickly became part of the Victorian establishment from which he had fought so hard to be different. Even after his breakdown Symons continued to write relentlessly, often by simply editing previous works or cutting and pasting them in new volumes or under new titles, but he never regained his former literary distinction. He lived to become an old man, unlike most of his contemporaries who had also been part of what Yeats famously named the 'Tragic Generation', and he even survived such Modernists as James Joyce and Virginia Woolf. At his death in 1945, the *Times Literary Supplement* significantly described him as 'the last of the eminent aesthetic writers', hinting unmistakably at his anachronistic status in the twentieth century.[10]

The story of Symons's rise and fall follows a narrative that is all too familiar to students of the literature of the late nineteenth century: once at the centre of literary modernity as an avant-garde poet and one of the most advanced and internationally recognised critics of the *fin de siècle*, Symons was marginalised by the modernist generation despite their indebtedness to him. This is the same fate that befell Pater, as well as A. C. Swinburne, Oscar Wilde, and Vernon Lee — all of whom were, incidentally, also deeply committed to building bridges between England and continental Europe. In Symons's case, though, the fall from fame was exacerbated by the stigma of the breakdown.[11] It is telling that in the *Romantic Agony* (1930), the first important critical revaluation of English aesthetic and Decadent literature in the early twentieth century, Mario Praz only makes a brief reference to him — along with Richard Le Gallienne, John Gray, Theodore Wratislaw, Lionel Johnson, Olive Constance, and Ernest Dowson — as a 'minor poet' dealing with 'themes of a decadent and perverse nature, at second hand'.[12] Praz would later note Symons's translations of Baudelaire and D'Annunzio, suggesting that his most lasting contribution was in the field of criticism.[13] Praz's ideas were then developed by his pupil Agostino Lombardo, a future leading figure of English studies in Italy, who investigated Symons's literary affiliations — from the Victorian poets to Pater, the French Symbolists, and Maurice Maeterlinck — and suggested that his originality lay in the unique merging of diverse intercultural inspirations.[14]

In general, though, if Symons's fortune was certainly at an ebb at the time of his death, it did not rise much in the 1950s and 1960s. The most notable exception to this widespread trend was Frank Kermode, who in his highly influential *Romantic Image* (1957) recognised Symons's unique role in the evolution from Romanticism to Modernism:

> Symons [...] more explicitly and more influentially than any of his contemporaries, saw how to synthesise the earlier English tradition — particularly Blake, on whom he wrote a good, and in this connexion revealing, book — with Pater and those European Symbolists he knew so well. Symons also had a considerable part in the associated revival of interest in Donne and the Jacobean dramatic poets. But above all he wrote the book out of which the important poets of the early twentieth century learnt the elements of French Symbolist poetic.[15]

Kermode is typical of this early phase, which concentrated first and foremost on Symons's place in the poetic tradition. The 1960s saw Roger Lhombreaud's and John M. Munro's biographies: the first rich in detail though sometimes imprecise, the second displaying a more critical approach to Symons's literary connections and influences.[16] Then, from the late 1970s, Symons found a devoted scholarly critic and editor in Karl Beckson, who played a major role in keeping his reputation alive, showing that Symons deserved to be considered as an artist in his own right, without simply appearing as one of the midwives of British Symbolism and Modernism.[17] Beckson is the author of the still-definitive biography, *Arthur Symons: A Life* (1987), and his co-authored bibliography remains an invaluable aid for navigating Symons's sprawling *oeuvre*. The late 1980s also saw the publication of Lawrence W. Markert's *Arthur Symons: Critic of the Seven Arts*, which opened up new avenues of research on Symons's criticism and his interest in drama, travel, the visual arts, and music.[18]

From the 1990s onwards, with the steady rise in academic interest in Aestheticism and Decadence, Symons has been making a slow return, even though, following the early critics, scholars have focused mainly on the poetry.[19] For instance, the recent collection *Decadent Poetics: Literature and Form at the British Fin de Siècle*, edited by Jason David Hall and Alex Murray, has foregrounded Symons's role as one of the main theorists of modernity at the *fin de siècle* and illuminated the complexity of Symons's ideas on language and prosody and their influence on contemporary and early twentieth-century poetics.[20] This formal approach is elaborated further in Vincent Sherry's *Modernism and the Reinvention of Decadence*, which devotes a chapter to the influence of Symons's poetic techniques on high Modernist poetry.[21] In larger thematic studies of Decadence, though, Symons is still given marginal roles.[22]

There is of course much in Symons's work to frustrate critics. The gender politics, for instance, can be as problematic from the perspective of today's feminist criticism as it was to Symons's first Victorian reviewers. In this sense, Symons has little to appeal to the interest in the queer and non-normative that animates much of the best recent work in this field. More importantly perhaps, his critical *oeuvre* is admittedly dotted with imprecisions that are the product of writing under pressure, which are amplified by Symons's habit of reusing his own work, constantly making small additions and slight modifications — in short, making it surreptitiously repetitive. Yet those same features that make Symons frustrating also make him ripe for revaluation. His publication practices are a case in point. For Symons provides a fascinating case of a writer navigating the periodical industry over several decades and in multiple languages and countries. If, as Laurel Brake reminds us, the study of Victorian periodicals alerts us to a plurality that is obscured by the deceitful uniformity of the single-authored book, Symons can be used as a window into the workings and aesthetics of that plurality.[23] Symons's amateurism — for he was a less rigorous critic than Pater, Matthew Arnold, or even the apparently more playful Wilde — could likewise be understood positively, as giving him a special kind of intellectual and social mobility that was more difficult to obtain for those contemporaries of his who had institutional affiliations to universities: the freedom of the 'vagabond' that he describes in 'A Prelude to Life'.

The same could be said for rethinking the familiar narrative of Symons as stuck in the literary forms, ideas, and values of the 1890s in a world that had moved on. Recent work on the *longue durée* of Decadence by Sherry and Kristin Mahoney encourages us to think of new temporalities to make sense of the connections between the *fin de siècle*, especially Decadence, and the literature of the twentieth century.[24] We should therefore not think of the twentieth-century Symons as simply an anachronistic phenomenon, but as revealing to us engagements between different presents and historical layers that overwrote each other in the early twentieth century before Modernism came to occupy the canonical status that it enjoys today. T. S. Eliot, who, as we have seen, was interested in Symons, thought as much in his essay 'Baudelaire in our Time', which was a review of Symons's 1926 translation *Baudelaire: Prose and Poetry*. Here Eliot was sceptical of the way in which Symons turned Baudelaire into 'a poet of the 'nineties', obsessed with nerves and sin, 'a contemporary of Dowson and Wilde', noting that while 'Dowson and Wilde have passed, [...] Baudelaire remains; he belonged to a generation that preceded them, and yet he is much more our contemporary than are they'.[25] And yet, at the same time, for all its period feel and 'smudgy botch[es]', Symons's Baudelaire also revealed to Eliot that the 1920s shared a more vital connection with the past of the 1890s than with the more recent literary generation of the early 1900s, which according to Eliot completely failed to appreciate Baudelaire's modernity.[26] From our vantage point in the twenty-first century it is easy to see that Eliot's effort in this review to turn Baudelaire into a Christian is as dated and anachronistic as

Symons's attempts to make the French poet sound like Swinburne. What matters, though, is that it shows that, even in the 1920s, Symons was not only being taken seriously as, to adapt the title of Pater's 1889 review, 'a poet with something to say' in his mediations of French literary modernity, but he became a vehicle to re-historicise the *fin de siècle* and find new meanings and challenges in its literary achievements.

Arthur Symons: Poet, Critic, Vagabond — the first collection of essays entirely dedicated to Symons — aims to project a new, nuanced image of Symons into the twenty-first century. The essays in this volume study his engagement with multiple literary genres (from poetry to criticism, fiction, and travel writing) as well as his journalistic activity; they examine his interest in aesthetics and the arts, as well as his incessant work of cultural mediation of material from Italy, France, and Belgium which he carried out by means of travel, reviews, and translations, and the cultivation of an impressive literary network that comprised, among others, Verlaine, Mallarmé, Villier de l'Isle-Adam, Remy de Gourmont, D'Annunzio, J.-K. Huysmans, Maeterlinck, and Verhaeren. The choice of presenting Symons within a comparative literature series is strategic, for we believe that Symons's contribution can best be examined afresh from a comparative perspective that throws light on his cosmopolitanism, transcultural engagement, and international profile. The book comes out at a moment in which Symons's works are starting to be available in reliable scholarly editions: Matthew Creasy's 2014 edition of *The Symbolist Movement in Literature* has been followed by a critical edition of *Spiritual Adventures* (1905) and the early prose writings by Nicholas Freeman; while a critical anthology of Symons's poetry by Jane Desmarais and Chris Baldwick has made available a wider selection of his verse than ever before, showcasing the variety of his poetic interests.[27] The critical essays in the present volume interact with the textual work of Symons's twenty-first century editors in order to indicate new directions in the study of his writings, and to suggest ways in which a revaluation of Symons can generate new perspectives on the literatures of the *fin de siècle* and early twentieth century.

Our choice to focus on a networked Symons stands behind the division of the book into three parts. The first, 'Artistic Connections', focuses on his writings on sculpture, music, and drama. After his poetic debut with *Days and Nights*, Symons embarked on a prolific journalistic career that included regular contributions to *The Athenaeum* and the *Star*, where he reviewed music hall performances under the pseudonym 'Silhouette'. Over the following decades he collected some of his pieces in a series of important volumes of criticism: *Studies in Two Literatures* (1897), *The Symbolist Movement in Literature* (1899), *Plays, Acting, and Music* (1903), *Studies in Prose and Verse* (1904), and *Studies in Seven Arts* (1906). Symons's comparative and transnational interests are very much in evidence in these volumes, but so is his ambition to establish himself as an aesthetic critic skilled at ranging across different art forms. As he writes in the preface to *Plays, Acting, and Music*, he believed that critics should acknowledge that each art has 'its own laws, its own capacities, its own limits' while at the same time endeavouring 'to master the universal science of beauty'.[28] This brought Symons to seek evocative connections between the arts, building on the experiments with synaesthesia, *correspondances*, and the fusion of different mediums that had characterised the critical writings of Théophile Gautier, Baudelaire, and of course Swinburne and Pater. Looking back on that tradition, Lene Østermark-Johansen focuses on the interrelationship between sculpture and dance, reconstructing Symons's exchanges with and writings about Auguste Rodin, and placing his work in the context of the experimental dance performances of Loïe Fuller and Isadora Duncan. Following the inter-artistic theme, Jane Desmarais unravels the complex associations of Symons's praise for the 'music' of Beardsley's drawings, analysing his conception of music as at the same time sensuous and spiritual. Their essays demonstrate that a full understanding of Symons's aesthetic theories needs to go beyond the critical writings, embracing different genres that range from poetry to the hybrid fiction of the *Spiritual Adventures*. At the close of this section, John Stokes shifts the discussion to drama, the art form on which Symons left his deepest mark as a critic. Stokes's analysis of Edward Gordon Craig's annotations to his copy of Symons's *Studies in Seven Arts* reveals a dialogue between Symons's criticism and Craig's influential dramatic innovations. All the essays in this section highlight the fact that Symons's participation in artistic Modernism was complex and anything but marginal, whether it be through his fascination with the moving body, the use of puppets and masks on the stage, or his insistence on the affective power of form that has still unexplored overlaps with the formalist approaches of Roger Fry and Clive Bell.

We have already seen that another modernist, T. S. Eliot, paid homage to Symons for his work on French Symbolism and grudgingly acknowledged his legacy. Yet, as the essays in the second part, 'International Mediations', make clear, the range and scope of Symons's activity of international literary mediation stretched far beyond his writings on Symbolism and remain understudied by his critics. Literary translation is a case in point. Symons translated very widely and always chose authors with whom he felt a strong affinity: his canon of translations is thus dominated by Symbolist and Decadent works, including the Austrian Hugo von Hofmannsthal's *Elektra*, which he translated in 1908, even though his knowledge of German was, by his own admission, rather poor. Translating foreign writers was not merely utilitarian work or a way to earn money: it manifests his enthusiasm for introducing new voices into the English literary landscape and forging international connections. In technical terms, Symons endeavoured to fuse his own voice with those of the foreign authors he translated, triggering a process whereby the translated text becomes an intertextual hybrid that embodies the dialogue between two authors across languages, dissolving the rigid border between original and copy, and probing the limits of the very concepts of authorship and subjectivity. Stefano Evangelista shows this process at work in Symons's translations of the controversial Italian Decadent author Gabriele D'Annunzio, whose writings Symons championed, as both translator and critic, in the early decades of the twentieth century; while Matthew Creasy examines Symons's translation of Villiers de l'Isle-Adam's *Contes cruels* (1883), unveiling an ambiguous and productive relationship between translation and adaptation. Both essays argue that translation was an integral part of Symons's broader mission as a critic, and suggest ways to re-situate translation at the heart of Symons's creative practices. The second part of this section re-evaluates Symons's deep engagement with Francophone literature, which earned him his reputation as cosmopolitan mediator. However, as Clément Dessy shows, Symons's critics have neglected the important fact that some of the French-speaking writers in which Symons was most interested, such as Maeterlinck, Charles Van Lerberghe, and Verhaeren, were in fact Belgian, and that Belgium occupied a special place in Symons's imagination; indeed, this ability to situate the distinctive achievement of Belgian writers within the larger French-speaking literary sphere made Symons unique among British critics of his generation. Another feature that distinguished him was his international journalistic career, examined by Bénédicte Coste, who shows that our understanding of Symons's formidable effort in the English press remains partial unless we consider it alongside his presence in French periodical culture. Symons was well-regarded in France at the end of the century, and as Coste shows, the French criticism of his work sometimes influenced his reception in England, both in the nineteenth and twentieth centuries. Read together, the essays in this section reveal the importance of looking at Symons from a point of view *outside* England: moving skilfully between languages and across the periodical presses in France, Belgium, and Britain, Symons operated on a trans-national level because he believed that literary modernity transcended, epistemologically and in material terms, the boundaries of national literature.

Symons's intellectual networks are also the subject of the third and final section, 'Places and Connections'. Nicholas Freeman reconstructs Symons's engagement with Venice, a city that he visited several times and that was the setting of his breakdown in 1908. Surveying the many essays, travel sketches, and poems connected with Venice, Freeman discovers a persistent interest in interiority and the uncanny, and reads these writings as a series of acts of psychological self-exploration. The Venetian essays and stories are part of Symons's substantial body of travel writing — a genre that is now largely marginalised but in fact constituted an important creative outlet (and often a good source of profit) for Symons, as for many of his late nineteenth-century contemporaries. In Symons's travel literature Italy at large occupied a privileged position. Elisa Bizzotto shows that Symons's writings on Italian cities and places are in dialogue with previous works by John Addington Symonds and Vernon Lee, on whom Symons modelled his impressionistic techniques of literary representation. The connection with Lee in particular is important, as it alerts us to his understudied interactions with women writers, for Symons has traditionally been viewed in relation to an exclusively male canon. As well as revealing networks of influence, Symons's travel writings constitute another important link between the *fin de siècle* and Modernism, as evidenced in his experimental *London: A Book of Aspects* (1908): this volume focuses on the cultural and social margins of the modern metropolis and contains a portrait of the vagrant and author Josiah Flynt (Frank Willard) as a paradigmatic vagabond/aesthete, which evokes a clearly autobiographical dimension. Katharina Herold shows that a similar sense of identification underlies Symons's interest in gypsies: Symons's 'gypsylorism' did not simply signal an interest in foreignness and marginality but provided the writer with a means to interrogate the identity and cultural politics of Decadence. The collection closes with a revaluation of Symons's connection with the most emblematic figure of English Decadence, Oscar Wilde, with whom Symons came into contact in the late 1880s, when he collaborated with Wilde's magazine the *Woman's World*. Laura Giovannelli traces their complex interaction, made of mutual appreciation, misunderstanding, and diffidence, which culminated with the publication of *A Study of Oscar Wilde* (1930), one of Symons's last works. Her essay takes us back to the overarching question of the persistence of the *fin de siècle* within the era of Modernism that also exercised T. S. Eliot in 'Baudelaire in Our Time'.

The essays in this volume thus (re)trace some of the most meaningful aesthetic networks, geographies, and literary and intellectual connections that characterised Symons's large and varied body of writings. As he mediated between the literatures of two centuries and brought English readers in dialogue with writers, artists, and trends from abroad, Symons retained his precarious identity as a 'vagabond', which fused the desire to 'search without an aim', as he puts it in 'A Prelude to Life', with the serious ambition to make English literary culture more outward-looking and international.

Notes to the Introduction

1. Arthur Symons, 'A Prelude to Life', in *Spiritual Adventures*, ed. by Nicholas Freeman, MHRA Critical Texts: Jewelled Tortoise, 3 (Cambridge: Modern Humanities Research Association, 2017), pp. 119–39 (pp. 119–20).
2. Ibid., p. 121. Symons's story has indeed been seen as a source of inspiration for Joyce's famous *Künstlerroman*; see Karl Beckson, 'Symons' "A Prelude to Life," Joyce's "A Portrait," and the Religion of Art', *James Joyce Quarterly*, 15:3 (Spring 1978), 222–28.
3. Symons, 'A Prelude to Life', p. 139.
4. Walter Pater, 'A Poet with Something to Say', *Pall Mall Gazette*, 23 March 1889, 3; repr. in Arthur Symons, *Selected Early Poems*, ed. by Jane Desmarais and Chris Baldwick, MHRA Critical Texts: Jewelled Tortoise, 2 (Cambridge: Modern Humanities Research Association, 2017), pp. 181–84 (pp. 182, 183). Pater was repaying a compliment, for Symons had previously compared Pater to Baudelaire in his signed review of *Imaginary Portraits* in *Time*, 6 (August 1887), 157–62, repr. in *Walter Pater: The Critical Heritage*, ed. by R. M. Seiler (London: Routledge & Kegan Paul, 1980), pp. 175–82 (pp. 176–77).
5. Arthur Symons, 'Preface' to the second edition of *London Nights* (1897); repr. in *Selected Early Poems*, pp. 200–01 (p. 200).
6. T. S. Eliot, 'The Perfect Critic', in *The Complete Prose of T. S. Eliot*, ed. by Ronald Schuchard and others, 8 vols (Baltimore, MD: Johns Hopkins University Press, 2014–), II (2014), 262–72 (p. 263). Eliot sees Symons as 'the critical successor' of Pater and Swinburne (p. 263).
7. Edmund Gosse to Arthur Symons, 7 March 1900, in *Arthur Symons: Selected Letters, 1880–1935*, ed. by Karl Beckson and John M. Munro (Basingstoke: Macmillan, 1989), p. 147. Amidst his compliments Gosse, however, also sounded a well-founded note of warning: 'such books must expect the maximum of negligence [...] partly because the temper of our fellow-citizens grows more and more indifferent and even hostile to the pure produce of the brain' (p. 147).
8. Eliot, 'The Perfect Critic', p. 264.
9. Allan Wade, 'Arthur Symons', *Times Literary Supplement* (10 March 1945), 115.
10. [Harold Hannyngton Child], 'Arthur Symons', *Times Literary Supplement* (3 February 1945), 55.

11. Biographers have certainly made much of this episode. See Roger Lhombreaud, *Arthur Symons: A Critical Biography* (London: Unicorn Press, 1963), pp. 240–70; John M. Munro, *Arthur Symons* (New York: Twayne, 1969), pp. 109–11; Karl Beckson, *Arthur Symons: A Life* (Oxford: Clarendon Press, 1987), pp. 250–78.
12. Mario Praz, *The Romantic Agony*, trans. by Angus Davidson, 2nd edn (London: Oxford University Press, 1951), p. 342.
13. Mario Praz, *Storia della letteratura inglese* (Florence: Sansoni, 1937), p. 350.
14. Agostino Lombardo, *La poesia inglese dall'estetismo al simbolismo* (Rome: Edizioni di storia e letteratura, 1950), pp. 155–88.
15. Frank Kermode, *Romantic Image* (London & New York: Routledge, 2004 [1957]), p. 127.
16. See n. 11. Beckson and Munro point out Lhombreaud's inaccuracies in transcribing Symons's letters in their 'Introduction' to *Arthur Symons: Selected Letters,* ed. by Beckson and Munro, pp. ix–xvi (p. xv).
17. *The Memoirs of Arthur Symons: Life and Art in the 1890s*, ed. by Karl Beckson (University Park & London: Pennsylvania State University Press, 1977); and Beckson, *Arthur Symons*. See also *Arthur Symons: Selected Letters*, ed. by Beckson and Munro.
18. Lawrence W. Markert, *Arthur Symons: Critic of the Seven Arts* (Ann Arbor: University of Michigan Research Press, 1987); *Arthur Symons: A Bibliography*, ed. by Karl Beckson and others (Greensboro, NC: ELT Press, 1990). Another important contribution to Symons criticism in this period is *Strangeness and Beauty: An Anthology of Aesthetic Criticism 1840–1910*, ed. by Eric Warner and Graham Hough, 2 vols (Cambridge: Cambridge University Press, 1983), II, esp. pp. 210–18.
19. See especially Petra Pointner, *A Prelude to Modernism: Studies in the Urban and Erotic Poetry of Arthur Symons* (Heidelberg: Universitätsverlag Winter, 2004); and Sebastian Hayes, *Arthur Symons: Leading Poet of the English Decadence* (Shaftesbury: Brimstone Press, 2007). More recently, Symons's poetry features prominently in Kostas Boyiopoulos's fine *The Decadent Image: The Poetry of Wilde, Symons, and Dowson* (Edinburgh: Edinburgh University Press, 2015).
20. Jason David Hall and Alex Murray, 'Introduction', in *Decadent Poetics: Literature and Form at the British Fin de Siècle*, ed. by Jason David Hall and Alex Murray (London: Palgrave Macmillan, 2013), pp. 1–25; see also, in the same collection, Nicholas Freeman, ' "The Harem of Words": Attenuation and Excess in Decadent Poetry', pp. 83–99.
21. Vincent Sherry, *Modernism and the Reinvention of Decadence* (Cambridge: Cambridge University Press, 2014), pp. 72–81.
22. See, for instance, *Perennial Decay: On the Aesthetics and Politics of Decadence*, ed. by Liz Constable, Dennis Denisoff, and Matthew Potolsky (Philadelphia: University of Pennsylvania Press, 1999); and Matthew Potolsky, *The Decadent Republic of Letters: Taste, Politics, and Cosmopolitan Community from Baudelaire to Beardsley* (Philadelphia: University of Pennsylvania Press, 2013).
23. Laurel Brake, *Subjugated Knowledges: Journalism, Gender and Literature in the Nineteenth Century* (Basingstoke: Palgrave Macmillan, 1994), esp. pp. 8–19 and 63–80.
24. See Sherry, *Modernism and the Reinvention of Decadence*; Kristin Mahoney, *Literature and the Politics of Post-Victorian Decadence* (Cambridge: Cambridge University Press, 2015); and the foundational David Weir, *Decadence and the Making of Modernism* (Amherst: University of Massachusetts Press, 1995).
25. T. S. Eliot, 'Baudelaire in our Time', in *The Complete Prose of T. S. Eliot*, ed. by Schuchard and others, III (2015), 71–82 (p. 71).
26. Ibid., p. 75.
27. Arthur Symons, *The Symbolist Movement in Literature*, ed. by Matthew Creasy (Manchester: Fyfield-Carcanet, 2014); *Spiritual Adventures* (2017); *Selected Early Poems*. Since the last two editions had not yet come out at the time in which the essays in this book were written, our authors as a rule refer to the first editions of Symons's works.
28. Arthur Symons, *Plays, Acting, and Music* (London: Duckworth, 1903), n. p.

PART I

Artistic Connections

CHAPTER 1

❖

The Rhythms of Life and Art

Symons and the Interrelationship between Rodin's Sculpture and Modern Dance at the *Fin de Siècle*

Lene Østermark-Johansen

> Rhythm, precisely, is a balance, a means of preserving equilibrium in moving bodies. The human body possesses so much volume, it has to maintain its equilibrium; if you displace its contents here, they may shift there; the balance is regained by an instinctive movement of self-preservation.
> ARTHUR SYMONS, 'Rodin'[1]

These observations occur at the beginning of Arthur Symons's essay on the French sculptor Auguste Rodin, a text which opens his influential volume *Studies in Seven Arts* of 1906. By the time Symons published his book, he was already a very well-established poet and critic, who had been moving fairly effortlessly within the English and French avant-garde for the past two decades, organising lecture tours in England for Verlaine, producing symbolist poetry alongside Yeats, Dowson, and Johnson in the Rhymers' Club, and writing journal articles on music, dance, painting, and literature in both English and French periodicals. His attempt to define the links and differences between the seven arts — sculpture, painting, architecture, music, drama, pantomime, and dance — begins and ends with a celebration of rhythm in sculpture and dance. From the opening essay on Auguste Rodin to the all-embracing exit, 'The World as Ballet', Symons hails the vital principle of pulsating rhythm as a unifying force connecting the spatial arts. Symons is essentially interested in economy of form when he discusses both sculpture and dance, an economy of form which is in many ways akin to what he explores in his poetry. In the gestures of both sculpture and dance he finds a compressed expression which resides in rhythm, and his initial observation on Rodin's ability to capture the rhythm of nature in a single gesture is full of insight. In the course of the volume his representation of rhythm evolves from a physical precondition of human balance into an evanescent image of the dancer as a symbol of human transcendence. The conclusion celebrates dance as an art form with the 'power of letting humanity drift into a rhythm so much of its own',[2] and focuses the reader's attention on the image of the solitary female dancer:

> Nothing is stated, there is no intrusion of words used for the irrelevant purpose of describing; a world rises before one, the picture lasts only long enough to have been there: and the dancer, with her gesture, all pure symbol, evokes, from her mere beautiful motion, idea, sensation, all that one need ever know of event. There, before you, she exists, in harmonious life; and her rhythm reveals to you the soul of her imagined being.[3]

Echoing Keats,[4] prefiguring Yeats.[5] Symons's dancer never lets us know the dancer from the dance, as she is both idea and image in the moment of her performance, encapsulating what Frank Kermode termed the 'Romantic Image'.[6] Sculpture and dance are both spatial arts, engaging in and exploring three-dimensional space. The one solid and static, the other evanescent and ephemeral, yet the state of sculpture and dance at the *fin de siècle* was one of constant approximation, as dancers and sculptors collaborated, befriended each other, and exhibited next to one another in the great Exposition Universelle in Paris in 1900.

This essay discusses Symons's life-long admiration of Rodin as the greatest of modern sculptors and contextualises his fascination within the framework of the development of modern dance, with Paris as the indisputable epicentre. At the turn of the century American dance pioneers like Loïe Fuller and Isadora Duncan headed for Paris, with London as a transitional stepping stone, where Rodin's status as French and European celebrity sculptor with expert knowledge of the expressive potential of the female body made him an obvious port of call. Antiquity and modernity merged in his art, as they did in the innovative scenographies and choreographies of Fuller and Duncan, and Symons, immersed in Parisian culture imbibed the *correspondances* between the arts with enthusiasm and perception. Having studied the movement of the female form during the 1890s, when he was a dance and theatre critic in London and Paris, Symons discovered Rodin's ability to capture the movement of the female body within the malleable medium of clay. The fluidity of Rodin's sculptural style appealed to Symons more than that of any other sculptor. With the exception of two late essays on the sculpture of Dora Gordine, Rodin was the only sculptor whose art inspired Symons to critical writing on sculpture.[7] By comparison, his many essays on nineteenth-century painting reflect a much more diverse awareness of the scope and variety of the art form of modernity, and they cannot easily be discussed collectively. Analyses of Symons as a critic of the visual arts tend to ignore his work on Rodin, and this piece is an attempt to address this imbalance, while also trying to locate Symons's fascination with Rodin more broadly in the *fin-de-siècle* cult of the moving body.[8]

Symons's encounter with the exotic Javanese dancers at the 1889 Exposition Universelle in Paris sparked off the early poem 'Javanese Dancers', in which the spectrally immobile faces of the dancers contrast with their rhythmically moving hands and feet.

> One, two, three, four step forth, and, to and fro,
> Delicately and imperceptibly,
> Now swaying gently in a row,
> Now interthreading slow and rhythmically,
>
> Still, with fixed eyes, monotonously still,
> Mysteriously, with smiles inanimate,
> With lingering feet that undulate,
> With sinuous fingers, spectral hands that thrill,
>
> The little amber-coloured dancers move,
> Like little painted figures on a screen,
> Or phantom-dancers haply seen
> Among the shadows of a magic grove.[9]

Considering that this is a poem about dance and movement, its shortage of finite verbs is intriguing. The main movement in the poem could be reduced to two lines: 'One, two, three, four step forth, and, to and fro, | The little amber-coloured dancers move'. A pile of qualifying subordinate clauses, weighed down by gerunds, adjectives, adverbs, and repetitions, postpones the main verb 'move'. Movement is delayed by immobility, by the ghostly expressionless faces which in their seductive monotony and seriality form a contrast to the undulating and serpenting extremities of the dancers. The countable individuals at the beginning transform into the collective, and real dancers become shadows or phantoms, two-dimensional projections on a screen, or ethereal ghosts in a magic world. The spectral artificiality of the Javanese dancers contributes to their seductive powers in the interplay between their own 'fixed eyes' and the mesmerised observing gaze of the poet.

Symons began his career as a dance critic in 1892, the same year as he became involved with the Rhymers' Club.[10] Writing under the pseudonym 'Silhouette', he contributed a long series of reviews of dance and music-hall entertainment in London and Paris for the *Star* and the *Sketch* in the course of the 1890s.[11] Together with the other members of the Rhymers' Club, such as Lionel Johnson, Ernest Dowson, and W. B. Yeats, he frequented the dance establishments in Leicester Square, and the cross-pollination between his poetry of the 1890s and his dance criticism is dense, as demonstrated by Heather Marcovitch.[12] The 'Prologue' to *London Nights* (1895) merges spectator and dancer, poet and performer, subject and object, in a way which is radically different from the strange otherness of the Javanese dancers. Although the majority of the poems that follow revolve around female figures, the poet/dancer in the opening scene is most likely male, in his impotent rage, his spellbound fascination with the turning (female) dancers and his puffs of smoke:

> My life is like a music-hall,
> Where, in the impotence of rage,
> Chained by enchantment to my stall,
> I see myself upon the stage
> Dance to amuse a music-hall.

> 'Tis I that smoke this cigarette,
> Lounge here and laugh for vacancy,
> And watch the dancers turn; and yet
> It is my very self I see
> Across the cloudy cigarette.[13]

The screen of smoke momentarily distorts the mirror image between the observing and the performing self; do we see a vision, a shadow, or a projection in this narcissistic splitting of the self? The staging of the self, on stage and off stage, follows the characteristic evolution in so many of Symons's writings from the concrete to the evanescent and spiritual. The two first stanzas of Symons's 'Prologue' portray an act of recognition. Like other *fin-de-siècle* split personalities, such as R. L. Stevenson's Dr Jekyll, Symons's poet must acknowledge that 'This, too, was myself'. The poems that follow take us into an artificial world where women emerge as exotic Baudelairean flowers, the only organic elements in an otherwise utterly inorganic universe.

Symons's first encounter with Auguste Rodin coincided with the beginning of his career as a dance critic; it took place in Paris in 1892, as he would later recall.[14] Another eight years would pass before Symons began to engage critically with the sculptor and his works, an ongoing involvement, bordering on hero-worship, which would last until 1931, some fourteen years after the sculptor's death.[15] The Auguste Rodin Collection at Princeton University holds twelve letters from the sculptor to Symons,[16] Tate Britain houses the small bronze sculpture of a woman on a column which the sculptor gave to Symons and his wife,[17] and after Symons's mental breakdown Rodin sent generous amounts to pay for his care.[18] From a first brief essay in French on Rodin's drawings for a French volume coinciding with Rodin's one-man show at the Exposition Universelle in 1900,[19] Symons repeatedly returned to the sculptor and his works in periodical and book publications.[20] He kept adding to his already existing essays on Rodin, smoothing over the transitions between old and new texts. The 1900 French essay on the drawings was incorporated in the 1902 essay on Rodin that he wrote for the *Fortnightly Review*, an essay which was republished as the opening chapter of *Studies in Seven Arts*. Where the opening essay on Rodin was the point of departure for Symons's discussion of the seven arts in 1906, the French sculptor became the culminating and concluding figure in the 1929 volume on modern art, *From Toulouse-Lautrec to Rodin with some Personal Impressions*. This late essay contained the major part of the 1902 essay (already incorporating the 1900 essay), padded with a few personal anecdotes. An unfriendly view of Symons's recycling of his own texts might see the process as one of cannibalisation; a more sympathetic approach might regard the texts in sculptural terms, in a process of continuing evolution (though not necessarily improvement) through an almost sculptural additive technique, from an early *bozzetto* towards an increasingly more finished version to which have been added meditations on painting, poetry, and architecture. Characteristic of the late essay is the strong presence of both the artist and the critic already in the opening paragraph:

> I met Auguste Rodin in Paris, 182 Rue de l'Université, in May 1892. The last time that I saw him was at a dinner given in Old Burlington Street in 1907. No one who has seen him can ever forget his singular appearance. There before me stood a giant of genius, with the timidity of the colossus; with a face in which strength struggled with passion; with veiled blue eyes that dilated like the eyes of the parrot when he spoke of anything that interested him deeply. He made few gestures; only when he sat, with his great hands folded on his knees, the gestures he made were for a purpose, never for an effect. I was struck by his quietness, his simplicity, a certain caution which comes from a suspicion that he is not being taken simply enough. When he talked of books or of his art of nature there was always the same freshness and profundity.[21]

Symons then moves effortlessly from sculpture via painting (Rodin's views on Gustave Moreau) to poetry (an observation by Rodin on Mallarmé's use of foreshortening) on to his own reading of Mallarmé's poetic technique. The fluid and associative style of the essay takes us through what may seem like digressions into the other arts to a meditation on the act and process of creation in poetry and in sculpture. The colossal genius of sculpture, famous for his rendering of the divine act of creation in such works as *La Main de Dieu*, is celebrated for his power over the clay, and at the same time humanised as a friend, fellow spectator, and reader. The image of the sculptor which opens *Studies in Seven Arts* is one of an artist in profound contact with the earth as he moulds organic shapes from the clay and makes them his own. Whether Christian God or Promethean deity, Rodin is master of life in art, and his moulding of the basest material into great art is in striking contrast to the Renaissance myths of Michelangelo, attacking the marble block directly. Symons saw Rodin as a direct descendant of the Greeks rather than a disciple of Michelangelo.[22] Reversing the conventional praise of sculpture as mimesis, he makes his sculptor a modern Pygmalion in mystic communication with the profoundest powers of nature:

> The art of Rodin competes with nature rather than with the art of other sculptors. Other sculptors turn life into sculpture, he turns sculpture into life. His clay is part of the substance of the earth, and the earth still clings about it as it comes up and lives. It is at once the flower and the root; that of others is the flower only, and the plucked flower. That link with the earth, which we find in the unhewn masses of rock from which his finest creations of pure form can never quite free themselves, is the secret of his deepest force. It links his creations to nature's, in a single fashion of growth.[23]

The organic, undulating rhythms of Rodin's flowerlike sculptures recall his well-known lifelong fascination with Baudelaire's *Flowers of Evil*, to be traced alongside his Dantesque motifs in both drawings and sculptures. As a highly literary sculptor, Rodin merges the arts imperceptibly in a manner which was bound to appeal to Symons, in search of Baudelairean *correspondances*. The organic images of earth, trees, and flowers were, however, part of the critical language in which Rodin's sculptures were being discussed at the time, perhaps even at the suggestion of the great sculptor himself whose role in the promotion of his art to a wider public at the 1900 Exposition Universelle was not inconsiderable.[24] Thus the preface to the official catalogue of the Rodin pavilion, authored by the sculptor's close friend, the painter Eugène Carrière, employed a series of very similar images that may well have inspired Symons.[25]

Throughout Symons's 1902 essay we perceive the presence of the sculptor himself, highly articulate about his art, in conversation with the English critic during a visit to his studio. The painter William Rothenstein, who had frequented Rodin's studio since 1897, had provided Symons with the introductory letter to Rodin which led to the friendship between the sculptor and the critic. For Rothenstein, Rodin likewise held a long and powerful fascination:

> To me Rodin's work combined an impassioned interest in tense and nervous form with a poetical vision — an artist's poetry. And, let it be confessed, there was added a certain paganism, a sensuality, a preoccupation with unusual sexual subject matter, a side of his temperament which became almost abnormally developed — which readily appeals to a young mind.[26]

The paganism, the sensuality, and the eroticism bordering on pornography were aspects to which Symons would also turn in his critical writings on the sculptor.

It is important to bear in mind that Symons was not the first English critic to engage with Rodin. Rodin already had a major reputation in England, thanks to figures like Alphonse Legros, J. A. M. Whistler, William Ernest Henley, Fredrick York Powell, and Frederic Leighton, who in many other ways bridged the French and English art worlds.[27] Since the early 1880s they had promoted Rodin's sculptures in England, making sure they were exhibited at avant-garde venues like the Grosvenor and Carfax Galleries and in more established circles like the Royal Academy. The new wealthy industrialists in both England and Scotland soon caught on to the European fashion for Rodin sculptures, and the wealthy middle classes flocked to Paris to have their portraits done by 'le Maître', to the extent that Rodin made more portraits of British sitters than of any other nationality.[28] As a consequence, several of Rodin's sculptures had found their homes in English collections, his works were strongly represented at the 1901 International Exhibition in Glasgow, and by 1908 even King Edward VII came to visit him at his home in Meudon.[29] Rodin's membership in 1898 of the International Society of Sculptors, Painters, and Gravers in London brought him into close contact with the international community of artists working in the English capital and cemented his status as a European celebrity sculptor with an appeal that reached far beyond Paris and France.

Rothenstein was, however, among the first to see the quality of the sculptor's graphic works and was keen to publicise those to an English audience around the turn of the century. He saw the drawings as:

> Very powerful, classical and romantic at the same time, evoking sculpture which no one, not even Rodin himself, had attempted. They were magnificent drawings, and I was enthusiastic about them, to Rodin's surprise — and pleasure, I think. No one, he said, had thought much of these scraps — certainly not enough to acquire them. I assured him that English collectors would jump at the chance, and he confided the drawings to my care.[30]

In his *Memoirs*, Rothenstein expressed his dislike of Rodin's celebrity status in Europe, while waspishly portraying Symons as 'a veritable amateur of artists', who 'collected them with the passion others have for china and pictures, poring over his impression of their characters like a connoisseur over his treasures'.[31] Symons here sounds like an unsympathetic collector in a piece of fiction by Henry James, gregarious and obsessive in his search for celebrities. The biographical nature of so many of Symons's essays on his contemporaries highlights the eyewitness account and the interrelationship between subject and object, allowing for a dialogic discourse on art and literature which never leaves the critic entirely out of sight. Yet Symons follows a long tradition: Vasari and Boswell spring to mind as forebears who in a similar way interwove their own personas with those of the friends and colleagues they were portraying.

There is no doubt that Rodin's status as 'Le Maître' encouraged such portraiture in which the disciple records the words of the Master. Symons's early writings about Rodin coincide in time with those of another foreign poet-critic, Rainer Maria Rilke, whose 1903 monograph — a distillation of conversations with Rodin leading up to Rilke's appointment as his private secretary in 1905 — contributed greatly to the sculptor's international fame.[32] Like Symons, Rilke is both spectator and interlocutor, observing the great man at work and listening to his theories about the art of sculpture and the interrelationship between life and art. Rilke's book had as an epitaph a quotation from Pomponius Gauricus's *De Scultura* (c. 1504): 'Writers work through words — Sculptors through matter'. One might think the author wants to suggest a separation of the two arts, but the text which follows constantly interweaves them and reveals their interdependence. Again, the sculptor is almost inseparable from his works, and the metonymic hands of creation become an entry gate into the exploration of the sculptor and his works:

> One thinks of how small man's hands are, how soon they tire, and how little time is given them to move. And one longs to see these hands that have lived like a hundred hands; like a nation of hands that rose before sunrise for the accomplishment of this work. One asks for the man who directs these hands. Who is this man?[33]

The search for the man ties Rilke's writings to those of Symons; neither the English nor the German poet-critic stopped writing about Rodin after just one essay.

It would seem that in Symons's writings the desire to capture the great man himself became even stronger after Rodin's death in 1917. In the 1929 essay Symons's English prose is interspersed with several of the master's maxims and *bons mots* in French in an attempt to evoke a voice that has now been silenced. A discussion of Judith Cladel's book *Auguste Rodin pris sur la vie* (1903) serves as a pretext for the inclusion of a range of Rodin's own theories about art in French, as a direct way of reaching across the grave, unmediated by translation. Symons also drew on Rodin's own artistic testament, *Les Cathédrales de France* [Cathedrals of France], published in 1914. Rodin's own definition of the interrelationship between architecture and sculpture takes us back to Symons's observations about rhythm and sculpture at the very opening of *Studies in Seven Arts*: 'Harmony in living bodies results from the counterbalancing of masses that move. A Cathedral is built on the principle of living bodies'.[34] Rodin's sculpture *La Cathédrale* (1908) — a *pas de deux*, two right hands confronting each other — bears some resemblance to the ribbed vault of a Gothic cathedral and combines empty space and the creator's hands into an organic structure which grows out of the earth. It revolves around notions of reflection: the two hands resemble each other, yet they are not mirror images. Similarly, Rodin's maxims about equilibrium would seem to echo Symons, or is it the other way around?

> Neither the light nor the mass of shadow are important; it is the modelling, the equilibrium that makes itself felt. When a figure is true in its contrasts, one feels the equilibrium, and if the equilibrium is good, one senses the possibility of movement, of life.[35]

Symons began his writings about Rodin with a discussion of the drawings exhibited inside the pavilion at the Place de l'Alma in 1900. At the other end of his career, the 1929 essay was illustrated solely with Rodin's drawings of women, one of which was a presentation drawing of a reclining woman given to Arthur and Rhoda Symons in August 1908, shortly before Symons's mental breakdown in September.[36] The vibrant outlines of Rodin's drawings reflect the process of capturing the movement of three-dimensional form in a two-dimensional medium. Symons's chosen focus on the drawings — both as individual works of art in their own right and as preparatory studies for sculpture — stresses rhythm and movement and reflects the new interest in Rodin's graphic works which was only just developing. In 1897 the so-called 'Album Goupil' was published in an exclusive edition of 125 copies with facsimiles of 142 of Rodin's early drawings.[37] The many photographs from inside Rodin's pavilion at the 1900 Exposition Universelle reveal how framed drawings could be seen alongside Eugène Druet's photographs of Rodin's sculptures, likewise framed and hung on the walls.[38] The Album Goupil was also on display and, together with the photographs of the sculptures, the facsimiles stressed modern methods of reproduction and raised issues of original versus copy and of the general proliferation and circulation of Rodin's *oeuvre* in a modern and increasingly technological world.

Symons emphasised the states of expressive ecstasy in these drawings of nude women, Baudelaire's *femmes damnées*, and the overwhelming sense of eroticism they conveyed. He responded to the anonymity of the women and to the sculptor's complete lack of interest in facial expression; as a consequence the women depicted became as serialised and strange as the Javanese dancers Symons had captured in his poem of 1889. As he evoked their ecstatic energy in terms of animals and devastating machines, the women lost every trace of humanity.[39] Twisting and turning around their own axes, around a pivot of desire, Rodin's women become mechanical puppets, phantasms, obsessive and terrifying in their monotony.[40] To Symons, Rodin's women are both profoundly primitive and products of the modern world and thus, in a sense, epitomes of the extremes which met at the Exposition Universelle, as the so-called savage representatives of the French Empire were displayed next to the very latest inventions in industry and technology.[41]

Just across from Rodin's exhibition at the Place d'Alma, the sculptor's friend, the American dancer Loïe Fuller, staged a one-woman show which was fully competitive with Rodin's elaborate self-promotion. Although, strictly speaking, a foreign pavilion, Fuller's dance exhibition was situated among the French and Parisian pavilions, thus testifying to the naturalised state of 'La Loïe' at the turn of the century. It combined sculpture and dance in the most intricate ways, as Rhonda Garelick has demonstrated:

> Her theatre at the Fair, designed by Henri Sauvage, was an Art Nouveau masterpiece adorned with a row of marble sculptures of Fuller by Pierre Roche. Its façade consisted of a sculpted stone replica of an undulating stage curtain, recalling Fuller's own sinuous stage costumes while simultaneously giving visitors the impression of walking through a curtain and onto a stage set themselves.[42]

More than anyone at the time, Fuller combined technological innovation with notions of woman as flower and animal. Her *danse serpentine* of the mid 1890s had been all the rage in America and Paris, and her transformations of self through dance into butterflies, black moths, lilies, orchids, and violets were processes of metamorphosis in which the dancer's body became the animal or flower forms which gave name to her dance. Her ephemeral sculptures in dance challenged gravity, as she hurled sails of white silk high into the air with the help of bamboo or aluminium rods:

> Underlying all the sculptural play with fabric was Fuller's system of hooked bamboo and aluminium rods that were sewn into the underside of the silk. These rods, patented in 1894, essentially became extensions of the dancer's arms, allowing Fuller to hold a costume as far as ten feet from her body.
> The overhead shapes formed by the fabric and rods required considerable force and control on Fuller's part. Once aloft, the shapes spun partly out of centrifugal force, in the manner of clay pots taking shape on a spinning wheel. In the case of her 1895 *Dance of the Lily*, a costume of five hundred yards of thin white Chinese silk reached a height of twenty feet over her head.[43]

As Garelick states, 'Fuller was neither entirely human, nor entirely machine, but an onstage enactment of the *fin de siècle*'s — and modernism's — newly blurred boundaries between these realms'.[44] She was, in effect, turning nineteenth-century ballet upside down, with her extended arms and hands as the counterparts of the modern ballerina's extended feet and legs, and rather than revealing her own body, she was concealing it behind swirls of white fabric, transforming her physical self into pure aesthetic form, moving towards a spiritual image which appealed to Symons.

The rhythmical hide and seek of her body — now you see it, now you don't — as she folded and unfolded her arms, allowed for a new kind of rhythmic viewing, much favoured by one of Symons's other French idols, Stéphane Mallarmé, whose repeated praise of Fuller celebrated her as the very essence of nothingness, as pure idea, a disembodied sign.[45] As an extension of Mallarmé's poetics of language working primarily through veiling and allusion, Loïe Fuller's art of dance played with spatial and aural rhythm in a manner which was entirely new. With its

Fig. 1.1. Loïe Fuller rehearsing, <https://commons.wikimedia.org/wiki/File:Houghton_MS_Thr_415_-_La_Loie_Fuller_rehearsing.jpg>.

merging of form and content, her dancing body provided the meeting ground for spatial and aural rhythm. Felicia McCarren points out how:

> Like music, like poetry at its best, Fuller's veils work rhythmically, shifting rhythm from sound to silk. For Mallarmé, rhythm makes evocation, allusion, or suggestion possible because it functions in language like the veil, seeming to hide, while in fact it reveals. And, like the veil, rhythm works through condensation; it is an overlapping rather than an excision or deletion.
>
> For Mallarmé, rhythm is a way to describe the form that structures both poetry and dance, language and the body: the form that structures but that cannot be seen.[46]

Unlike much nineteenth-century dance, Fuller's dances were non-narrative, moving towards the abstraction of the sign in a way not unlike what Symons was trying to achieve with some of his poetry. Fuller may have approached ideal nothingness for Mallarmé and soared towards the realm of the spiritual, but the heavy physical presence of the far from sylph-like woman should not be forgotten. The many Art Nouveau sculptures of Fuller elongate her into a lithe, swaying spirit, turning around her own pivotal centre with her arms and draperies into ideal form, yet for a spectator like Jean Cocteau, not engaged in erotic fantasies about the female form, the experience of the dancer in performance was different. She may have been the spirit of the age, the epitome of the *fin de siècle*, but the actual voluminous body of Fuller resounds in Cocteau's description:

> I retain only one vibrant image from the *Exposition Universelle* [...]. Mme Loie Fuller [...] a fat, ugly American woman with glasses atop a pedestal maneuvering great waves of supple silk [...] creating innumerable orchids of light and fabric unfurling, rising, disappearing, turning, floating [...]. Let us all hail this dancer who [...] created the phantom of an era.[47]

Fuller's entrepreneurial nature went beyond the staging of herself, and at her own initiative she staged the first exhibition of the sculptor's works at the National Arts Club in New York in 1903, an exhibition which admittedly only lasted a week, but which displayed a range of Rodin's sculptural works, many of them in Fuller's own possession.[48] Already in 1896 a journalist had pointed out that Fuller broke significantly with centuries of dance tradition: 'Since prehistoric periods dancers have danced with their feet, but Loie dances with her hands';[49] and, like Rodin, she was fascinated by the expressive powers of the hand. He took bronze casts of her hands, and in 1914 she had a series of photographs of her hands taken in which she created sculptural shapes, evoking some of the organic shapes of Rodin's *oeuvre*.[50] The same year she choreographed *La Danse des mains* in homage to the sculptor and his exploration of the expressive potential of the hand: her entire body was shrouded in darkness, leaving only her hands to dance in the light from strong projectors, giving the audience a puppet show minus the puppets, as her hands danced and evoked different emotional states of mind.[51] The event itself, and the carefully posed hands in the arty gelatine print photographs, invite comparisons to Rodin's fragmented hands and his use of photography as a means of circulating his art to a wider audience. The dancer and the sculptor employed the same photographer, Eugène Druet, who had been Rodin's court photographer since 1896. He also photographed Fuller dancing, or posed next to some of Rodin's sculptures, and the archives in the Musée Rodin hold about a hundred photographs of Fuller in Rodin's possession, testifying to the exchange of ideas between the dancer and the sculptor, with photography as a mediating element.[52] In her *Danse des mains*, Fuller's hands, detached from the rest of the body, take on a life of their own somewhere between nature and art. In the spotlight they perform according to the very latest technological inventions. Electricity enabled a new fragmented version of the dancer's body, a different kind of hide and seek, leaving only a partial view of the performer. Celebrated in 1900 as 'la fée éléctricité', heralding the rhythm and energy of the new century, Fuller was already famous for her use of special light effects, sometimes employing up to thirty specially trained electricians for her performances. The rhythm of the modern pervaded every aspect of her performance.

One cannot overestimate the importance of the Exposition Universelle as a forum for cultural and artistic exchange. This was where Symons encountered the full range of Rodin's works and this was also where the young Isadora Duncan, fresh from America, encountered the art of both Fuller and Rodin. Duncan had moved to Europe in 1900 with her brother Raymond, first settling in London, where she took a rather unusual approach to the study of dance:

> We spent most of our time in the British Museum, where Raymond made sketches of all the Greek vases and bas-reliefs, and I tried to express them to whatever music seemed to me to be in harmony with the rhythms of the feet and Dionysiac set of the head, and the tossing of the thyrsis.[53]

Similar scenes played themselves out in the Louvre, where the guards found the behaviour of the dancing and drawing duo highly suspect.[54] Duncan's methods may well have been inspired by Maurice Emmanuel's *La Danse grecque antique* (1896) which drew a series of parallels between the postures seen on vases, bas-reliefs, and Tanagra figurines and the postures and positions of modern dance with special reference to the interrelationship between graphic and bodily rhythm.[55] The book was illustrated with primitive line engravings from antique art and stylised outlines of modern dance positions, alongside a few specimens of modern chronophotography of a woman dancing, in the dress and postures of a Tanagra dancer and her modern equivalent. The path from antiquity to modernity was short in *fin-de-siècle* Paris, and soon Duncan was touring with 'la fée électricité' and entering the studio world of Rodin, who also paid the dancer a reciprocal visit. The latter experience was nothing short of an erotic pagan encounter with the Great God Pan and a missed opportunity of the complete merging of sculpture and dance:

> He gazed at me with lowered lids, his eyes blazing, and then, with the same expression that he had before his works, he came toward me. He ran his hands over my neck, breast, stroked my arms and ran his hands over my hips, my bare legs and feet. He began to knead my whole body as if it were clay, while from him emanated [a] heat that scorched and melted me. My whole desire was to yield to him my entire being and, indeed, I would have done so if it had not been that my upbringing caused me to become frightened, and I withdrew, threw my dress over my tunic, and sent him away bewildered. What a pity! How often I have regretted this childish miscomprehension which lost to me the divine chance of giving my virginity to the Great God Pan, the mighty Rodin. Art and all Life would have been richer thereby![56]

In Duncan's account of the cultural clash between the puritan American and the sensuous Frenchman we sense the maenad in the making. The savage god, seeing through his hands, approaches the organic world through touch and transforms cold flesh into melting desire. Duncan's swift feet, however, soon took her back to the great sculptor, and they struck up a life-long friendship. In 1908 the present Musée

Fig. 1.2. Isadora Duncan at the Theatre of Dionysus, Athens, <https://commons.wikimedia.org/wiki/Category:Isadora_Duncan#/media/File:Isadora_Duncan_1903.jpg>.

Rodin at the Hôtel Biron, in the rue de Varenne, housed one of Duncan's dance studios while also providing studio space for Cocteau, Rodin, Rilke, and Matisse. The place became 'the site of such raucous entertainments, "Roman" parties, and fêtes champêtres that the French government, which owned the building, shut it down'.[57]

Duncan's natural dance — on bare feet, in thin Greek-inspired tunics which revealed the contours of the body underneath and allowed maximum freedom of movement — formed an interesting counterpart to Fuller's veiled metamorphoses of her techno-body into butterflies and lilies. The freely flowing rhythms of paganism revived moved in quite other directions than the technologically adept Fuller, who employed fluorescent paints, x-rays, and enormous amounts of kilowattage for her performances. Inspired by Friedrich Nietzsche's *The Birth of Tragedy* (1872) and the Cambridge Ritualists, Isadora Duncan saw a strong interconnection between the choric dance of Greek tragedy and the ritual dances in honour of Dionysus, and her Greek dance forms part of the revival of the figure of the maenad at the *fin de siècle*.[58]

Poets and scholars like A. Mary F. Robinson, 'Michael Field', and Jane Harrison were all drawing parallels between the unleashings of sexual and creative energy of the maenads and the phenomenon of the 'New Woman'. Duncan's free dance was part of the liberation of the female body from the constraints of corsets, shoes, or the schools of classical ballet, and in the Greek cult of the nude and in the direct contact with the earth she found a universal freedom transcending time. In her artistic manifesto, 'The Dancer of the Future' (c. 1902) she made it clear that her project was not a revivalist one, but an international, aesthetic, and feminist movement, striving towards complete harmony between soul and body, self and society:

> The dance of the future will be a new movement, a consequence of the entire evolution which mankind has passed through. To return to the dances of the Greeks would be as impossible as it is unnecessary. We are not Greeks and therefore cannot dance Greek dances.
> But the dance of the future will have to become again a high religious art as it was with the Greeks. For art which is not religious, is mere merchandise.
> The dancer of the future will be one whose body and soul have grown so harmoniously together that the natural language of the soul will have become the movement of the body. The dancer will not belong to a nation but to all humanity. She will dance not in the form of a nymph, nor fairy, nor coquette, but in the form of a woman in her greatest and purest expression. She will realize the mission of woman's body and the holiness of its parts. She will dance the changing life of nature, showing how each part is transformed into the other. From all parts of her body shall shine radiant intelligence, bringing to the world the message of the thoughts and aspirations of thousands of women. She shall dance the freedom of woman.[59]

As in Symons's 'The World as Ballet', Duncan's notion of the dancer is gendered. The radiant image of the female dancer, who blends soul and body into pure expression, is an idealised abstraction of woman, but unlike Symons's symbolist, aestheticised image, Duncan's vision is highly politicised. The fact that the silent image had now been given a voice, and even an articulate one, stressed the gendered tension between male spectator/critic/poet and female dancer, and male sculptor and female model. The 'radiant intelligence' of Duncan's dancer of the future is one which applies both to the command of her body and her mind. Change, transformation, and the notion of one movement leading to another, are all part of the imagined choreography of Duncan's dancer, who is a modern maenad in control of her movements. Her art is self-begotten, and she is at once both dancer and choreographer, artist and work of art.

The new sculpture and the new dance at the *fin de siècle* broke with conventions of schooling and academies; neither Rodin nor Fuller nor Duncan were the products of established art or ballet schools. Their innovative developments of art forms which had existed since antiquity sprang from complete artistic freedom and a lack of the constraint imposed by a formative professional training. Yet, once they had established their idiosyncratic styles and methods in the art world, they all set up schools of disciples who perpetuated their art. '"Rodin surrounds himself in his studio with slabs of marble", Isadora said. "I want to surround myself also; my block of marble — my pupils"'.[60] Her disciples, popularly known as the Isadorables, trained by her in Germany and France, became clones of herself in their dresses and modes of dancing, and when in 1908 'La Loïe' formed her ensemble Les Ballets Loïe Fuller, the company consisted of girls whose physiognomies resembled the founder's own. The girls were not known under their own names, but were given the names of some of Fuller's dances, and thus became reflections of both herself and her art. The desire to see and stage the self, in a constant rhythmical alternation between veiling and unveiling, is a fundamental aspect of the flux of the *fin de siècle*. As the fluid rhythms of dance and sculpture met and merged, the ancient dream of the moving statue took new forms. It was no longer the cold marble statue of Pygmalion turning into flesh, but rather the malleable organic material of clay modulating into great lengths of white silk and air, assisted by the shaping powers of electricity into an altogether ethereal act of begetting.

Shaped by his activities as a poet and critic in the 1890s, Symons was highly perceptive to the changes in the exploration of the expressive potential of the female body at the *fin de siècle*. His hero-worship of the semi-divine modern male creator retained a very gendered notion of subject-object, which also finds expression in his poetry: the powers of looking and creating are associated with a predominantly masculine force, while the female is primarily erotic and performative, carrying a seductive lure which retains a mysterious secrecy of its own. Symons never engaged critically with either Fuller or Duncan at any length, thus never granting them full credit for the extraordinarily creative powers they possessed. Although their innovative influence on the development of modern dance was no less ground-breaking than the changes Rodin brought about in modern sculpture, Symons celebrated the named individual in a critical study of artistic male genius while leaving the flimsy figure of the anonymous female dancer as a suggestive image on which to conclude his *Studies in Seven Arts*. While the French sculptor himself embraced both the techno-body of 'La Loïe' and the maenadic bare-footed classicism of Isadora Duncan, the English critic proved far more conservative in his tastes, at least one step removed from the truly cutting edge of the avant-garde.

Notes to Chapter 1

1. Arthur Symons, 'Rodin', in *Studies in Seven Arts*, pp. 3–30 (p. 5).
2. Ibid., p. 390.
3. Ibid., p. 391.
4. See the last stanza of John Keats's 'Ode on a Grecian Urn' (1819): 'O Attic shape! Fair attitude! with brede | Of marble men and maidens overwrought, | With forest branches and the trodden weed; | Thou, silent form, dost tease us out of thought | As doth eternity: Cold Pastoral! | When old age shall this generation waste, | Thou shalt remain, in midst of other woe | Than ours, a friend to man, to whom thou say'st, | "Beauty is truth, truth beauty, — that is all | Ye know on earth, and all ye need to know"' (*The Poems of John Keats*, edited by Jack Stillinger (London: Heinemann, 1978), p. 373).
5. See the last stanza of W. B. Yeats's 'Among School Children' (1926): 'Labour is blossoming or dancing where | The body is not bruised to pleasure soul, | Nor beauty born out of its own despair, | Nor blear-eyed wisdom out of midnight oil. | O chestnut tree, great rooted blossomer, | Are you the leaf, the blossom or the bole? | O body swayed to music, O brightening glance, | How can we know the dancer from the dance?' (*Yeats's Poems*, edited and annotated by A. Norman Jeffares (London: Macmillan, 1989), p. 325).

6. Kermode, *Romantic Image*.
7. See *Arthur Symons: A Bibliography*, ed. by Beckson and others, nos. C.1933.1 and C.1938.1.
8. See Markert, *Arthur Symons*; Susan Azar Porterfield, 'Symons as Critic of the Visual Arts', *English Literature in Transition, 1880–1920*, 44:3 (2001), 260–74.
9. Arthur Symons, 'Javanese Dancers', in *Silhouettes* (London: Mathews & Lane, 1892), p. 42 (stanzas 3–5).
10. Beckson, *Arthur Symons*, pp. 82–83.
11. A selection of Symons's dance criticism has been made available: '"More Natural than Nature, more Artificial than Art": The Dance Criticism of Arthur Symons, introduced and annotated by Jane Pritchard', *Dance Research*, 21:2 (Winter 2003), 36–89.
12. See Heather Marcovitch, 'Dance, Ritual, and Arthur Symons's London Nights', *English Literature in Transition, 1880–1920*, 56:4 (2013), 462–82.
13. Arthur Symons, 'Prologue', in *London Nights* (London: Smithers, 1895), p. 3 (stanzas 1–2).
14. Arthur Symons, 'Rodin', in *From Toulouse-Lautrec to Rodin with Some Personal Impressions* (London: John Lane, 1929), pp. 219–42 (p. 219).
15. See Symons's remark to his friend, the painter Augustus John, in a letter of April 1910, as he was recovering from his mental illness: 'Only one woman exists for me, who is here [his wife, Rhoda]. Only two men exist for me: Rodin and you. So let there be eternal luck for these famous four!' (*Arthur Symons: Selected Letters*, ed. by Beckson and Munro, p. 215).
16. Princeton University, Auguste Rodin Collection, Box 1, Folder 16A (C0195).
17. The small bronze is entitled *Femme sur une colonne* [Woman on a Column], c.1900–03, and inscribed 'Hommage à Madame et Monsieur Arthur Symons. A. Rodin' around the top of the column. Tate registration no N06070.
18. Beckson, *Arthur Symons*, p. 261.
19. Arthur Symons, 'Les Dessins de Rodin', trans. by Henry D. Davray, in *Auguste Rodin et son œuvre* (Paris: Éditions de 'La Plume', 1900), pp. 47–48.
20. *Arthur Symons: A Bibliography*, ed. by Beckson and others, nos A.19, A.54, B.22, C.1902.78, C.1903.32, C.1904.41, C.1917.19, C.1922.15, C.1931.2.
21. Symons, 'Rodin', in *From Toulouse-Lautrec to Rodin*, p. 219.
22. Symons, 'Rodin', in *Studies in Seven Arts*, p. 5. In fact, Rodin's admiration for Michelangelo has been amply demonstrated, see Flavio Fergonzi and Maria Lamberti, *Rodin and Michelangelo: A Study in Artistic Inspiration* (Philadelphia: Philadelphia Museum of Art, 1997).
23. Symons, 'Rodin', in *Studies in Seven Arts*, p. 3.
24. See *Rodin en 1900: l'exposition de l'Alma*, ed. by Antoinette Le Normand-Romain, Musée du Luxembourg (Paris: Réunion des Musées Nationaux, 2001).
25. Eugène Carrière: 'L'art de Rodin sort de la terre et y retourne, semblable aux blocs géants, rochers ou dolmens qui affirment les solitudes et dans l'héroïque grandissement desquels l'homme s'est reconnu. [...] Ainsi la terre projette au dehors ses formes apparentes, images, statues qui nous pénètrent du sens de sa vie intérieure [...]. Les arbres, les plantes, lui ont révélé leur analogie avec ces belles jeunes femmes aux jambes lisses montant en frêles colonnes' [Rodin's art springs from the earth and returns to it, like giant blocks of stone, rocks or megaliths which confirm their solitudes and in whose heroic grandeur man recognises himself. [...] Thus the earth projects its visible forms, its images and statues which penetrate us with its sense of inner life. [...] The trees, the plants have revealed to him the resemblances to those beautiful young women with smooth legs which rise up like frail columns] ('Préface', in *L'Œuvre de Rodin: exposition Rodin*, Pavillon de Hanovre (Paris: Société d'Édition Artistique, Imprimerie D. Dumoulin, 1900), pp. 10–11 (p. 10)). All English translations are the author's own unless otherwise stated.
26. William Rothenstein, *Men and Memories: Recollections of William Rothenstein 1872–1900*, 2 vols (London: Faber & Faber, 1931), II, 322.
27. Legros had, for example, introduced Rothenstein to Rodin. See Tomoko Ando, 'Rodin's Reputation in Great Britain: The Neglected Role of Alphonse Legros', *Nineteenth-Century Art Worldwide: A Journal of Nineteenth-Century Visual Culture*, 15:3 (Autumn 2016), <http://www.19thc-artworldwide.org/index.php/autumn16/ando-on-rodin-reputation-in-great-britain-neglected-role-of-alphonse-legros> [accessed 30 November 2016].

28. See Antoinette Le Normand-Romain, '"When I Consider the Honours that Have Been Bestowed Upon Me in England"', in *Rodin*, ed. by Catherine Lampert, exhibition catalogue (London: Royal Academy of Arts, 2006), pp. 118–31 (p. 127).
29. Ibid., pp. 123 and 125.
30. Rothenstein, *Men and Memories*, I, 321.
31. Ibid., II, 47. Rothenstein prints Symons's letter begging for an introduction to Rodin and repeatedly highlights his own friendship with the French sculptor and his efforts to introduce him to the English art world.
32. See Rainer Maria Rilke, *Auguste Rodin*, trans. by Jessie Lemont and Hans Trausil (London: Pallas Athene, 2006).
33. Ibid., pp. 17–18.
34. Auguste Rodin, *Cathedrals of France*, trans. by Elisabeth Chase Geissbuhler (London & New York: Country Life, 1965), p. 3.
35. Ibid., pp. 68–69.
36. The drawing is now in the British Museum. It is signed and inscribed on the front: 'en hommage à | Madame & Monsieur | Symons | Rodin' (British Museum, Department of Prints and Drawings, registration number 1937, 0213.7).
37. *Les Dessins de Auguste Rodin reproduits en fac-similé par la Maison Goupil*, ed. by Maurice Fenaille (Paris: Boussod, Manzi, Joyant et Cie, 1897).
38. See Claudrie Judrin, 'Dessins: l'obscur et le clair', in *Rodin en 1900*, ed. by Le Normand-Romain, pp. 344–51.
39. Symons would speak of 'la femme animal, et, dans un sens assez étrange, la femme idole' [the animal woman, and, in such a strange sense, the woman idol]; 'C'est une machine en mouvement, monstrueuse et dévastatrice, agissant automatiquement et possédée de la rage de l'animal' [She's a machine in movement, monstrous and destructive, which acts automatically and is possessed by the rage of an animal] (Symons, 'Les Dessins de Rodin', pp. 47–48).
40. 'Chaque mouvement de son corps, violemment agité par le souvenir ou l'attente du plaisir sensuel, est fixé dans un moment expressif. Elle tourne sur elle-même en cent attitudes, toujours sur le pivot central de son sexe qui accentue avec une fantastique et terrifiante monotonie, comme une obsession' [Every movement of her body, violently agitated by the recollection or expectation of sensuous pleasure is fixed into an expressive moment. She revolves around herself in a hundred attitudes, always around the central pivot of her sex which she accentuates with a fantastic and terrifying monotony, like an obsession] (Symons, 'Les Dessins de Rodin', p. 48).
41. See Jean-Christophe Mabire, *L'Esposition Universelle de 1900* (Paris: l'Harmattan, 2000).
42. Rhonda K. Garelick, *Electric Salome: Loie Fuller's Performance of Modernism* (Princeton, NJ: Princeton University Press, 2007), p. 81.
43. Ibid., p. 40.
44. Ibid., p. 6.
45. See Stéphane Mallarmé, 'Autre étude de danse' (1893–96), from *Divagations* (1897), in *Igitur, Divagations, Un coup de dés*, ed. by Bertrand Marchal (Paris: Gallimard, 2003), pp. 206–11. See Susan Jones, '"Une écriture corporelle": The Dancer in the Text of Mallarmé and Yeats', in *The Body and the Arts*, ed. by Corinne Saunders, Ulrika Maude, and Jane Macnaughton (Basingstoke: Palgrave Macmillan, 2009), pp. 237–53.
46. Felicia M. McCarren, 'The "Symptomatic Act": Mallarmé, Charcot, and Loie Fuller', in *Dance Pathologies: Performance, Poetics, Medicine* (Stanford, CA: Stanford University Press, 1998), pp. 113–71 (p. 124).
47. Jean Cocteau, *Souvenirs* (1935), quoted by Garelick, *Electric Salome*, p. 14.
48. See Hélène Pinet, 'Loïe Fuller and Auguste Rodin: Dancer and Impresario', in *Body Stages: The Metamorphosis of Loïe Fuller*, ed. by Emma Cavazzini and Doriana Comerlati (Milan: Skira, 2014), pp. 55–63.
49. Review of Loïe Fuller at Koster and Bial, *New York Sun*, 23 February 1896, quoted by Garelick, *Electric Salome*, p. 146.
50. Garelick, *Electric Salome*, p. 7.

51. See Hélène Marraud, *Rodin: Revealing Hands* (Paris: Éditions du Musée Rodin, 2005), pp. 57–59.
52. See Juliet Bellow, 'Beyond Movement: Auguste Rodin and the Dancers of his Time', in *Rodin and Dance: The Essence of Movement*, ed. by Alexandra Gerstein, Courtauld Gallery and Musée Rodin (London: Paul Holberton, 2016), pp. 41–59 (p. 48).
53. Isadora Duncan, *My Life* (London: Victor Gollancz, 1928), p. 63.
54. Ibid., pp. 76–77.
55. See Maurice Emmanuel, *La Danse grecque antique* (Paris: Librairie Hachette et Cie, 1896).
56. Duncan, *My Life*, p. 100. The English edition of the text is expurgated, stops at 'bewildered', and thus leaves out the last revealing sentences which seem very heartfelt from Duncan's pen. Peter Kurth, *Isadora: A Sensational Life* (New York & London: Little, Brown, 2001), quotes the full passage from the American edition on p. 76.
57. Kurth, *Isadora*, pp. 244–45.
58. See Fiona Macintosh, 'Dancing Maenads in Early Twentieth-Century Britain', in *The Ancient Dancer in the Modern World: Responses to Greek and Roman Dance*, ed. by Fiona Macintosh (Oxford: Oxford University Press, 2010), pp. 188–208; Yopie Prins, 'Greek Maenads, Victorian Spinsters', in *Victorian Sexual Dissidence*, ed. by Richard Dellamora (Chicago: University of Chicago Press, 1999), pp. 43–82. For the Dionysiac in a poetic context, see Charlotte Ribeyrol, 'Poetic Podophilia: Gautier, Baudelaire, Swinburne, and Classical Foot-Fetishism', *Journal of Victorian Culture*, 20:2 (2015), 212–29. Symons was himself a great admirer of Nietzsche, as was his close friend Havelock Ellis, who was one of the foremost promoters of Nietzsche to English audiences. See Marcovitch, 'Dance, Ritual, and Arthur Symons's London Nights'.
59. Isadora Duncan, 'The Dancer of the Future', quoted from *The Twentieth-Century Performance Reader*, ed. by Michael Huxley and Noel Witts (London: Routledge, 2002), pp. 164–69 (p. 169).
60. Quoted by Kurth, *Isadora*, p. 366.

CHAPTER 2

Symons, Beardsley, and the 'Minims and Crotchets' of Art

Jane Desmarais

> Music speaks no language known to us, has nothing of ourselves to tell us, but is shy, alien, and speaks a language which we do not know. It comes to us as a divine hallucination, chills us a little with its 'airs from heaven' or elsewhere, and breaks down for an instant the too solid walls of the world, showing us the gulf.
>
> ARTHUR SYMONS, 'Pachmann and the Piano'[1]

In the preface of *Plays, Acting, and Music* Arthur Symons describes his aim as 'working my way towards the concrete expression of a theory, or system of aesthetics, of all the arts'.[2] 'System of aesthetics' or 'musical aesthetics': these terms may be too definitive for a music amateur such as Symons, who according to the leading British music critic Ernest Newman lacked a 'musical brain', but his ambition should not be disregarded.[3] Of all the arts, music was for Symons both the supreme expression of the imaginative life and a 'divine hallucination', full of foreignness and mystery. His reflections on the 'interpenetration of substance and form' and his concern with what he called the 'universal science of beauty' represented a new direction in modern aesthetics, towards greater freedom of association between the arts.[4] He claimed:

> I do not understand the limitation by which so many writers on aesthetics choose to confine themselves to the study of artistic principles as they are seen in this or that separate form of art. Each art has its own law, its own capacities, its own limits; these it is the business of the critic jealously to distinguish. Yet, in the study of art as art, it should be his endeavour to master the universal science of beauty.[5]

Symons's pursuit of the 'science of beauty' and his openness to Baudelairean correspondences between the arts mark him out as a distinctive voice in English art criticism at the turn of the twentieth century. He was as comfortable with traditional Romantic and Victorian perspectives as he was curious about modern Continental theories, and in his critical writings from the 1890s we encounter a broad range of preoccupations and practices. Symons was a catalyst not only in the emergence of major poetic developments in the early twentieth century, but in aesthetic thinking and in writing about the arts.

Within Symons's critical *oeuvre* one essay stands out as a turning point in the evolution of his writing about the arts. In his obituary notice for Aubrey Beardsley in the *Fortnightly Review* in May 1898 Symons relates the innate musicality of Beardsley's decorative designs to the 'unemotional intellect' of the young artist, declaring it 'emotional only in perhaps the highest sense, where emotion almost ceases to be recognisable, in the abstract, for ideas, for lines'.[6] 'Using the puff-box, the toilet-table, the ostrich-feather hat, with a full consciousness of their suggestive quality [...]', Symons goes on,

> [Beardsley] put these things to beautiful uses, because he liked their forms, and because his space of white or black seemed to require some such arrangement of lines. They were the minims and crotchets by which he wrote down his music; they made the music but they were not the music.[7]

Symons's correspondence between Beardsley's art and musical composition was high praise indeed for a controversial illustrator whose working life had begun only five years earlier and whose creative output in the previous year and a half had been restricted to limited-circulation publications. Not only did it draw special attention of critics and the public to what was fairly obvious about Beardsley's style — black lines and stipples on white paper — but it emphasised a defining juxtaposition in his work between sensuality of form and abstraction of style. 'The conventional draughtsman, any Academy student, will draw a line which shows quite accurately the curve of a human body', Symons comments, 'but all his science of drawing will not make you *feel* that line, will not make that line pathetic' (my emphasis).[8] By focusing on the suggestiveness of form, its ability to make the viewer *feel* rather than merely acknowledge its truth to material fact, Symons was directing appreciation to and formulating a language for an issue at the heart of modern aesthetics, the significant *affective* power of form. How and why does art *move* us? This was the question that preoccupied Symons and for which he attempted to articulate a response in his critical writings. As I aim to show here, his obituary inspired numerous later critics of Beardsley who used the metaphor of music to situate Beardsley's achievement outside late-Victorian book illustration and within the realm of modern art.

In this chapter, I consider Symons's conceptualisation of music as both a sensuous and spiritual experience from different perspectives. I look at the fusion of music, perfume, and memory in his early poetry and critical prose writing, and with close reference to Symons's appreciation of Beardsley's 'musicality', go on to discuss Symons's influence on the artist's critical reception after 1898. I argue that while Symons's music criticism was, as Nicholas Freeman has commented, 'largely poetic appreciation', his application of a musical metaphor to Beardsley's art had far-reaching influence and prefigured some of the radical formulations of formalist critics like Roger Fry and Clive Bell at the turn of the twentieth century.[9]

For many artists and writers in the late nineteenth century, music was the aesthetic ideal, revered for what Hegel termed its 'abstract subjectivity', its detachment from the 'objective' world, its consummate expressiveness.[10] Symons regarded music as the ideal art. In his critical writing from the late 1890s to 1908, he pondered the abstract and somewhat mysterious power of music, and claimed it as the 'one absolutely disembodied art when it is heard, and no more than a proposition of Euclid, when it is written'.[11]

The principal reference-points for *fin-de-siècle* aesthetes like Symons were, of course, Walter Pater and James McNeill Whistler. While Pater's dictum that 'All art constantly aspires towards the condition of music'[12] was taken by many as an endorsement of the fusion of the arts and a signal to express the content of art *through* the 'imaginative perception' of form, Whistler (following Gautier's lead) synthesised the practices of painting and music.[13] His titles (arrangements, harmonies, nocturnes, symphonies) effectively recalibrated the way in which the Victorian public looked at art, drawing attention away from representation and signification to the art of picture-making itself and encouraging a more blended view of the arts as in complementary relation to one another.

Music is 'disembodied' and abstract, a 'language', Symons maintained, 'in which birds and other angels may talk', but it was also for him a highly sensual (syn)aesthetic experience. Symons *saw* sounds.[14] In his critical prose writings, he frequently invokes music in visual and tactile terms and vice versa described the supremely affective quality of visual art in musical terms. In its sensuous appeal, autonomy, and abstraction, Symons conceived music to have the potential — much like 'an articulate perfume'[15] — to stimulate the faculties of memory and 'imaginative reason', sometimes, as in his own case, to the point of madness.[16] In the summer of 1908, while in Italy, he suffered a mental breakdown, 'an illness that he partly attributed to (Wagner's) music', and ceased writing about music.[17] In *Confessions: A Study in Pathology* (1930), Symons recalls the torment of music in Venice:

> The gondoliers' hoarse shouting comes violently through the music. Two or three phrases, poignant and piercing, monotonous and profound, rise suddenly out of the luminous night of waters. It was this cry that Wagner heard from the balcony on that fortunate night when he found the melody for his shepherd's pipe. Inspiring, disconnected scraps of song, harsh expressive voices, abrupt pauses and repetitions, but with a strange fantastic beauty; songs that decorate and illumine the night, cries out of the depth of the secret heart of Venice, songs instinctive and remote, melancholy and passionate, what strange and obscure secrets you conceal![18]

To understand Symons's use of the musical metaphor in Paterian and Whistlerian terms alone is to underplay Symons's complex conceptualisation of music and his significant contribution to modern aesthetic criticism. In the years following the publication in March 1900 of *The Symbolist Movement in Literature*, Symons worked at an exhausting pace, writing drama and music reviews for various papers. In 1902 he wrote 'Christian Trevalga', a short story about a concert pianist (collected in *Spiritual Adventures*, 1905), followed by his first attempt to write for the stage: *Tristan and Iseult* (1902–03), a verse tragedy in four acts inspired by a recent visit to Bayreuth. In 1903 and 1906 two books dedicated to non-literary arts appeared: *Plays, Acting, and Music* and *Studies in Seven Arts*, alongside music reviews in various journals that intensified in 1907 and 1908 in regular contributions to the *Saturday Review*.

Symons was a passionate amateur of music, sensitive to the challenges of musical craftsmanship and performance and alert to the contemporary debates about 'absolute' and 'programme' music. According to the musicologist Sarah Collins in her fascinating essay on Symons's 'Theory of Musical Aesthetics', 'he was the only aesthetic critic to engage directly with the musical repertory, as opposed to an abstracted concept of music', positioning himself against the tendencies of 'modern music'.[19] Symons's outlook was distinctly cosmopolitan. He looked abroad — as he did for most things — for musical and artistic greatness. His favourite composers were Wagner, Beethoven, and Richard Strauss, and Chopin was his favourite composer for the piano. About contemporary English music he was fairly silent and he was positively disparaging about the English concert-goer. In a Letter to the Editor of the *Pall Mall Gazette* in 1890 entitled 'Are the English People Musical?' his exasperation is evident: 'It proves, and proves finally', he barked, 'that the nation which took naturally to Mendelssohn [...] has, after all, no intelligent interest in music as music [...]. It stamps us, in the face of musical Europe, a definitely non-musical nation'.[20]

By all accounts, including those ventriloquised through Trevalga in *Spiritual Adventures*, Symons himself was a decent pianist, able to sight-read and improvise. One of the first things he did when he moved into Fountain Court in 1891 was to have an upright piano hauled up several flights of stairs to his rooms. He was modest, however, and faintly erotic, about his own musical ability: 'I never acquired the technique to play a single piece correctly', he averred, 'but I learned to touch the piano as if one were caressing a living being [...] it answered me in an intimate and affectionate voice'.[21] The listening experience for Symons was physically stimulating; it was visual, tactile, and olfactory. Many Victorians experienced music in this way, of course, as in spite of various inventions and developments (including, for example, the phonograph cylinder in 1877 and the gramophone disc in 1881), music continued to be a loud, live, close-up experience. But for Symons the listening experience was more than sensory, it was *inter*sensorial.

In *Plays, Acting, and Music*, Symons corresponds the senses with Baudelairean panache. He refers to himself as a 'passionate spectator' of music, listening to 'Mozart in the Mirabell-Garten [...] with the full consent of my eyes'.[22] Of Eugène Ysaÿe's performance of Beethoven's Kreutzer Sonata on the violin, he writes that:

> An invisible touch seemed to pass over it; [...] the eyelids and the eyebrows began to move, as if the eyes saw the sound, and were drawing it in luxuriously, with a kind of sleepy ecstasy, as one draws in perfume out of a flower.[23]

And in his essay on 'Pachmann and the Piano' (Vladimir de Pachmann was regarded by Symons as the 'greatest living pianist')[24] he appends a sonnet, 'The Chopin Player', evoking the performance of the Russian-German pianist:

> The sounds torture me: I see them in my brain;
> They spin a flickering web of living threads,
> Like butterflies upon the garden beds,

> Nets of bright sound. I follow them: in vain.
> I must not brush the least dust from their wings:
> They die of a touch; but I must capture them,
> Or they will turn to a caressing flame,
> And lick my soul up with their flutterings.
>
> The sounds torture me: I count them with my eyes,
> I feel them like a thirst between my lips;
> Is it my body or my soul that cries
> With little coloured mouths of sound, and drips
> In these bright drops that turn to butterflies
> Dying delicately at my fingertips?[25]

Here Pachmann's performance is described as affecting all the senses, particularly touch, but in its intensity and transience this musical experience hints tantalisingly at capturing a fugitive spiritual realm, like chasing butterflies with an immaterial net ('Nets of bright sound').[26] The physical effects of the music dematerialise and leave the listener tortured by desire and loss (the 'bright drops that turn to butterflies').

Desire and loss are familiar themes in Symons's volumes of verse from the 1890s. They contain few unmediated references to musical works, but in the poems about dancers and dancing (which is the visual expression of music after all), the swirling and hypnotic dance rhythms are evoked by metre and form. In 'La Mélinite: Moulin Rouge', for example, a poem singled out by Yeats as 'one of the most perfect lyrics of our time',[27] the restless movement of the poem culminates in a double reference to a 'dance of shadows' in the final stanza. A single, twirling dancer narcissistically 'dances for her own delight' in a dream-like succession of circles, roses, mirrors, and shadows.[28] As Katharina Herold comments in her essay, 'Dancing the Image: Sensoriality and Kinesthetics in the Poetry of Stéphane Mallarmé and Arthur Symons':

> The poem plunges the reader into a vortex of movement, music, colour, and twirling bodies [...]. The image of 'the dance returning | Rounds the full circle, rounds' in the second stanza produces a sense of disorientation placing the reader in the centre of this 'dance of shadows'. This is stressed in the poem by the dizzying density of prepositions such as '*down* the long hall', '*into* the circle', '*apart*', '*before* the mirror', '*between* the robes' and '*back to* a shadow', which direct the reader's 'gaze'. The swift change of sensory attention demanded by the text, creates a flip-book of dancing images that rapidly pass before the mind's eye.[29]

Caught up in the word patterns and circuitous phrasings, repetitions, and refrains, we are engaged in a multi-sensory spectacle. We watch from the stalls and loiter outside stage-doors where 'Faces flicker and veer' in expectant desire.[30] However, in spite of the musicality of Symons's poetic form, inspired by the poetry of Verlaine and to a lesser extent the more radical symbolism of Mallarmé, the emphasis is on looking and seeing as portals to attraction and desire. Symons's erotic lyrics are evocations of the scintillating metropolitan theatre-land as a sphere of visualised longing, a space of countless looks and glances, both desirous and arousing desire.

Music, along with other vaporising phenomena like perfume and memory, is a recurrent trope embedded in the verse structures of Symons's early poetry. Impossible to contain or fix, music represents the sensation of the fleeting moment and thereby intensifies the poet's emotions.[31] Like a remembered moment or the whiff of a particular perfume, the sensation of listening to music is a reminder of the impossibility of being able to possess that memory or that fragrance for longer than it lasts. Above all, in its all-encompassing affective power, music suggests the overwhelming insatiability of libidinal desire.

In an early impressionist poem about music entitled 'Music and Memory', composed on 20 February 1891 and dedicated to 'K. W.', Katherine Willard, a young American woman studying singing in Berlin whom Symons befriended in 1890, Symons situates the remembrance of 'K. W.' in an intoxicatingly liquid realm of memory that, like the tide and the refrain of the poem itself ('in the night'), comes and goes rhythmically and suggestively:

> Across the tides of music, in the night,
> Her magical face,
> A light upon it as the happy light
> Of dreams in some delicious place
> Under the moonlight in the night.
>
> Music, soft throbbing music in the night,
> Her memory swims
> Into the brain, a carol of delight;
> The cup of music overbrims
> With wine of memory, in the night.
>
> Her face across the music, in the night,
> Her face a refrain,
> A light that sings along the waves of light,
> A memory that returns again,
> Music in music, in the night.[32]

Symons derived his literary Impressionism from Verlaine whom he had met in Paris in 1890 on one of his trips across the Channel with his friend Havelock Ellis. Symons admired Verlaine's evocative verse, the 'perfumed shadows', the 'hushed melodies', and he applauded his unshackling of French versification from the classical Alexandrine form and his sensitivity to the musical cadences of popular language.[33] Not everyone shared his view. In England, where many viewed the Continent as a hotbed of revolutionary idealism, such innovation was regarded as bordering on the reckless. Verlaine's musicality was viewed with great scepticism by conservative critics keen to prevent English art from being 'affected by the disease of the French School'.[34]

In the 1890s, the 'French School' caused much confusion among English art critics about the terms of engagement for evaluating modern art. There was a sharp divide between the patriotic Old Guard who championed verisimilitude and narrative and New Art critics who, sympathetic to French tendencies, realised the insufficiency of describing art in representational terms alone. With Beardsley in the mix, debates about modern art became quite heated, because on the one hand his drawings had a recognisable and often grotesque subject matter and on the other they seemed to privilege the art of decoration for its own sake. The autonomy of his illustrations, in particular, created a storm in the art press, and it was not until after his death in March 1898 that critics found a proximate language to describe his designs.[35]

This shift in aesthetic thinking was inspired by Symons's obituary tribute to Beardsley in the *Fortnightly Review*, which was published in book form in 1898 and followed by an expanded version in 1905. Symons was not the first critic to describe modern art in musical terms. The metaphor of music had been circulating in art journals and magazines since the mid-nineteenth century. The editor of *Portfolio* and an authority on etching, Philip Gilbert Hamerton (1834–94), spent many years trying to understand and articulate the primacy of form in contemporary French art, and in his popular review columns he frequently experimented with a musical analogy. In his book, *Contemporary French Painters* (1868), he described form as 'the visible melodies and harmonies, — a kind of visible music, — meaning as much and narrating as much as the music which is heard in the ears, and nothing whatever more'.[36] Hamerton focused on French artists' preoccupation with 'organic form' and, recalling Whistler's aestheticism, he claimed:

> When they paint a woman they do not take the slightest interest in her personally, she is merely, for them, a certain beautiful and fortunate arrangement of forms, an impersonal harmony and melody, melody in harmony, seen instead of being heard.[37]

Although, to a certain extent, Symons was drawing on the extensive use of synaesthesia by Swinburne and Pater in their criticism of the visual, his application of synaesthesia to music was more experimental, more suggestive. Not only was he the first author to use a synaesthetic approach in both his poetry and critical writing, but he was the first to seriously assess Beardsley's contribution to late nineteenth-century visual culture and also the first to deploy the metaphor of music in relation to Beardsley's art. Robert Ross called the essay 'the most sympathetic and introspective account of this strange artist's work', and believed that 'it [would] always remain the terminal essay'.[38] Symons 'approaches Beardsley', Ross went on:

> as he would John Bunyan or Aquinas. Art, literature and life are all to this engaging writer a scholiast's pilgrim's progress. Beside him Walter Pater, from whom he derives, seems almost flippant — and to have dallied too long in the streets of Vanity Fair.[39]

It is not surprising that Symons was drawn to the genius of Beardsley. They were both tuned in to a cosmopolitan bohemianism and shared many passions, including for contemporary French art and music. Beardsley was a musical prodigy, who, 'before he was twelve months old [...] used to beat with a brick to his mother's playing of a Beethoven sonata'.[40] Before tuberculosis rendered him weak and febrile at the age of seven, his ambition was to become a great pianist; in his draft for *Who's Who* Beardsley described himself as having taken up music first as a profession. In his obituary, Symons highlights this musical tendency in the young artist, describing him in terms that might also be applied to himself: 'he seemed to know more, and was a sounder critic, of books than of pictures; with perhaps a deeper feeling for music than for either'.[41]

Symons's obituary is more than an account of the artist's life and work. It is a singularly poetic piece of writing in which Symons meditates on Beardsley's 'intensely spiritual art' ('sin transfigured by beauty'), particularly the primacy of form in his drawings and his line.[42] 'After all,' he writes, 'the secret of Beardsley is there; in the line itself rather than in anything, intellectually realised, which the line is intended to express. With Beardsley everything was a question of form'.[43] Symons described the work of other artists and writers in musical terms — Verlaine, Mallarmé, Adolphe Monticelli[44] — favouring Whistler in particular for his visual Impressionism and his ability to go 'clear through outward things to their essence', but his appreciation of Beardsley was two-pronged.[45] Beardsley's lines, his 'minims and crotchets', were not only evocative and suggestive in the same way as Whistler's ghostly paintings or Verlaine's visual poetry, but signified great art, *fine* art. For Symons, Beardsley was more than a lowly illustrator in service to the written word; he was an artist genius composing his own visions, who used the musical language of line to express both the sensuous and the spiritual realms.[46]

A keynote essay in Beardsley's critical reception, Symons's obituary stands apart from mainstream educative Victorian art writing.[47] Symons was part of a more highly individual, impressionistic school of writing and thinking. After 1900, critics on both sides of the Channel borrowed his musical analogy to describe Beardsley's art. In France, the painter and student of Renoir, Jacques-Émile Blanche, and aesthete and dandy, Robert de Montesquiou — habitués of the bohemian scene in Paris and Dieppe — both took up Symons's musical baton. They referred to the English artist's ability to create pure and bizarre harmonies and likened his genius to that of Mozart.[48] Closer to home, writer and art critic, W. G. Blaikie Murdoch enthused over the first *Savoy* title-page and maintained that the 'whole is full of rhythm and melody equal to anything in Mozart',[49] while journalist and art critic, Haldane MacFall continued in the same vein as Symons, asserting (in a typically long-winded way) that Beardsley was 'wholly concerned with decorative schemes as a musician might create impressions in sound as stirred in his imagination by the suggestion of the play'.[50]

Of all Beardsley's critics perhaps the one who comes closest to Symons's evaluation of the young artist's work is the painter and critic, Roger Fry, who attempted to articulate what he termed in 1909 as 'aesthetic emotion'.[51] Influenced by his study of Tolstoy's expressive theory of art (*What is Art?*, 1898) and Bernard Berenson's *The Florentine Painters of the Renaissance* (1896), Fry came to believe that the function of art is expressive, and that the emotions of the artist's imaginative life are communicated by formal means — by the manipulation of rhythm and mass, space, chiaroscuro, and colour — which evoke physical responses in the viewer (this is what he termed 'significant form', i.e. the ability of the visual arts to address themselves directly to the imagination through the senses). As J. B. Bullen attests, 'Fry stresses again and again the autonomy and the importance of the imaginative, aesthetic life of man as opposed to the practical, quotidian aspects of his mental activity'.[52] In his 1911 lecture, given at the close of the exhibition 'Manet and the Post-Impressionists' at the Grafton Galleries in London, and subsequently printed in the *Fortnightly Review*, Fry applied the idea of 'significant form' to his description of the exhibition's pottery:

> Particular rhythms of line and particular harmonies of colour have their spiritual correspondences, and tend to arouse now one set of feelings, now another. The artist plays upon us by the rhythm of line, by colour, by abstract form, and by the quality of the matter he employs.[53]

Writing about Beardsley seven years earlier, in 1904, Fry clearly identified in the artist's work the presence of 'significant form'. He claimed that Beardsley expressed his imagination — his 'diabolism' as Fry called it — through a '*mesquinerie* [meanness] of line, this littleness and intricacy of the mere decorator', and as a result the sensation produced by seeing a Beardsley drawing was 'expressive of muscular tension and virile force'.[54] He proposed that Beardsley's line could even deliver a sense of colour: 'each tone produces the sensation of something as distinct from the others as do flat washes of different tints. The Frontispiece to *Salome* is an excellent example of this'.[55]

Symons and Fry shared a vision of art as associative and affective, and in Beardsley they identified a confluence of line and emotion. Symons's use of a musical analogy pioneered a vision of Beardsley's designs that underscored the young artist's mastery of rhythm and line, and consequently elevated the status of the decorative and applied arts. It was a vision shared by Fry struggling in the early 1900s to articulate the effects of abstract form on the senses. Symons may not have been a visual artist, but in his writings he shows remarkable prescience and insight into what he called the 'interpenetration of substance and form'. In 'Christian Trevalga', for example, Symons evokes the experience of synaesthesia. Trevalga *sees* his own playing of Chopin:

> Something in the curve of the music, which he had always seen as a wavy line, going on indefinably in space, spreading itself out elastically, but without ever forming a pattern, seemed to become almost externally visible, just above the level of the strings on the open top of the piano.[56]

The convergence between Symons's musical analogy as applied to Beardsley's art — his ongoing preoccupation with the artist's line in particular — and Fry's aesthetic theorising in the early years of the twentieth century is thought provoking, especially as there appears to have been little connection between Symons and the Bloomsbury Group. As Karl Beckson notes in his biography, Symons 'seemed to take no interest in the newer artistic developments. [...] there are no references in his essays or letters to such figures as D. H. Lawrence, Virginia Woolf, E. M. Forster or T. S. Eliot, despite the latter's praise'.[57] Symons was perhaps too cosmopolitan in outlook to bother much about the English avant-garde, but his critical writings on art and music represent a critical moment in the evolution of nineteenth-century aesthetics. They catalyse Hegel's ideas about music's 'abstract subjectivity', mediate the Paterian notion of the interrelationship of the arts, and — perhaps most significantly — reveal unmapped common ground, not only between Symons and formalist critics like Fry and Bell, but other journalist-critics like Haldane MacFall (who is not mentioned in the literature on Symons, but who exchanged notes about Beardsley in letters to Symons in the 1920s).[58] These critics, from their different vantage points, were pushing at the boundaries between low and high art. Symons and Fry in particular were instrumental in modernising aesthetic discourse. In privileging an intuitive, personal response to art, and in focusing on the way in which art arouses powerful sensations and deep emotions, they brought art and its audience into a closer relationship.

Notes to Chapter 2

1. Arthur Symons, 'Pachmann and the Piano', in *Plays, Acting, and Music: A Book of Theory* [1903] (London: Constable, 1909), pp. 237–57 (pp. 240–41). This passage was not included in the first edition.
2. Symons, 'Preface' (written July 1903), in *Plays, Acting, and Music* (1909), pp. vii–ix (p. vii).
3. See Sarah Collins, 'Absolute Music and Ideal Content: Autonomy, Sensation and Experience in Arthur Symons's "Theory of Musical Aesthetics"', *Australasian Journal of Victorian Studies*, 19 (2014), 45–66 (p. 63). Cautious about accrediting Symons with too much expertise in this area, Collins refers to Symons's '"musical aesthetics", such as it is' (p. 45).
4. Symons, 'What is Poetry?', in *Studies in Prose and Verse* (London: Dent, 1904), pp. 192–95 (p. 194); 'Preface', p. ix.
5. Symons, 'Preface', p. ix.
6. Symons, 'Aubrey Beardsley', *Fortnightly Review*, 63 (May 1898), 752–61 (p. 752).
7. Ibid., p. 760.
8. Ibid., p. 760.
9. Nicholas Freeman, '"Mad Music Rising": Chopin, Sex, and Secret Language in Arthur Symons's *Christian Trevalga*', *Victoriographies*, 1 (2011), 157–76 (p. 160). In 'Mr. Arthur Symons on Richard Strauss', *Speaker: The Liberal Review*, 8 (11 April 1903), 35–36, Ernest Newman referred to the way that Symons made musical criticism 'a really readable performance' (p. 35).
10. Georg Wilhelm Friedrich Hegel, *Aesthetics: Lectures on Fine Art (1835–8)*, trans. by T. M. Knox, 2 vols (Oxford: Clarendon Press, 1975), II, 891.
11. Symons, 'On Writing about Music', in *Plays, Acting, and Music* (1909), pp. 229–31 (p. 229).
12. Walter Pater, 'The School of Giorgione', in *The Renaissance: Studies in Art and Poetry*, ed. by Donald L. Hill (Berkeley: University of California Press, 1980), pp. 102–22 (p. 106).
13. Patricia Herzog, '"The Condition to Which All Art Aspires": Reflections on Pater on Music', *British Journal of Aesthetics*, 36 (April 1996), 122–34. Herzog is insistent on the 'negative and positive interpretation of Pater's thesis': 'The ideal matter of music or any other art is revealed not *as* form but *through* form, or more precisely, through the *imaginative perception* of form' (p. 130). We find a synthesis of painting and music in Théophile Gautier's *Émaux et camées* (1852, enlarged in 1872), especially in his poem 'Symphonie en blanc majeur' (1849).
14. Symons, 'On Writing about Music', p. 231.
15. Symons, 'Beethoven' [1904], in *Studies in Seven Arts*, pp. 191–222 (p. 197).
16. Pater's term in 'The School of Giorgione'; see Herzog, '"The Condition to Which All Art Aspires"', p. 123.
17. See Stoddard Martin, *Wagner to 'The Waste Land': A Study of the Relationship of Wagner to English Literature* (London: Macmillan, 1982), pp. 74–76; cited in Emma Sutton, *Aubrey Beardsley and British Wagnerism in the 1890s* (New York: Oxford University Press, 2002), p. 78.
18. Symons, *Confessions: A Study in Pathology* [1930] (New York: Haskell House, 1972), pp. 7–8.
19. Collins, 'Absolute Music and Ideal Content', pp. 46, 50.
20. Symons, 'Are the English People Musical?', Letter to the Editor, *Pall Mall Gazette*, 15 December 1890, 2.

21. Symons, 'A Prelude to Life', in *Spiritual Adventures* (London: Constable, 1905), pp. 3–50 (p. 27).
22. Symons, 'Mozart in the Mirabell-Garten', in *Plays, Acting, and Music* (1909), pp. 290–96 (p. 291).
23. Symons, 'Technique and the Artist', in *Plays, Acting, and Music* (1909), pp. 232–36 (pp. 234–35).
24. Freeman, '"Mad Music Rising"', p. 162.
25. Symons, 'Pachmann and the Piano', pp. 249–50, and collected in *The Fool of the World and Other Poems* (London: William Heinemann, 1906), p. 74. 'Have you ever tried to catch a butterfly without brushing the dust off its wings?' notes Trevalga in 'Christian Trevalga' (1902–03), in *Spiritual Adventures* (1905), pp. 85–113 (p. 111).
26. 'In the interpretation of music all action of the brain which does not translate itself perfectly in touch is useless' (Symons, 'Pachmann and the Piano', p. 238).
27. W. B. Yeats, *Uncollected Prose, Volume II: Later Reviews, Articles and Other Miscellaneous Prose 1897–1939*, ed. by John P. Frayne and Colton Johnson (London: Macmillan, 1975), p. 40.
28. Symons, 'La Mélinite: Moulin Rouge', in *London Nights*, p. 24.
29. Katharina Herold, 'Dancing the Image: Sensoriality and Kinesthetics in the Poetry of Stéphane Mallarmé and Arthur Symons', in *Decadence and the Senses*, ed. by Jane Desmarais and Alice Condé (Oxford: Legenda, 2017), pp. 141–61 (p. 150, my emphasis).
30. Symons, 'At the Stage-door', in *London Nights*, p. 16.
31. 'Music can prolong, reiterate, and delicately vary the ecstasy itself: and its voice is all the while speaking to us out of our own hearts' (Symons, 'Beethoven', p. 196).
32. Symons, 'Music and Memory', in *Silhouettes* [1892], 2nd edn (London: Smithers, 1896), p. 46.
33. Symons, 'Notes on Paris and Paul Verlaine', in *Colour Studies in Paris* (London: Chapman & Hall, 1918), pp. 161–201 (pp. 171–72).
34. John Trevor, *French Art and English Morals* (London: Sonnenschein, 1886), p. 43.
35. Jane Haville Desmarais, *The Beardsley Industry: The Critical Reception in England and France, 1893–1914* (Aldershot: Ashgate, 1998).
36. P. G. Hamerton, *Contemporary French Painters* (London: Seeley, Jackson and Halliday, 1868), p. 37.
37. Ibid., p. 37.
38. Robert Ross, 'Aubrey Beardsley', *Academy and Literature*, 70 (1906), 95–96 (p. 95).
39. Ibid., p. 96.
40. *A Beardsley Miscellany*, ed. by R. A. Walker (London: Bodley Head, 1949), p. 75.
41. Symons, 'Aubrey Beardsley', p. 752.
42. Ibid., p. 757.
43. Ibid., p. 759.
44. Munro, *Arthur Symons*, pp. 91–92.
45. Symons, 'Impressionistic Writing' [1923], in *Dramatis Personae* (Indianapolis, IN: Bobbs-Merrill, 1923), pp. 343–56 (p. 345).
46. Freeman makes a similar observation in '"Mad Music Rising"': 'In writing on art, Symons invariably works around these polarities; the ability to create is valued alongside but ultimately above the ability to enact' (p. 169).
47. For more on Victorian music conventions, see Emma Sutton, '"The Music Spoke for Us": Music and Sexuality in fin-de-siècle Poetry', in *The Figure of Music in Nineteenth-Century British Poetry*, ed. by Phyllis Weliver (Aldershot: Ashgate, 2005), pp. 213–29; Phyllis Weliver, *The Musical Crowd in English Fiction, 1840–1910: Class, Culture, and Nation* (Basingstoke: Palgrave Macmillan, 2006); and Phyllis Weliver, *Women Musicians in Victorian Fiction, 1860–1900: Representations of Music, Science and Gender in the Leisured Home* (London: Routledge, 2016).
48. Jacques-Émile Blanche, 'Aubrey Beardsley', *L'Antée*, 11 (1 April 1907), 1103–22 (p. 1105); Robert de Montesquiou, 'Beardsley en Raccourci', *Assemblée de Notables* (Paris: Societé d'Edition et de Publications Librairie Felix Juven, s.d. [1908]), pp. 17–27 (p. 20).
49. W. G. Blaikie Murdoch, *The Renaissance of the Nineties* (London: Alexander Moring, 1911), p. 11.
50. Haldane MacFall, *Aubrey Beardsley: The Man and His Work* (London: John Lane, 1928), p. 49. During periods of revived interest in Beardsley's work — in the 1940s, '60s through to the '90s

— critics continued to refer to the musicality of his line. In 1946 Robin Ironside commented on the 'melodious fulfilment, of some linear rhythm or from the tonal or atonal harmonies that may be produced by the painstaking disposition and variation of darks and lights' ('Aubrey Beardsley', *Horizon*, 14 (September 1946), 190–202 (p. 198)); Annette Lavers, in 1967, declared of Beardsley's illustrations for *The Rape of the Lock* (1897) that the 'variation in thickness of line' was 'equivalent to musical *pianissimo* and *fortissimo*' ('Aubrey Beardsley: Man of Letters', in *Romantic Mythologies*, ed. by Ian Fletcher (London: Routledge, 1967), pp. 243–70 (p. 256)); Brigid Brophy maintained that like all great tunes Beardsley's lines went up and down in beautiful places (*Black and White* (London: Cape, 1968), p. 11); and Simon Wilson in 1983 described his designs as 'musical structures' (*Beardsley* (Oxford: Phaidon, 1983), p. 9). For more detail see Jane Desmarais, 'The Musical Analogy in Beardsley Criticism 1898–1914', *Journal of Pre-Raphaelite Studies*, 6 (Spring 1997), 64–90.
51. Roger Fry, 'An Essay in Aesthetics', *New Quarterly*, 2 (April 1909), 171–90.
52. J. B. Bullen, 'Introduction', in Clive Bell, *Art* (Oxford: Oxford University Press, 1987), pp. xxi–l (p. xxxiv).
53. Roger Fry, 'Post Impressionism', *Fortnightly Review*, 89 (May 1911), 856–67 (p. 862).
54. Roger Fry, 'Aubrey Beardsley's Drawings', *The Athenæum*, 4019 (5 November 1904), 627–28 (p. 628).
55. Ibid., p. 628.
56. Symons, 'Christian Trevalga', pp. 104–05.
57. Beckson, *Arthur Symons*, p. 2.
58. The correspondence between MacFall and Symons is housed in the Canaday Library at Bryn Mawr College, Pennsylvania.

CHAPTER 3

❖

'A New Art of the Stage': Edward Gordon Craig and the Seven Arts of Arthur Symons

John Stokes

> We are the puppets of a shadow-play.
> ARTHUR SYMONS, 'Prologue: Before the Curtain'

In the early years of the twentieth century thinking about theatrical practice passed through a visionary phase to which Arthur Symons and the director and designer Edward Gordon Craig both made significant contributions. Craig's reputation as a prophet and innovator has survived and has, if anything, grown over the decades, but Symons's role has subsequently been overlooked. As a working journalist he wrote enthusiastically about the performing arts throughout his career and he had extremely wide tastes. His reviews for the *Star* newspaper from 1898 until 1902 dealt judiciously with run-of-the-mill West End comedies while paying fervent tributes to visiting stars such as Sarah Bernhardt and Eleonora Duse. In addition, and unusually among professional critics, he appreciated the physical skills on display in London music-halls, especially dance. Symons's most far-sighted writing, however, was inspired by playwrights in the Symbolist tradition, in particular Maurice Maeterlinck. In this respect alone it might be possible to see him as playing the Evangelist to Craig's Messiah, a status that Craig would happily have taken as his due.[1]

Although it seems unlikely (if not inconceivable) that later theatrical pioneers such as Vsevolod Meyerhold, Bertold Brecht, Antonin Artaud, and Peter Brook would have read Symons, we do know that they were very much aware of Craig and that Craig, in turn, had once been very much aware of the author of *Plays, Acting, and Music* (1903) and, crucially, *Studies in Seven Arts*. The latter volume appeared in 1906 and Craig seems to have read it soon after publication as he inscribed the year in black ink in his own personal copy and made plentiful pencil annotations throughout.[2] He was puzzled by the title and wrote the following at the very top of the contents page: 'But surely there can be 70 arts or 700 or fewer. I find it easier firmer [? Illeg.] to see but 3 Architecture — Music — & the art of Movement'.[3] Craig had his own reasons for raising the question of number, and supplying an alternative, but it was a good question nonetheless. Although the contents of the volume reflect Symons's comprehensive interests up until that time, why should there be seven arts in particular? There is no definite article in the title — it is not '*The* Seven Arts' — and in the dedicatory preface to his wife Rhoda, Symons goes some way in suggesting that the number might actually be arbitrary. 'With the art of poetry, or of literature in general, I am not here concerned', he writes:

> That is my main concern in most of my other books of criticism. In this book I have tried to deal with the other arts, as I know or recognise them; and I find seven: painting, sculpture, architecture, music, handicraft, the stage (in which I include drama, acting, pantomime, scenery costume, and lighting), and separate from these dancing. (pp. v-vi)

He 'finds' seven, we might note, so there could actually be more than that or there could even, should Symons have misjudged, be fewer. Is the choice of the number seven scientific or superstitious? There are, after all, seven days of the week and seven seas; according to Newton there are seven colours in the rainbow. On the other hand, it is the dance of the seven veils and there are, of course, seven deadly sins.

Studies in Seven Arts is made up of fifteen chapters which range from Rodin to mediaeval cathedrals and Arts and Crafts, from Beethoven to Wagner and Strauss, from the actress Eleonora Duse to the playwright Alfred Jarry and to the arts of ballet and puppetry, taking in a chapter on Craig himself along the way. This is entitled 'A New Art of the Stage'. In additional annotations to the contents page Craig attempted to group these fifteen chapters under five or six generic headings, bracketing them together with his own pencil marks. The first essay, on Rodin, obviously represents sculpture; the next four essays make up painting; 'Cathedrals' and 'Craftsmanship' are linked to make a third group; the essays on Beethoven, Wagner, and Strauss are clearly music. There appears to be some indecision in Craig's mind about the remaining six. At first he seems to have put them together as 'theatre' leaving the last as a sixth art — ballet — but at some point to have changed this so that they came together, including ballet, to form a fifth and final group.

Behind this concern with taxonomy lies a long history that stretches back through the nineteenth century to Lessing's *Laocoon* (1766) and, always in the minds of both Symons and Craig, the essayist Charles Lamb. Walter Pater, another admirer of Lamb, had made his own distinctive contribution to the topos and Symons's dedicatory preface to *Studies* quotes the first two sentences of 'The School of Giorgione', calling them 'a kind of motto to my book'. Pater had written:

> It is the mistake of much popular criticism to regard poetry, music, and painting — all the various products of art — as but translations into different languages of one and the same fixed quantity of imaginative thought, supplemented by certain technical qualities of colour, in painting, of sound, in music, of rhythmical words, in poetry. In this way, the sensuous element in art, and with it almost everything in art that is essentially artistic, is made a matter of indifference; and a clear apprehension of the opposite principle — that the sensuous material of each art brings with it a special phase or quality of beauty, untranslatable into the forms of any other, an order of impressions distinct in kind — is the beginning of all true æsthetic criticism.[4]

This is not an argument for similarity, actual or desired, between the arts (the notion of *Anders-streben* and the formula 'all the arts aspire to the condition of music' come later in Pater's essay and pose their own problems). Nor is it an appeal for convergence of the arts into one overwhelming whole associated with Wagner's notion of *Gesamtkunstwerk* — but rather for the uniqueness of each independent element. Yet, as Karl Beckson observed in his biography, no sooner has Symons quoted Pater than he would seem to contradict him by speaking of his own 'endeavour to master what I have called the universal science of beauty' (p. vi). Beckson asks:

> What did Symons mean by his curious, uncharacteristic, un-Paterian phrase 'the universal science of beauty'? Pater had cautioned, in his preface to *The Renaissance*, not to seek a universal formula of beauty. Symons seems to be restating what he had said in his preface to *Plays, Acting, and Music* (1903) — that he was 'gradually working [his] way towards the concrete expression of a theory, or system of aesthetics, of all the arts' — a 'system' never developed.[5]

Beckson is right: there does seem to be a philosophical conflict here but it is particularly acute wherever the theatre is concerned. When it comes to performance, the Paterian attempt to tease out each 'special phase or quality of beauty' is inevitably paradoxical. How to respect and celebrate the individual elements of each art when they are practised simultaneously and in an exact spatial and temporal relationship? How to draw the line between the contributions made by artists and craftsmen? How to permit, or actively encourage, transgression of those boundaries? Is theatre always a coming together that is not, and can never be, a synthesis, where priorities will always be contested? The 'comparison of the arts' is, above all, a matter of borders — highly practical in terms of professional function and control (of 'job description') — that remain permeable in aesthetic theory.

Questions of similarity and difference nevertheless played an important part in the protracted battle against theatrical realism where the co-conspirators of Craig and Symons included, around the turn of the century, Adolphe Appia, Stéphane Mallarmé, and W. B. Yeats, all of them anxious to replace the fulfilment of textual detail by material objects with more evocative, poetic methods. Although *Studies in Seven Arts* relates to this tendency, it was not a campaign manifesto but rather a symptom of anti-realist feeling in general and, in the case of 'A New Art of the Stage', of a relationship that is still not easy to describe.[6] Neither Craig nor Symons was the dominant partner; it was never a Socratic dialogue. It was more of a sporadic, semi-spontaneous conversation or *causerie*: two voices speaking on common themes, sometimes in unison, aware of each other, but rarely indulging, publically at any rate, in a direct exchange. It was more like a series of encounters between two people in the process of discovering that they had a great deal in common as they went along. Yet both men could be wilfully secretive, writing as if they were the holders of some esoteric wisdom that they would only disclose on their own terms.

Intellectual contact had begun in the spring of 1901, when Craig directed and designed a staging of *The Masque of Love* (adapted from Henry Purcell's *Diocletian*, 1690) together with a revival of Purcell's *Dido and Aeneas* (1687/8). Symons reviewed these productions pseudonymously in the *Star*, 26 March 1901, writing that:

> The mounting which was arranged by Mr Gordon Craig, was quite original, and on the whole remarkably good. The stage was generally in shadow, at times almost in darkness; a purple backcloth suggested a background of dark and clear sky, masses of figures moved tumultuously across the scene, rising and groveling, rushing and creeping, with what promised to be a really mysterious and terrifying effect.[7]

In April 1902 Craig went on to direct Handel's *Acis and Galatea* (1718) together with a revival of *The Masque of Love*. As far as we know, Symons did not review these productions in the *Star* or anywhere else but he did publish an essay entitled 'A New Art of the Stage' in the *Monthly Review*, June 1902, that he was to reprint with the same title in *Studies in Seven Arts* as 'Part I' of the chapter on Craig. 'Part II' of that Craig chapter was to include portions of a piece by Symons entitled 'Mr. Gordon Craig and the Painters in Tempera' which had appeared in the *Outlook* in June of 1905, together with a résumé of Craig's polemical pamphlet, *The Art of the Theatre*. The amalgamation was typically strategic.

In addition to being great absorbers of other people's ideas, Symons and Craig were both self-cannibalisers, juggling pieces of text long before computers made 'cut and paste' easy. Their books were compilations that were also summations — and publication tended to announce a completed sequence that was at the same time a projection into the future. *Studies in Seven Arts* is a volume of this kind. The title of the composite chapter on Craig evokes those other annunciatory titles of the *fin de siècle* such as 'the New Journalism', 'the New Drama', and 'the New Woman', though Symons was at first still quite hesitant, unsure of precisely what might be coming.

Even in 1906 the opening to the discussion of Craig (originally dating, of course, from 1902) begins like this:

> In the remarkable experiments of Mr. Gordon Craig, I seem to see the suggestion of a new art of the stage, an art no longer realistic but conventional, no longer imitative, but symbolical. In Mr. Craig's staging there is the incalculable element, the element that comes of itself, and cannot be coaxed into coming. But in what is incalculable there may be equal parts of inspiration and of accident. How much, in Mr. Craig's staging, is inspiration, how much is accident? That is, after all, the important question. (p. 349)

The essay continues with a highly attentive account of Craig's designs which are based on principles of draughtsmanship: the use of lines, of squares (not curves), and of sharp angles. This applies not only to set design but to acting styles whether of the group or the individual. Symons goes on to see Craig's techniques as born of a kind of fantasy, driven by rules of form rather than the need to reproduce an external reality — a priority that extends even to the costumes in *The Masque of Love*. Although made of rough sacking, Symons is now ready to pay a more appreciative tribute to their effect than he had been able to do in 1901: 'Under the cunning handling of the light, they gave you any illusion you pleased, and the beggars of the masque were not more appropriately clothed than the kings and queens. All had dignity, all reposed the eye' (p. 351). It follows that the art of Craig must be opposed to the highly skilled materialist art that simply gives us a 'crude illusion of reality': 'Mr. Craig aims at taking us beyond reality; he replaces the pattern of the thing itself by the pattern which that thing evokes in his mind, the symbol of the thing' (p. 352). And with the introduction of that word 'symbol' Symons is primed, at least tacitly, to associate Craig's art with a trend that he has hailed in other arts.

It is also apparent that Symons has studied Craig's drawings for productions as yet unstaged. In the analyses that follow — of designs for *The Masque of London* and ideas for *Hamlet* — Symons discovers environments in which 'a drama of Maeterlinck might find its own atmosphere awaiting it' (p. 355). This positions Craig in two ways: not only might his designs inspire a new kind of drama (reversing the more normal sequence in which designs follow the text), plays already existed that prefigured his approach. In due course Symons will return to Maeterlinck, the author of 'plays which exist anywhere in space, which evade reality, which do all they can to become disembodied in the very moment in which they become visible'. Such plays 'have atmosphere without locality, and that is what Mr. Craig can give us so easily' (p. 358).

Meanwhile, Symons goes on to part blame, part praise Wagner's dictatorial ideal of *Gesamtkunstwerk*. The composer's great error was, he says, to pursue the hopeless realist goal of recreating nature largely by insisting on detail. The same goes for modern Shakespeare productions in England that bury poetry under bric-a-brac. By contrast, Craig, who stimulates the imagination of the spectator, is able to release the otherwise hidden imagination of writers and composers. In the hands of Craig two great artists of the late nineteenth century, Wagner and Ibsen, might finally succeed where Wagner himself at Bayreuth had failed. By abolishing the footlights and releasing instead a more ghostly kind of light in the manner of Craig it might be possible to liberate the music-drama on the one hand and bring the mood of the fjord into Ibsen's typically domestic 'room' on the other. Yet the essay ends with personal hesitancy:

> What might not Mr. Craig do with that room! What precisely, I do not know; but I am sure that his method is capable of an extension which will take in that room, and if it can take in that room, it can take in all of modern life which is of importance to the playwright. (p. 360)

In his copy of *Studies in Seven Arts*, Craig wrote alongside that: 'Here's a man I like — he looks <u>through</u> the eye'.[8]

This much was first published, as I have noted, in 1902 as part of 'A New Art of the Stage' and it makes up Part I of the essay on Craig as it appears in *Studies in Seven Arts* in 1906. Part II is entirely taken up with the 1905 essay on Craig, ostensibly a review of designs on show at an art gallery, but mainly concerned with Craig's own *The Art of the Theatre*. 'Most people begin with theory, and go on, if they go on, to carry their theory into practice', says Symons introducing Craig's short book, but Craig has worked in reverse, from practice, 'on the actual boards of the theatre', to theory. Moreover, it is now clear that Craig's work is indeed based on intention and not just on 'accident'. His grand vision is becoming apparent since he defines theatre, in his own words, as 'a place in which the entire beauty of life can be unfolded, and not only the external beauty of the world, but the inner beauty and meaning of life'. The theatre is a 'temple', a ceremonious and religious place (p. 361).

Because theatre can serve this sacred and transcendent function it can — indeed, it must — consist of all the elements that make up the other arts: action (from acting), words (from the play), line and colour (from scenic design), rhythm (from dance). What follows is for the most part Symons's digest of Craig's ideas in which the various arts are said to be subservient to the visual imagination of the director as he responds to the 'spirit of the play' by selecting and foregrounding objects, positioning actors, selecting costumes, making decisions about lighting, and movement, in that order.

Yet, as Symons allows, a fundamental question about priorities persists:

> The question is this: whether the theatre is the invention of the dramatist, and of use only in so far as it interprets his creative work; or whether the dramatist is the invention of the theatre, which has made him for its own ends, and will be able, when it has wholly achieved its mechanism, to dispense with him altogether, except perhaps as a kind of prompter. (p. 365)

Almost inevitably Symons invokes Lamb, who had argued that performance coarsened Shakespeare's poetic texts, and suggests that Craig's own position is that *Hamlet*, for instance, is actually not designed for 'all that the theatre has to offer; not, that is, that it is greater or less in its art, but that it is different'. This might well have been an accurate account of Craig's position (though he was to contradict himself with his famous production of *Hamlet* in Moscow in 1912), but personally Symons opts for compromise: 'the technique, which Mr. Craig would end with, might, if it were carried out, be utilised by the dramatist to his own incalculable advantage' (p. 367).

Again, this is characteristically opaque, but the implication must be that the playwright might benefit by giving the designer/director (Craig understood) control over the whole theatrical enterprise while, at the same time, reaffirming the importance, though no longer the priority, of his own contribution. That, at any rate, seems to be how Craig understood the matter, for at the very end of the essay he wrote two questions in his own copy of Symons's book: 'But does he know of what consists this technique which I would end with? and does he then know what material such a technique would permit' (p. 367). It may be that Craig is thinking here of the 'techniques' that he would go on to evolve, such as the abstract but mobile 'screens' that he developed for Yeats. Or it may be that by 'material' he is asking what kind of play would benefit from his way of doing things. In which case, the answer must surely be suggestive mood pieces that would enable theatre to serve its true function. As for now, 1906, Craig simply adds a grateful pencilled tribute: 'But Symons is a clever fellow & besides I am fond of him' (p. 367).

Following on from 'The New Art of the Stage', *Studies in Seven Arts* concludes with three related essays on theatrical performance: 'A Symbolist Farce' (about

Jarry's *Ubu Roi*), 'Pantomime and the Poetic Drama', and 'The World as Ballet'. As usual they had all been published before. At the end of 'A New Art of the Stage' as it appears in *Studies in Seven Arts* on p. 367, Craig has pencilled: 'Symons has written somewhere about pantomime'. This suggests that he was reading and noting the chapters of the book in sequence since 'Pantomime and the Poetic Drama' appears quite soon after, on p. 381.

In fact, the final two chapters of the book had originally appeared as parts of a single piece entitled 'Ballet, Pantomime, and Poetic Drama' in the first volume of a periodical called the *Dome* in October 1898. In *Studies in Seven Arts* the second part of the *Dome* essay, which is entitled 'Pantomime and the Poetic Drama', becomes the penultimate chapter of the book and the first part of the *Dome* essay, which is entitled 'The World as Ballet', becomes the book's final chapter. The switch around might seem merely a matter of convenience but, in fact, is highly significant because it is programmatic. 'The World as Ballet' now stands as a culminating manifesto in which wordlessness, rhythm, and sensuality are the supremely creative forces, a symbolic evocation of 'life' itself.[9]

'In every art', writes Symons in 'The World as Ballet':

> Men are pressing forward, more and more eagerly, farther and farther beyond the limits of their art, in their desire to do the impossible: to create life. Realising all humanity to be but a masque of shadows, and the solid world an impromptu stage as temporary as they, it is with a pathetic desire of some last illusion, which shall deceive even ourselves, that we are consumed with this hunger to create, to make something for ourselves, of at least the same shadowy reality as that about us. (p. 390)

And this air of euphoria is now prepared for by what has become the previous chapter, where the word 'pantomime' refers not to Christmas entertainments but to the ancient art of mime itself, a purely gestural drama, entirely silent that, because it exists before speech intervenes, addresses itself, in Symons's words, 'by the artful limitations of its craft, to universal human experience' (p. 381). Far from a flawed imitation of nature (i.e. far from realism), its wordless gestures are rather a 'transposition', a new form of 'life'. Although Maeterlinck is not mentioned, his presence is palpable in Symons's claim that watching mime is like dreaming, and that the mute actor is possessed by 'a nervous exaltation which has its subtle, immediate effect upon us, in tragic and comic situation' (p. 383). It follows that, if silence can exert this power, then the only form of language that can come close is poetry: the saying of beautiful things, 'the only things worth saying' (p. 384). And yet, with an odd and unexplored hint at the very end, Symons suggests that even the poetic drama waits for its 'ideal presentment, the interpretative accompaniment of music, which Wagner will give it, in what is so far the most complete form of art yet realised' (p. 384).

Craig's pencilled comments on this chapter praise Symons for his inability to separate the ancient from the modern: 'Show him a work of art and he will speak with understanding. Others have to ponder — & compare — & hear what the rest have to say first' (p. 379). With Symons, by contrast, 'his heart speaks through his head'. And on the following page Craig adds the comment: 'Arthur Symons in this short 3 page note on Pantomime does more honour to the theatre than any other writer of this age' (p. 380). 'The World as Ballet' is only very lightly annotated by Craig. Nevertheless, it is apparent that he read the closing chapters of *Studies in Seven Arts* with considerable, if self-reflecting, attention. Later on, in January 1912, Craig paid tribute to the then ailing Symons by reprinting passages from 'Pantomime and Poetic Drama' in his usually egotistical, downright solipsistic, periodical, the *Mask*. Along with the Symons passages he printed an additional 'note' of his own. This opened with:

> All great drama moves in silence. Events of the greatest magnitude and significance pass in silence; there is nothing to be said. [...] it is possible that the present age will replace action on its stage-throne and that that throne will be remade and replaced in its temple.[10]

And concluded: 'It is an essay which in my opinion will do more to help us to understand the lost art of the stage than that of any writer of modern times'.[11] Silence creates or renews our sense of life. In which case, wordless dance and mime are the supremely 'symbolist' arts To which might be added another: the art of puppetry.

The first public expression of this mutually shared enthusiasm is Symons's 1897 essay 'An Apology for Puppets', reprinted in *Plays, Acting, and Music* of 1903, which, although heavily influenced by Maeterlinck, was apparently prompted by Symons's experience of puppets at the Costanzi Theatre in Rome sometime in late 1896 or early the following year. Here puppets are compared to the masks of the ancient theatre and preferred to the modern actor, whose characteristics include egotism, a casual approach to his art, and an indulgence in audience relationships. In contrast:

> The marionette may be relied upon. He will respond to an indication without reserve or revolt; an error on his part (we are all human) will certainly be the fault of the author; he can be trained to perfection. As he is painted, so will he smile; as the wires lift or lower his hands, so will his gestures be; and he will dance when his legs are set in motion.[12]

Which brings us, by a circuitous route (but that is the only way with these two authors), to Craig's most celebrated essay: 'The Actor and the Über-Marionette', probably commenced in 1906 (the year of Symons's *Studies in Seven Arts*), dated March 1907, first published in the *Mask* in April 1908, and then reprinted in Craig's volume entitled *On the Art of the Theatre* in 1911. This is one of the most revered — and most puzzling — documents of modern theatre. Its title plays a game, of course, with Nietzsche's concept of the *Übermensch* or superman (Nietzsche was, we know, also of considerable interest to Symons at the time). But the epigraph to the essay is from Eleonora Duse, and its source is given as *Studies in Seven Arts*: 'To save the theatre the theatre must be destroyed, the actors and actresses must all die of the plague... They make art impossible'.[13] The opening sequence, and to some extent Craig's essay as a whole, belongs once again firmly in the context of 'the comparison of the arts'. The question to be asked is 'whether or no Acting is an art'. Although ancient the topic has rarely 'disturbed the minds of the leaders of thought'. Had it done so, they might have 'applied to it the same method of inquiry as used when considering the arts of Music and Poetry, of Architecture, Sculpture and Painting'.[14] This is similar to, but not identical with, the revised taxonomy that Craig had pencilled on the contents page of his copy of *Studies in Seven Arts*.

The problem for Craig is that the actor can never be an artist because he is prone to 'accident' whereas Art 'arrives only by design'.[15] 'Accident' is an important word here, as it is for Symons, standing for something like the human, the natural, the bodily, that which cannot be controlled. 'The actor must go, and in his place comes the inanimate figure — the Über-marionette we may call him, until he has won for himself a better name'. 'Much has been written about the puppet or marionette', says Craig, thinking perhaps of Symons. 'There are excellent volumes upon him, and he has also inspired several works of art'.[16]

Craig's advocacy of the *Übermarionette* caused some consternation among a professional community always worried about unemployment. Did Craig really mean that human actors should be replaced by wooden puppets? The answer is both yes and no, since Craig also saw:

> A loop-hole by which in time the actors can escape from the bondage they are in. They must create for themselves a new form of acting, consisting for the main part of symbolical gesture. Today they *impersonate* and interpret; tomorrow they must *represent* and interpret; and the third day they must create.[17]

No-one would ever claim that Craig is a stylistically inhibited writer, let alone a consistent thinker, but the conclusion to this extraordinary essay is bizarre even by his own standards. He had recently delved into eastern religion (Buddhism in particular) and into ancient Egyptian rituals in which puppets played a key part. His final peroration is wildly metaphysical:

> I pray earnestly for the return of the image — the über-marionette to the Theatre; and when he comes again and is but seen, he will be loved so well that once more will it be possible for the people to return to their ancient joy in ceremonies — once more will Creation be celebrated — homage rendered to existence — and divine and happy intercession made to Death.[18]

An oracular superman indeed, yet the idea only develops in an extreme way a tendency that had long been present in Maeterlinck. In his *Symbolist Movement in Literature*, Symons had praised the Flemish writer's work because it was 'founded on philosophical ideas, apprehended emotionally; on the sense of the mystery of the universe, of the weakness of humanity'.[19]

If you had been reading Symons — as we know that Craig had been doing — then the dramatic shift into the metaphysical is not nearly so unexpected. The puppet cult belongs with the alternative religions of the *fin de siècle*: with mysticism, spiritualism, and a dramatic reappraisal of the relation of soul to body, with deathliness. Like symbolism itself, the puppet is a symptom of the process through which Paterian psychological materialism became wedded to a spiritual quest. The manifesto-like introduction to *The Symbolist Movement* credits symbolism with an eschatological role: 'in speaking to us so intimately, so solemnly, as only religion has hitherto spoken to us, it becomes itself a kind of religion, with all the duties and responsibilities of the sacred ritual'.[20] As with the art of theatre itself, puppets involve border-crossing. Inanimate manifestations of the human condition, they are 'uncanny', to apply a word we associate most of all with Freud but which forms the subtitle for Kenneth Gross's remarkable book on puppets of 2011, *Puppet: An Essay on Uncanny Life*. Gross writes that puppet theatre:

> May also remind us that we do not yet know what it means to be inanimate, that we do not know fully the different kinds of death that humans own, or the shapes of the lives that can be lived by inanimate things. That is why locating precisely the life of the puppet, or the source if its charm and fascination is so complex, so elusive a matter, and is endlessly suggestive of the paradoxes of our own lives.[21]

More specifically the puppet is, in a dreadfully overused word, an 'icon' of the morbid *fin de siècle*. In fact, the word has a more literal application than usual since puppets, like icons, are made of painted wood and they inspire both reverence and fear. The great difference being that, unless a miracle is taking place, icons never move and for puppets movement is everything, an idea that Craig would take much further with his belief that movement is predicated upon life itself and is at the heart of theatre, a conviction also to be found in the work of Artaud, in Peter Brook's notion of 'holy theatre', in Jacques Lecoq's litany of *tout bouge*, in Simon McBurney's use of shadow puppets with Theatre de Complicité, and in Beckett's early mimes.

What we have in the *causerie* of Arthur Symons and Edward Gordon Craig, in their theory of the death-defying/death-embracing marionette, is a loosely collaborative moment in the history of a quasi-sacramental idea of theatre. As an aesthetic experience the sheer beauty of theatre can satisfy our appetite for the transcendent and yet, since it employs mortal actors, its very physicality simultaneously challenges that possibility. Symons's decision to concentrate on just 'seven' arts (why not, as Craig noted, seventy or seven hundred?) may well have been superstitious, but then around the turn of the century the whole business of theatre was — as for many it has remained — pervaded by the belief that this supremely composite art must in some way occupy the space left by religion, be part of life itself.

Notes to Chapter 3

1. As Lawrence W. Markert says, 'the relationship between Craig and Symons works in both directions; Symons senses the embodiment of his artistic ideals in Craig's productions, and Craig draws upon the theoretical foundations Symons suggests in his various essays for part of his own theories of drama and dramatic presentation' (Markert, *Arthur Symons*, p. 29).
2. Craig's personal copy of *Studies in Seven Arts*, which surfaced in a Paris flea-market in 1984, is in my possession. All subsequent references to Craig's annotations are to this particular copy.
3. Symons, *Studies in Seven Arts*. Subsequent references to this work are in the main body of the text.
4. Pater, *The Renaissance*, p. 102.
5. Beckson, *Arthur Symons*, p. 245.
6. It is not clear when they first met, although according to Karl Beckson they were in contact in 1903. See Beckson, *Arthur Symons*, pp. 225, 367.
7. 'Silhouette' [Arthur Symons], 'Purcell and Ellen Terry', *Star*, 26 March 1901, p. 1.

8. Christopher Innes reports a piece of marginalia that appears in one of Craig's scrapbooks of press cuttings. Alongside Symons's sentence beginning 'Mr. Craig aims at taking us beyond reality' Craig wrote (though we presumably do not know when), 'Right, right so!' (Innes, *Edward Gordon Craig* (Cambridge: Cambridge University Press, 1983), pp. 69, 227).
9. At the very end of the chapter, following Symons's apostrophe to the figure of the dancer ('There, before you, she exists in harmonious life; and her rhythm reveals to you the soul of her imagined being'), Craig adds: 'Unfortunately the Dancer damns her art for the sake of £20,000' — presumably aimed at Isadora Duncan, with whom he had been involved since 1904 (Symons, *Studies in Seven Arts*, p. 391).
10. Arthur Symons, 'Ballet, Pantomime, and Poetic Drama', *Mask*, 4 (1912), 188–89 (p. 188).
11. Ibid., p. 189.
12. Symons, *Plays, Acting, and Music* (1903), p. 193.
13. Edward Gordon Craig, *On the Art of the Theatre* (London: William Heinemann, 1911), p. 54; quoting Symons, *Studies in Seven Arts*, p. 336.
14. Craig, *On the Art of the Theatre*, p. 54.
15. Ibid., p. 55.
16. Ibid., p. 81.
17. Ibid., p. 61.
18. Ibid., p. 94.
19. Symons, *The Symbolist Movement in Literature*, p. 81.
20. Ibid., p. 8.
21. Kenneth Gross, *Puppet: An Essay on Uncanny Life* (Chicago: University of Chicago Press, 2011), p. 47.

PART II

International Mediations

CHAPTER 4

Symons and D'Annunzio: Decadence in Translation

Stefano Evangelista

Arthur Symons's mission to internationalise English literary culture was driven and dominated by French literature. France and its modern writers pervade 'The Decadent Movement in Literature' (1893), *The Savoy* (1896), *The Symbolist Movement in Literature* (1899), *Studies in Two Literatures* (1897), and *Studies in Prose and Verse* (1904), to name some of his most important critical works. His translations included works by Zola, Baudelaire, Verlaine, Mallarmé, Pierre Louÿs, Villiers de l'Isle-Adam, and the French-speaking Belgian symbolist Émile Verhaeren. It is therefore somewhat surprising that the foreign author whom Symons translated most extensively was in fact not French, but Italian: the controversial poet, novelist, and playwright Gabriele D'Annunzio (1863–1938), whom Symons met in Rome in 1896, and whose growing fame he followed closely, from its early days in the 1890s to the interwar period.[1]

D'Annunzio — an author whose international reputation sank in the second half of the twentieth century and who is certainly not well-known in the English-speaking world today — occupied a central position in the literary landscape of the turn of the century as the chief exponent of Italian literary Decadence and an international celebrity. Already in 1893 Symons had got wind of D'Annunzio's rising star and in 'The Decadent Movement in Literature' he included D'Annunzio among a handful of European authors who represented the up-and-coming Decadent school outside France (the only English authors listed in this same context are Walter Pater and W. E. Henley). It is highly likely that Symons, who kept a vigilant eye on the French press, was alerted to D'Annunzio by the serialisation of a French translation of his novel *L'innocente* (1892) as *L'Intrus* in the periodical *Le Temps*, starting from September 1892 (the novel was then published in book form the following year). Nonetheless, he singled out a work that was yet untranslated into any foreign language, D'Annunzio's first novel *Il piacere* (1889), praising it as 'marvelous' and 'malarious', and calling it 'a triumph of exquisite perversity'.[2] By the end of the decade, the Danish critic Georg Brandes, who was always sensitive to the transnational dimension of literature, would list D'Annunzio, together with Kipling, as the representatives of a new trend in world literature that propelled living authors to global fame.[3]

How had this international fame come about? The answer to this question lies in a series of controversial novels on which D'Annunzio embarked after an early debut as poet which had attracted the attention of domestic (Italian) literary circles: these include *Il piacere*, to which Symons refers in 'The Decadent Movement in Literature', *L'innocente*, *Il trionfo della morte* (1894), *Le vergini delle rocce* (1895), and *Il fuoco* (1900). All these works concentrate on autobiographical male protagonists — artistic, hyper-aesthetic, and sexually curious young men — caught in stories of perverse psycho-sexual development. They deploy characteristic Decadent devices, such as a close focus on interiority at the expense of dialogue and action, a non-moralising portrayal of perversion and morbidity, and a juxtaposition of artistic beauty and moral and physical degeneracy, eros and death. They are written in an elaborate prose style marked by the use of elevated, complex, and highly lyrical literary language, full of archaisms, artifice, and decorative elements. Thematically, several of the novels draw heavily on Nietzsche's philosophy, especially the well-known theory of the *Übermensch*, which in fact D'Annunzio helped popularise by way of his fiction.

These Decadent novels launched D'Annunzio's brilliant international career, which was aided by the constant efforts and dedication of his French translator Georges Hérelle: after being deeply struck by the Italian serialisation of *L'innocente* during a holiday in Naples, Hérelle translated all of D'Annunzio's major works in the years around 1900, securing their publication in prestigious French venues such as the *Revue de Paris*, the *Revue des deux mondes*, and the influential publisher Calmann-Lévy. Italian author and French translator developed a friendship of sort — Hérelle visiting D'Annunzio in Italy several times and even joining him on an ill-fated yachting holiday around Greece. Their long correspondence shows that D'Annunzio took a very active interest in the French publication of his works and, as we shall see, tried to influence the process of translation, giving Hérelle insistent and sometimes impertinent advice on technical matters.[4] D'Annunzio's success in France was remarkable. According to Giovanni Gullace, 'No other Italian writer, with the exception of Dante, attracted so much attention and aroused so much discussion in French literary circles'.[5] Gullace attributes this success to a growing weariness among French readers, in the course of the 1890s, of 'the vulgarity of naturalism and the somber psychology of northern literatures' coupled with the rise in interest in a so-called 'Latin renaissance', of which the influential critic and academician Eugène-Melchior de Vogüé hailed D'Annunzio as a harbinger.[6] Indeed, writing in the *Revue des deux mondes*, Vogüé presented D'Annunzio as a new turning point in a cosmopolitan literary modernity that had so far been fuelled by the northern points of view of Ibsen, Nietzsche, and the Russian novelists; according to Vogüé, D'Annunzio now replaced these with a welcome burst of Latin spirit of which French readers could more easily and, as it were, naturally partake. He concluded with a veritable ovation: 'Et puis, l'immunité ethnique de cet enfant du soleil, de ce beau félin [...]! Et la joie de saluer en Italie un présage certain de la Renaissance latine, une éclosion nouvelle du doux génie dont le clair sourire nous a si souvent réchauffés!' [And then, the ethnic immunity of this child of the sun, of this beautiful feline creature [...]! And the joy of saluting in Italy a definite presage of the Latin Renaissance, a new blossoming of the gentle genius whose pleasant smile has so often warmed us].[7] Vogüé also freed D'Annunzio from the accusations of vulgarity with which he was frequently targeted (the implicit comparison throughout is with Zola, whom Vogüé disliked), arguing that the Italian language enjoys, thanks to its proximity to Latin, the privilege of staying close to popular idiom without ever becoming coarse; and he therefore regretted that no French translation 'n'a osé donner integralément les inventions de ce terrible homme' [has dared to convey the fantasies of this terrible man in full].[8] Of course in France D'Annunzio had his detractors as well as his powerful admirers. In any case, if we accept Pascale Casanova's argument that at this point Paris was 'the chief place of consecration in the world of literature' — that is, the place where universal standards were set that drove authors' international reputations — then we can see how the French success was D'Annunzio's card to international recognition.[9]

In a perceptive essay that appeared in the *Fortnightly Review* in 1897, the sensation novelist Ouida, who like Symons was close to English aesthetic circles, predicted that the French 'adoption' of D'Annunzio would have both advantages and disadvantages for his reputation: 'for one reader outside Italy who would read him in the original text, ten thousand will know him only in the French version, and twenty thousand will accept de Vogüé's description of his works without attempting to judge those for themselves'.[10] Ouida's essay, which is a direct response to Vogüé, was the first sustained and authoritative critical engagement with D'Annunzio's novels in English. According to her, French translator and critics had conspired to render D'Annunzio less prolix and obscene, but in this process had also made him 'much less vigorous, virile, impassioned, and furiously scornful'.[11] Ouida, who was based in Italy and prided herself on her authentic knowledge of Italian life, contrasted Vogüé's opinions and criticised Hérelle's translations in an attempt to give English readers a more authentic impression of D'Annunzio, unmediated by his French reception. To this purpose, she provided a selection of her own translations from several of his novels, including passages that had been excised by Hérelle. Her main purpose seems to have been to tease English readers by giving them a taste of a forbidden fruit: she feared that, with the exception of *Le vergini delle rocce*, D'Annunzio's novels 'could not be reproduced in English' because they were too indecent for English taste.[12]

Ouida would soon be proved wrong for, between 1896 and 1900, all the five major novels translated by Hérelle also appeared in English. She was right, though, in envisaging that the English translations would follow in the footsteps of the French. The first to come out, with Heinemann, in 1896 — and therefore in fact, before Ouida's essay, though she seems to have been unaware of it — was Georgina Harding's translation of *The Triumph of Death,* a novel that had originally been published in Italian in 1894 and then serialised in the *Revue des deux mondes* (in Hérelle's translation) in 1895. Harding, who became the most prolific English translator of D'Annunzio's novels, was an interventionist translator, who manipulated the originals liberally (much more so than the faithful Hérelle, whose cuts, bemoaned by Vogüé, were often made in consultation with D'Annunzio) in order to make them more palatable to the English public. For instance, in *The Triumph of Death*, the most openly Nietzschean of D'Annunzio's novels, she removed all references to Nietzsche, including the epigraph from *Beyond Good and Evil*, softened the anti-Christian and misogynistic elements of the original, and toned down the sensuality of the novel.[13] The result was a bowdlerised version that was widely attacked in the press, where it was described as lacking 'a fine sense of style [...] in every page, every paragraph, every line'.[14] Disappointed that the first English version of D'Annunzio had turned out to be a failure, Symons joined the ranks of Harding's hostile critics. Writing in the *Saturday Review*, he lamented the erasure of the philosophical content from the novel and declared his 'shock' at Harding's use of a linguistic register fit for a penny dreadful, concluding that she was 'not an artist in translation', and that her cuts perversely worked to increase the perceived immorality of the novel.[15] Seemingly undeterred by such rebukes, Harding followed similar practices in her later versions of *Il piacere* (*The Child of Pleasure*, 1898) and *L'innocente* (*The Victim*, 1899).[16]

After such an open declaration of hostility, it is somewhat surprising to see Symons enter the scene later that same year as collaborator of Harding on the English translation of *Il piacere*. In fact, Symons's role in the collaboration was somewhat limited, being confined to the translation of the occasional verse contained in the novel, and in particular of a sonnet cycle that appears as the work of the hyper-refined amoral protagonist, the aesthete Andrea Sperelli. As he explained in the introduction, Symons had been asked directly by the publisher (Heinemann), who undoubtedly hoped thereby to raise the literary credentials of the translation by having the name of an established poet on the cover. The original of *Il piacere* is indeed filled with poetic references, notably to Shelley and to English Pre-Raphaelite and Aesthetic cultures, which D'Annunzio absorbed in the cosmopolitan circles of *fin-de-siècle* Rome.[17] Symons was in this sense an apt choice because of his own proximity to English Aesthetic and Decadent circles, as well as his obvious interest in D'Annunzio.

Symons's input was mostly paratextual rather than textual. He was responsible for the English title, *The Child of Pleasure*, which followed the evocative French *L'Enfant de volupté* chosen by Hérelle, and for the decision to adopt the re-ordered chapter sequence and cuts of the French version, which Hérelle had agreed in consultation with the author.[18] His most important contribution was, however, the short introduction, which, as often with him, would be taken up again and refashioned in different contexts many times in years to come. Here Symons provides one of the earliest and most authoritative, positive assessments of D'Annunzio in English, following on from Ouida's pioneering essay. In the light of his previous criticism of Harding's work, it is unsurprising that Symons opened his introduction by distancing himself from her, claiming, somewhat tendentiously, not to have seen her translation and limiting his 'own responsibility in the matter', as he puts it (p. v). The implication was that, while Harding dumbed down and bowdlerised, the *other* translator stayed true to the author by refusing to read anything but the original, not even the French translation of which D'Annunzio had so heartily approved. His brief introduction must therefore be taken as an act of restitution of the content with which the official translation had silently done away.

Symons presented D'Annunzio as the proponent of a refined materialist philosophy ('the idealist of material things', p. vi) and a hypersensitive aesthete who felt 'more passionately than others, the juicy softness of a ripe fruit, the texture of women's hair, and also the distress of rain, of rough garments, of the cloud that interrupts the sunlight' (pp. vi–vii). According to Symons, D'Annunzio's chief ambition was to free fiction from 'the bondage of mere "truth"' and thus transform the novel into an art form which had 'beauty as its highest aim' (p. x). Within this radical aesthetic programme, his sexual licentiousness had to be understood as part of the most elevated Italian tradition of eroticism 'coming up from a root in Boccaccio, through the stem of Petrarch, to the very flower of Dante' (p. vi), which was of course also a powerful source of inspiration for the English Pre-Raphaelites.

It is clear that Symons, like Ouida before him, had read Vogüé on D'Annunzio and the Latin Renaissance. He borrowed from the French critic the idea that the perceived immorality of D'Annunzio's writings was in fact a misreading, from a foreign point of view, of an essentially Italian (and more generally Latin) lack of reticence in articulating physical sensations, 'which races drawn further from nature by civilisation have thought it needful to invent in their relations with nature' (p. vii). He also borrowed from Vogüé the image of D'Annunzio as a revenant from the Italian Renaissance:[19]

> Beginning by that intent waiting upon sensation in the first place, he ends by expanding the creature of acute sensation into a kind of Renaissance personality, in which sensation becomes complex, cultivated, the flower of an elaborate life. The Italy of the Renaissance cultivated personalities as we cultivate orchids; and, there also, the rarest beauty came from a heightening of nature into something not quite nature, a perversity of beauty which might be poisonous, as well as merely curious. ('Introduction', p. vii)

And again:

> To him, as to the men of the Renaissance, moral qualities are variable things, to be judged only by aesthetic rules. Is an action beautiful, has it that intensity which, in the stricter sense, is virtue? Other considerations may, if you please, come afterwards, but these are the essential. For to D'Annunzio life is but a segment of art, and aesthetic living the most important thing for the artist who is not merely an artist in words, or canvas, or marble, but an artist in life itself. (p. viii)

If the reference to orchids alerts us to the family likeness between D'Annunzio's Decadent heroes and Des Esseintes in Huysmans's *À rebours* (1884), who also has a perverse passion for orchids as the most unnatural of nature's creations,[20] the conjunct references to the Renaissance and the aesthetic life cannot but point English readers to Pater, who had famously argued that the Renaissance should be understood as a spirit that travels across time, rather than a discreet historical period, and had postulated a rekindling of that spirit in the present by means of a life of heightened sensation, which he memorably described as the act of burning with a 'hard, gem-like flame'.[21] Pater too had argued that the making and appreciation of art (including literature) ought to be driven by aesthetic rules rather than moral concerns, and had hinted — very problematically for his hostile critics — that it could be possible to transfer these rules to the social sphere.

The reference to Pater becomes explicit later in the essay when Symons remarks that 'with *Il piacere* [D'Annunzio] has begun, a little uncertainly, to mould a form of his own, taking the hint, not only from some better French models, but also from an Englishman, Pater' (p. x). This striking throwaway comment is pregnant with undeveloped ideas. In the first instance, it suggests that we could see *Il piacere*, an Italian Decadent novel that records the life of an amoral aesthete in nineteenth-century Rome, as a sequel of sorts to *Marius the Epicurean* (1885), an English Decadent novel that records the 'sensations and ideas' of a Roman proto-aesthete in the second century AD. The two works are indeed linked by prominent thematic overlaps, such as the fascination with paganism and the mingling of sex and death, as well as stylistic similarities in the two writers' use of a learned and deliberately literary prose style, rare in nineteenth-century fiction, which introduces a sense of stasis that delays the action of the plot. Symons, in other words, traces a tradition of innovation in the novel form that goes directly from Pater to D'Annunzio, and which consists in abandoning exteriority in favour of perception and the exploration of the inner life or, as he writes in the introduction, 'the hidden, inner self which sits silent through all our conversation' (p. ix), which we have now come to appreciate as a vital link between Decadence and Modernism.

The comparison between *Il piacere* and *Marius the Epicurean* had already been suggested by the Italian critic Enrico Nencioni (a close friend of Vernon Lee) in a review of 1889 that Symons, ever an omnivorous reader of foreign journals, might have known.[22] In any case, the argument on the continuity between Pater and D'Annunzio acquired an especially provocative resonance in the British context, as is easy to see if we turn briefly to one of the reviews of *Il piacere* in the British press. In an anonymous notice in *The Academy*, the reviewer dismissed Harding's bland translation, claiming that it makes criticism 'beside the mark', but nonetheless got worked up by the 'voluptuousness' of the novel, which allegedly makes the book 'tedious and stifling' and 'nothing but heavy perfume', and concluded: 'A study of Latin lasciviousness so minute and intimate as this is surely for Latins only. The Northerner is not competent to judge. For ourselves, we have been bored by it'.[23] What is particularly striking here is the emphasis on (bad) translation and the idea of untranslatability. The reviewer wants D'Annunzio's Decadence to remain a foreign idiom, incomprehensible to the English. In this sense Harding's failed translation appears natural and almost to be welcomed. By contrast, Symons shows that there is a direct link between Pater's aesthetic materialism and its radicalised form in D'Annunzio, with all its Latin, perfumed, and oversexed elements that British reviewers found so unpleasant. By encouraging English speakers to approach the novel through the familiar prism of English aestheticism, the paratextual intervention of the sympathetic translator/critic stands out as an uncomfortable act of domestication.

This move has important consequences for readers' understanding of Pater, as well as D'Annunzio, though, for it retrospectively implicates Paterian aestheticism within D'Annunzio's more markedly Decadent brand. In doing this Symons goes directly against other guardians, as it were, of Pater's legacy, such as Vernon Lee, who in those very years was busy denouncing D'Annunzio's work as dangerous because fundamentally untrue to the artistic and ethical ideals of an earlier moral aestheticism represented by the likes of Pater.[24] It must be remembered, in this context, that D'Annunzio's novels were entering English literary culture not long after the scandalous demise of Oscar Wilde, when the idea of Decadence had become compounded, in the press and in the mind of the general public, with all manners of undesirable social practices linked to its moral provocations including, prominently, male homosexuality. Symons himself, as is well known, would shy away from the term when he recast 'The Decadent Movement in Literature' into the book-length *Symbolist Movement in Literature* shortly after his collaboration on the translation of *Il piacere*. In his introduction to this novel there is likewise no mention at all of this term that had been so thoroughly contaminated. Yet, one of the most interesting offshoots of Symons's analysis is precisely in terms of gender politics. Symons encourages us to see a link between, on the one hand, the effeminate and somewhat understated tradition of sexual radicalism represented by Paterian aestheticism, recently exposed in its implications with the homosexual counterculture in the Wilde trials; and, on the other, the hyper-aesthetic and hyper-masculine heterosexuality represented by D'Annunzio. Different as these two traditions will appear to most readers, Symons is perceptive in suggesting a contiguity between them centred around the ambiguous figure of the over-refined male aesthete — a culturally unstable figure latent with gender indeterminacy and queerness. This reading gains further weight when we consider that D'Annunzio's French translator Hérelle — who, as we have seen, was one of the key agents behind the internationalisation of his fame — was at the same time a pioneering historian and theorist of male love, who might well have spied that D'Annunzio's Decadent eroticism could be hospitable to other modes of sexual desire.[25] In other words, after the Wilde trials, in a period in which writers were subjected to increased public censure in matters of public morality, especially in relation to gender, Symons finds, by way of D'Annunzio, a language to praise and revive the radicalism of the English aesthetic and Decadent schools, with which he was of course closely associated.

The focus on D'Annunzio's sexuality became more explicit in a rewriting of the introduction to *The Child of Pleasure* that Symons included in *Studies in Prose and Verse* as an essay simply entitled 'Gabriele D'Annunzio'. Here Symons spelled out the symbiotic relationship between aestheticism and libido in D'Annunzio: 'His adoration of beauty is a continual fever, and in the intoxication of physical desire he is conscious that passion, also, is a supreme art'.[26] The additions to this later essay emphasised further D'Annunzio's materialism and his grounding in the world of the senses, as well as reinforcing the Paterian connection by glossing D'Annunzio's 'lust of the eye' with a quotation from the central scene in 'The Child in the House' (1878), in which Pater describes his protagonist's epiphany of the beauty of the material world as leaving a 'seemingly exclusive predominance in his interests, of beautiful physical things, a kind of tyranny of the senses over him'.[27] The quotation strengthens both the hypothesis of a continuity between Pater's inward-looking art of fiction and D'Annunzio's, and the impression of a shared sensibility between the two authors, given that 'The Child in the House' is credited as one of Pater's most autobiographical pieces. Now Symons also spoke of D'Annunzio's debt to Nietzsche, which, as we have seen, was excised from the English translations, although he had reservations about the extent to which D'Annunzio's Latin temperament could fully grasp the theory of the *Übermensch*. These new strands of argument were supported with references to other works that had appeared in English in the meantime, such as *The Flame of Life* and some of D'Annunzio's dramas, which, as we shall shortly see, Symons was responsible for translating. The reissuing of this essay in enlarged form was strategic: it catered for the growing interest in D'Annunzio among English-speaking readers in the first years of the twentieth century but it also marked D'Annunzio as Symons's own territory, reclaiming ownership of this controversial writer whose works Symons had advocated in the early days.

The collaboration on the translation of *Il piacere*, with its resulting critical writings, represents a crucial moment in Symons's mediation of D'Annunzio for English readers. It would lead on to the translation of five of D'Annunzio's dramas, which Symons undertook in the early years of the twentieth century, at the height of the Italian writer's international popularity. In the late 1890s, emboldened by the success of his novels, D'Annunzio decided to try his hand as dramatist, an enterprise that was to achieve mixed results in the long run, for his theatrical works never attracted the same amount of attention as his novels. Starting from 1900, Symons translated in close succession *La città morta* (1896; trans. *The Dead City*, 1900), *La gioconda* (1899; trans. *Gioconda*, 1901), and *Francesca da Rimini* (1902; trans. *Francesca da Rimini*, 1902). Further translations were made of *La figlia di Iorio* (1903, *The Daughter of Ioris*) and *La fiaccola sotto il moggio* (1905, *The Torch under the Bushel*) but these did not see the light of day — somewhat ironically, for these last two plays, set in D'Annunzio's native Abruzzi and more naturalist in character, have enjoyed more critical success than the ones which Symons actually published.[28]

D'Annunzio's decision to start writing for the theatre was motivated by the fact that, in 1896, he had started a rocky affair with the celebrated Italian actress Eleonora Duse, which was to last until 1904. Duse's international fame helped further to promote D'Annunzio beyond Italy, as she took his plays around the world, from European capitals to North and South America, broadcasting his reputation.[29] There is no doubt that Symons's own fascination with Duse, whose performances he reviewed in several articles dating from this period, acted as both cause and effect of his decision to translate D'Annunzio's dramas. More generally, though, Symons's translations of D'Annunzio's plays must be placed within his longstanding interest in contemporary drama, which had already resulted in his translation of the Belgian Symbolist Émile Verhaeren's *Les Aubes* (1898; trans. *The Dawn*, 1898), analysed by Clément Dessy in this volume. A note by the publisher (Duckworth) at the back of that book explains that the volume is part of a series on

European drama in translation, conceived because, 'though translations seem to be more in demand every day, the greater number of the Continental dramatists are at present little known in this country'.[30] Symons must have sensed the opportunity to be the first to introduce D'Annunzio's plays to English audiences, maybe hoping to ride the wave of the 'New Drama' into the twentieth century, replicating the success enjoyed in the previous decade by translations of Ibsen and Maeterlinck. In the event, D'Annunzio's plays had none of Ibsen's popularity on the stage (in the English-speaking world as everywhere else) and, although they were frequently compared to those by Maeterlinck because of their Symbolist resistance to dramatic action, they were widely perceived as less original and powerful than Maeterlinck's, lacking the latter's haunting quality. Nonetheless, it is undeniable that Symons was at this point breaking new ground in introducing English readers to avant-garde literary material that was attracting widespread international curiosity.

The first of his translations, *The Dead City*, was also, chronologically, the first play that D'Annunzio wrote. It is a neoclassical tragedy inspired by a trip to Greece where D'Annunzio had visited the recently opened archaeological site at Mycenae. The action is set in modern-day Argos and incorporates the episode of the excavations at Mycenae and the finding of the famous golden artefacts. The male protagonist, Leonardo, is an archaeologist who is caught in a tragic plot of adulterous and incestuous love, clearly driven by the legacy of the classical past, which comes back to haunt the present as its material remains are excavated from the soil. Symons's translation was dedicated to D'Annunzio — a gesture that enabled Symons to project his own voice into the text and, in a sense, take ownership of it in a way that had been unthinkable for Harding, signalling an intellectual dialogue between translator and author, whom he addressed as a fellow poet. The notion of a 'dead city', which D'Annunzio used to characterise a once-prosperous centre of the ancient world that had now become a decaying periphery of Europe, appealed to Symons's sensibility as a travel writer: in his dedication Symons compared D'Annunzio's Argos with Arles and Toledo, 'the two dead cities which I love most in Europe', where the translation was, we are told, begun and finished, in order to suggest that author and translator shared a similar Decadent vision of history as a kind of death-in-life.[31] Symons's travel sketches of these cities, published in 1898 and 1901, absorbed the Decadent atmosphere of D'Annunzio's novels, furthering the dialogue between the two authors.[32]

English reviews were quick to condemn the Decadence of the play with all the usual complaints about 'decay', 'corruption', and 'a mortal and ruinous loveliness, which shines as putrescence shines'.[33] Yet, there is no doubt that the appearance of *The Dead City* inaugurated a new phase in D'Annunzio's English reception, for now, instead of the customary accusations of bowdlerisation and betrayal directed at Georgina Harding, critics pointed out the correctness and beauty of Symons's translations. If we consider, for instance, the reviews of the three dramas that appeared in *The Academy*, we can see that Symons's translation effort attracted increasing praise over the years or, in other words, his presence gained visibility at the expense, as it were, of the author: the culmination was the anonymous review of *Francesca da Rimini*, where the critic cast a retrospective glance at Symons's work of translating D'Annunzio's theatre and compared it to Alfred Sutro's important translations of Maeterlinck, praising the way in which Symons carried out the difficult task of rendering D'Annunzio's language 'with the cunning grace and formal perfection [...] which only the practised hand, the sympathetic and plastic mind of a poet could compass'.[34] Such assessments projected the view that, thanks to Symons's technical ability and his fellow-poet's 'sympathy' with the original, English-speaking readers could now, through the plays, access a more powerful and authentic D'Annunzio than was available in the English versions of the novels; even though, paradoxically, the dramas were widely held to be less accomplished than the fictions.

D'Annunzio's dramas certainly present challenges for translators: first and foremost his use of an overwrought and archaic language, which slows down the dramatic exchanges between the characters, forcing the reader/viewer to concentrate on the language and thereby delaying the action of the play. In his dealings with Hérelle over the years, D'Annunzio had been very insistent that the peculiarities of his style should be rendered into French as faithfully as possible. He checked and corrected the draft translations before they went to press; and in his letters he repeatedly criticised Hérelle's tendency to domesticate him and make him sound prosaic in French, urging him to avoid 'i *modi di dire* comuni e prosastici di cui abbonda l'idioma francese moderno' [the common and prosaic *manners of expressions* that abound in modern French].[35] The question of stylistic faithfulness was of paramount importance to him and for this reason he advocated an ideal of translation, as far as his own works were concerned, that would preserve the foreign character of the original — what, in his own case, he called the '*accento* dannunziano'[36] — even if this meant introducing elements of disruption in the target language:

> Per fortuna, i traduttori odierni hanno compreso che un'opera tradotta *non deve* entrare a far parte della letteratura nazionale ma deve conservare la sua impronta d'origine, magari *contro* il genio della nazione che l'ospita. Una traduzione, oggi, non può essere se non *un modo ingegnoso* di far indovinare — a colui che dall'ignoranza della lingua straniera è impedito di averne una rivelazione diretta — *un modo ingegnoso* di far indovinare le qualità dell'opera originale.[37]
>
> [Luckily modern translators have understood that a translated work *must not* enter a national literature, but rather preserve its original character, even if this goes *against* the specific genius of the host nation. A translation today cannot but be an *ingenious way* of enabling those, whose ignorance of a foreign language prevents from having a direct revelation, to guess the qualities of the original.]

Such comments reveal a fundamental scepticism towards translation. Moreover, it is evident that D'Annunzio's ideal translator would have to be a poet like himself: in the same passage he goes on to cite with approval Mallarmé's translations of Edgar Allan Poe and Gabriel Mourey's translations of Swinburne. When it came to *La città morta*, D'Annunzio wanted his first drama to be disrupted as little as possible, believing that 'al teatro questa parola — *traduzione* — sembra quasi mettere un velo tra l'opera e gli spettatori. Sembra che gli spettatori, a traverso una traduzione, non debbano ricevere una emozione *diretta*' [in the theatre this word — *translation* — almost seems to place a veil between the work and the audience. It seems that the audience, through a translation, should not be able to receive a *direct* emotion].[38] He therefore even managed to persuade Hérelle to omit his name from the text, in order deliberately to give the impression that the work had been composed directly in French — something that he was later to do with his Decadent 'mystery' *Le Martyre de St Sébastien* (1911) and lyric play *La Pisanelle ou la mort parfumée* (1913), in which the '*accento* dannunziano' came through in the French unmediated.

Symons's English translations went against such principles in that, as we have seen, they foregrounded the mediating role of the translator/interpreter in the eyes of the critics. Symons also domesticated D'Annunzio into English in ways that the author would not have tolerated in French. But D'Annunzio was far less interested in his English reception than in his French one and, besides, his command of English was poor in comparison to his fluency in French, so he did not interfere with Symons's work as he did with the long-suffering Hérelle. Indeed, when Hérelle was working on *Francesca da Rimini* in 1903, D'Annunzio sent him a copy of Symons's translation (the only English translation of a work by D'Annunzio to have been published earlier than its French equivalent), encouraging him to draw inspiration from it, telling him that 'il poeta Symons è riuscito talvolta a rendere il colorito speciale del testo' [the poet Symons has at times succeeded in rendering the special colouring of the text].[39] The seemingly casual word 'poeta' carried a special force of rebuke. Indeed, in his introduction to the English version of the play, Symons went into much detail about the technicalities of blank verse and prided himself on his translation being 'alike in [...] rhythm' to the original.[40] By comparison D'Annunzio thought Hérelle's draft to have totally failed to capture the rhythm and 'colore *linguistico*' [*linguistic* colour] of the original. This might simply have been a provocation on D'Annunzio's part, as he went on to add, in characteristic fashion, that *Francesca da Rimini* 'è opera così profondamente italiana che non è possibile trasportarla in altra lingua né *farla sentire* a uomini d'altra razza' [is such a profoundly Italian work that it is not possible either to transpose it into another language or to make persons of another race *feel* it].[41] Yet his comments show that he trusted that Symons's reputation as a poet would equip him to pierce through at least some of these unsurmountable barriers posed by language and 'race'.

A fundamental reason behind D'Annunzio's wish to make *La città morta* appear as French as possible was that he had persuaded Sarah Bernhardt to stage the premiere of the play in her *Théâtre de la Renaissance* in Paris (it took place on 21 January 1898). While *La città morta* is connected with the name of the French actress, *La gioconda* and *Francesca da Rimini* are closely linked with Duse, the dedicatee of both plays and their lead female role in performances around the globe. Symons admired Duse intensely and felt a voyeuristic fascination with her tempestuous relationship with D'Annunzio, which was widely reported in the international press. In this sense his translations of D'Annunzio's dramas were also a way to get close to Duse. Symons saw Duse perform and met her several times, and he published a book about her after her death in 1924 (as ever, partly collated from previous essays and reviews), in which he explored her dramatic talent and presented her as a Symbolist artist, on a par with Verlaine and D'Annunzio himself. Her relationship with D'Annunzio he compared to Choderlos de Laclos's notoriously scandalous *Les Liaisons dangereuses* (1782).[42] In this late book, which is in fact as much about D'Annunzio as it is about Duse, Symons clearly wanted to distance himself from D'Annunzio's work, calling his poetry 'a hard, positive thing, in which there is little underneath his favourite sounds, colours and form, which exist for their own sake, and not for the sake of what they have to express' (p. 121). It was, however, the dramas that were the object of Symons's harshest censure. In an anecdote, he revealed that Duse herself told him 'in the Savoy in 1900' that D'Annunzio was never a real dramatist, only a mere talented lyricist (p. 112). Of the plays that he himself translated, only *Francesca da Rimini* was presented in a fully positive light, as possessing a 'personal style' that is otherwise lacking from D'Annunzio's poetry (p. 120). By contrast, in *The Dead City* D'Annunzio failed to create 'a wholly new and satisfying form' like Maeterlinck, merely transplanting 'the novel to the stage' without achieving a satisfyingly dramatic effect; when Symons saw it played in Zurich three years after the publication of his translation, Duse's performance was the only thing that mitigated his disappointment (p. 161). A similar judgement was reserved for *La gioconda*, which was redeemed only by Duse's acting, being 'at its best [...] lyrical rather than dramatic, and at its worst [...] horrible with a vulgar material horror' (p. 10).

In *Eleonora Duse*, Symons recycled much material that he had used in his earlier essays on D'Annunzio, but his overall judgement was decidedly more negative than in any of the earlier writings. The motivation for this was, at least in part, political. D'Annunzio's work had been appropriated by the Fascists, who had come to power in Italy in 1922, in order to bolster their nationalist ideology (while D'Annunzio himself, although undoubtedly on the political far right, always remained ambivalent towards Fascism and the figure of Mussolini).[43] After the First World War, D'Annunzio had been heavily involved in several military exploits, including, most spectacularly, the occupation in 1919 of the city of Fiume (or Rijeka, as it is known in Croatian), which he governed as a dictator for a period of about one year. Symons ventured the hypothesis that D'Annunzio had been seized by 'a kind of insanely egotistical madness', which brought him to kill his own genius in a drug-fuelled suicide ritual (p. 126). Symons here revisited his former characterisation of D'Annunzio as a revenant from the Italian Renaissance in a perverse key:

> As in Pietro Aretino, so in D'Annunzio, there flashes before one's vision the image of an exotic undergrowth of the Renaissance becoming if anything more exotic as it flowers on Italian soil, tormented and twisted and tortured into forms of unimaginable abnormality by this creature whose furious passions and whose exasperations drive him onward towards some unknown abyss, elaborately and utterly himself (as I have said before) as he weaves his fictions, never out of human entrails, but out of the bare physical facts, like a subtle spider turned animally human. [...] So, as Aretino was the last, the most perfect, if also the most vitiated product of the Renaissance manners, so, in a sense, the

> modern Italian seems to end a period; he is essentially decadent and might be said to end the movement we call decadent. (p. 128)

Taking leave of D'Annunzio in 1926 is thus Symons's way of marking the end of Decadence, a movement he had himself introduced to English readers exactly thirty-five years earlier. Yet this remarkable image of *mise en abyme* — D'Annunzio as the decadence of Decadence — at the same time testifies to the survival of Decadence into what we now know as the age of Modernism, not least thanks to Symons's own efforts.

In conclusion, it is worth noting that the archive of D'Annunzio's monumental last residence, Il Vittoriale degli Italiani, contains records of the correspondence between D'Annunzio's Italian publishers, Mondadori, and the London firm Putnam & Co. concerning the translation of D'Annunzio's last major work, *Il libro segreto* (1935). Evidently pleased with Symons's previous work, D'Annunzio wanted Symons to undertake the task. But, after some amusing misunderstandings created by the Italians' wrong spelling of Symons's name, Putnam & Co. informed the Italian publishers that Symons 'has now largely retired from writing and in connection with his age and state of health, he would clearly not be available'. Echoing the opinions of Victorian critics, they added that, 'while we are assured of its merit and a certain grandeur, we have been forced to recognise that the author's most exceptional style and the character of the narrative not only render it almost impossible of translation, but would make it very difficult of comprehension for the ordinary English reader'. It predictably followed that they would not be able to pay what they called 'a competitive advance, or even an exceptionally high royalty'.[44]

The most conclusive remark, however, was made by the anonymous reader commissioned by Putnam & Co., whose otherwise positive evaluation — somewhat cattily forwarded to Mondadori by Putnam & Co. — states that 'it is useless to shut our eyes to the fact that, of all living great authors, d'Annunzio is comparatively the most out of fashion. [...] And this book is for the erudite, the select. For the poets [sic.] admirers and students, — not for the crowd'.[45] While it would be wrong to claim that Symons had tried to make D'Annunzio into an author for the crowd, it is certainly true that his work shaped D'Annunzio's reputation in the English-speaking world. As Modernism came to dominate British literary culture in the 1920s and '30s, the two authors went out of fashion together. D'Annunzio was now deemed more untranslatable than ever. But Symons's translations survive as a reminder of the often obscured continuities between English aestheticism, Italian Decadence, and the international Modernist canon.

Notes to Chapter 4

1. Beckson, *Arthur Symons*, p. 160. Symons gives an account of his first meeting with D'Annunzio in *Eleonora Duse* (London: Elkin Mathews, 1926), pp. 113–14. After their first meeting the two kept a sporadic correspondence.
2. Arthur Symons, 'The Decadent Movement in Literature', *Harper's New Monthly Magazine* (November 1893), 858–67 (p. 866), repr. in Symons, *The Symbolist Movement in Literature*, pp. 169–83 (p. 181).
3. '[Kipling and D'Annunzio] er efter al Sandsynlighed berømtere end de største af deres For-

gængere nogensinde i levende Live har været' [Kipling and D'Annunzio are in all likelihood more famous than the greatest of their predecessors have ever been during their lifetime]. Georg Brandes, 'Verdensliteratur' [1899], in *Samlede Skrifter*, 18 vols (Copenhagen: Gyldendal, 1899–1910), XII, 23–28 (p. 27), <http://adl.dk/adl_pub/pg/cv/ShowPgImg.xsql?nnoc=adl_pub&p_udg_id=20&p_sidenr=23> [accessed 15 January 2017]. All translations are the author's own, unless otherwise stated.
4. Their correspondence was first collected and translated by Guy Tosi, *Gabriele D'Annunzio à Georges Hérelle: correspondance accompagné de douze sonnets cisalpines* (Paris: Éditions Denoël, 1946); and has more recently appeared in the Italian original in *Carteggio D'Annunzio-Hérelle (1891–1931)*, ed. by Mario Cimini (Lanciano: Rocco Carabba, 2004).
5. Giovanni Gullace, *Gabriele D'Annunzio in France: A Study in Cultural Relations* (Syracuse, NY: Syracuse University Press, 1966), p. x.
6. Ibid., pp. ix and 19–25.
7. Eugène-Melchior de Vogüé, 'La Renaissance latine: Gabriel D'Annunzio, poèmes et romans', *Revue des deux mondes* (1 January 1895), 187–206 (p. 206), <http://rddm.revuedesdeuxmondes.fr/archive/article.php?code=66236> [accessed 10 January 2017].
8. Ibid., p. 205.
9. Pascale Casanova, *The World Republic of Letters*, trans. by M. B. DeBevoise (Cambridge, MA, & London: Harvard University Press, 2004), p. 127.
10. Ouida, 'The Genius of D'Annunzio', *Fortnightly Review*, 61:363 (March 1897), 349–73 (p. 349).
11. Ibid., p. 350.
12. Ibid., p. 361.
13. See John Woodhouse, 'Il *Trionfo della Morte*: traduzioni, reazioni e interpretazioni anglosassoni', in *Trionfo della Morte: atti del III convegno internazionale di studi dannunziani*, ed. by Edoardo Tiboni and Luigia Abrugiati (Pescara: Centro nazionale di studi dannunziani, 1981), pp. 239–58.
14. [Anon.], 'D'Annunzio in English', *The Academy* (5 February 1898), 141–42 (p. 141).
15. Symons, 'D'Annunzio in English', *Saturday Review*, 85 (29 January 1898), 52–53.
16. Of D'Annunzio's other major novels, *Le vergini delle rocce* was translated by Agatha Hughes (*The Virgins of the Rocks*, 1899); and *Il fuoco* by Kassandra Vivaria, pseudonym for Magda Sindici (*The Flame of Life*, 1900). Both were published in Britain by Heinemann. Vivaria/Sindici was William Heinemann's wife.
17. See Giuliana Pieri, *The Influence of Pre-Raphaelitism on Fin de Siècle Italy: Art, Beauty, and Culture* (London: Modern Humanities Research Association, 2007), pp. 67–78.
18. See Arthur Symons, 'Introduction', in Gabriele D'Annunzio, *The Child of Pleasure*, trans. by Georgina Harding and Arthur Symons (London: Heinemann, 1898), pp. v–xii (p. v). Further references to this work will be made in the main body of the text. Guy Tosi explains that some of the cuts to the French translation were motivated by the fact that in the original D'Annunzio had drawn liberally from French authors, notably Joséphin Péladan, and that such borrowings would have become problematically glaring when rendered 'back' into French. Tosi, *Gabriele D'Annunzio à Georges Hérelle*, pp. 94–95.
19. Vogüé had described Andrea Sperelli, the protagonist of *Il piacere*, as 'un phénomène d'atavisme trés caractérisé: il est un survivant ou un revenant du XVIe siècle, de la Renaissance italienne' [a very characteristic phenomenon of atavism: he is a survival or revenant of the sixteenth century, of the Italian Renaissance] ('La Renaissance latine', p. 199).
20. J. K. Huysmans, *Against Nature*, trans. by Robert Baldick (London: Penguin, 1959). Des Esseintes's interest in orchids is described in Chapter 8. The comparison with *À rebours* would become something of a bone of contention among D'Annunzio scholars, who have disagreed on whether *Il piacere* was in fact inspired by Huysmans's novel. See for instance Ilvano Caliaro, 'Fra Trinità dei Monti e Fontenay-aux-Roses: intorno a Sperelli e a Des Esseintes', in *Da Bisanzio a Roma: studi su Gabriele D'Annunzio* (Verona: Fiorini, 2004), pp. 11–25.
21. Walter Pater, 'Conclusion', in *The Renaissance*, p. 189.
22. Enrico Nencioni, 'Due nuovi romanzi', *Nuova Antologia* (16 June 1889); repr. as 'Il piacere' in Nencioni, *Nuovi saggi critici di letterature straniere e altri scritti* (Florence: Le Monnier, 1909), pp. 391–404 (pp. 397–98).

23. [Anon.], '*The Child of Pleasure* by Gabriele D'Annunzio', *Academy* (26 November 1898), 333.
24. Lee takes D'Annunzio as an example of the failures of art for art's sake, attacking the 'poverty of thought and feeling [and] the vacuity of the *man*', Vernon Lee, 'The Nature of Literature, II', *Contemporary Review*, 86 (1 July 1904), 645–61 (p. 656).
25. A full exploration of Hérelle's sexological and queer interests is available in *Georges Hérelle: archéologie de l'inversion sexuelle 'fin de siècle'*, ed. by Clive Thomson (Paris: Éditions du Félin, 2014). Thomson notes that, in Naples in 1890, Hérelle discovered D'Annunzio at the same time as his first experiments with male prostitution (p. 34).
26. Arthur Symons, 'Gabriele D'Annunzio', in *Studies in Prose and Verse*, pp. 129–42 (p. 134). Symons had previously reissued a version of the same essay in the *Imperial and Colonial Magazine Review*, 1 (December 1900), 242–49.
27. Symons, 'Gabriele D'Annunzio', p. 136; cf. Walter Pater, 'The Child in the House', in *Imaginary Portraits*, ed. by Lene Østermark-Johansen, MHRA Jewelled Tortoise 1 (London: Modern Humanities Research Association, 2014), p. 91.
28. The manuscript translations have survived among the Symons papers in Princeton University Library. For early praise of *La figlia di Iorio* in English by a noted translator and critic, see Helen Zimmern, 'D'Annunzio's *La Figlia di Iorio*', *North American Review*, 41 (1 January 1905), 41–47.
29. See John Woodhouse, *Gabriele D'Annunzio: Defiant Archangel* (Oxford: Clarendon Press, 1998), pp. 139–40.
30. Émile Verhaeren, *The Dawn*, trans. by Arthur Symons (London: Duckworth, 1898), n. p.
31. Gabriele D'Annunzio, *The Dead City*, trans. by Arthur Symons (London: Heinemann, 1900).
32. Arthur Symons, 'Arles', *Saturday Review*, 86 (22 October 1898), 528–29; and 'A Study of Toledo', *Monthly Review*, 2 (March 1901), 144–54.
33. [Anon.], '"And Yet — He is a Master"', *The Academy* (2 June 1900), 464–65 (p. 464).
34. [Anon.], 'An Atmospheric Tragedy', *Academy and Literature* (12 January 1903), 48.
35. Gabriele D'Annunzio to Georges Hérelle, [between 6 and 15 March 1896], in *Carteggio D'Annunzio-Hérelle*, ed. by Cimini, p. 369.
36. D'Annunzio to Hérelle, 16 March 1896, in *Carteggio D'Annunzio-Hérelle*, ed. by Cimini, p. 372.
37. D'Annunzio to Hérelle, 4 January 1905, in *Carteggio D'Annunzio-Hérelle*, ed. by Cimini, p. 588.
38. D'Annunzio to Hérelle, [before 19 October 1896], in *Carteggio D'Annunzio-Hérelle*, ed. by Cimini, p. 419.
39. D'Annunzio to Hérelle, [end of February 1903], in *Carteggio D'Annunzio-Hérelle*, ed. by Cimini, p. 556.
40. Arthur Symons, 'Introduction', in Gabriele D'Annunzio, *Francesca da Rimini*, trans. by Arthur Symons (London: Heinemann, 1902), vii–xiv, p. xi.
41. D'Annunzio to Hérelle, in *Carteggio D'Annunzio-Hérelle*, ed. by Cimini, p. 556.
42. Symons, *Eleonora Duse*, p. 43. Further references to this work will be made in the main body of the text.
43. On D'Annunzio and Mussolini see Woodhouse, *Gabriele D'Annunzio*, pp. 360–71.
44. Putnam & Co. to Mondadori, 24 July 1935, Fondazione Il Vittoriale degli Italiani, Archivi del Vittoriale, AG XLIX, 2.
45. Reader's report for Putnman & Co. on *Il libro segreto*. Archivi del Vittoriale, AG XLIX, 2.

CHAPTER 5

The Sinister Guest: Arthur Symons, Villiers de l'Isle-Adam, and Post-Victorian Decadence[1]

Matthew Creasy

As the narrator of 'Le Convive des dernières fêtes' recognises, social situations can rapidly turn awkward:

> Le Commandeur de pierre peut venir souper avec nous; il peut nous tendre la main! Nous la prendrons encore. Peut-être sera-ce lui qui aura froid.
> Un soir de carnaval de l'année 186..., C★★★, l'un de mes amis, et moi, par un circonstance absolument due aux hasards de l'ennui 'ardent et vague', nous étions seuls, dans une avant-scène, au bal de l'Opéra.
> Depuis quelques instants nous admirions, à travers la poussière, la mosaïque tumultueuse des masques hurlant sous les lustres et s'agitant sous l'archet sabbatique de Strauss.[2]

> [The statue of the Commendatore may come to dine with us; he may hold out his hand to us! We will still take it. Perhaps it will be his turn to feel a chill.
> One evening during carnival in the year 186..., through circumstances absolutely due to the vagaries of an 'impassioned and obscure' boredom, one of my friends, C★★★, and I found ourselves alone in a box at the Opera ball.
> For a short while we admired through the dust the tumultuous mosaic of maskers howling under the chandeliers and frisking under the sabbatine baton of Strauss.]

The opening allusion to the *Commendatore* from Mozart and Da Ponte's *Don Giovanni* anticipates the events that follow. Bored by the scene before them, the two protagonists accept an invitation by three ladies from the Parisian demi-monde to abandon the ball and join them in a private room at the Maison Dorée. On their way out, the narrator bumps into a mysterious gentleman he encountered whilst holidaying previously in Germany. Through an odd mixture of embarrassment and curiosity, he invites this stranger to join their private festivities. Even as the party attempt to escape social life, it seems, they find themselves governed by its constraints.

Having been invited to dine, the unsettling behaviour and demeanour of this stranger, who insists on adopting the name 'M. Saturne', recalls the *Commendatore*, whose statue comes to life in Mozart's opera to invite his murderer, Don Giovanni, to a supper at which he drags him down to hell. As M. Saturne departs, another friend, Docteur Les Églisottes, arrives and reveals that their mysterious guest suffers from an obsession with participating in executions. He is leaving, it turns out, in the hope of operating the guillotine that morning upon a convicted murderer known to one of the party. Hence the reversal in the story's opening lines — 'Peut-être sera-ce lui qui aura froid' [perhaps it will be his turn to feel a chill]: having entertained him, the party feel complicit in the actions of their strange guest. But this complicity reverberates throughout the story, which hints at deep suspicions of writers and writing. Narrated in the first person, the story is told by a character close to that of the author, who confesses that he likes to attend a café where he can observe the behaviour of the former official public executioner of Paris for inspiration. Writing, death, and awkward social situations are all intimately linked within the fabric of the story.

First published in the *Revue du monde nouveau* in March 1874, 'Le Convive des dernières fêtes' was collected in *Contes cruels* (1883), where Arthur Symons encountered it whilst reading Villiers's work for the first time during 1887. Enthusing privately to correspondents, Symons felt Villiers deserved an English audience and, shortly after the French writer's death in 1889, he appealed publicly in the *Athenaeum* for 'some thoroughly competent hand' to translate the *Contes cruels*.[3] At the same time, he seems to have worked on his own version, writing to Ernst Rhys in 1890 that Elkin Mathews had:

> Practically promised to publish my translation of the *Contes Cruels* of Villiers de l'Isle-Adam. This is an immense relief to me. I hope to do something of the same service to English readers that Baudelaire did to French readers by his translation of Poe.[4]

Although his translation of 'Le Secret de la musique ancienne' ('The Secret of Ancient Music') was printed in the first issue of *Black and White* during February 1891, Symons never published a full translation of *Contes cruels*. Instead, he wrote critical appreciations of Villiers's work for *Woman's World*, *Illustrated London News*, and *Fortnightly Review*. A period of severe mental illness during 1908–10 forced a halt to his literary career, but as he recovered Symons turned again to the possibility of translating Villiers. He produced a translation of 'Le Convive des dernières fêtes' in July 1915, but did not find a publisher until 1919, when a heavily revised version appeared in the *English Review* as 'The Sinister Guest'.[5] Symons then went on to publish translations of two other stories from *Contes cruels* in 1925 and 1926, as well as Villiers's short novel, *Claire Lenoir* (1925).

Unusually, Symons did not credit Villiers directly for 'The Sinister Guest'. But his debt to the French author is clear from the opening paragraphs:

> It is a Carnival night in Paris, and I am in a box in the Opéra Français with Count Nayrac. Below us whirl the masked dancers to the sound of diabolical music, in a tumultuous mosaic, as if the figures of the mosaics in San Marco had come to life over again. It is a *Bal Masqué* after my own heart. How can one do otherwise than admire ardently the painted webs of light of the women's

costumes and this Eastern Sultan who dances with a white Circassian girl, he
with his turban and she with her veils? Does not this mad world seem to tie my
senses to some dubious dream, as doubtful as dusk?[6]

Despite abandoning Villiers's aphoristic allusion to *Don Giovanni*, the setting is clearly the same and Symons renders key phrases such as 'la mosaïque tumultueuse' directly. 'The Sinister Guest' retains the narrative arc of 'Le Convive de dernières fêtes', but converts the sequestered festivities of the original group into the occasion — in the mode of Boccaccio's *Decameron* — for members of the party to relate a series of anecdotes and stories about murder and adultery.

In this way 'The Sinister Guest' challenges conventional categories: whilst it contains directly translated elements, its departures seem closer to a free adaptation of Villiers rather than a translation. As such it provides a useful focal point for my account of the unconventional and varying nature of Symons's response to Villiers. The peculiarities of 'The Sinister Guest' point to the wider resonance of this literary relationship beyond the contours of Symons's own career. For the break forced by his mental health very roughly coincided with broader social and historical upheavals. Symons's treatment of Villiers is not just revealing about the reception of Decadent French writing within anglophone culture during the *fin de siècle*; I shall argue that it reflects the fate of what Kristin Mahoney has described as 'post-Victorian Decadence' during the Modernist era.[7]

His loose approach to adapting 'Le Convive des dernières fêtes' in 1919 contradicts some of Symons's previous statements of principle regarding translation. Prefacing his version of Baudelaire's *Petites poèmes en prose* in 1905, Symons announced his intention to be 'absolutely faithful to the sense, the words, and the rhythm of the original'.[8] An article for the *Bookman's Journal and Print Collector* in 1922 erects this as a general principle:

> Translation from prose into prose should be within the power of every skilled man of letters. All that is required of him is that he should render the sense and follow the cadence of every sentence. Paraphrase, in a prose translation, is unpardonable; or can be pardoned only when a man of genius translates a person of mediocrity, and transforms his leaden prose into gold.[9]

Observing the scarcity of 'genius', Symons urged 'extreme fidelity' upon translators of prose before describing the technical difficulties of translating poetry.[10] In contrast, addressing the same topic three years later, Symons cited Dante Gabriel Rossetti's distinction between 'fidelity' and 'literality' in translation. Contrary to his previous disdain for paraphrase, Symons argued that 'literality is rarely possible in any translation, either from prose or from verse'.[11] The work of Villiers de l'Isle-Adam may constitute a special case here, since these remarks preface his translation of *Claire Lenoir*. Having noted that 'literality is rarely possible', Symons continued: 'certainly not in the case of Villiers; for this man of passionate and lofty genius [...] invented a style which is entirely of his own creation'.[12] The challenges of rendering the lexical shifts of Villiers's prose may have forced a change of mind upon Symons.

Translation and the technical and theoretical challenges posed by translation articulated by Symons played a central role in Decadence, which was, as Matthew Potolsky notes, 'fundamentally international in origin and orientation'.[13] Adapting the work of Benedict Anderson and Jean-Luc Nancy, Potolsky conceives of Decadence as characterised by an unorthodox 'imagined community' or 'literary communism' whereby ostensibly alienated or isolated figures forge a sense of collective endeavour through the tastes and interests they share with other similarly isolated writers: 'Works are "decadent" not because they realize a doctrine or make use of certain styles and themes but because they move within a recognizable network of canonical books, pervasive influences, recycled stories, erudite commentaries, and shared tastes'.[14] 'The Sinister Guest' is a case in point. Symons's structural alterations extend the story's connection with Villiers's work beyond 'Le Convive des dernières fêtes'. The first nested story Symons added, related by the courtesan, Marcelle Maulle, draws upon 'L'Enjeu' from Villiers's third collection, *Nouveau contes cruels* (1893). Marcelle describes a disreputable priest embroiled in a gambling circle, who reveals 'a secret of the Church', that there is no Purgatory (pp. 107–08). There are passing references to other stories from *Contes cruels* too: Symons adopts a simile from 'À s'y méprendre' to describe the weather (p. 114); and a striking image when the narrator catches sight of his face in the reflection from a shop window derives from 'Le Désir d'être un homme' (p. 115). In this way, Symons creates a composite response to Villiers's short stories. The 'sinister guest' underscores this by referring to his own contribution to the tales being told amongst the group as a 'cruel story' (p. 108).

The 'imagined community' within 'The Sinister Guest' is not limited to relations between Symons and Villiers: his choice of names forges broader connections. Re-christening the narrator's companion 'C★★★' as 'Count Nayrac' recalls Paul Bourget's novel *La Terre promise* (1892), in which 'Francis Nayrac' finds himself drawn back to an older former mistress and their illegitimate child, rupturing his engagement with a younger woman (the promised land). Instead of the Verlainian 'Baron Saturne,' Symons's sinister guest adopts the pseudonym, 'Baron Hulot', alluding to the philandering nobleman from Balzac's *La Cousine Bette* (1846). Both allusions point to the story's running preoccupation with various kinds of marital infidelity. But Symons also changes Villiers's 'Florian Les Églisottes', into 'Flavian Des Esseintes', combining direct allusion to the protagonist of Huysmans's *À rebours* (1884) with Roman history and an echo of Marius's companion, Flavian, in Walter Pater's *Marius the Epicurean* (1885).

In this way, Symons's alterations and interpolations transform Villiers's story into one of the canonising allusive works that Potolsky describes as characteristic of Decadence. The fluctuations in Symons's views on translation elsewhere, however, point to the potential complexities and contradictions of such a Decadent Republic of Letters, where 'community' rests on contact between texts rather than individuals. Translating another author involves, from one point of view, imaginatively inhabiting their work with an intimacy that surpasses most other forms of influence. It means surrendering to another writer, to try and find a voice for them within the formal and linguistic constraints of your own language and culture. Symons described the 'vital heat' that a translation aims to capture, explaining that his choice of material was an expression of partiality: 'Why did I translate Verlaine? Because he was a man who loved life more passionately than any man I ever knew'.[15] On the other hand, translation may imply a very different relationship, whereby translators impose their own linguistic choices and preferences upon their source material. Hence the punning Italian saying, *traduttore traditore*, which associates translation with treachery, and the loaded vocabulary of 'fidelity' used by Symons, which implies a concomitant anxiety about infidelity.

It is fitting, then, that the nested narratives of 'The Sinister Guest' turn upon adultery and betrayal. Instead of offering tribute, Symons's adaptation of his source could be read as a means of surpassing or writing-over Villiers de l'Isle-Adam. This possibility becomes stronger as the extent to which Symons interpolated previously published material of his own within 'The Sinister Guest' becomes apparent. The fourth nested story told by Juliette Vairy, for example (p. 110), is lifted straight out of 'Extracts from the Diary of Henry Luxulyan', from Symons's only collection of short fiction, *Spiritual Adventures* (1905).[16] Similar to the story's Decadent allusions, connections with Symons's works occur at a local level too, as in the opening paragraph, quoted above, where the image of 'the Sultan' derives from Symon's poem 'Bal Masqué', which describes 'such pearls | As none but white Circassian girls | Wear in some sullen Sultan's sight'. The interrogative mode of this poem ('What is this living wheel that twirls?') may also help to determine the repeated questions ('How can one', 'Does not this') which characterise the narrative at this point in 'The Sinister Guest'.[17]

At times, quotations from his previous works occur in rapid succession:

> An intense curiosity has always been mine, an inexhaustible one; so that I have been apt to look on the world as a puppet show, and all the men and women merely players, whose strings we do not see as they move them. These, like the marionettes, may be relied on, even in their gestures. So, for these reasons, my desire is to fathom the perhaps unfathomable secrets in our stranger, to deprive him of some of his illusions, not his illusions of himself; and, having found these, to intrude no further into his destiny. ('The Sinister Guest', p. 106)

This passage echoes the ambivalence about writing and creativity found in Villiers's hint in 'Le Convive des dernières fêtes' that writers are somehow morally compromised by the detachment required by their art. Upon closer inspection, it combines material from two separate essays by Symons. First, a general observation from *London: A Book of Aspects*: 'I have always been apt to look on the world as a puppet-show, and all the men and women merely players, whose wires we do not see working'.[18] And then Symons's essay, 'An Apology for Puppets':

> The marionette may be relied upon. He will respond to an indication without reserve or revolt; an error on his part (we are all human) will certainly be the fault of the author; he can be trained to perfection. As he is painted, so will he smile; as the wires lift or lower his hands, so will his gestures be; and he will dance when his legs are set in motion.[19]

Lifted out of their original context with only minor verbal changes, these passages are recombined into a single, continuous line of narrative. Such practice may be symptomatic of the generally derivative and repetitive nature of the later phase of Symons's career remarked by Karl Beckson and several of the contributors to this volume.[20] Symons had always republished his periodical writings in different formats, but did this with greater frequency after recovering from his breakdown. So, having published 'An Apology for Masks' in the *Saturday Review* during 1897, he republished it in *Plays, Acting, and Music* (1903). When the second edition of this collection was printed 1909, he added further essays and repositioned 'An Apology for Masks' to form an introduction.[21] His work on 'The Sinister Guest' marks a third return to that essay.

This relationship to his own previously published work points to another difficulty or complication with reading Symons's version of Villiers de l'Isle-Adam in relation to Potolsky's 'Decadent Republic'. For 'The Sinister Guest' was not published until 1919, a period more usually associated with Modernism than Decadence. The distance between such 'literary generations' is central to T. S. Eliot's account of Symons as a translator in 'Baudelaire in Our Time': 'Mr Symons has made a good translation, in the Symons style. If our point of view to-day was the point of view of thirty years ago, or even of twenty years ago, we should call it a good translation'.[22] As I have noted elsewhere, Eliot's attitude towards Symons was highly ambivalent and the praise he offers here is qualified, even arch, depending on the kind of pause implied by the comma in the first sentence.[23] In the review that follows, Eliot presents two serious criticisms of 'the Symons style'. Firstly, he claims that Symons holds a trivial conception of 'sin' and 'vice' in relation to Baudelaire. From Eliot's perspective, Symons treats them as aesthetic matters rather than moral or ethical questions that might form the basis of authentic religious belief. Secondly, Eliot criticises Symons's deviation as a translator into paraphrase, most notably his failure to render the word *soeur* as 'sister' when translating 'Invitation au voyage'.[24] Both charges stem from Eliot's basic complaint that Symons turns Baudelaire into 'a poet of the 'nineties, a contemporary of Dowson and Wilde'.[25] For Eliot, Symons's presentation of 'vice' reflects 'the childish attitude of the 'nineties' and his linguistic choices 'envelop[e] Baudelaire in the Swinburnian violet-coloured London fog of the 'nineties'.[26]

In many respects, Eliot's criticisms of Symons anticipate his broader rejection of nineteenth-century Aestheticism in the work of Walter Pater (referred to as a 'remoter spectre' in this review) and Matthew Arnold on the grounds that they substitute art for religion.[27] But his repeated insistence upon the obsolescence of 'nineties' values staunchly identifies 'the Symons style' as an anachronism for a readership in 1927. Still, if his Baudelaire sounds to Eliot like a poet of the 'nineties', that may be because Symons recycled material that had been translated much earlier. The target of Eliot's ire, *Baudelaire: Prose and Poetry* (1926) incorporates work previously published in *Poems in Prose from Charles Baudelaire* as part of Elkin Mathews's Vigo cabinet series. Symons's versions of Villiers de l'Isle-Adam are similar in this respect. Manuscripts at Princeton University and the British Library confirm Symons's statement in 1925 that the translations published in the 1920s had been written 'at long intervals, in various years'.[28] And in the case of 'The

Sinister Guest', it is clear that Symons's translation *sounds* like the 1890s because it incorporates material that he himself wrote during that period, including passages from his critical writings on Villiers.

This is a source of weakness for Eliot, who seems to confirm Carl Van Vechten's observation: 'To be 1890 in 1890 might be considered almost normal. To be 1890 in 1922 might be considered almost queer'.[29] But, as Kristin Mahoney has argued, sounding 'queer' in this way was — contrary to Eliot — a source of value for some writers and thinkers in the 1920s and 1930s. 'The rebellious spirit of critique' associated with Decadence and the *fin de siècle*, Mahoney claims, offered the twentieth century 'a method of subtly communicating distaste for the methods and values of the present'.[30] She traces this in the work of writers who survived from the nineteenth into the twentieth century:

> Vernon Lee's Paterian critique of jingoistic biosociology in the years following World War I and Max Beerbohm's dandyish radio broadcasts during World War II relied on a sense of connectedness to the late-Victorian past to theorise a way out of early-twentieth-century violence.[31]

Mahoney also explores the attraction of *fin-de-siècle* aesthetics for a younger generation, describing how allusions to the style and subject matter of Aubrey Beardsley offered Beresford Egan a way of mocking contemporary campaigns for sexual purity. As Mahoney shows, Egan shared with A. J. A. Symons (who was fascinated by the work of Frederick Rolfe, 'Baron Corvo') an interest in the general association of Decadence with sexual transgression. Mahoney classifies both types of artist within 'post-Victorian Decadence', a category which is also useful in relation to Arthur Symons — another survivor from the nineteenth century. It is notable here that 'The Sinister Guest' appeared alongside 'Satan the Waster', one of Vernon Lee's pacifist texts discussed by Mahoney, in the same issue of the *English Review* of August 1919.

Mahoney's suggestion that the 1920s saw a renewed interest in Decadent texts may help account for publishers' mixed responses to Symons's translations. Writing to James Dyke Campbell during January 1888, Symons joked that a translation of *Contes cruels* might not be 'indecent enough' to appeal to the publisher, Henry Vizetelly, who had acquired a reputation for publishing risqué texts by French authors, such as Émile Zola.[32] A year later, Symons sounded a more cautious note in public: 'Contemporary French literature just now is a subject which the Vigilance Committee should make one chary of recommending to English readers; and perhaps the impeccable "Demoiselles de Bienfilâtre" would not find favour in the eyes of Mr. Coote'.[33] The discrepancy corresponds to events: during May 1888 Vizetelly's translation of Zola's *La Terre* was cited during a debate on 'Corrupt Literature' in the House of Commons and in June the National Vigilance Association (William Alexander Coote became secretary of this organisation in 1885) brought a prosecution against Vizetelly for obscenity which he lost at trial during October.[34] Symons's initial failure to publish his translation of *Contes cruels* may reflect the inhibiting effects of the Vizetelly trial upon publishing experimental or supposedly transgressive French texts in translation during the 1890s.

The circumstances under which Symons found an outlet for his translation of Villiers's 'impeccable' story, 'Les Demoiselles de Bienfilâtre', confirm a shift in publishing conditions and the 'post-Victorian' fascination with Decadence identified by Mahoney. For Symons placed his translation in *Two Worlds*, an American quarterly run by Samuel Roth, a publisher best known for the scandal and international protest he prompted by serialising parts of James Joyce's *Ulysses* in another of his periodicals, *Two Worlds Monthly*.[35] Roth met Symons in person during a visit to London in the winter of 1920, recruiting him as a 'contributing editor' to *Two Worlds*. Consequently, Symons published six items in *Two Worlds* and one essay on Joyce in *Two Worlds Monthly* between September 1925 and September 1926. Unfortunately, information about his arrangements with Roth is limited to the American's own account, which is not always reliable. As well as his disregard for author's rights, Roth acquired a shady reputation for publishing and selling erotic and pornographic works. Describing their first meeting as 'restful', Roth announced that it laid the basis of a 'fruitful friendship which was to be extended by correspondence and an author-publisher relationship until Symons' death'.[36] But in the same memoir, Roth claimed he was posted to London by the *New York Herald*, whereas his biographer records that he fled America in the face of bankruptcy and obtained press credentials from the *Herald*, but held no salaried position from the paper.[37] Likewise, Roth's claim about their 'fruitful friendship' does not acknowledge Symons's recoil from the *Ulysses* piracy. 'Joyce has genius', Symons wrote to Sylvia Beach in 1927, 'and Roth is a fraud', adding his signature to a letter of protest about Roth's unauthorised publication of *Ulysses*.[38]

Although Roth appeared at a time when Symons was anxious to find an outlet for his work (Beckson records that his patron, the American lawyer, John Quinn was increasingly irritated by Symons's requests for support), the relationship may still have been exploitative.[39] Also listed as a contributing editor to *Two Worlds*, Ford Madox Ford remained uncertain about what was expected of him and warned a potential contributor about Roth's 'lugubrious' reputation and unreliability on financial matters.[40] According to Beckson, Roth valued Ford and Symons on the front covers as names 'calculated [...] to attract attention' alongside that of Ezra Pound.[41] As such, the tenor of Symons's contributions is highly suggestive. For, aside from translations of Villiers and poetry by Paul Verlaine, Symons's contributions mostly consisted of biographical or autobiographical memoirs relating to the *fin de siècle*. In each case, Symons emphasises the connection between Decadent art and 'vice' that Eliot found so shallow. His account of Toulouse-Lautrec suggests he 'had a devil in him' and details the French artist's interest in creating pictures and paintings of licentious figures from the Parisian demi-monde.[42] Symons's article on Verlaine begins by contrasting the poet's 'sensuality, brutal as it could sometimes be', with the 'perverse, complicated and ferocious' sensuality of his lover, Rimbaud.[43] He then explores biographical connections between Verlaine's poetry and 'dissolute prostitutes' (in the words of his editor, Adolphe van Bever).[44] In both articles, Symons makes a point of his personal connections with the subject of his 'notes', mixing details of Verlaine's highly fraught relations with Philomène Boudin and an account of his visit to Oxford and London in 1893, during which the French poet stayed briefly with Symons.

If Roth deployed Symons as a source of direct, salacious gossip about key figures from French Decadent culture, Symons allowed himself to be co-opted into this process too, publishing two fragments of autobiography under the title of 'Confessions'. Whilst the second of these offers a partial account of his mental breakdown in 1908, the first details his relationships with prostitutes and extra-marital affairs in London during the 1890s. He notes with pride that he acquired an 'evil reputation' comparable to that of Verlaine, boasting: 'My aesthetic instinct became perverted. I relished nothing that was not vicious, morbid, fantastic, abnormal'.[45]

Advertised as 'especially written for publication in *Two Worlds*', these confessions and their vocabulary ('perverted', 'morbid') show Symons creating a retrospective Decadent identity for himself, under Roth's encouragement.[46] But this was not always the case. As Vincent Sherry has remarked recently, Symons rejected Decadence at the close of the nineteenth century in favour of Symbolism.[47] This shift of aesthetic affiliation is clearly reflected in his critical writings on Villiers de l'Isle-Adam and especially the significance accorded to *Contes cruels*. During 1890 and 1891 he was emphatic that this collection was the French writer's highest achievement, describing it in the *Illustrated London News* as 'the most delightful thing in modern French fiction':

> I record a deliberate judgement in saying that for exquisite subtlety of spirit and form, for a delicate and etherealized perversity entirely modern and entirely personal, for sheer effect alike of charm, of terror, of grotesque and ironical humour, these tales must be assigned a place among the finest French work.[48]

Eight years later in the *Fortnightly Review*, however, Symons shifted attention onto Villiers's much revised and uncompleted play, *Axël*, which he identifies as 'the Symbolist drama'.[49] Instead of 'perversity', Symons stresses Villiers's Catholic mysticism, construing his 'belief' through a series of quotations from *Axël* and dividing Villiers's *oeuvre* between works which present 'the ideal world, or the ideal in the world', such as *Axël*, and those works offering 'satire, the mockery of reality'.[50] Consigned to the latter category, *Contes cruels* receives much less attention. In closing, Symons announces that Villiers 'had been preparing the spiritual atmosphere of the new generation. [...] he had been creating a new form of art, the art of the Symbolist drama and of Symbolism in fiction'.[51] The persona Symons offered twenty-five years later in his 'Confessions', then, coincides with his return, through translation, to the stories from the *Contes cruels*, indicating a new turn, after the First World War, away from the Symbolist aesthetics of his article for the *Fortnightly Review* and back to Decadence.

Symons's autobiographical writings in *Two Worlds* belong amongst what Kirsten MacLeod describes as 'a host of memoirs in the 1910s and 1920s [that] glorified the Decadents as wrongfully neglected revolutionaries in arts and letters'.[52] And yet the frank heterosexuality that characterises Symons's presentation of himself as a sexual adventurer, despite proclaiming his tastes 'abnormal', may temper any reading of his work as 'queer' or transgressive. Yeats supposedly observed that 'Symons has always had a longing to commit a great sin, but he has never been able to get beyond ballet girls'.[53] There is a risk that, unlike Mahoney's other 'post-Victorian' Decadent writers, Symons merely perpetuates a sexual status quo, instead of offering critique.

His choice of 'Les Demoiselles de Bienfilâtre' for translation may help to recuperate Symons's writings (if not his behaviour) here, for its transgressive power lies in its style rather than its content. Although it features two prostitutes, Henriette and Olympe Bienfilâtre, the story is deliberately oblique about what they do. Its satire depends upon applying the language of conventional morality to their careers as sex workers. The two girls allude, for example, to their freedom from sexual disease as 'a state of grace'.[54] When Olympe falls in love with a young student called Maxime, she is ostracised for contravening professional ethics by her family (who rely on her income from prostitution) and the broader society of the café in which they meet their regular clients. Henriette urges Olympe to 'Respect [...] appearances' and their father is revolted by Maxime's 'cynicism' when he asks for permission to marry Olympe.[55] As these examples indicate, Symons's translation of this work is more literal than 'The Sinister Guest', respecting Villiers's lexical ironies as a means of indicting sexual and social hypocrisy. His translation aims at conveying a satirical linguistic relativity about sexual values in the original that Linda Dowling argues is characteristic of Decadence more generally.[56]

If his return after the war to *Contes cruels* as a source of inspiration represents Symons's 'post-Victorian' return to Decadent values, 'The Sinister Guest' confirms that this was a deliberate, reflexive process. Just as Villiers incorporates reflection upon his predilections as a writer into 'Le Convive des dernières fêtes', so Symons's narrator also contemplates his professional habits and relationship to his own characters:

> As for my creations, I never spare them; I have the cruelty of my race; I study their iniquities, their monstrous deeds, their slips from virtue, their descent into vice. They are abnormal. I love them and I hate them with a multiplicity of meaning — which disconcerts many of my readers and makes them think some of my prose is obscure. I cannot pardon stupidity; for I see that stupidity is more criminal than vice, if only because vice is curable, stupidity incurable. (p. 113)

Once again Symons is quoting from his own previous writings. The irony is that this account of Villiers's Decadent interest in 'vice' and the 'abnormal' transposes remarks from the Symbolist account of Villiers de l'Isle-Adam in Symons's article for the *Fortnightly Review*, shifting them from the third to the first person.[57]

The incorporation of such critical material into 'The Sinister Guest' confirms an ambition for the story which exceeds literal translation. It becomes an embodied form of critical response: one that provides a generic account of the French writer as an author of cruel and Decadent tales. But a fundamental awkwardness within this story makes it difficult to affirm this achievement without qualification.

The juxtaposition of his own writings with those of Villiers might suggest an intimate relationship of influence, as Symons's voice merges with that of his source material. But as they proliferate, such juxtapositions become a little queasy, as if Symons were trying to out-do his source material or felt that he had absorbed the French writer into his own personality. The instability of these identifications within the narrative of 'The Sinister Guest' seems to confirm the verdict of Symons's biographer on the frequency with which he re-purposed previously published critical material. For Beckson, a tendency to re-hash his own work provides evidence of Symons's 'impaired judgement' and 'intellectual impairment [...] a basic thought disorder that plagued him for the remainder of his life'.[58]

Writing off Symons's authorial persona in this story as 'impaired,' however, overlooks the fact that 'The Sinister Guest' deliberately sets out to present authorship as something pathological and prone to mental instability. This is Symons's correlative to the presentation of the imaginative complicity between art and death in 'Le Convive des dernières fêtes'. To make this point, Flavian Des Esseintes cites the example of Gérard de Nerval: 'every artist lives a double life in which he is for the most part conscious of the illusions of the imagination' (p. 114). Nerval's mental breakdown, it is claimed, 'lit up the hidden links of distant and divergent things' (p. 114). In Symons's version, the guest's preoccupation with executions is cognate with a Romantic myth about the madness which lies at the heart of artistic creativity and inspiration.

The resonance of this comparison is fraught with difficulty: once again, Symons turns out to be quoting himself without acknowledgement, drawing on the article from the *Fortnightly Review* that he re-published in *The Symbolist Movement*.[59] And his personal circumstances introduce further complexity: subsequent reference to Nerval in a memoir of his own mental collapse suggests that Symons discerned parallels between the French writer and his own situation.[60] Symons's repeated self-borrowings leave it unclear whether this story is a deliberate, reflective mediation upon his own experiences or whether it represents an obsessive re-cycling of his previous writings under the exercise of some compulsion. Instead of a confident re-imagining of Villiers de l'Isle-Adam, 'The Sinister Guest' may embody Symons's anxieties about his own fate after his breakdown and the heyday of the 1890s.

Such questions of intention or control are not merely biographical: they affect our understanding of his failure to acknowledge his sources when quoting from himself and others. Citing Peter Shaw's definition of plagiarism as 'using the work of another *with an intent to deceive*', Christopher Ricks identifies circumstances when a failure to acknowledge a quotation may yet be excusable.[61] T. S. Eliot, for example, explained that even though his poem 'Cousin Nancy' quoted from a poem by George Meredith 'without quotation marks [...] the whole point was that the reader should recognise where it came from'.[62] Some texts are so well-known that a failure to recognise them might be considered a fault in the reader.

Symons plays with similar expectations in 'The Sinister Guest':

> This has been written by a man of immense genius: 'Every man may make for himself, and must allow that he cannot pretend to impose upon any other, his own image of the most wicked man ever created by the will of man or God.' Certainly our man has made for himself his own monstrous image in the form of what to him is wickedness. (p. 118)

Whilst the quotation here from A. C. Swinburne's essay on *Othello* is not fully credited, the use of inverted commas and reference to 'a man of immense genius' suffice to acknowledge openly the existence of a debt.[63] This is not, however, true of the observation at the start of the same paragraph:

> Can one even question what is the hereditary horror of doom once imminent over the house of Atreus to this instant imminence of no supernatural but a more woefully natural fate? He is not actually cursed and cast out of existence, but figuratively he is. He does not go beyond the presumable limits of human evil. (p. 117)

There are no quotation marks around the description of 'the house of Atreus' which derives from another essay by Swinburne, on *King Lear*.[64] The acknowledgement of Swinburne's 'genius' that follows may mitigate this otherwise surreptitious borrowing. In context, Symons might expect his readers to recognise retrospectively that Swinburne's 'immense genius' is at play throughout whole the passage. But this does seem perilously close to plagiarism and 'the intent to deceive'.

There is a risk here that an 'imagined community' of grateful indebtedness to other writers becomes tainted by accusations of theft. A more startling example occurs towards the end of the story, when Flavian prefaces his account of the sinister guest's mental disorder by observing:

> Have any of you during the crisis of a terrible illness felt, as you watched the sunlight creep over the wall opposite, first, that the sensation of the slow black flies that crawl across the path of warmth seem to be crawling over your raw nerves? Have you ever expected the surface of the wall to contract like a skin and switch them off, and feel your own skin doing that out of mere sympathy? (pp. 115–16)

This clearly derives from F. Tennyson Jesse's *The Secret Bread* (1917):

> He lay and watched the spring the sunlight creep over the whitewashed wall opposite, and every slow black fly that crawled across the patch of warmth might have been crawling over his raw nerves. He almost expected the surface of the wall to contract like a skin and twitch them off, as he felt own skin doing out of sympathy.[65]

Symons may have encountered Jesse through mutual links with the *English Review* which had launched her literary career in 1912 by publishing her short story 'The Mask', when she was twenty-four.[66] Perhaps they shared an interest in Cornwall, the setting of *The Secret Bread,* where Jesse had studied in the Newlyn painters' community.[67] Or perhaps Symons heard an echo of Villiers de l'Isle-Adam's life in the opening of Jesse's novel, where a character marries the working-class mother of his children on his deathbed to legitimate an heir, since the French writer had married Marie Dantine under the same circumstances, for similar reasons. But such connections do not explain why Symons chose to borrow from Jesse's novel without acknowledgement.

This passage is not found in the original version of 'The Sinister Guest' from 1915, held at the Harry Ransom Center, Austin, Texas: Symons added it deliberately when revising the story at the beginning of 1919. Jesse's work was undoubtedly better known in 1919 than it is now, but it is hard to believe that her celebrity was such that Symons expected readers of the *English Review* to recognise the source of this passage. Such a clear example of plagiarism throws into doubt Symons's allusive practice throughout the story, including the failure to acknowledge his fundamental debt to Villiers de l'Isle-Adam.

Once Symons's allusive practices and textual borrowings are uncovered, an awkward quality about 'The Sinister Guest' emerges that evokes Villiers's interest in the pitfalls of polite society and the haunted nature of authorship without ever quite being harmonious. This is epitomised by the general slippage between translation and free adaption within the story, which clouds our understanding of its authorship. Yet this text has a power that is somehow more than the sum of its parts. From one perspective, Symons's versions of Villiers de l'Isle-Adam are timely: they cater to a retrospective taste for the 1890s after the First World War. From another angle, they are ahead of their time: if we could be confident of Symons's intentions, we might acclaim the collage of quotation in 'The Sinister Guest' as Modernist in technique. At the same time, they are also hopelessly out of date: sad relics of a neglected Decadent writer filtered through 'the Symons style'. As such, the uneven tones and unacknowledged debts of 'The Sinister Guest' epitomise the more general awkwardness that characterises the 'strange and conflicted' works ascribed by Mahoney to 'post-Victorian Decadence'.[68]

Notes to Chapter 5

1. I am grateful to Jon Watson and Sasha Dovzhy for research assistance, and to the Carnegie Trust for a travel grant which allowed me to consult primary materials at the Firestone Library in Princeton.
2. Villiers de l'Isle-Adam, 'Le Convive des dernières fêtes', in *Oeuvres complètes*, ed. by Alan Raitt and Pierre-Georges Castex, 2 vols (Paris: Gallimard/Pléiade, 1986), 1, 607–27 (p. 607). All translations are the author's own, unless otherwise stated.
3. [Arthur Symons], 'Villiers de l'Isle-Adam', *The Athenaeum*, 3229 (14 September 1889), 354.
4. Arthur Symons to Ernest Rhys, 8 March 1890, Princeton University, Arthur Symons Papers, C0182, Box 24, Folder 16.
5. The Harry Ransom Center in Austin, Texas, holds an unpublished manuscript and typed copy of this. The King's School, Canterbury, holds a manuscript copy of Symons's second version. I am grateful to the librarian at King's School, Peter Henderson, for sharing information about this with me. A typescript of this second version is also held at Princeton University, Arthur Symons Papers.
6. Arthur Symons, 'The Sinister Guest', *English Review*, 129 (August 1919), 105–19 (p. 105). Further references to this work are given in the text. For comparison, the same passage in the draft at Austin, Texas, (with running changes corrected silently) reads: 'In the winter of 1889 I was seated beside Toulouse-Lautrec, on a certain Carnival night, in a box at the Opera. From there we looked down on the tumultuous mosaic of the masked dancers as they whirled in close circles to the *Valse des Roses*, Olivier Metra's; that passionate, sensual, erotic dance-music which he only, in our age, created. We were admiring this magical evocation of turning figures, ghosts of no actual reality, when the door of the box opened, and in rush three women, who, as they took off their masks cried: *Bonjour!*' (MS 414 B51 8.6, fol. 1ʳ). Although this is closer to the French original, it is clear that Symons's translation of the story was always free, involving considerable adaptation and addition.
7. Mahoney, *Literature and the Politics of Post-Victorian Decadence*.

8. Arthur Symons, 'Preface', in Charles Baudelaire, *Poems in Prose from Charles Baudelaire*, trans. by Arthur Symons (London: Elkin Mathews, 1905), p. 5.
9. Arthur Symons, 'Should Translators Improve Their Authors?', *Bookman's Journal and Print Collector*, 5:4 (January 1922), 109–12 (p. 109).
10. Ibid., p. 109.
11. Arthur Symons, 'Preface', in *Claire Lenoir by Villiers de l'Isle-Adam*, trans. by Arthur Symons (New York: Albert & Charles Boni, 1925), pp. vii–x (p. ix). This cites D. G. Rossetti on the distinction between 'literality of rendering' and 'fidelity', from *The Early Italian Poets* (London: Smith, Elder & Co, 1861), pp. viii–ix.
12. Symons, 'Preface', in Villiers de l'Isle-Adam, *Claire Lenoir*, p. ix.
13. Potolsky, *The Decadent Republic of Letters*, p. 1.
14. Ibid., p. 5.
15. Arthur Symons, 'Preface', in Charles Baudelaire, *Baudelaire: Prose and Poetry*, trans. by Arthur Symons (New York: Albert & Charles Boni, 1926), pp. v–ix (p. v).
16. Arthur Symons, 'Extracts from the Journal of Henry Luxulyan', in *Spiritual Adventures* (1905), pp. 241–314 (pp. 276–78).
17. Arthur Symons, *Knave of Hearts, 1894–1908* (London: William Heinemann, 1913), p. 51.
18. Arthur Symons, *London: A Book of Aspects* (London & Minneapolis, MN: Privately Printed, 1909), p. 28.
19. Arthur Symons, 'An Apology for Puppets', *Saturday Review*, 84 (17 July 1897), 55–56 (p. 55).
20. Beckson, *Arthur Symons*, pp. 290–95.
21. *Arthur Symons: A Bibliography*, ed. by Beckson and others, pp. 21–23, 161.
22. T. S. Eliot, 'Baudelaire in Our Time', in *The Complete Prose of T. S. Eliot*, ed. by Schuchard and others, III (2015), 71–82 (p. 71).
23. Regarding Eliot's public expression of indebtedness to Symons for introducing him to the work of Jules Laforgue and others, mixed with doubts about the lasting value of Symons's critical judgements, see Matthew Creasy, 'Introduction', in Symons, *The Symbolist Movement in Literature*, pp. ix–xxix (pp. ix–xiii).
24. Eliot, 'Baudelaire in Our Time', pp. 74–75.
25. Ibid., p. 71.
26. Ibid., pp. 73–74.
27. Ibid., p. 72. For Eliot's criticisms of Pater, see 'An Experiment in Criticism' (1929), in *The Complete Prose of T. S. Eliot*, ed. by Schuchard and others, III (2015), 753–59; and 'Arnold and Pater' (1930) in *The Complete Prose of T. S. Eliot*, ed. by Schuchard and others, IV (2015), 176–89.
28. Symons, 'Preface', in Villiers de l'Isle-Adam, *Claire Lenoir*, p. vii.
29. Quoted in Mahoney, *Literature and the Politics of Post-Victorian Decadence*, p. 11.
30. Mahoney, *Literature and the Politics of Post-Victorian Decadence*, p. 3.
31. Ibid., p. 5.
32. Arthur Symons to James Dyke Campbell, 2 January 1888, in *Arthur Symons: Selected Letters*, ed. by Beckson and Munro, p. 35.
33. Symons, 'Villiers de l'Isle-Adam', *The Athenaeum*, p. 354.
34. See Anthony Cummins, 'Émile Zola's Cheap English Dress: The Vizetelly Translations, Late-Victorian Print Culture and the Crisis of Literary Value', *Review of English Studies*, 60:243 (2008), 108–32.
35. Richard Ellmann, *James Joyce*, 2nd edn (Oxford: Oxford University Press, 1984), pp. 585–87.
36. Samuel Roth, 'Adrift in London: An Extract from *Count Me Among the Missing*', *Journal of Modern Literature*, 3:4 (April 1974), 922–27 (p. 926).
37. Jay A. Gertzman, *Samuel Roth, Infamous Modernist* (Gainesville: University Press of Florida, 2013), pp. 56–61.
38. Robert Spoo, *Without Copyrights: Piracy, Publishing and the Public Domain* (Oxford: Oxford University Press, 2013), p. 233.
39. Beckson, *Arthur Symons*, pp. 289–92, 300–01.
40. Max Saunders, *Ford Madox Ford: A Dual Life. Volume II — The After-War World* (Oxford: Oxford

University Press, 1996), p. 118; see also Ford Madox Ford to Edgar Jepson, 1 July 1922, in *Letters of Ford Madox Ford*, ed. by Richard Ludwig (Princeton, NJ: Princeton University Press, 1965), pp. 140–41.
41. Beckson, *Arthur Symons*, p. 311.
42. Arthur Symons, 'Notes on Toulouse Lautrec and his Lithographs', *Two Worlds*, 1.2 (December 1925), 162–69.
43. Arthur Symons, 'Notes on Verlaine's Adventures and Sensations', *Two Worlds*, 1.3 (March 1926), 267–79 (p. 270).
44. Ibid., p. 272.
45. Arthur Symons, 'Bohemian Years in London', in *The Memoirs of Arthur Symons*, ed. by Beckson, pp. 70–74 (p. 72).
46. Preliminary material, *Two Worlds Monthly*, 1.3 (September 1926), iii.
47. Sherry, *Modernism and the Reinvention of Decadence*, pp. 2–20, 72–87.
48. Arthur Symons, 'Villiers de l'Isle-Adam', *Illustrated London News*, XCVIII (2701) (24 January 1891), 118.
49. Arthur Symons, 'Villiers de l'Isle-Adam', *Fortnightly Review*, 66 (August 1899), 197–204 (p. 199). This essay was reproduced in *The Symbolist Movement in Literature*, first published in 1899.
50. Symons, 'Villiers de l'Isle-Adam', *Fortnightly Review*, pp. 198–99.
51. Ibid., p. 204.
52. See Kirsten MacLeod, *Fictions of British Decadence: High Art, Popular Writing and the Fin de Siècle* (Basingstoke: Palgrave Macmillan, 2008), p. 7.
53. Stanislaus Joyce, *My Brother's Keeper*, ed. by Richard Ellmann (London: Faber & Faber, 1958), p. 198. For a critical account of Symons's 'aggressive' heterosexuality, see Laurel Brake, 'The Savoy: 1896. Gender in Crisis?', in *Subjugated Knowledges: Journalism, Gender and Literature in the Nineteenth Century* (New York: New York University Press, 1994), pp. 148–65.
54. Arthur Symons, 'Les Demoiselles de Bienfilâtre', *Two Worlds*, 1.1 (September 1925), 100–07 (p. 102).
55. Ibid., p. 104.
56. Linda Dowling, *Language and Decadence in the Victorian Fin de Siècle* (Princeton, NJ: Princeton University Press, 1986), pp. 107–74.
57. Symons, 'Villiers de l'Isle-Adam', *Fortnightly Review*, pp. 202–03.
58. Beckson, *Arthur Symons*, pp. 287, 292, 295.
59. Arthur Symons, 'Gérard de Nerval', *Fortnightly Review*, 63 (January 1898), 81–91 (p. 86).
60. Arthur Symons, 'Mental Collapse in Italy', in *The Memoirs of Arthur Symons*, ed. by Beckson, pp. 234–53 (p. 236).
61. Quoted by Christopher Ricks, 'Plagiarism', in *Allusion to the Poets* (Oxford: Oxford University Press, 2002), pp. 219–40 (p. 220).
62. Ibid., p. 232.
63. A. C. Swinburne, 'Othello', *Harper's Monthly Magazine*, 109 (October 1904), 659–67 (p. 659).
64. A. C. Swinburne, 'King Lear', *Harper's Monthly Magazine*, 106 (December 1902), 3–8 (p. 4). This essay and 'Othello' were reprinted in *Three Plays of Shakespeare* (New York: Harper and Brothers, 1909).
65. F. Tennyson Jesse, *Secret Bread* (London: William Heinemann, 1917), p. 181.
66. Jesse went on to provide the *English Review* with first-hand accounts of the frontline in France and Belgium during the First World War. See Martha S. Vogeler, *Austin Harrison and the English Review* (Columbia: University of Missouri Press, 2008), pp. 207–08.
67. Joanna Colenbrander, *A Portrait of Fryn: A Biography of F. Tennyson Jesse* (London: André Deutsch, 1984), pp. 41–42.
68. Mahoney, *Literature and the Politics of Post-Victorian Decadence*, p. 166.

CHAPTER 6

Arthur Symons, a Mediator of Belgian Symbolist Writers[1]

Clément Dessy

For Patrick McGuinness

When studying Arthur Symons's special relationship with Belgian art and literature, the obvious starting point is his chapter 'Maeterlinck as a Mystic', which covered the new literary trends from France at the close of *The Symbolist Movement in Literature* (1899). Yet, however important this single item might be in the history of Maurice Maeterlinck's English reception, if we limited our assessment to it we would grossly underestimate the full range of the relationship between Symons and Belgian Symbolist writers. Symons played a central role as cultural mediator between England and Belgium. As a critic, he may have been preceded by William Archer in the discovery of Maeterlinck or by his friend Osman Edwards in that of Émile Verhaeren, but he certainly made use of the prestige he acquired as a poet to increase the credit of Belgian writers within London literary circles. The following pages demonstrate that Belgium occupied a distinctive place in Symons's imagination, as he was well informed on specific issues relating to Belgian authors within the French-speaking literary sphere and on the status of these peripheral authors in their relationship to the Parisian centre. This chapter considers Symons's activities both as critic and translator and shows how these commitments were fully absorbed into his promotional activities. It traces the evolution of the relationship between Symons and the French-speaking writers of Belgium — Maurice Maeterlinck, Charles Van Lerberghe, and Émile Verhaeren — from the 1890s until 1907.

The Brussels Fair and the Bruised Bodies

The first obvious connection with Belgium that emerges from Symons's works is his interest in the artist and engraver Félicien Rops (1833–98), who inspired one of the poems included in the collection *Days and Nights* (1889). 'The Temptation of Saint Anthony (After a Design by Félicien Rops)' is an ekphrastic poem, following on from other adaptations 'from the French' from Leconte de Lisle, Théophile Gautier, and Villiers de l'Isle-Adam. The poem refers to one of the most famous

FIG. 6.1. Félicien Rops, *La Tentation de Saint Antoine*, 1878, Royal Library of Belgium, Brussels.

works by the Belgian engraver and presents the transfiguration of Christ as a lascivious woman or femme fatale, in Saint Anthony's vision:

> The Cross, the Cross is tainted! O most Just,
> Be merciful, and save me from this snare.
> The Tempter lures me as I bend in prayer
> Before the sacred symbol of our Trust.
> Yea, the most Holy of Holies feeds my lust,
> The body of thy Christ; for, unaware,
> Even as I kneel and pray, lo, She is there,
> The temptress, she the wanton; and she hath thrust
> The bruised body off, and all her own,
> Shameless, she stretches on the cross, arms wide,
> Limbs pendent, in libidinous mockery.
> She draws mine eyes to hers — ah, sin unknown!
> She smiles, she triumphs; but the Crucified
> Falls off into the darkness with a cry.[2]

Rops gained recognition in Belgium and France thanks to his illustrations for Charles Baudelaire's collection of poems, *Les Épaves* (1866). Since then, and especially after moving to Paris in 1875, his reputation had been growing in Parisian literary milieus; Joris-Karl Huysmans, for instance, praised his work in his book of art criticism *Certains* in 1889, that is to say at the same time as Symons's poem was published. Rops's reputation of perversity and immorality in works such as the *Tentation de Saint-Antoine* (1878), *Pornocratès* (1878), and the *Sataniques* (1882) appealed to the young Symons. The poet probably knew of Rops in Paris. Even though their very first meeting might not have taken place in Belgium, they did meet at least once in Brussels in 1896, as Symons wrote to John Quinn, an Irish American lawyer and art patron in 1915:

> I have an etching of Félicien Rops that he gave me in Brussels in 1896 — I was with Dowson. Huysmans praises it in his *Certains*. It is eight and a half inches broad — ten and a half high. It is quite indecent. A prostitute of the Parisian kind stands half-naked — with the usual black stockings gartered at the knees — showing her sex; in an amazing attitude of self-admiration before her mirror. Behind the glass is an infamous monkey holding in its hand its Priapus. The whole thing is prodigiously fine.[3]

The cited etching, entitled *Impudence*, closely combines Symons's favourite poetic interests in prostitution, eroticism, and scandalous atmospheres — interests that he shared with Rops.

In the same letter, Symons also mentions the presence of his friend, the poet Ernest Dowson (1867–1900), in Brussels. In a memoir enclosed with a posthumous edition of Dowson's poems, Symons jots down a few words about their visit to the Belgian capital:

> At Brussels, where I was with him at the time of the Kermesse, [Dowson] flung himself into all that riotous Flemish life, with a zest for what was most sordidly riotous in it. It was his own way of escape from life.[4]

In a later article on Bruges, he relates how he crossed from Newhaven to Antwerp

Fig. 6.2. Félicien Rops, *Impudence*, c. 1878, Royal Mariemont Museum, Morlanwelz.

together with the publisher Leonard Smithers and Dowson, before going to Bruges and then to Brussels, where he describes the fair as 'the Kermesse of Rubens'.[5] This remark would be merely anecdotic if it did not echo a short story published (anonymously) by Symons: 'Bertha at the Fair' (1896).[6] This 'exquisite and personal sketch' or 'study', as Dowson himself referred to it,[7] depicts the special atmosphere of the fair in Brussels:

> This was in Brussels. It was in the time of the Kermesse, when, as you know, the good Flemish people are somewhat more boisterously jolly than usual; when the band plays in the middle of the market-place, and the people walk round and round the band-stand, looking up at the Archangel Michael on the spire of the Hôtel de Ville, to see him turn first pink and then green, as the Bengal lights smoke about his feet; when there are processions in the streets, music and torches, and everyone sets out for the Fair. (p. 87)

Immersed in this popular scene, the narrator recognises 'something quite Flemish in the solid gaiety of its shows and crowds, as solid as the "*bons chevaux de bois*," Verlaine's "*bons chevaux de bois*," that go prancing up and down in their rattling circles' (p. 87). The narrator recounts his strange encounter with Bertha, a Flemish working-class girl: 'she fascinated us all: the mild Flemish painter, with his golden beard; our cynical publisher, with his diabolical monocle [Smithers]; my fantastical friend, the poet [Dowson]; and [...] myself' (p. 87). Bertha's bruised female body is disturbingly eroticised, a bewitching femme fatale:

> She was scarred on the cheek: a wicked Baron, she told us, had done that, with vitriol; one of her breasts was singularly mutilated; she had been shot in the back by an Englishman, when she was keeping a shooting-gallery at Antwerp. And she had the air of a dangerous martyr, who might bewitch one, with some of those sorceries that had turned, somehow, to her own hurt. (p. 87)

Although not good-looking, the Flemish girl seduces and confuses the narrator. But there is a more striking element about her: illiterate, she ignores what a poet is and the nearest thing she can relate to that concept is a '*café-chantant* singer' (p. 88). This naïveté causes the narrator to be surprisingly enthusiastic: 'Never did any woman so charm me by so celestial an ignorance. The moments I spent with Bertha at the Fair repaid me for I know not how many weary hours in drawing-rooms' (p. 88). By comparison with London, where the 'poet' was recognised as such wherever he went, with the Flemish girl the narrator finds himself delivered from his own identity for the duration of his stay in Brussels. He regains access to another self, a more genuine one, freed from its literary and social status. In Brussels, he is not a poet any more but a simple human being enjoying life.

Symons's representations of Belgium are partly based on Rops and the Kermesse. Combining Naturalist and Symbolist elements more closely than their French neighbours, Belgian authors indeed proved capable of appealing to Symons, as he remained open to many different French cultural currents from the Goncourts and Zola to Verlaine and Mallarmé.[8]

The Belgian Literary Renaissance

In 1902, Symons was invited by Edmund Gosse, literary editor of the tenth edition of the *Encyclopaedia Britannica*, to contribute to the new volumes. Among articles mainly dedicated to French writers (Goncourt, Mallarmé, Verlaine, and Villiers de l'Isle-Adam, as well as Thomas Hardy), he was asked to offer an overview of the whole contemporary literary movement in Belgium. It is worth remembering that, until the First World War, even if a Flemish literature did exist in Belgium, the Belgian literary space was not divided into two sets of equal status, as it is today. Since its independence in 1830, Belgium had been using French as the official and dominant language, Flemish and Walloon being perceived as dialects. When referring to this period, the whole Belgian literary space is thus often described as a sub-section of the larger French field,[9] subjected to the magnetic attraction of Paris.[10] Up until today, every French-speaking Belgian writer has always had to tread a careful path between two allegiances: fidelity to the small institutions and readership of his country and ambition to succeed in the French literary field by targeting its centre — Paris. Symons's article on Belgian literature for the encyclopaedia clearly shows his accurate knowledge:

> Beginning unconsciously, and under definitely French influences, Baudelaire, Zola, for example, a group of Belgian writers began to detach themselves from the various schools of France; their first public proclamation of a new literature may be dated from the banquet given in 1883 to Camille Lemonnier. Lemonnier had already found out a way for himself, on definitely Flemish soil; Maeterlinck began to concern himself with the soul; Eekhoud with the strange passions of the body; Verhaeren with whatever was most coloured and violent in body and soul and the external world; Rodenbach with the aged quietude of the little dead cities of his country. It was as if a sluggish body had become possessed of an unexpectedly powerful life; as if restless nerves had come to awaken a stolid nature. It was thus a new quality, of imagination which seemed to reveal itself, as the soul became conscious of the mystery of the universe, and the body shivered at new fears, apprehensions, the haunting of a forgotten spiritual sense. It was the soul coming into a literature of mind, and at once the literature of Belgium was distinguished from the literature of France.[11]

Using multiple impressionist metaphors, Symons describes here the search for autonomy conducted by Belgian writers. From the 1880s, a new generation of writers, the Symbolist generation, succeeded in gaining greater independence from France. As Symons explains, they started selecting their literary models from within their national canon (Charles De Coster, Camille Lemonnier, etc.) and created their own institutions of recognition and consecration ranging from literary journals (*La Jeune Belgique*, *L'Art moderne*, etc.) to publishers (Edmond Deman, Paul Lacomblez, etc.).

Because of the shared French language, things could be even more difficult for Belgian writers in Paris, where they were more likely to be perceived as provincial.[12] There, they did not benefit from the potential aura conferred on a writer by a major foreign language. In this respect a Belgian writer in *fin-de-siècle* Paris would have been quite unlike Oscar Wilde, for instance, whose origins made him attractive to a French audience. Still, Belgian writers constructed their own distinctive literary identity, which was largely perceived through a mythic lens in France: it was a unique Nordic identity mixing Germanic and Latin components. The idea of a 'Belgian soul', theorised by Edmond Picard, aimed to demonstrate the central position of Belgium in Western Europe, located at an intermediate point between German-ness and Latin-ness.[13] This distinctive identity was also perceptively described by Symons:

> Belgian literature, as distinguished from French, has come about through a fusion of two elements, the Flemish and the Walloon, which make up what we call the Belgian race; and it is only somewhat recently that any attempt has been made in literature to fuse these two elements. The Walloon, which is related to the French, brings a nervous sensibility, a delicate mental energy, while the Flemish, which is related to the Dutch, brings a slow, profound faculty of meditation, an almost fervour, deeply rooted in the earth.[14]

Pascale Casanova has noted that, at this time, Brussels tried to emerge as a new artistic and literary centre, positioning itself as a rival to Paris.[15] In order to distinguish themselves, Belgian Symbolists particularly targeted London and the British Isles in their efforts to internationalise themselves. Around 1900, there existed a real anglomania in Belgium, particularly in Brussels, which stretched beyond Symbolist circles. The wish to appear ahead of their French neighbours propelled the Belgians to import new trends from Britain to the Continent: from Pre-Raphaelite painting to the Arts and Crafts movement.[16]

Maurice Maeterlinck, from Decadent Fear to Symbolist Mysticism

Symons can be counted among the most fervent supporters of Maeterlinck in Britain. One of the most intense moments of this commitment occurred in the letter of protest, written by Symons himself and signed by many other prominent authors, including George Meredith, Algernon Charles Swinburne, Thomas Hardy, and W. B. Yeats, which was published in *The Times* on 20 June 1902, after performances of *Monna Vanna* were censored for immorality (on the grounds that Monna Vanna was supposed to be 'nude under her mantle' according to the stage directions).[17] Laurence Alma-Tadema, Maeterlinck's translator and daughter of the well-known painter, helped Symons gather signatories for the letter. In the following days and weeks, several objections to the ban appeared in various periodicals and among them were two other texts by Symons published in *The Academy*: 'The Question of Censorship' and '"Monna Vanna"'.[18] These were reprinted in *Plays, Acting, and Music* (1903) — which Symons dedicated 'To Maurice Maeterlinck in friendship and admiration' —, along with several notes on *Pelléas et Mélisande* and 'An Apology for Puppets', discussed more fully by John Stokes in this volume (Chapter 3).[19] The censorship and the charge of immorality against the Belgian dramatist represented a clear opportunity for Symons, often the victim of similar accusations himself, to raise his voice against Victorian society and reaffirm himself publicly as a provocative writer.

However, a decade earlier, it was not Symons, but the Irishman William Archer (1856–1924) who published the first significant English essay on Maeterlinck in the *Fortnightly Review*, under the title 'A Pessimist Playwright'.[20] The critic acknowledged the discovery of the Belgian dramatist by the French writer Octave Mirbeau in a famous article in *Le Figaro*, in which Mirbeau compared *La Princesse Maleine* (1889) to 'the finest parts of Shakespeare', judging it 'more tragic than *Macbeth*; more extraordinary in its thought than *Hamlet*' ('ce qu'il y a de plus beau dans Shakespeare [...] plus tragique que "Macbeth," plus extraordinaire de pensée que "Hamlet"').[21] Although Archer also admired Maeterlinck's work, he did not dare to reiterate Mirbeau's complimentary comparison. Instead, he opted to use the image of a 'Webster who has read Alfred de Musset',[22] which was more nuanced and less provocative, adding all the same: 'In reading the last two acts, we feel that M. Mirbeau was not so utterly astray in citing the name of Shakespeare, if only he had used it more discreetly'.[23]

A few months later, in April 1892, Symons, recently appointed literary critic at *The Athenæum*, wrote a very detailed review of the first complete translations of *The Princess Maleine* and *The Intruder* (originally published in 1890). More accurate in his information, he reminded readers that the Belgian Paul Fredericq had already cited Maeterlinck's name in the pages of *The Athenæum* in July. Symons judged that Archer's article 'was interesting by reason of its novelty, it was valuable for its quotations, but it was somewhat tentative as a criticism'.[24] He compensated by providing details of the French and English performances of *The Intruder* as well as of other works by Maeterlinck, ranging from his early poetry in *Les Serres chaudes* (1889) — 'apparently modelled upon Walt Whitman' with 'memories of Baudelaire, echoes of Verlaine, echoes of Poe' — to his more recent translations 'from the Flemish of the mystical work of Ruysbroeck l'Admirable, "L'Ornement des Noces Spirituelles"'.[25] According to Symons, Maeterlinck showed a continuity of forms ('calculated' and 'monotonous repetitions', 'simplicity', and 'childishness') that went from the poems to the dramas; he also highlighted the visual features in the plays, referring to shadow theatre. For Symons, *La Princesse Maleine*, a drama for marionettes, indeed contained no characters as such: Maeterlinck's characters are 'no realizable persons', they are 'a masque of shadows, a dance of silhouettes behind the white sheet of the "Chat Noir"'.[26] This analysis reveals how well informed Symons was on the new forms of shadow theatre created at the Chat Noir, where he might also have become aware of new staging techniques, such as the use of tulle and lights to highlight the silhouettes of the actors, which would be used in the 1893 performance of *Pelléas et Mélisande* by Aurélien Lugné-Poe[27].

In his review Symons also stressed a 'particular skill' of Maeterlinck's, that is, his ability to create an atmosphere of fear and to communicate 'the *nouveau frisson*'.[28] This idea is also at the core of the paragraphs he dedicated to the Belgian dramatist in his famous article 'The Decadent Movement in Literature' in 1893. Here Symons argues that 'to find a new personality, a new way of seeing things, [...] we must turn from Paris to Brussels — to the so-called Belgian Shakespeare, Maurice Maeterlinck'.[29] Like Archer, he makes a gentle revision of Mirbeau's outrageous comparison: 'In truth, M. Maeterlinck is not a Shakespeare, and the Elizabethan violence of his first play is of the school of Webster and Tourneur rather than of Shakespeare. As a dramatist he has but one note, that of fear; he has but one method, that of repetition'.[30] He re-uses the ideas of 'terror', of 'shadows' and 'marionettes', and of 'monotony', to which he had already referred in 1892. A major part of the text is indeed repeated almost word for word from his first article in *The Athenæum*. However, when referring to Maeterlinck's translation of Ruysbroeck, Symons starts evoking what is for him the 'real character' of 'Maeterlinck's dramatic work', which is 'dramatic as to form, by a sort of accident, but essentially mystical'.[31] He expands this last idea when reviewing *Le Trésor des humbles* (1896) in 'Maeterlinck as a Mystic', in 1897.[32] Focusing on the philosophical aspects of the writer's production, this article was later included within the different editions of *The Symbolist Movement in Literature* (1899, 1908, and 1919). Symons is convinced that Maeterlinck's philosophical essay goes further than the dramas by meditating on the essence of souls and going beyond the surface of things: 'To Maeterlinck the theatre has been, for the most part, no more than one of the disguises by which he can express himself, and with his book of meditations on the inner life, *Le Trésor des Humbles*, he may seem to have dropped his disguise'.[33] He adds that 'in some of his plays he would seem to have apprehended this mystery as a thing merely or mainly terrifying'.[34] Through his analysis of Maeterlinck, we can observe how Symons conceptualises the shift from what might be seen as a Decadent perception of 'fear' and 'terror' to a more Symbolist one of mysticism (reflected in the change of title between his two essays of 1893 and 1899).[35] Symons even brings his comparison between the essays and the dramas to the level of literary form: 'And what may seem curious is that this prose of the essays, which is the prose of a doctrine, is incomparably more beautiful than the prose of the plays, which was the prose of an art'.[36] *The Bookman* totally disagreed with this idea: 'How can Mr. Symons, with his exquisite sensibility, speak of Maeterlinck's prose [...] as surpassing his dramas? The general reader holds with him, of course. But the general English reader prefers sermons to high imaginative literature'.[37]

This slight deprecation of Maeterlinck's style as viewed by Symons might seem surprising, especially when we remember that in the following years Symons would write a one-act play, 'Barbara Roscorla's Child', inspired by Maeterlinck's method. The text remained unpublished until 1917 when it appeared in the *Little Review*.[38] Princeton University Library holds several versions of the play (one typescript and two manuscripts), the typescript being dated 21–23 January 1902, that is to say following Symons's translations of Verhaeren's and D'Annunzio's dramas.[39] 'Barbara Roscorla's Child' does not only draw its inspiration from Maeterlinck: it is a veritable remake, if such a cinematographic concept can be applied to literary works. The brief form of the play in a single act and its story of an anxious wait for death to strike, as well as the character of Barbara, a pregnant woman located in a room beyond the stage, recall *L'Intruse* exactly. The rivalry between the Roscorla brothers and the references to the uncontrollable temper of the elder one, Peter, also echo the relationship between Pelléas and Golaud in *Pelléas et Mélisande*. The location of the play is transposed from a remote Flemish castle to a Cornish manor on the seashore. The opening lines reflect Maeterlinck's writing principles — simple or incomplete sentences and expressive repetitions or silences, suggesting invisible presences and mysterious past events:

> SISTER A[GATHE] (*with a start*)   Asenath, Asenath, is that only the wind?
> ASENATH (*rousing herself*)   Eh?
> SISTER A.   Is that the wind?
> ASENATH   It is the wind from the sea. It blew all night. You can hear the sea out beyond; sometimes you can hear it louder than the wind. There's always been wind at sea when the Roscorlas were born; they bring trouble.
> SISTER A.   The wind frightens me. I have never been quite myself since I came here.
> ASENATH   Yes, yes, the Roscorlas come with the wind; they bring trouble.[40]

The influence of Maeterlinck's plays on Symons can be seen through the references to 'fear' (Barbara's fear of giving birth to a child and of reproducing an inherited curse, or Peter's fear of seeing his brother coming back if he does not produce a male heir) and the idea of a mystical connection between the material world and the 'inner truth' of the soul:

> DR. T[REVITHICK]   Do you know I sometimes wish we physicians had the power that our rival, the priest, has; the power of getting at the truth, the real, inner truth of our patients. The body is so often little more than the slave of the mind.[41]

Symons's transposition of Maeterlinck proved to be rather unsuccessful, as he only published his play much later in a periodical. However, it reveals the strong impact that Maeterlinck had on Symons's conception of theatre. It demonstrates that Symons was not only hoping to promote the Belgian dramatist, but also wished to import new forms of writing into British theatre. In 1906, in the Belgian journal *Antée*, Symons presented Maeterlinck as one of the most acclaimed writers in Britain ('un de nos écrivains favoris'). He claimed that Maeterlinck's plays had more readers there than in the playwright's own country. He noted nevertheless that Maeterlinck is mostly *read* rather than *performed*.[42] The attempt to imitate Maeterlinck's style shows the extent to which Symons's creative writing could be driven by his critical practices.

Charles Van Lerberghe, one of Maeterlinck's Masters

Although he never denied Maeterlinck's originality, Symons was aware that the 'Belgian Shakespeare' was not the very first 'initiator' of his dramatic conceptions:

> First in order of talent, he is second in order of time to another Belgian, M. Charles van Lerberghe [...]. It was M. van Lerberghe (in 'Les Flaireurs', for example) who discovered the effect which might be obtained on the stage by certain appeals to the sense of hearing and of sight, newly directed and with new intentions.[43]

Symons was right. Van Lerberghe's *Les Flaireurs* was indeed published in Liège in 1889 and Maeterlinck, who was a close friend of his, paid tribute to his work by dedicating *Les Aveugles* to him. Van Lerberghe remained nevertheless much less famous than Maeterlinck. By pleading in his favour, Symons displays his familiarity with Belgian literary culture. He seems to be the first to have cited the name of Van Lerberghe in Britain, even before the Scottish critic William Sharp, who translated *Les Flaireurs* into English (as *The Night-Comers*) and published a substantial study, 'La Jeune Belgique,' in the *Nineteenth Century* in 1893.[44]

During his lifetime, Van Lerberghe had often been associated with the English Pre-Raphaelites for his aestheticism centred on the primitive and coloured atmosphere of legend, and on mysterious and hieratic female figures.[45] He had felt attracted to London since the 1880s. It was only in 1898, however, that he realised his wish to move to London, where he intended to acquaint himself with English literature and to teach French literature at University College.[46] None of these projects materialised in the end, although the poet did manage to strengthen his literary network and make some contacts in the British capital. To facilitate his move, Olivier-Georges Destrée had previously written to his close friend Laurence Binyon, asking him to introduce Van Lerberghe to London literary milieus.[47] In London from early May 1898, Van Lerberghe regularly met up with Symons, who wrote a substantial article on his *Entrevisions* (1898) in the *Saturday Review* in August 1898 entitled 'A Belgian Poet'.[48] After reminding readers that Van Lerberghe had invented the techniques used in *L'Intruse* and that he had played a crucial role in shaping 'the art of the future in Belgium', Symons developed an impressionistic criticism, highlighting the same features in Van Lerberghe's 'great Symbolist art' as in Maeterlinck's early writing:

> That, or something even less substantial than that, is the *décor* through which very gentle shadows move drowsily to the sound of a faint piping, so remote that it may be no more than the wind stirring the reeds or rustling the leaves and the trees. [...] You hear words whispered, echoed back, a shadowy conversation. There are long silences, and indeed all this coming and going is a kind of suspense between something, scarcely even imagined, which has happened before and something, hardly to be conjectured, which is to happen afterwards. [...] it is really to the credit of M. van Lerberghe's technique that he has been able to produce that very sensation of uniformity — monotony as it may seem — from beginning to end of a book which has in consequence a perfectly individual atmosphere.[49]

Symons clearly establishes strong connections between the two dramatists' works, suggesting an aesthetic proximity as well as a national one. He later produced two reviews of Van Lerberghe's *La Chanson d'Ève* (1904) and *Pan* (1906).[50] Even if Van Lerberghe's stay in London did not achieve all that he had hoped for by the time he left in July 1898, it resulted at least in the publication of several articles by Symons, which contributed to strengthening the Belgian poet's reputation in Britain. The two kept up close relations after Van Lerberghe left London, as is shown by a postcard Symons sent him in 1906: '*Pan* is adorable, and I am only not writing you about it because I have written what I think for the *Saturday Review*. I am sending you a tiny set of verses of mine, which I hope, you will accept as a little sign of gratitude'.[51] The premature death of Van Lerberghe in 1907 put an end to these small efforts to promote his work, but Symons certainly continued to be influenced by him in his ideas for a new theatre.

Émile Verhaeren, the Poet-Dramatist

Symons's translation of *The Dawn* in 1898 was a defining factor for Verhaeren's reception in English. It was only after this first volume was translated that Verhaeren acquired a higher profile in Britain.[52] His name had however been circulating for a few years in small literary circles and some of his poetic works had already been translated in journals by Alma Strettell and, especially, Osman Edwards. Letters from the latter indicate that Verhaeren chose Edwards as his 'official' translator, limiting Strettell's work to some specific poems.[53] Edwards was a very close friend of Symons. A cosmopolitan, unstoppable traveller, and passionate about Japan, where he lived for some time, he wrote a major study on Verhaeren in the *Daily Chronicle* in 1895.[54] In 1896 he published an even more substantial study in *The Savoy* under Symons's editorship.[55]

Because of his translation of *The Dawn*, Symons might seem to overshadow Edwards, to whom he owed his discovery of the Belgian poet. One of his letters to Verhaeren however reveals that Symons received the original book he needed for the translation from Edwards himself, who was then writing for *The Savoy*.[56] In full agreement with Edwards, the more famous Symons took over and used his name in order to boost Verhaeren's promotion. He had previously read *Les Aubes* when it was first published in the *Mercure de France* and asked his own publisher to contact the Brussels publisher of the volume before it came out in book form.[57] This is how the English translation came to be published only a few months later than the French original.

Thanks to Symons's intervention, *The Dawn* had a strong impact in Britain. Some reviews foregrounded Symons even more than the poet himself.[58] As the critic of the *St. James's Gazette* wrote: 'M. Verhaeren is happy in finding a translator with so considerable an original gift in verse and criticism as Mr. Arthur Symons'.[59] Up till now Symons had already translated several works: *The Drunkard* (*L'Assommoir*) by Émile Zola in 1894 and the poems included in *The Child of Pleasure* (*Il piacere*) by Gabriele D'Annunzio in 1898. However, before Verhaeren's play he had never translated any drama. As Stefano Evangelista shows in this volume (Chapter 4), in the following years he would devote himself more to the theatre, translating D'Annunzio's plays: *The Dead City* (*La città morta*) in 1900, *La gioconda* in 1901, and *Francesca da Rimini* in 1902, as well as Hofmannsthal's *Electra* in 1907. It is worth recalling that it was probably at this same period that Symons wrote 'Barbara Roscorla's Child'.

Les Aubes constitutes the third and last part of a trilogy that includes the two collections of poems, *Les Campagnes hallucinées* (1893) and *Les Villes tentaculaires* (1895). This symbolic and utopian drama shows the conflicts between the countryside and the city, tradition and industrial modernity. It is set in Oppidomagne, an imaginary city beleaguered by the complaints of the peasants, a workers' strike, and the siege of a foreign army. The local aristocracy, the Regents, seem more vulnerable than ever. Hérénien, a tribune of the people and a kind of Christ figure, reconciles the different factions but is nevertheless basely murdered at the end of the play.

In the preface he wrote for *The Dawn*, Symons showed more interest in the

Fig. 6.3. Théo Van Rysselberghe, design for the cover of *Les Aubes* by Émile Verhaeren (Brussels: Edmond Deman, 1898).

evolution of Verhaeren's career than in the actual play, as the volume was included in a new series devoted to foreign dramatists ('Modern Plays' at Duckworth) where Ibsen, Stepniak, Ostrovsky, Strindberg, Maeterlinck, Villiers de l'Isle-Adam, Brieux, and Sienkiewicz would also appear. Starting from the early 'Naturalistic' poems of *Les Flamandes*, Symons showed how Verhaeren's poetry had become more abstract in outlook culminating in *Les Villes tentaculaires*, where 'the hallucinations become entirely external'.[60] He observed a shift from Naturalism to Symbolism: 'Contrast these poems with those early poems, so brutal, so Flemish, if you would see at a glance all the difference between the Naturalistic and the Symbolistic treatment'.[61] As for the play, Symons commented on its formal aspect, alternating verses and prose, 'which, in France, is a very novel experiment indeed. To English readers, accustomed to the Elizabethan drama, nothing can seem more natural than such an alternation'.[62] In agreement with Verhaeren, the English version abandoned the original rhyming scheme in favour of a more literal translation, which preserved the internal rhythm of free verse:

> Mon principe est ceci: de traduire la prose en prose et le vers en vers, mais en vers sans rimes, quelques morceaux exceptés, où les strophes à peu près régulières, demandent la rime [...]. Tout le reste je traduis rythme pour rythme, et presque mot par mot, avec au moins, je crois, le résultat de vous faire parler en d'assez beaux vers anglais! Dites-moi si vous approuvez de [*sic*] cette méthode. Il me semble que cela vous donne un peu l'air 'élisabéthain,' et surtout par la suppression de la rime, qu'on ne trouve dans le drame de ce temps-là que très rarement, et presque seulement dans certaines pièces écrites avant Shakespeare, ou dans les pastorales.[63]

> [My principle is this: to translate prose into prose and verse into verse without rhymes, apart from some passages where the lines are more or less the same length and demand rhyme [...]. All the rest I translate almost word for word, keeping to the original rhythm, with at least the result, I think, of making you speak in rather beautiful English verse. Tell me if you approve of this method. It seems to me that this gives you a slight 'Elizabethan' aura, especially through the suppression of rhyme, something found only rarely in the drama of that period and almost only in certain pre-Shakespearean plays or pastorals.]

In Britain, the translation was generally well received. For *The Athenæum*, which described the play as Verhaeren's 'maturest work', 'Mr. Symons [...] achieved his version with more self-suppression than is common in translators'.[64] In contrast, *The Academy* mocked Symons's choice of a very literal translation.[65] Several articles noted how Symons's translation rendered 'the "free verses" of the modern school of symbolical writers'.[66] Verhaeren's play was also often described as a masterpiece. For *The Speaker*, 'Present-day English literature has no parallel for this amazing energetic, ardent, and moving dramatic spirit'.[67] However, *The Dawn* looked essentially like a poem. Thus Edmund Gosse wrote that 'the new poem of M. Verhaeren is in dramatic form', adding: 'The subject of "Les Aubes" is the conquest of a new existence at the cost of infinite sorrow and the blood of a world of victims. Oppidomagne is one of the great capitals of humanity; it is Paris or Berlin'.[68] This is one of the reasons why, according to *The Stage*, the play was 'never likely to be represented on the English boards except by such organisations as the Independent Theatre and the New Century Theatre'.[69] In the event *The Dawn*, unlike other Verhaeren plays such as *The Cloister*, was never performed in English.

Symons did not translate any other works by Verhaeren; he left the field clear for Edwards. He nevertheless carried on praising him through his reviews for the *Saturday Review*. In a letter of 1902, Symons thanked him for sending him *Les Forces tumultueuses*, paying him the highest tribute: 'What I always find in your work, and in so little of the work of others, is *l'énergie, la grâce littéraire suprême*, as Baudelaire called it, so justly. That is why I prefer your work to that of any other French living poet'.[70] In his letters to Verhaeren Symons was deferential, writing to him as if to a master. Symons became closer to Verhaeren than to any other Belgian writer, indeed their names would become permanently bound together. The *Manchester Guardian* even recognised Verhaeren among Symons's influences when reviewing his collection *Poems* (1902).[71] After Verhaeren's sudden death in 1916, Symons wrote a tribute to him in the *English Review*.[72]

A Late Belgian Connection: The London Publisher Arthur Herbert in Bruges

The history of Symons's relationship with Belgium also includes the publishing house Arthur Herbert. This was founded in Bruges in 1906 by a London publisher, Herbert Arthur Doubleday (1867–1941), in collaboration with an anglophile Bruges printer, Édouard Verbeke. The two men joined forces in editing an avant-garde French-speaking literary journal called *Antée* (1905–06) before starting an actual publishing house.[73] Arthur Herbert published the works of Belgian and French authors (Joseph Bossi [Christian Beck], Henri Vandeputte, Louis Piérard, Paul Spaak, Eugène Montfort, Saint-Georges de Bouhélier, and Francis de Miomandre). It also aimed to publish French translations rather than English books, making translations of Oscar Wilde's and Arthur Symons's works available in French. This unusual publishing endeavour however ceased in 1907, very shortly after its creation.

Short though its existence was, Arthur Herbert's publishing house acted as an important mediator between English and French writing. Symons published several translations of his works (*Poèmes* and *Portraits anglais* translated by Louis Thomas) with Herbert and also contributed to *Antée*.[74] This journal published French and Belgian writers and was circulated in both countries. Conversely, the Belgian writer André Ruyters sent an appraisal of Symons's criticism and his *Portraits anglais* to the journal, while the French Symbolist writer (of American origin) Stuart Merrill wrote a critique of his poetry.[75] Thus the network around *Antée* enabled Symons to connect with both Belgian and French authors. Since the publication of Georges Rodenbach's novel, *Bruges-la-Morte* (1892), and the rediscovery of the Flemish primitives in the big exhibition of 1902, Bruges, the home of the journal, had become symbolic of Belgian literature itself. This might explain why Symons reused the content of his article for the *Encyclopaedia Britannica* together with a poetic description of the city in an article published in 1918.[76]

This example shows, more broadly, how Belgian networks acted as a useful intermediary between Britain and France. During the same years, Symons contributed to another cosmopolitan and left-wing periodical established in Belgium, *La Société nouvelle*.[77] Created in 1884, this journal had already published every important Belgian Symbolist writer (including Lemonnier, Maeterlinck, Verhaeren, Rodenbach, and Eekhoud) and many French authors (Huysmans, Cladel, Barrès, Kahn), as well as translations of Nietzsche, Morris, Emerson, Kropotkin, and Bakunin. Together with Verhaeren, Symons also contributed to the ephemeral French journal *Psyché* (1906), edited by Louis Thomas, his translator at Arthur Herbert.

Conclusion

To Symons, the Bruges episode of the early twentieth century already seemed very distant from the atmosphere of the 1890s, as he makes clear in his reply to Stuart Merrill, who, in April 1907, asked him to send him a few lines about his life: 'It is like good old times to hear from you — times that I have recalled in dedicating my translated poems to Verhaeren'.[78] Symons indeed dedicated the volume published by Arthur Herbert to the poet. He had previously asked his permission and in return was promised a dedication in one of his books.[79] This promise would be fulfilled in 1910, when Verhaeren placed Symons's name at the head of his collection *Les Villes à pignons*.

Symons felt a particular rapport with Belgian authors, as if he identified other versions of himself in them. Belgians wished to be perceived as distinct from and ahead of their French neighbours in the eyes of a British readership, and indeed Symons acknowledged the independence of Belgian contemporary literature from the French Symbolist movement. As an English-speaking and francophile writer, he might have felt a closeness to these French-speaking and anglophile Belgian authors. This closeness can be sensed from his 1907 dedication to Verhaeren:

> Dans la bonne et amicale lettre où vous acceptez la dédicace de cette première traduction en français de quelques-uns de mes poèmes, vous me rappelez nos anciennes rencontres dans 'ce Londres prodigieux et formidable' que nous avons également aimé. C'est déjà un lien entre nous. Mais vous ajoutez : 'Avec vous, je me sentais en France ou en Belgique.' Vous ne pouviez certes rien dire qui me donnât plus de plaisir.[80]

> [In the kind and amicable letter in which you accept the dedication of this first translation into French of some of my poems, you reminded me of our former meetings in 'ce Londres prodigieux et formidable' that we both loved equally. That is already a bond between us. You added, however: 'With you, I felt as if I was in France or Belgium.' You could certainly have said nothing that would have given me more pleasure.]

Notes to Chapter 6

1. I would like to thank Jill Fell and Stefano Evangelista for their comments and suggestions in the writing of this chapter.

2. Arthur Symons, 'The Temptation of Saint Anthony (After a Design by Félicien Rops)', in *Days and Nights* (London: Macmillan, 1889), p. 50.
3. Arthur Symons to John Quinn, 10 August 1915, in *Arthur Symons: Selected Letters*, ed. by Beckson and Munro, p. 236.
4. *The Poems of Ernest Dowson*, with a memoir by Arthur Symons (London: Bodley Head, 1922), p. xvi.
5. Arthur Symons, 'Bruges', *Nation*, 2791 (28 December 1918), 796–97 (p. 796).
6. [Arthur Symons], 'Bertha at the Fair: An Encounter', *The Savoy*, 3 (July 1896), 86–88. Further references to this work are given in the text.
7. Ernest Dowson to Arthur Symons, 5 July 1896, in *The Letters of Ernest Dowson*, ed. by Desmond Flower and Henry Maas (Rutherford, NJ: Fairleigh Dickinson University Press, 1967), p. 355.
8. Guy Ducrey, 'Le Passeur du symbolisme français: Arthur Symons', in *'Curious about France': visions littéraires victoriennes*, ed. by Ignacio Ramos Gay (Bern: Peter Lang, 2014), pp. 137–52.
9. This terminology refers to Pierre Bourdieu's theory developed in his work *The Rules of Art*, trans. by Susan Emanuel (Stanford, CA: Stanford University Press, 1995).
10. See Benoît Denis and Jean-Marie Klinkenberg, *La Littérature belge: précis d'histoire sociale* (Brussels: Labor, 2005).
11. A[rthur] Sy[mons], 'Belgium. Literature', in *The New Volumes of the Encyclopædia Britannica*, 10th edn (Edinburgh & London: A. & C. Black, 1902), XXVI, 203–04 (p. 203).
12. Jacques Dubois and Pierre Bourdieu, 'Champ littéraire et rapports de domination', *Textyles*, 15 (1999), 12–16.
13. Edmond Picard, 'L'Âme belge', *Revue encyclopédique*, 7:207 (24 July 1897), 595–99.
14. Symons, 'Belgium. Literature', p. 203.
15. Casanova, *The World Republic of Letters*, p. 131.
16. Laurence Brogniez, *Préraphaélisme et symbolisme: peinture littéraire et image poétique* (Paris: Champion, 2003).
17. See *Arthur Symons: Selected Letters*, ed. by Beckson and Munro, p. 125.
18. Arthur Symons, 'The Question of Censorship', *The Academy*, 63 (28 June 1902), 21–22; and '"Monna Vanna"', *The Academy*, 63 (5 July 1902), 45.
19. Symons, *Plays, Acting, and Music* (1903).
20. William Archer, 'A Pessimist Playwright', *Fortnightly Review*, 50:297 (September 1891), 346–54.
21. Octave Mirbeau, 'La Princesse Maleine de M. Maeterlinck', *Le Figaro*, 24 August 1890, p. 1. All translations are the author's own unless otherwise stated.
22. Archer, 'A Pessimist Playwright', p. 346.
23. Ibid., p. 354.
24. [Arthur Symons], '*The Princess Maleine* and *The Intruder*', *The Athenæum*, 3365 (23 April 1892), 525–26 (p. 525).
25. Ibid., p. 525.
26. Ibid., p. 525.
27. Denis Laoureux, 'Maurice Maeterlinck et l'invention d'un théâtre de l'image', in *Les Arts de la scène à l'épreuve de l'histoire: les objets et les méthodes de l'historiographie des spectacles produits sur la scène française (1635–1906)*, ed. by Roxane Martin and Marina Nordera (Paris: Champion, 2011), pp. 113–21.
28. [Symons], '*The Princess Maleine* and *The Intruder*', p. 525.
29. Symons, 'The Decadent Movement in Literature', *Harper's New Monthly Magazine* (November 1893), repr. in *The Symbolist Movement in Literature*, p. 177.
30. Ibid., p. 178.
31. Ibid., p. 180.
32. Arthur Symons, 'Maeterlinck as a Mystic', *Contemporary Review*, 72 (1897), 349–54.
33. Symons, *The Symbolist Movement in Literature*, p. 80.
34. Ibid., p. 82.
35. To know more of what is at stake in Symons's revision of the title, see Matthew Creasy's introduction in Symons, *The Symbolist Movement in Literature*, pp. xv–xviii.
36. Ibid., p. 83.

37. Agnes Macdonell, 'The Symbolist Movement in Literature', *The Bookman*, 18:105 (June 1900), 94.
38. Arthur Symons, 'Barbara Roscorla's Child', *Little Review*, 4 (October 1917), 25–36.
39. See Anne Cnudde-Knowland, 'Maurice Maeterlinck and English and Anglo-Irish Literature: A Study of Parallels and Influences' (unpublished doctoral thesis, University of Oxford, 1984), pp. 126–39.
40. Symons, 'Barbara Roscorla's Child', p. 26.
41. Ibid., p. 31.
42. 'J'ai nommé Maeterlinck; il est un de nos écrivains favoris; il a probablement plus de lecteurs dans notre pays que dans le sien, mais il y est lu, non joué; exception faite pour les rares tentatives de l'actrice anglaise la plus capable de l'interpréter: Mc Patrick Campbell' [I have mentioned Maeterlinck, who is one of our favourite writers. He probably has more readers in our country than in his; however, he is read and not performed, with the exception of some rare attempts by the English actress who is most capable of performing his works: Mrs Patrick Campbell] (Arthur Symons, 'Dieu à Londres: l'art et le public anglais', *Antée*, 5 (1 October 1906), 475.
43. Symons, '*The Princess Maleine* and *The Intruder*', p. 525.
44. William Sharp, 'La Jeune Belgique', *Nineteenth Century*, 34 (September 1893), 416–36. See also Charles Van Lerberghe, 'The Night-Comers (Englished by William Sharp)', *Evergreen, The Northern Seasonal*, 2 (Autumn 1895), 59–71.
45. Laurence Brogniez, 'Charles Van Lerberghe, préraphaélite flamand? Tradition anglophile et héritage flamand', *Textyles*, 22 (2003), 94–108.
46. Jacques Detemmerman, 'Van Lerberghe et la pédagogie: rêveries et velléités', in *Littératures en contact: mélanges offerts à Vic Nachtergaele*, ed. by Jan Herman, Steven Engels, and Alex Demeulenaere (Leuven: Presses universitaires de Louvain, 2003), pp. 75–88 (p. 82).
47. Marysa Demoor and Frederick Morel, 'Laurence Binyon and the Belgian Artistic Scene: Unearthing Unknown Brotherhoods', *Victorian Periodicals Review*, 44:2 (2011), 184–97.
48. Arthur Symons, 'A Belgian Poet', *Saturday Review*, 86 (20 August 1898), 243.
49. Ibid.
50. Arthur Symons, 'Reviews', *Saturday Review*, 98 (1 October 1904), 432; 102 (7 July 1906), 16–17.
51. Arthur Symons to Charles Van Lerberghe, postcard, London, 2 June 1906, Brussels, Archives et Musée de la littérature, MS ML 770/2.
52. For more information, see Clément Dessy, 'Les Vies britanniques d'Émile Verhaeren', *Textyles*, 50–51 (2016), 119–36.
53. See Jacques Marx, 'Verhaeren et ses traducteurs anglais', *Revue de littérature comparée*, 299:3 (2001), 443–54.
54. Osman Edwards, 'Émile Verhaeren', *Daily Chronicle*, 16 May 1895, 3.
55. Osman Edwards, 'Émile Verhaeren', *The Savoy*, 7 (November 1896), 65–78.
56. See *Arthur Symons: Selected Letters*, ed. by Beckson and Munro, p. 125.
57. Arthur Symons to Émile Verhaeren, [early 1898], Brussels, Archives et Musée de la littérature, MS FS XVI 148/1193.
58. [Anon.], 'Mr. Arthur Symons as Translator', *The Academy*, 1387 (3 December 1898), 370–71.
59. W. P. James, 'The Literary World', *St James's Gazette*, 5 November 1898, 12.
60. Arthur Symons, 'Introduction', in Verhaeren, *The Dawn*, pp. 1–8 (p. 5).
61. Ibid., p. 6.
62. Ibid., p. 7.
63. Arthur Symons to Émile Verhaeren, [early 1898], in *Arthur Symons: Selected Letters*, ed. by Beckson and Munro, p. 125 (Brussels, Archives et Musée de la littérature, MS FS XVI 148/1194).
64. [Anon.], 'Translations', *The Athenæum*, 3725 (18 March 1899), 336.
65. [Anon.], 'Mr. Arthur Symons as Translator', p. 370.
66. [Anon.], 'New Books', *The Scotsman*, 24 October 1898, 3. *Manchester Guardian* also noted the use of the '*vers libre*', in [Anon.], 'Books of the Week', 6 December 1898, 4.
67. [Anon.], 'Recent Poetry and Verse', *Speaker: A Review of Politics, Letters, Science and the Arts*, 19 (7 January 1899), 26. See also *Illustrated London News*, 94 (7 January 1899), 20.
68. Edmund Gosse, 'M. Verhaeren's New Poem', *Saturday Review*, 85 (23 April 1898), 560.

69. [Anon.], 'Chit Chat', *The Stage*, 920 (3 November 1898), 14.
70. Arthur Symons to Émile Verhaeren, 12 February 1902, Brussels, Archives et Musée de la littérature, MS FS XVI 148/1190.
71. [Anon.], 'Books of the Week', *Manchester Guardian*, 26 August 1902, 7.
72. Arthur Symons, 'Émile Verhaeren', *English Review*, 26 (March 1918), 234–39.
73. See Andries Van den Abeele, 'Une maison d'édition brugeoise: Arthur Herbert (1906–1907)', *Textyles*, 23 (2003), 95–101.
74. Arthur Symons, 'Sur un air de Rameau', *Antée*, 2 (July 1906), 111; 'Dieu à Londres'; 'Robert Buchanan', *Antée*, 7 (December 1906), 648–52.
75. Stuart Merrill, 'L'Œuvre poétique d'Arthur Symons', *Antée*, 13 (June 1907), 66–82.
76. Symons, 'Bruges'.
77. Arthur Symons, 'Poèmes', *La Société nouvelle*, 2nd series, 13:2 (August 1907), 245–51; 'Christian Trevalga', *La Société nouvelle*, 2nd series, 13:7–8 (January-February 1908), 145–57.
78. Arthur Symons to Stuart Merrill, 26 April 1907, Brussels, Archives et Musée de la Littérature, MS ML 7065/182.
79. Arthur Symons to Émile Verhaeren, 19 and 22 March 1907, Brussels, Archives et Musée de la Littérature, MS FS XVI 148/1191 & 1192.
80. Arthur Symons, *Poésies* (Bruges: Arthur Herbert, 1907), pp. 49–50.

CHAPTER 7

Arthur Symons in France: Transnational Journalism and the French Reception[1]

Bénédicte Coste

> J'éprouve un vif intérêt pour la littérature française contemporaine, je suis toujours heureux d'entendre dire qu'on étudie nos auteurs en France. Dans le monde moderne, il n'y a que deux grandes littératures — la vôtre et la nôtre — j'y vois là plus d'une raison pour que nous nous étudiions mutuellement.
> ARTHUR SYMONS to Remy de Gourmont[2]

Full of praise for both French and English literature in an 1889 letter to Remy de Gourmont, Arthur Symons was not yet engaged in introducing French Symbolism in Britain; he was trying instead to get himself introduced to French Symbolist writers. Symons never met Auguste Villiers de L'Isle-Adam with whom, as Matthew Creasy shows in this volume (Chapter 5), he had such a close textual relationship; but he did encounter Gourmont and other French writers during his regular trips to the Continent in the 1890s, and this laid the foundation for his lifelong interest in French literature. Although Symons's poetry and criticism have continuously elicited critical discussions, his literary activity in France and his reception there, from 1890 to the twenty-first century, have remained largely unexplored.

Symons's extensive interest in France was a constant in his literary career. He translated Stéphane Mallarmé, with the poet's approval, triggering a distinctive Anglo-Saxon approach to his poetical works,[3] and he is rightly considered a mediator of French Symbolism in Britain;[4] but he was also actively involved in Anglo-French cultural exchange on the other side of the Channel, enjoying recognition in France and contributing to a wide array of periodicals during the remarkably cosmopolitan period that marked the end of the nineteenth century.[5] As early as 1888, Gourmont was mentioning Symons's forthcoming article on Villiers to the ailing writer;[6] and in June 1890, he discussed Symons's *Days and Nights* in the *Mercure de France*, providing a translation of 'A Litany of Lethe'.[7] Soon Symons himself contributed to the dissemination of contemporary French and British writing in both countries thanks to his impressive journalistic activity that took the form of hundreds of reviews. From 1891 onwards, he published in French periodicals and was hailed as an impressive British poet and critic by his French peers. In the twentieth century he continued to appear as a persistent, if discreet, presence in French letters, notably through a steady stream of translations of his works; these included the complete translation of *Spiritual Adventures* into French by Pierre Leyris (1907–2001), a distinguished heir to Symons's early translators, Henry-D. Davray (1873–1944) and Paul Verlaine.

What follows is a discussion of both Symons's presence and his deeper recognition as a poet and literary critic in French periodicals, especially those with a strong cosmopolitan bent, including the *Mercure de France* (1890–1965) and the *Navire d'argent* (1925–26). The chapter then moves on to consider his academic reception from the 1920s onwards. When viewed from France, Symons — who translated some of Verlaine's poems as early as 1890 and was lauded as the French poet's 'most active supporter' after he arranged his visit to Britain in 1893 — presents a different picture than he does in Britain.[8] He certainly played a major role in introducing Symbolism to Britain but, in this new picture, he appears against a backdrop of literary cosmopolitanism, translation and translators, avant-garde periodicals, journalistic networks, failed opportunities, and the development of a new aesthetics that ultimately evolved into twentieth-century Modernism.

A Vibrant Début

Even before setting foot on French shores, Symons had started to laud French artists in British periodicals, translating Villiers de l'Isle-Adam's 'L'Aveu' in *Days and Nights* and offering his opinions on the French Symbolist lithographer and painter Odilon Redon (1840–1916).[9] During his first trip to Paris in 1889, he befriended Gourmont, met Decadent and Symbolist poets, and soon found himself reviewing an astonishing range of writings in French: he discussed not only the most respected authors, such as Victor Hugo, but also the most avant-garde, such as Tristan Klingsor (1874–1966) and André Fontainas (1865–1948).[10] The well-known story of the summer of 1895 in Dieppe during which Symons designed *The Savoy* with the help of Aubrey Beardsley and Leonard Smithers, may be further illuminated by Gourmont's 1904 article 'Les Décadents'. Here, he describes Symons's astonished reaction on learning that, when publishers turned down their work, French-speaking poets responded by creating new, sometimes ephemeral magazines of their own.[11] Symons would obviously remember this when he collaborated on launching *The Savoy*.

On 1 January 1890, the *Mercure de France*, France's oldest periodical, reappeared under the editorship of Alfred Valette (1858–1935), and soon became known as the 'Revue des Deux Mondes des Jeunes'.[12] It gathered many Symbolists under its banner, ultimately gaining recognition for its literary cosmopolitanism and promotion of avant-garde poetry in various languages. As part of the journal's internationalist mission, in March 1892, the pseudonymous 'The Pilgrim' published a short article entitled 'Un manifeste littéraire anglais', which celebrated the first *Book of the Rhymers' Club* and praised 'a common love of art' ('un amour commun de l'art'), 'a sense of Catholic mysticism' ('un sens du mysticisme catholique'), a common interest in 'la rime riche', and the Parnassianism of its contributors.[13] The article featured a good selection of the Rhymers' poetry both in English and in French, including Symons's 'Music and Memory', which was translated as 'La Musique et le souvenir'. From June 1890, Gourmont's short pieces in the 'Revue des revues' and 'Littérature anglaise' sections of the *Mercure de France* made Symons familiar to French readers, both as a poet and translator. During 1892 Gourmont partly translated Symons's *Fortnightly Review* article on Joris-Karl Huysmans, mentioned his *National Review* article on Verlaine, and even referred to his *Athenaeum* article on the translation of Maurice Maeterlinck's *La Princesse Maleine*.[14] Thanks to Gourmont and later to Davray, Symons's name continued to appear in the *Mercure* until the 1910s, in sections devoted to foreign literature and periodicals. In 1908, the distinguished folklorist Arnold Van Gennep hailed the first volume of the new series of the *Journal of the Gypsy Lore Society* and Symons's article 'In Praise of Gypsies', discussed by Katharina Herold in this volume (Chapter 10).[15]

It is possible that Gourmont convinced Symons to submit translated essays to the *Mercure de France*. Symons's most important contributions in the 1890s provide interesting insights into his journalistic practice: 'La Littérature anglaise', for example, was a panorama of the British literary publications of 1893.[16] Published in February 1894, it was a translation of 'English Literature in 1893', originally written for the *Athenaeum*, the English weekly that, in the 1890s, published most of his reviews of French literature.[17] Throughout the 'Yellow Nineties', Symons's literary reputation seems to have fared better in France than in Britain: if the reception of *London Nights* was controversial in Britain, Symons's third volume of poetry was approvingly reviewed both by Gourmont in the *Mercure* and by Verlaine himself in the *Revue encyclopédique*.[18]

In March 1896 Davray noted that *The Savoy* was acclaimed in Britain for its 'very endearing content' ('contenu très attachant'); meanwhile, its editors — Smithers and Symons — were both said to be 'very sympathetically known in France' ('très sympathiquement connus en France').[19] He added that the 'very luxuriously published' *Savoy* would be an 'excellent magazine' and prove to be 'a very complete record of the current artistic effort in Britain'.[20] In August 1896, Davray insisted that *The Savoy* was 'the protagonist of the current movement that will frame English art for a while', a view clearly at odds with the lukewarm attitude to the venture in Britain.[21]

In 1897, Franco-American poet and translator Stuart Merrill (1863–1915) devoted an article to Symons's writings in *L'Aube* (1896–97), another avant-garde cosmopolitan literary magazine. This article offers one of the best assessments of Symons's place in the literary scene of the 1890s. Merrill described Symons as 'one of the unquestioned leaders of young English literature' ('un des chefs incontestés de la jeune littérature anglaise'), belonging to no school — which was seen as an oddity in France — along with other independent promising poets still overshadowed by the tutelary figures of Victorian poetry.[22] He praised Symons's interest in music halls, arguing that this fostered a new aesthetics, and lauded his writings on the performing and visual arts. Merrill translated some of the verses from *London Nights* and declared the 'Preface' to the second edition to be 'of a rare courage in England' ('d'un rare courage en Angleterre'), where the sovereign taste of the Young ('Jeune Personne') was either for self-censorship or more daring publications; the controversial 'Stella Maris' belonged among the latter (p. 153). Interestingly, Merrill believed that Symons was on the cusp of greater achievements, concluding that he ranked 'high among the young English poets' ('haut parmi les jeunes poètes anglais') (p. 153). Those views were later echoed in Britain by an anonymous reviewer in *The Academy*, who noted that Symons was 'an authority on *les jeunes*' — the expression showing the French influence on Britain's literary sphere.[23]

Symons in Translation

Surprisingly, given his mastery of written French, Symons does not seem to have published directly in that language. In February 1898, the *Mercure de France* published his essay 'Walter Pater', translated by the Belgian writer Georges Khnopff (1860–1929).[24] At this time, though, Symons's regular translator for the *Mercure* was also one of the most productive and distinguished of the period: Davray, whose work included versions of H. G. Wells, Laurence Housman, Frank Harris, Edmund Gosse, Oscar Wilde, and Maurice Hewlett. Davray translated Symons's essay on George Meredith for the *Mercure*'s newly established publishing house, and thanked Symons 'for [his] precious advice and the authority of [his] name' ('pour vos précieux conseils et l'autorité de votre nom').[25] Davray met Symons again in 1900 in Fountain Court and translated an essay on Auguste Rodin that first appeared in *La Plume*, another cosmopolitan magazine and house mainly publishing 'les jeunes' in 1900.[26] He followed this by translating an essay on Casanova in 1903 and remained a constant supporter of Symons in the *Mercure*.[27]

Symons's other French translators at the turn of the century were Louis Thomas and his father Édouard.[28] They were responsible for the translations of Symons's 'Appendice' to his edition of the *Poésies de Choderlos de Laclos*,[29] 'William Morris',[30] and the essay on Oscar Wilde published in *La Plume*.[31] Along with Jack Cohen, the Thomases translated *Aubrey Beardsley* in 1906 and were credited accordingly,[32] as they were for 'Chopin', which appeared in the *Mercure musical* the following year.[33] Other publications were less respectful of translators: Symons's essay on Dante Gabriel Rossetti, which appeared in 1912 in a collection of art monographs, *L'Art et le beau*, did not credit any translator, but its appearance proved that Symons's fame was undiminished on this side of the Channel. As the editors of Symons's bibliography note, the history of *Dante Gabriel Rossetti by Arthur Symons* is unclear, but it nonetheless confirms the role of translations in the dissemination of literary cosmopolitanism.[34]

Symons's many contributions to various kinds of publications — art, Symbolist, avant-garde — enabled him to build and develop journalistic networks with French-speaking writers. His networks were unusually wide in comparison to those established by his British contemporaries. He signed no less than twenty-seven articles between April 1903 and March 1904 in the short-lived Anglo-French

Weekly Critical Review, to which W. B. Yeats and Gourmont also contributed regularly; these included a three-part essay on Whistler, another cosmopolitan artist with strong ties to France.[35] Symons's short pieces in the bilingual *Weekly Critical Review* discussed either art or cities such as Moscow and Rome; they were translated by the rather obscure Mahaut (Comtesse Mathilde de la Tour).[36]

The *Weekly Critical Review Devoted to Literature, Music and the Fine Arts* (to give it its full title) is an intriguing participant in the late nineteenth-century wave of Anglo-French relations. Owned and edited by Arthur Blès, who presented himself as a translator and teacher of English and a recipient of the 'Palmes académiques', each issue provided cultural news from Britain and France across a dozen pages.[37] French contributors included established figures such as Jules de Clarétie, Melchior de Voguë, Alfred Capus, Gourmont, Huysmans, Catulle Mendès, Rodin, J. H. Rosny, and the Comtesse de Courson, a Catholic writer. Their British counterparts — Theodore Watts-Dunton, John Gurdon, Housman, Ernest Newman, Francis Thompson, and Yeats — were a miscellaneous group, enjoying different degrees of recognition and representing different literary movements. An illustrated and rather mainstream magazine, the *Weekly Critical Review* published poetry (including Symons's 'Hymn to Earth'), travelogues, pieces on music ('London Notes'), art, and fashion, as well as social life snippets ('Place aux Dames' signed 'La Parisienne') next to the sports and finance sections.[38] A section entitled 'Chips Caught Flying' presented a selection of excerpts from British newspapers and magazines such as the *Standard*, the *Manchester Guardian*, and the *Evening News*. Advertisements for the *Mercure de France* testify to the existence of a comprehensive literary Anglo-French network in which Symons was fully immersed. On 8 April 1904, the *Weekly Critical Review* announced its transformation into a monthly publication designed both to be the French counterpart of the *Review of Reviews* and to provide a teaching aid for English and French through excerpts.[39] Contributors to the forthcoming 'La Revue franco-anglaise' were again to include Gourmont and Symons, who had just reviewed Gourmont's *Épilogues: réflexions sur la vie* in the *Saturday Review*, but the project seems not to have materialised.[40] Anglo-French cultural relations would later be given a new lease of life through the *Anglo-French Review* (1919–20), a bilingual monthly edited by the Englishman James Lewis May and the enduringly anglophile Davray, designed to 'consolidate the union between England and France immediately after the Great War'.[41]

The Belgian Moment

Symons's Belgian connections are the subject of Clément Dessy's article in this volume (Chapter 6); however, it is important to consider here how the Belgian reception functions in the context of Symons's participation in French culture. If Symons's contributions to the *Weekly Critical Review* showcase his engagement with transnational journalism, the same is true of the pieces he wrote in 1907 for the Belgian literary magazine *Antée*, which was less interested in Symbolism than in publishing Belgian and French writers of a 'naturist' bent.

Like other magazines, *Antée* soon set up a publishing house — in this case under the name of 'Arthur Herbert', which was the Belgian-sounding pseudonym of Herbert Arthur Doubleday, who was in fact a British citizen.[42] One of the first volumes issued by the Collection d'Antée was *Portraits anglais*, an anthology of Symons's articles on British writers (1907).[43] All had previously appeared in British magazines and in *Studies in Verse and Prose* (1904), and some had been published in translation in the *Mercure de France*. Thanks to this beautifully produced translation, Symons inched further into the French-speaking literary community as a mediator of modern British literature.[44] The Collection d'Antée's second book was Symons's *Poésies*,[45] made up of ninety-five poems translated by Verlaine, Merrill, Mahaut, Léon Balzagette (a friend of Gourmont), and Édouard and Louis Thomas. Some of these had already appeared: for instance Verlaine's translations had been published in the periodical *Vers et prose* in 1905–06.[46] Arguably, *Poésies* can be seen as a further attempt on Symons's part to gain recognition from the French-speaking community, this time as a poet and by following the established publishing pattern. *Portraits anglais* was duly reviewed in *Antée* by André Ruyters (1876–1950), a banker and friend of André Gide, in return for Symons's review of his collection of essays *Le Mauvais-Riche*. Noting that Symons's position in criticism was 'considérable', Ruyters highlighted his method of blurring the boundaries between criticism and art and concluded that his place in avant-garde culture was secure.[47]

In June 1907, Merrill devoted a comprehensive article in *Antée* to Symons's writings in order to publicise the forthcoming publication of *Poésies, précédées d'une préface par Louis Thomas et d'un portrait en héliogravure de l'auteur de Jacques-Émile Blanche*. In this — an opportunity to update his 1897 assessment of Symons — Merrill discusses Symons's poems and view of gender relations and mentions the performance of *Cleopatra in Judea* by the Drama Society in London on 6 May, as well as *The Symbolist Movement in Literature, Studies in Two Literatures*, and Symons's criticism of Robert Browning, Beardsley, and William Blake.[48] Reminiscing how he had met Symons in 1895 in London, Merrill situates him in a generation of poets noticeable for their individuality; he specifically names Yeats, Ernest Dowson, Lionel Johnson, and Vincent O'Sullivan. He records the group's close, friendly relationships with the French Symbolists, acknowledges the role played by *The Savoy* in Symons's reputation, and praises his poetic sincerity. Merrill also translates some of Symons's poems on urban life into French ('Paris', 'Mains'), but deems his later work on nature untranslatable because it is steeped in the British tradition. Obviously, by this stage, Symons's poetry was embracing a more national vein and the poet was no longer an up-and-coming writer; instead, he was facing down competition from a new generation. Merrill's commentary testifies to the progressive relegation to history of both French Symbolism and British Decadent poetry of the 1890s. Soon Davray would offer an even more alarming analysis: in February 1914 he declared that the 'period of transition' of the 1890s, in which Symons was a key figure, 'had failed to produce the expected results'.[49]

Symons's breakdown in 1908 and subsequent disappearance from the forefront of the literary scene put an end to a fruitful connection with French-speaking writers at what was already a charged moment of literary history. *Antée* and its publishing house foundered at the close of 1907 despite André Gide's attempts to rescue them.[50] The following year, Gide became one of the contributors to the *Nouvelle Revue Française* (*NRF*). Launched anew in February 1909, after an aborted attempt in November 1908 under Eugène Montfort's editorship, the *NRF* was to change the French literary landscape. It adopted the pattern of appearing first as a periodical before Gaston Gallimard set up the famous publishing house in 1911. Under Gide's mentorship, the *NRF* also introduced the dominant French literary aesthetics of the twentieth century (Gourmont was banished to literary purgatory for some time due to his enmity with the journal's editors). Symons may thus have lost an opportunity to be part of the redesigned French map. In a 1918 article on Verlaine and Britain, Georges Jean-Aubry — a musicologist and translator of Joseph Conrad into French — paid tribute to Symons on Verlaine's behalf.[51] Jean-Aubry (1882–1950) belonged to a generation for whom Symons had been influential, especially as far as Franco-British literary relations were concerned. The Modernist period had begun, and with it a new, second phase of these relations.

The Unfortunate Modernist

Symons was characterised as a late-Victorian author in the short-lived *Navire d'argent*, which appeared between June 1925 and May 1926. Under the ownership and editorship of Adrienne Monnier (1892–1955), this literary review, as financially unsuccessful as it was highly influential, made a resounding debut by publishing Monnier and Sylvia Beach's French translation of T. S. Eliot's 'The Love Song of J. Alfred Prufrock' (1915). A draft of James Joyce's *Finnegan's Wake* (publ. in book form 1939) and an excerpt of Yeats's *The Trembling of the Veil* (1922) soon followed in its pages.[52] The *Navire d'argent*'s French contributors included Paul Claudel, Paul Valéry, André Chamson, Joseph Delteil, Valéry Larbaud, and Ramon Fernandez. Indeed, the review was particularly remarkable for its internationalist spirit: it embraced 'a pleiad of Anglo-Saxon writers' such as e. e. cummings, Ernest Hemingway, and, surprisingly, Symons. A selection of Symons's translated writings were listed in its second issue, including the 'Preface' to *William Blake* (1907), which had just appeared in the September issue in a translation by Georges Luciani.[53] The *Navire d'argent* reinforced Symons's association with poetry and the visual arts, and, in doing so, possibly sidelined his more comprehensive interest in the 'seven arts'. It also pre-empted any recognition of Symons as a contemporary writer by listing his publications in a recapitulative bibliography of late-Victorian writings ('les derniers Victoriens') translated into French.[54] Simultaneously, Frédéric Roger-Cornaz, who had worked on Walter Pater's *The Renaissance*, translated Symons's 'The Journal of Henry Luxulyan' and 'The Death of Peter Waydelin' in the *Revue européenne* (1923–31), which was published by the Éditions du Sagittaire.[55] Cornaz's translation attests to an enduring readership for Symons in France, at least in Modernist cosmopolitan publications. Another transnational venture, the Hours Press owned by the British émigrée and Modernist muse Nancy Cunard specialising in limited print runs and beautifully designed books, published Symons's *Mes souvenirs* (1929). This was certainly in response to his dedication of the nostalgic *Café Royal and Other Essays* (1923) to Cunard whom Symons had also encouraged to found her private press. The last translated text released in Symons's lifetime was 'Philip Massinger', from his 1919 collection *Studies in the Elizabethan Drama*; it was printed in the high-brow *Revue politique et littéraire* in 1933.[56] Symons's journalistic practice of giving the maximum visibility to his writings by having them translated and circulated in France may have persisted, but the literary world was no longer particularly responsive to it. Academe was even colder in its reception of the collections he published in the 1920s.

The Academic Reception

As Symons was issuing the initial volumes of his *Complete Works*, Thomas Earle Welby published the first monograph on the poet and critic: *Arthur Symons: A Critical Study* (1925). Welby's laudatory language reads less easily nowadays, but his early appreciation paved the way for scholars to review Symons's writings; this, in turn, made his *oeuvre* an integral part of the British literary heritage and academic syllabi. André Koszul, a Professor of English Literature at the University of Strasburg, reviewed Welby's study in the *Revue anglo-américaine*, a newly created university journal with a 'livres' section and a 'comité de patronage' that included the British Ambassador in France, Henri Bergson, Gustave Lanson, André Chevrillon, Mary Duclaux (*née* Robinson), Edmund Gosse, and Rudyard Kipling.[57] In October 1923, Louis Cazamian and Charles Cestre, respectively professors of English and American Literature at the Sorbonne, became the journal's editors.

In the same journal, the 'agrégé' André Brulé described *From Toulouse-Lautrec to Rodin with Some Personal Impressions* (1929) as 'a picture of a certain literary state of mind of the closing years of the nineteenth century' ('la peinture d'un certain état d'esprit littéraire des dernières années du XIXe siècle').[58] Symons's tendency to recycle material elicited 'a sort of saddened irritation' ('une sorte d'irritation attristée') as the reviewer noted 'too many repetitions' ('trop de redites').[59] Now a mature writer, Symons seemed nonetheless to have 'remained the man he was between twenty and thirty years old' ('il est resté l'homme qu'il était entre 20 et 30 ans'), returning to 'pleasures' that 'seem quite out of date nowadays' ('qui paraissent bien périmés maintenant').[60] As in Britain, Symons appeared old-fashioned because French mores had changed.[61] A living incarnation of a long-departed spirit, Symons, when he appeared at all, now seemed an oddity. In 1939, William Rothenstein mentioned seeing an elderly Symons during a concert by Yvette Guilbert, one of his 1890s muses. He concluded that Symons had not truly survived the 1890s — a period he had once so brilliantly embodied — and even admitted to believing the poet had died long ago.[62]

The following year, Albert Farmer's *Le Mouvement esthétique et 'décadent' en Angleterre (1873–1900)* (1931) considered Decadence quite favourably, but restricted its evaluation of Symons's achievements to his editorship of *The Savoy* and his 1890s poetry: for Farmer, Symons's verse embodied 'the acute modernism, the complacent artificiality, and the eroticism heralding a fashion already prepared by

Wilde' ('le modernisme aigu, l'artificialité complaisante et l'érotisme anon[çant] une mode déjà préparée par Wilde').[63] Farmer's seminal monograph established the academic study of British Aestheticism in France, but it was possibly limited in its argument: in choosing to focus on books, it passed over the aesthetes' hundreds of articles, essays, and reviews and ignored the journalistic basis of the movement.[64] Here, Symons's contribution began and ended with some notable 1890s British pieces; the collections he was in the process of arranging in the 1920s faded into the background. At the same time, Madeleine Cazamian, a scholar of British literature, published *Le Roman et les idées en Angleterre: l'anti-intellectualisme et l'esthétisme (1880–1900)*. This study contained numerous errors about Symons even as it judged him worthy of a lasting place in literary history.[65] Cazamian and her husband, Louis, occupied a key position in the French academic world: they were distinguished scholars who helped to widen the scope of university syllabi, championing modern texts and embedding them in the larger context of literary history. Their work coincided with the late 1920s revival of Decadence; this manifested itself in Remy de Gourmont's 1929 re-publication of *Promenades littéraires*, for instance, which included 'Les Décadents'.[66] Symons, then, was being read as a minor critic and poet in the academic world, hovering somewhere between Decadence and Symbolism; at the same time, Symbolism itself was undergoing a process of reassessment, mainly thanks to an exhibition at the Bibliothèque nationale de France in 1936. The role of foreign influences on the movement was noted, and Symons appears at several points in the extensive catalogue: as a participant in Mallarmé's *mardis* and as a mediator of French Symbolist poetry abroad.[67] *The Symbolist Movement in Literature*, *Images of Good and Evil*, and *Aubrey Beardsley* are also listed here.

Partial Recognition

When Symons died on 22 January 1945 no one seemed very willing to discuss the 'Yellow Nineties' or his *oeuvre*, except in a few obituary notices. In France, it took Roger Lhombreaud's 1963 biography to spark fresh interest from scholars and translators. While Richard Ellmann was dismissive, Pierre Leyris wrote a glowing review: he recounted how Ezra Pound's praise of *Spiritual Adventures* triggered his own interest in Symons's collection of short stories, which he could no longer find in France.[68] Educated alongside Pierre Klossowski at the renowned Lycée Jeanson de Sailly, Leyris became a prominent translator of 'untranslatable writers' — Herman Melville, Blake, Thomas de Quincey, Yeats — and less canonical modernist writers such as Djuna Barnes, Jean Rhys, and Kathleen Raine. He published these translations in the 'Domaine anglais' collection he had set up in the Mercure de France publishing house.[69] Leyris had read some of Symons's prefaces, his *William Blake*, and his translations of Baudelaire; he also remembered Yeats's biography. He belonged to a generation who received Symons's writings second-hand, transmitted via the Modernists. In his 1964 review, 'Pour Arthur Symons', Leyris drew a nuanced picture: here, Symons was a man who replaced his father's Methodism with an 'aesthetic religion' and, following a personal acquaintance with most of the *fin-de-siècle* poets, developed a sustained and genuine interest for France. Mentioning *The Savoy* and *The Symbolist Movement*, Leyris translated excerpts from Symons's portraits of Verlaine and Mallarmé and praised his penetration of these poets, comparing it to the work of a spiritual medium. Symons was a great essayist, he argued, until 'the terrible turning-point of his forty-fourth year' ('le tournant terrible de sa quarante-troisième année') in 1908, when he experienced a bout of psychosis.[70] Symons recounted the episode afterwards, Leyris noted, before translating a quotation from *Confessions: A Study in Pathology* (1930) which appeared in Lhombreaud's biography. *Spiritual Adventures*, however, was no study in pathology. Drawing a parallel between Symons and his fictional characters, Leyris was struck by their loneliness.[71] Each of Symons's heroes was a solitary figure, and like Symons, each was 'a pilgrim of the absolute who is also a knight of paradox' ('un pèlerin de l'absolu qui est aussi un chevalier du paradoxe').[72] Like Merrill, Leyris praised Symons's sincerity and he introduced his translation of an excerpt from 'Seaward Lackland' by comparing it to Hawthorne and to Hogg's *Confessions of a Justified Sinner* (1824) noting its 'dark theological or psycho-theological atmosphere' ('sombre atmosphère théologique ou psycho-théologique').[73] As a contributor to the *Mercure de France*, Leyris acknowledged that he was heir to Symons and paid tribute to his contributions by publishing a full translation of *Aventures spirituelles* in 1964, in which he called for an English re-edition of the best of his writings.[74]

Over the last few decades, French-speaking scholars have taken their cue from Leyris's translation just as they have been indebted to Farmer's and Louise Rosenblatt's landmark monographs.[75] Contemporary scholars interested in *fin-de-siècle* Anglo-French exchanges have furthered Symons's cause. Besides French translations of some of his critical writings, studies of Symons mainly come from scholars of comparative literature, who either read him as a Symbolist poet or as a man of the 1890s; Symington, for example, discusses his translations of Mallarmé and complicates the definition of Symbolist criticism as 'a second-degree symbolization, *i.e.* the symbolization of an object already functioning as a symbol'.[76] Now more than ever, Symons's place as a key mediator between French and British Symbolism appears unquestionable. As this chapter has delineated, though, his cosmopolitanism also materialised in his activity as a journalist on both sides of the Channel. Symons's transnational journalistic practices far exceeded his editorship of *The Savoy* and continue to await further studies.

Notes to Chapter 7

1. I would like to thank the reviewers of the first version of this chapter for their stimulating comments and careful reading.
2. Arthur Symons to Remy de Gourmont, 16 January 1889, in Remy de Gourmont, *Correspondance*, ed. by Vincent Gogibu, 3 vols (Paris: Éditions du Sandre, 2010), I, 173. All translations are the author's own unless otherwise stated.
3. See Stéphane Mallarmé to Arthur Symons, 12 January 1897, in *Correspondance*, ed. by Henri Mondor and Lloyd James Austin, 11 vols (Paris: Gallimard, 1983), IX, 42; and Miceala Symington, *Écrire le tableau: l'approche poétique de la critique d'art à l'époque symboliste* (Bern: Peter Lang, 2006), p. 190.
4. See Ducrey, 'Le Passeur du symbolisme français'.

5. Madeleine Cazamian, *Le Roman et les idées en Angleterre: l'anti-intellectualisme et l'esthétisme (1880–1900)* (Paris: Champion, 1935), p. 225.
6. In a letter dated 30 October 1888, Gourmont reminds Villiers that Symons, 'jeune écrivain écossais [*sic*], plein de talent, collaborateur de la *Westminster Review*' asks for permission to translate *L'Eve future*, and solicits permission to respond to the young writer because, 'un Anglais, même au courant de nos littératures peut se trouver embarrassé par bien des petits détails, et l'intérêt de votre gloire [...] exige qu'il soit renseigné'; see Gourmont, *Correspondance*, I, 169, 171. The article Gourmont refers to is: Arthur Symons, 'Villiers de l'Isle-Adam', *Woman's World*, 24 (October 1889), 657–60. No other letters between Symons and Gourmont appear.
7. See also Remy de Gourmont, 'Littérature anglaise', *Mercure de France*, 1:6 (June 1890), 219–20.
8. Arthur Waugh, 'London Letter', *Critic*, 20 (9 December 1893), 383. Between 1890 and 1896, Symons devoted twelve articles to Verlaine, whom he had first met in Paris on 29 April 1890. They included 'Verlaine in London', *Star*, 22 November 1893, 2; and 'Paul Verlaine', *New Review*, 9:55 (December 1893), 609–17. This publicised Verlaine's visit to London, which Symons organised with William Rothenstein. See also Symons, 'Tears in my Heart', *The Academy*, 38 (12 July 1890), 31.
9. Symons's first article was 'Frédéri Mistral', *National Review*, 8 (December 1886), 659–70; see also 'A French Blake: Odilon Redon', *Art Review*, 7 (July 1890), 206–07; repr. 'Odilon Redon', *Revue indépendante*, 18 (March 1891), 390–96.
10. [Arthur Symons], 'Some French Verse', *Saturday Review*, 84 (24 July 1897), 94–95. Symons mainly reviewed French writings, translations, and performances for the *Saturday Review* and *The Athenaeum*.
11. Remy de Gourmont, 'Les Décadents', 'Anecdotes littéraires', in *Promenades littéraires*, 7 vols (Paris: Mercure de France, 1929), I, 191–97 (p. 196).
12. [Anon.], 'Historique', <http://www.mercuredefrance.fr/unepage-historique-historique-1-1-0-1.html> [accessed 14 May 2016].
13. 'The Pilgrim', 'Un manifeste littéraire anglais', *Mercure de France*, 4:27 (March 1892), 200.
14. See Gourmont's review of *Days and Nights*, 'Littérature anglaise'; R[emy de] G[ourmont], 'Journaux et revues', *Mercure de France*, 5:29 (May 1892), 82–85; 'Journaux et Revues', *Mercure de France*, 5:31 (July 1892), 276–77; and 'Les Livres', *Mercure de France*, 5:31 (July 1892), 274–75; cf. Arthur Symons, 'J.-K. Huysmans', *Fortnightly Review*, 51 (March 1892), 402–04; and 'Paul Verlaine', *National Review*, 19 (June 1892), 501–15.
15. Arnold Van Gennep, 'Revue de la quinzaine', *Mercure de France*, 74:268 (August 1908), 697.
16. Arthur Symons, 'La Littérature anglaise', *Mercure de France*, 10:50 (February 1894), 105–11. No translator is mentioned.
17. Arthur Symons, 'English Literature in 1893', *The Athenaeum*, 3454 (6 January 1894), 17–19.
18. Remy de Gourmont, 'Livres', *Mercure de France*, 15:68 (August 1895), 243; Paul Verlaine, 'Deux poètes anglais', *Revue encyclopédique*, 114 (July 1895), 325–26.
19. Henry-D. Davray, 'Revues et journaux', *Mercure de France*, 17:75 (March 1896), 438.
20. Ibid.: 'Très luxueusement édité, *The Savoy* sera un excellent périodique, et un document très complet sur l'effort artistique actuel en Angleterre'.
21. 'Le *Savoy* s'affirme comme protagoniste du mouvement qui a lieu actuellement et qui fixera pendant une époque l'Art anglais' (Henry-D. Davray, 'Lettres anglaises', *Mercure de France*, 19:80 (August 1896), 373).
22. Stuart Merrill, 'Arthur Symons', *Aube*, 2 (January 1897), 151–53 (p. 151). Subsequent references in the main body of the text.
23. [Anon.], 'Mr. Arthur Symons as Translator', p. 370.
24. Arthur Symons, 'Walter Pater', *Mercure de France*, 25:98 (February 1898), 450–62. George Khnopff later translated *Imaginary Portraits* into French as *Portraits imaginaires* (Paris: Société du Mercure de France, 1898).
25. George Meredith, *Essai sur la comédie: de l'idée de comédie et des exemples de l'esprit comique précédé d'une introduction par Arthur Symons*, trans. by Henry-D. Davray (Paris: Société du Mercure de France, 1898), p. 12. Symons's essay was first published as 'A Note on George Meredith', *Fortnightly Review*, 62 (November 1897), 673–78.

26. Henry-D. Davray, 'Lettres anglaises', *Mercure de France*, 34:125 (May 1900), 553–59; Arthur Symons, 'Les Dessins de Rodin', *La Plume*, 12 (June 1900), 383–84, repr. in Octave Mirbeau and others, *Auguste Rodin et son œuvre*, trans. by H.-D. Davray (Paris: Éditions de la Plume, 1900), pp. 47–48. *La Plume littéraire, artistique et sociale* (1889–1914) had been founded by Léon Deschamps and organised dinners at Café du Soleil d'Or for contributors and subscribers. Against the division between 'les jeunes', i.e. avant-garde writers, and more established writers, the magazine supported Verlaine. In the periodical, Symons rubbed shoulders with Gustave Kahn, Stuart Merrill, Camille Mauclair, and Octave Mirbeau.
27. See Arthur Symons, 'Casanova à Dux: un chapitre d'histoire inédit', *Mercure de France*, 48:166 (October 1903), 60–88. Between 1900 and 1914 Davray mentioned Symons's publications, including his periodical articles, in the sections entitled 'Revue du mois', 'Variétés', 'Lettres anglaises', and 'Revue de la quinzaine'. See, for instance, Davray, 'Lettres anglaises', *Mercure de France*, 64:228 (15 November 1906), 298–302, which praised Symons's 'masterly critical study' ('magistrale étude', p. 300) of Ibsen in 'Henrik Ibsen', *Quarterly Review*, 409 (October 1906), 375–97.
28. Louis Thomas (1885–1962) published *Les Dernières Leçons de Marcel Schwob sur François Villon* (Paris: Éditions de Psyché, 1906), and later translated from English, German, and Hungarian. Sometimes publishing under several pseudonyms, he edited the letters of Chateaubriand and other eighteenth-century writers. He embraced antisemitism during the 1940s and was accordingly blacklisted in 1945; see Andries Van den Abeele, <http://www.andriesvandenabeele.net/index.htm> [accessed 1 October 2016].
29. *Poésies de Choderlos de Laclos*, ed. by Arthur Symons and Louis Thomas (Paris: chez Dorbon l'Aîné, 1908), and Symons's 'Appendice: une édition perdue des Liaisons dangereuses' (pp. 89–96). The appendix was first published by Symons in *Outlook* (9 and 16 September 1905). Symons had relied on Jean de Gourmont's new edition of the *Liaisons*. 'Une édition perdue des "Liaisons dangereuses"', written in French and signed 'Arthur Symons', was mentioned in 'Variétés', *Mercure de France*, 58:204 (15 December 1905), 633–38.
30. Arthur Symons, 'William Morris's Prose', *Saturday Review*, 84 (11 December 1897), 669–70, repr. in Symons, *Studies in Prose and Verse*; translated by Édouard and Louis Thomas as 'William Morris' in *Mercure de France* (15 December 1896), 221–32, repr. in Arthur Symons, *Portraits anglais*, trans. by Jack Cohen and others (Bruges: A. Herbert, 1907).
31. Arthur Symons, 'Un artiste dans ses attitudes: Oscar Wilde', *La Plume*, 371 (1 May 1905), 397–400.
32. Arthur Symons, *Aubrey Beardsley*, trans. by Jack Cohen, Édouard and Louis Thomas (Paris: Floury 1906). The Thomases translated the 'Preface' to the 1905 edition (pp. 13–24); Jack Cohen and Louis Thomas translated Symons's 1898 essay (pp. 25–48).
33. Arthur Symons, 'Chopin', trans. by Édouard and Louis Thomas, *Mercure musical*, 3:1 (January 1907), 323.
34. See *Arthur Symons: A Bibliography*, ed. by Beckson and others, p. 37.
35. Arthur Symons, 'Whistler', *Weekly Critical Review*, 28 (30 July 1903), 36–37; 29 (6 August 1903), 49–50; and 30 (13 August, 1903), 81–82.
36. Arthur Symons, 'The Improvements of Rome', *Weekly Critical Review*, 61 (18 March 1904), 215–16.
37. The *Weekly Critical Review* had offices in both London and New York, but was printed in France.
38. Arthur Symons, 'Hymn to Earth', *Weekly Critical Review*, 53 (22 January 1904), 15.
39. 'La meilleure façon d'acquérir la connaissance pratique d'une langue étrangère est de lire les journaux écrits dans cette langue' [the best way to acquire the practical knowledge of a foreign language is to read newspapers written in that language], [Anon.], *Weekly Critical Review*, 65 (8 April 1904), 279.
40. [Arthur Symons], 'Remy de Gourmont', *Saturday Review*, 96 (November 1903), 675–76. Symons's review also discussed Pierre de Querlon's *Remy de Gourmont*. Symons had reviewed Gourmont's *Le Livre des masques* in 'A Book of French Masks', *Saturday Review*, 82 (21 November 1896), 550–51.

41. On the *Anglo-French Review* see Birgit Van Puymbroeck, 'Anglo-French Relations in the *Anglo-French Review*: "Bien en Advienne"', *English Literature in Transition, 1880–1920*, 55 (2012), 69–93 (p. 69).
42. On Arthur Herbert, see Van den Abeele, 'Une maison d'édition brugeoise', <https://textyles.revues.org/796> [accessed 2 October 2016].
43. The collection was dedicated to Remy de Gourmont and reprinted Symons's 'Walter Pater', 'George Meredith', and essays from *Studies in Prose and Verse* (1904). Since Gourmont appeared to be less of a Symbolist proponent at the time, he also contributed to *Antée*.
44. Each of the Collection d'Antée's volumes was priced 5 francs and aimed at 'cette élite qui recherche des œuvres inédites qui ne se vendront jamais à 100.000 [*sic*] exemplaires, même à 0,95 cmes [*sic*] [...] et elle exige qu'on les lui serve en de belles éditions durables' [that elite which seeks out unpublished works that will never sell 100,000 [*sic*] copies, even at 95 centimes [*sic*] [...] and it demands to read them in fine, lasting editions]; *Antée*, 11 (1 March 1907), 1086. The list of forthcoming publications included 'Le Mouvement symboliste dans la littérature' and 'Les Aventures intellectuelles' by Symons.
45. Symons, *Poésies* (1907).
46. Arthur Symons, 'Quatre poèmes', trans. by Paul Verlaine, *Vers et prose*, 4 (1906), 10. *Vers et prose* (1905–28) was another new literary periodical; its contributors were mostly French turn-of-the-century writers. Symons showed his support by reviewing the first issue: see 'A New French Quarterly', *Outlook*, 15:383 (3 June 1905), 797. Symons's other contributions to *Vers et prose* included 'Qu'est-ce que la poésie', trans. by Edouard and Louis Thomas, *Vers et prose*, 3 (1905), 29–33; 'Le Chant du vagabond', trans. by Edouard and Louis Thomas, *Vers et prose*, 3 (1905), 97.
47. André Ruyters, 'La Critique d'Arthur Symons', *Antée*, 11 (April 1907), 1153–58 (p. 1155). The same issue includes a tribute to Beardsley by J.-E. Blanche, who also cites Symons's book on Beardsley. Cf. Arthur Symons, 'Le Mauvais-Riche', *Antée*, 13 (June 1907), 1269–74. Symons saw the book as a satire and interpretation of Nietzsche's writings.
48. Stuart Merrill, 'L'œuvre poétique d'Arthur Symons', *Antée*, 13 (June 1907), 66–82. Merrill included a letter by Symons of 26 April 1907, which provided a brief account of his life and travels (p. 72).
49. 'Le bel effort de cette période de transition n'a pas donné les résultats qu'on pouvait attendre de tant d'ardeur dépassée', Henry-D. Davray, 'Revue de la quinzaine', *Mercure de France*, 107:400 (16 February 1914), 862–66 (p. 864).
50. See Pascal Mercier, 'André Gide stratège ou tacticien?', *La Belle Époque des revues, 1880–1914*, ed. by Jacqueline Pluet-Despatin, Michel Leymarie, and Jean-Yves Mollier (Paris: Éditions de l'IMEC, 2002), pp. 93–100 (p. 94).
51. Georges Jean-Aubry, 'Paul Verlaine et l'Angleterre: 1872–1892', *Revue de Paris*, 6 (1 December 1918), 600–20.
52. See Laure Murat, *Passage de l'Odéon: Sylvia Beach, Adrienne Monnier et la vie littéraire à Paris dans l'entre-deux-guerres* (Paris: Gallimard/Folio, 2005), p. 111.
53. Arthur Symons, 'La Place de William Blake', trans. by Georges Luciani, *Navire d'argent*, 4 (September 1925), 371–82. It was followed by short texts by A. C. Swinburne and Marcel Brion, along with a 'Choix de poèmes' translated by Anne Hervieu and Auguste Morel, and 'La Critique française de William Blake' (pp. 437–40).
54. [Anon.], 'Bibliographie. La Littérature anglaise traduite en français. VI Les Derniers Victoriens, les Edwardiens et les Georgiens', *Navire d'argent*, 6 (1 November 1925), 22.
55. Arthur Symons, *Journal de Henry Luxulyan*, trans. by Frédéric Roger-Cornaz (Paris: Kra, Coll. Carnets littéraires, Série cosmopolite, 1928). The Éditions du Sagittaire specialised in *fin-de-siècle* writers in limited print runs before turning to contemporary literature and becoming a forum for the Surrealists. See François Laurent and Béatrice Mousli, *Les Éditions du Sagittaire, 1919–1979* (Paris: Éditions de l'IMEC, 2003). The publishing house founded by Simon Kra had various appellations: Éditions du Sagittaire Simon Kra, Simon Kra, or simply Kra.
56. Arthur Symons, 'Philip Massinger', trans. by Georges Darondeau, *Revue politique et littéraire*, 15 (5 August 1933), 472–76.

57. André Koszul was a Mary Shelley scholar; he translated Mary and Percy Bysshe Shelley, Shakespeare, and Elizabethan drama into French; see <http://irhis.recherche.univ-lille3.fr/00-SiteUniversite/htdocs/koszul-andre.html> [accessed 1 September 2016]. See also Koszul, 'Review of *Arthur Symons, A Critical Study* by T. Earle Welby', *Revue anglo-américaine*, 4:3 (December 1926), 255–56. The *Revue anglo-américaine* was published by the Presses universitaires de France from 1923 to 1936. Between 1923 and 1935, Symons is mentioned on eight occasions.
58. André Brulé, 'Review of *From Toulouse-Lautrec to Rodin* by Arthur Symons,' *Revue anglo-américaine*, 8:1 (1930), 185–86 (p. 185).
59. Ibid., p. 186.
60. Ibid., p. 186.
61. Cf., for example, Kineton Parkes, 'The Decadence' [review of *From Toulouse-Lautrec to Rodin* by Arthur Symons], *Bookman*, 77.459 (December 1929), 226.
62. William Rothenstein, *Since Fifty: Men and Memories, 1922–1938: Recollections of William Rothenstein* (London: Faber, 1939), p. 305.
63. Albert Farmer, *Le Mouvement esthétique et 'décadent' en Angleterre (1873–1900)* (Paris: Champion, 1931), p. 282.
64. Floris Delattre, 'Review of Albert Farmer, *Le Mouvement esthétique et décadent en Angleterre (1873–1900)*', *Revue belge de philologie et d'histoire*, 13 (1934), 273.
65. Cazamian, *Le Roman et les idées en Angleterre*, p. 225.
66. In Britain, this revival materialised, for instance, in *An Anthology of 'Nineties Verse'*, ed. by A. J. A. Symons (London: Elkin Mathews and Marrot, 1928), with ten poems by Symons.
67. *Cinquantenaire du symbolisme; exposition de manuscrits autographes, estampes, peintures, sculptures, éditions rares, portraits, objets d'art*, ed. by André Jaulme and Henri Moncel (Paris: Éditions des Bibliothèques nationales, 1936), pp. 37, 243.
68. Pierre Leyris, 'Pour Arthur Symons: à propos d'une biographie', *Mercure de France* (January 1964), 3–10; cf. Richard Ellmann, 'Dangerous Acquaintances', *New York Review of Books*, 4:12 (15 July 1965), <http://www.nybooks.com/articles/1965/07/15/dangerous-acquaintances/> [accessed 14 April 2016].
69. See Pierre Leyris, *La Chambre du traducteur* (Paris: José Corti, 2007).
70. Leyris, 'Pour Arthur Symons', p. 7.
71. Ibid., p. 9.
72. Ibid., p. 10.
73. Ibid., p. 10.
74. Pierre Leyris devotes some lines to his arrival in the 'old dusty' offices of the *Mercure de France* in *Pour mémoire: ruminations d'un petit clerc à l'usage de ses frères humains et des vers légataires* (Paris: Corti, 2002), p. 246; Arthur Symons, *Aventures spirituelles*, trans. by Pierre Leyris (Paris: Mercure de France, 1964), p. 9.
75. Louise Rosenblatt, *L'Idée de l'art pour l'art dans la littérature anglaise pendant la période victorienne* (Paris: Champion, 1931), initiated a vein of studies of Symons in comparative literature. See for instance, Robert Guiette, 'Un cas de symbiose dans le Symbolisme en France', *Comparative Literature Studies*, 4 (1967), 103–07.
76. Symington, *Écrire le tableau*, p. 220. Besides the already cited articles by Ducrey and Symington, see also Arthur Symons, 'Le Mouvement symboliste: introduction' and 'Stéphane Mallarmé', trans. by Bénédicte Coste, in *Les grands mouvements littéraires anglo-saxons*, ed. by Christine Reynier, (Paris: Houdiard, 2009), 72–85; Arthur Symons, 'Aubrey Beardsley', trans. by Michèle Duclos, *Temporel* (25 April 2009), <http://temporel.fr/Arthur-Symons-version-francaise> [accessed 21 April 2016]; and Régine Sargeant-Quittanson, 'Arthur Symons et les mouvements décadents des années 1890' (unpublished doctoral thesis, University of Rheims, 1981).

PART III

Places and Connections

CHAPTER 8

'They Keep Mad People There': Symons and Venice

Nicholas Freeman

> Que c'est triste Venise
> Au temps des amours mortes
> Que c'est triste Venise
> Quand on ne s'aime plus
> Les musées, les églises
> Ouvrent enfin leurs portes
> Inutile beauté
> Devant nos yeux déçus.
>
> [How sad Venice is
> When loves have died
> How sad Venice is
> When we love no longer
> The museums and churches
> Open their doors
> Useless beauty
> Meets our disappointed eyes.]
>
> CHARLES AZNAVOUR, 'Que c'est triste Venise' (1964)

> Songs of Venice, poignant, passionate, melancholy and gay songs of Venice, what is really your meaning, what lies under the beauty of your melodies?
>
> ARTHUR SYMONS, *Confessions: A Study in Pathology* (1930)

Arthur Symons visited Venice four times between 1894 and 1908. The floating city bewitched and fascinated him; its 'soft and entangling enchantments' were irresistible.[1] As a connoisseur of the urban, Symons was astonished and overwhelmed, and having 'devoutly practised' what he called 'the religion of the eyes',[2] found himself akin to the child in Browning's poem who 'gazed and gazed and gazed and gazed, | Amazed, amazed, amazed, amazed' at a painting of Venus.[3] Daniel Roserra, the protagonist of Symons's 'An Autumn City' (1905), typically has 'no interest in historical associations or in the remains of ugly things that happened to be old, or in visiting the bric-à-brac museums of the fine arts which make some of the more tolerable countries tedious'.[4] This was very much Symons's usual attitude when travelling around Europe, but Venice was quite unlike anywhere else he had even been, and he 'spent weeks' in its churches, 'climbing upon ladders, and propping myself against altars, and lying on my back to look at pictures'.[5] The city's rich history, the 'superb, barbaric patchwork' of its architecture, and its absorbing literary, artistic, and musical associations delighted him.[6] 'Only to live, only to be | In Venice is enough for me', he wrote in March 1894.[7] He was equally effusive in letters home. 'But Venice! There is certainly nothing like Venice', he told his friend, James Dykes Campbell two months later. 'I have made a sort of vow to go there every year, if I can'.[8]

Symons had only been back in England for a few weeks when his mentor, Walter Pater, died in late July 1894. Pater was a profound and life-long influence on the younger writer, who used the notorious 'Conclusion' of *The Renaissance* (1873) to license his unending quest for new experiences and his rejection of 'facile orthodoxy'.[9] As Karl Beckson notes, it was Pater who showed Symons how 'creative intelligence' could structure 'random impressions into a unified aesthetic'.[10] Underlying this was the crucial question Pater asked in the 'Preface' to his controversial study: 'What is this song or picture, this engaging personality presented in life or in a book, to *me*? What effect does it really produce on me?'[11] In answering this, Symons was rarely interested in engaging with representations of his chosen cities by others: his 'London: A Book of Aspects' (1918) passes over Dickens in a single impatient line. He preferred to explore what he called in the title of his first article on Venice, and elsewhere, 'impressions and sensations', and was unapologetically subjective, even egotistical, in his responses to the places he saw.[12] The Venice of Tintoretto, Bellini, and Goldoni, and later of Ruskin, Musset, Wagner, and Browning, interested him far less than the city he fashioned from his own perceptions. Ruskin's *The Stones of Venice* (1851–53) concentrated on the evolution of Venetian architecture, combining detailed studies of individual buildings such as St Mark's with a wider treatment of the inter-relationship between the fabric of the city and its spiritual decline. Symons however had no artistic or architectural training, and only a limited knowledge of Venetian history. He sought instead a personal relationship with the places he visited, his analyses and evocations foregrounding his perceptions of the moment rather than attempting to place those perceptions in a more precise topographical or historical context. 'For me', he wrote in 1903, 'cities are like people, with souls and temperaments of their own, and it has always been one of my chief pleasures to associate with the souls and temperaments congenial to me'.[13] Venice, along with Rome and Seville, he adored. 'What a delight it was to me merely to be alive, and living in them', he declared; 'what a delight it is to me to think of them, to imagine myself in their streets and on their waters!'[14]

This personalised version of Venice prompted a series of essays and poems during the 1890s and early 1900s, works in which Symons reiterated his 'impression of that unreality which is Venice, the masque or ballet',[15] sought to convey the unique experience of travelling by gondola, and depicted the city as somewhere free from the hectic industry and technology which characterised modernity's development in London and Paris, though by 1907 he feared that 'the modern spirit' was beginning to destroy Venice 'with a literal, calculated destruction'.[16] Symons funded his travels in part with essays about the places he visited, and his bibliography reveals not only his itinerary but also the extent to which he moved between public and more private forms of expression, cannibalising and recycling material in order to maximise its financial reward. He was a mixture of hyper-refined aesthete and connoisseur and commercially-driven journalist who 'placed' essays and articles to best advantage: he did not employ an agent until 1907. He was on good terms with leading magazine editors such as Frank Harris of the *Saturday Review*, and might earn £15 to £20 for an essay requiring only a few days' work. Travel writing was therefore doubly appealing, since it allowed him to combine his European explorations with a steady income. Symons may have had no interest in finance beyond his personal balance sheet, but he undoubtedly profited from sterling being the most powerful currency in the world. British economic power let him live far more cheaply in Italy than he could ever have done in London, even when renting a palazzo on the Giudecca.

The first fruits of Symons's Venetian explorations were 'Venice in Easter', published in the popular American periodical *Harper's New Monthly Magazine*, and the four poems of 'Intermezzo: Venetian Nights', published in *London Nights* in June 1895, a more exclusive collection with a print run of only 500 copies.[17] His next trip, in 1897, led in due course to the impressionistic essay 'Venetian Glamour' for the *Saturday Review* (14 October 1899), and 'Venetian Night', a poem collected in *Images of Good and Evil* (1900). His lengthiest account of the city is 'Venice' in *Cities of Italy* (1907), which began as 'Venice in Easter' and 'The Soul of Venice', another contribution to the *Saturday Review* (9 November 1901), before being enlarged for *Cities* (1903) and expanded further four years later in order to incorporate material from 'Venetian Sensations' (*Saturday Review*, 6 August 1904), a piece written following his third visit, this time made in the company of his wife, Rhoda. They returned in 1908, with Symons publishing a curious account of his responses to Venetian music. Appearing once again in the *Saturday Review* (17 October 1908), it was Symons's final publication that year, and the last essay he wrote before his breakdown. Although he never again went to Italy, his memories informed poems and articles for years afterwards.[18] Even his final book, the misprinted *Amoris victimia* [sic] which appeared in 1940 when he was seventy-five, continued to testify to his two enduring but tormenting loves: Lydia, his mistress during the mid-1890s, and, in 'Venice 1897', the place where he had experienced such joy and terror.

Despite his initially blissful impressions of Venice, it was not long before Symons began to dwell upon its darker aspects. Invoking an image from his recurrent nightmares, he found it was disconcertingly easy to lose oneself in the 'coil of entangling alleys, which seemed to be tightening about me like a snake'.[19] 'In Venice one is as if caught in an immense network, or spider's web, which, as one walks in its midst, seems to tighten about one', he added when revising the essay for *Cities of Italy*.[20] Images of constriction and confinement became increasingly prevalent in his accounts of the streets and subsidiary canals, and the open water of the lagoon only added to the oppressive character of the whole, leaving him with a sense of being marooned or cut off. 'There is no more bewildering city', he wrote, 'and as night comes on the bewilderment grows almost disquieting. One seems to be turning in a circle, to which there is no outlet, and from which all one's desire is to escape'.[21] London was insufferably noisy and motorised. It 'was once habitable', he said, but 'the machines have killed it'.[22] Venice was hushed and muted, its backwaters silent, melancholy, and desolate; Symons's excellent command of Italian meant that any loneliness he endured was not attributable simply to linguistic isolation.

A subtly menacing environment, clearly an ancestor of the city depicted by Patricia Highsmith, Daphne Du Maurier, and Ian McEwan is evident even in 'Venice in Easter'. 'There is no city in Europe which contains so much silence as Venice', Symons writes, 'and the silence of Giudecca' — the island to the south which seems to stare longingly across the Giudecca Canal to St Mark's Square — 'is more lonely than any silence in Venice'.[23] In 'Venetian Glamour', 'glamour' used here in its sense of magic or enchantment, his feelings had intensified. He told his readers:

> The scene is permeated with an indescribable and exquisite sadness. When the black gondolas go by with their black-covered coffin-shaped cabins, the sense of sadness becomes nigh unbearable. Their aspect is lugubrious, as that of a catafalque, and explains, along with the sad dark canals and the mournful lagoons, the dislike, amounting to horror, which Venice inspires in some breasts.[24]

A prose version of Liszt's *La Lugubre Gondola* (1883) or Böcklin's *The Isle of the Dead* (1880–86), the essay was far removed from the Venice of Symons's letter to Campbell, insisting that 'you begin to forget your soul' in a city that, despite its profusion of churches, was always profane rather than sacred, offering 'every grace of the flesh but not a hint of spirituality'.[25] It also demonstrates how he had moved away from a treatment of Venetian melancholy that was, as Catherine Maxwell says, 'less a personal emotion than a kind of aesthetic effect'.[26] Feeling that nothing was to be gained from attempting to picture Venice's appearance, since it was already 'a finished, conscious work of art', Symons turned his gaze inward, employing the city as a visual index of his own fears and fantasies.[27] This took him ever further from touristic belles-lettres and into far more disturbing terrain.

His final visit to Venice in the sweltering autumn of 1908 saw Symons working on what he called 'very obscene'[28] poems and 'Music in Venice', a hastily-written piece which evoked 'strange and obscure secrets' and 'the dungeons under the "Bridge of Sighs", a water prison where men languished without hope'.[29] According to the dates in his *Collected Works*, he also composed 'Venice', a poem subtitled 'Minuet: The Masque of the Ghosts' (26 August) which blends Wilde's 'The Harlot's House' and the *commedia dell'arte*, in addressing 'the tyrant of the years' who 'Commands you to perpetuate [...] The sunken splendours of her state'.[30] By the time 'Music in Venice' appeared, Symons was in the sunken splendour of his own former state, and seemed hopelessly insane. He would later judge the essay as 'a document in which my madness is most evident', a view shared by contemporaries such as Max Beerbohm, and subsequently, his biographers Roger Lhombreaud and Karl Beckson.[31]

Hélène Cixous calls Venice 'a name for countless interior and exterior mysteries', and the city is the ideal place for acts of self-exploration and analysis.[32] Taken as a whole, these essays and poems show Symons powerfully attuned to a sense of duality which echoed the unresolved tensions in his own character. At times populous and festive, as in 'A Masque of Kings', an account of the meeting between King Umberto and Kaiser Wilhelm in 1894, Venice's benign theatricality masked, to use an appropriately Venetian image, profound social inequality, political unrest, and even, as it became difficult to distinguish between objects and their reflections, perceptual instability. Uninterested in politics, Symons saw the poverty of Venetian fishermen as essentially picturesque, even when its squalor repelled him, and he certainly did not denounce the city as he did the apparently irredeemable Naples or Moscow. A significant proportion of Symons's urban aesthetic was based upon his sensitivity to mood and the relationship between the environment and his perception of it. He therefore found it difficult to negotiate between states of mind which mapped his perceptions onto his surroundings, and others in which he responded to external suggestion. As the *Athenæum*'s reviewer observed, he was 'afflicted with super-consciousness of life' and 'turn[ed] away from exteriority towards its own organization', a shift which saw his life 'playing with itself, exasperating itself, torturing itself'.[33]

Symons's catastrophic nervous collapse has encouraged his critics to read his work teleologically, with each reference to madness, imprisonment, or sensory derangement being prophetic, or in Lhombreaud's phrase, a moment of 'unconscious fore-knowledge'.[34] Instead of seeing his work as foretelling his fate, however, it would be more useful to understand it as a means by which he negotiated and explored his worries and unease, mediating them through his different personae (critic, poet, translator, essayist) or, to put it another way, using his work as an early variant of Breuer and Freud's 'talking cure', though Symons's 'writing cure' was more a means of inoculating himself against his fears than a banishing of the fears themselves. In this sense, his creativity operated as a temporary vaccine, whereby writing strengthened his resistance to contagion, but did not grant lasting immunity and needed to be all but constant to remain effective. This was why he repeatedly explored the same preoccupations. Andrew Mangravite remarks that Symons 'had been living off of his nerves for years, working himself up about things so that he could then sit down and write about it [*sic*]. It was only a matter of time before the nerves snapped'.[35] An urbane and personable exterior only partially concealed a plethora of anxieties; the serpent nightmares outlined in 'A Prelude to Life' (1905) and elsewhere indicate this very clearly. Fearing, as Mangravite says, that the overstrained strings would one day snap, Symons tested and inspected them relentlessly. His 'super-consciousness of life' was not therefore merely the egotistical narcissism of a self-obsessed Paterian (as those unsympathetic to his methods were wont to claim), but a vital means of keeping anxieties at bay. Transformed into art and placed upon paper, they were, for a while at least, unable to harm him. Edwin Block concludes that in 'dramatizing the privately unbearable truth, he helps to exorcise certain fears of madness and failure'.[36] Unfortunately, such strategies were not a permanent solution to his psychological malaise. The end result underscores Christopher Isherwood's claim: 'The normal healthy boy does not worry very much about his soul. And perhaps he is right. You will not make a plant grow in the earth if you are always digging it up to look at the roots'.[37]

In essays and poems, Symons tended to use 'I' to refer to a stylised version of himself. His travel writing constructs an image much like the character of Daniel Roserra, a leisured connoisseur who is free from quotidian responsibilities and drifts through Europe's cultural pleasures as his whims dictate. That he was invariably accompanied on these trips by friends such as Frank Willard, Havelock Ellis, or, following his marriage, Rhoda, goes unsaid. Financial and logistical concerns are almost never mentioned, and though he does at one point admit to losing his guidebook, he uses its absence as a stimulus for exploration rather than simply visiting a stationer's and purchasing a replacement.[38] His poems portray him as an amoral impressionist, observing life with painterly detachment, or else brooding solipsistically on his emotions. In his fiction, however, he adopts different methods of self-analysis, a point demonstrated at length in 'Extracts from the Journal of Henry Luxulyan', the final story in his *Spiritual Adventures*.

'Henry Luxulyan' is a complex and disconcerting blend of autobiography and invention. In his unpublished notes, 'The Genesis of Spiritual Adventures', probably written in the 1920s, Symons recalled that the story was 'mostly founded on actual facts' and 'not entirely imaginary'. 'I put much of my own temperament into it', he admitted, 'many of my impressions and adventures'.[39] Other material was supplied by his friend, the French aristocrat Mathilde, la Comtesse Victor Sallier de la Tour, to whom he dedicated *Cities*, and his reading of contemporary English and French fiction and newspapers.

Luxulyan is an amateur historian, living in London on a small private income and writing a never-to-be completed book on Attila the Hun — the link between Attila and Venice is not explicit, though its presence is significant for readers with a knowledge of Venetian history. He is the friend of a German Baroness, and when he is ruined by the collapse of the Argonaut Building Society to which he has entrusted his funds, she employs him as her librarian. The Baroness von Eckenstein, whose Christian name we never discover, is a woman of considerable intelligence and learning, but her face is horribly scarred, causing Luxulyan to recoil. Having been alone since the end of a relationship with Clare, a woman about whom the journal tells us almost nothing, Luxulyan is emotionally wounded, obsessively self-analytical, and misogynistic.[40] He is also troubled by 'nerves' which destabilise the supposed masculine rationality associated with historians and archivists.

Luxulyan discovers that the Baroness's injuries were inflicted by her philistine and distant husband, who, discovering her affair with a young Frenchman, threw vitriol in her face and then, when she had partially recovered after months of suffering, invited her lover to dinner so that he might behold the full extent of her injuries.

The Baroness falls in love with her librarian, who stifles his physical repugnance but remains self-absorbed. Caught between the demands of a necessarily furtive liaison and his desire to help Clare, who has nameless troubles of her own, Luxulyan's nerves begin to get the better of him. He holidays with the von Eckensteins in Cornwall, growing increasingly fond of the Baroness but finding her friendship and then love stifling in their intensity.

After a breakdown of sorts emphasised by a ten-month-gap in the journal, Luxulyan is in Italy, recuperating. 'Surely one gets well of every trouble in Venice', he writes, 'where, if anywhere in the world, there should be peace, the oblivion of water, of silence, the unreal life of sails?'[41] Even here though, he is haunted, finding the city threatening and mysterious. At last, he believes the Baroness has come to him, but whether this is actually the case is impossible to determine. When the journal comes to its abrupt end, he is reading Balzac and ill with fever. A year later, the narrator calls on the von Eckensteins in Rome, only to find that the Baroness is dead, having 'succumbed to a protracted illness' (p. 313). The implication is that she has either died from a broken heart, or that the Baron has murdered her.

As this outline suggests, Luxulyan is one of the many authorial doubles who haunt Symons's fiction: the title of *Spiritual Adventures* reverses its author's initials. 'A Prelude to Life' is an unacknowledged self-portrait, which makes liberal use of events from Symons's Cornish childhood and adolescence. 'Esther Kahn' features Philip Haygarth, the playwright and dramatic theorist who teaches a young Jewish actress about love and the arts of the stage. 'Christian Trevalga' depicts a Cornish pianist who succumbs to hallucination and madness while playing Chopin, Symons's favourite composer, while in 'An Autumn City' Roserra, another Cornishman, shares his love for the French town of Arles, and is Symons as he might have been with a larger income and enhanced social standing. Luxulyan however is the closest to Symons in terms of his interest in literature, and his affection for London, Cornwall, and Venice. The story makes a number of allusions to Symons's literary output, notably in the way the Baroness's injuries recall those in 'Bertha at the Fair: An Encounter', a piece Symons published in *The Savoy* nine years earlier, in which 'a wicked Baron' throws vitriol in his lover's face.[42]

The story's final section makes the most detailed use of Symons's own life. His surviving diaries are largely records of deadlines, payments, recitals, and theatrical performances, but if he had ever kept a more reflective journal, Luxulyan's gives a fair idea of what it may have been like.[43] Luxulyan's voice is indistinguishable from his creator's, and his observations could be (and occasionally are) taken from his essays. Like Symons, he lives in a Palladian house on the Giudecca, observing that 'To sit still, in Venice, is to be at home to every delight' (p. 301), a line from 'Venetian Sensations'. The sense that the story facilitated its author's self-exploration is encouraged by Luxulyan's confession that the best way to 'quiet' himself is 'by writing down all these fears and scruples of mine, as coldly as I can, as if they belonged to somebody else, in whose psychology I am interested' (p. 262). This calms his 'uneasiness', but he fears such solutions are but temporary and contingent. 'Who knows if I am only wrapping the blanket round my head once more', he ends the entry, 'in order that I may run through fire and not see it?' (p. 262). In his critical writing, Symons is rarely so candid, but the obvious similarity between himself and Luxulyan implies that the librarian's tactics were those he himself deployed.

Henry James's preface to *The Princess Casamassima* (1907), considered the difficulties of urban representation when the writer moved through the metropolis 'as with his head in a cloud of humming presences', accumulating impressions that slowly overwhelmed him, and vulnerable always to the 'mystic solicitation, the urgent appeal, on the part of everything to be interpreted and, so far as possible, reproduced'.[44] For Symons, who had met James in Venice during his first visit there, the problem was still more serious, for the 'humming presences' and 'mystic solicitations' were within as well as without, and interpretation was at once an issue of self-analysis and the scrutiny of external affairs.

One solution to this crisis was passive surrender. Luxulyan floats on the lagoon in a gondola, 'perfectly happy, not thinking of anything, hardly conscious of [him]self' (p. 304). This is the 'animal content which comes over one in Venice', Symons writes in *Cities of Italy*, taking away 'the desire of action and the need of excitement which way-lay the mind and the senses'.[45] It is also another borrowing from 'Venetian Sensations', emphasising the close kinship between author and character. Unfortunately, denied the solace of spiritual meditation by his rejection of his Methodist upbringing, unwilling to 'trip agnostically along the slightly perilous borders of heretical occultism' as W. B. Yeats did, and having taken on the financial responsibilities of marriage, Symons could not remain in this blissful condition.[46] Luxulyan may insist that 'The art in life is to sit still, and let things come towards you' (p. 301), but 'that sympathetic submissiveness to things' which in 'An Autumn City' constitutes 'so much of the charm of life' (p. 193) was ever more difficult to practise. Symons was troubled by headaches, sleeplessness, and neurasthenia. 'Overexcitable and overstrained', he was also dealing with eyestrain.[47] Luxulyan writes of 'that other self, which lay on the sofa with half-shut eyes and a forehead eaten away by the little sharp teeth of nerves' (p. 263). For a time, he ceases to write altogether.

As a convalescent, the tired and weakened librarian seems newly receptive to both sides of the city, giving himself over to 'enchantment' (p. 302) and, 'sink[ing] into this delicious Venice, where forgetfulness is easier than anywhere in the world' (p. 303). Yet less than a fortnight later, he has begun to worry. 'Does the too exciting exquisiteness of Venice drive people mad?' he asks, after seeing the asylum on the island of San Servolo. 'Two madhouses in the water! It is like a menace' (p. 304). Out on the lagoon, he hears a 'kind of moaning sound' coming from a walled garden. 'It is San Clemente', his gondolier tells him; 'they keep mad people there, mad women' (p. 13). After this incident, he is never able to regain his equilibrium, fearing the 'insidious coiling of water about one' and 'a subtle terror' emerging from the deep (p. 306). The Doges' Palace glitters in the darkness with 'the beauty of witchcraft' (p. 306), dogs bark, steamers shriek. Luxulyan begins to miss the Baroness but senses 'a vague, persistent image of death, implacable, unintelligible, not to be shaken off' (p. 308). 'I know not what I am dreading', the entry concludes, 'not the mere fear of water [...] but some terrible expectancy, which keeps me now from getting any rest' (p. 308). A heavy storm leaves the lagoon deserted and Luxulyan feeling he is 'on the shore of some horrible island', waiting for a boatman to row him across 'the sea, which there was no crossing' (p. 310). The gondolier has become Charon, and Luxulyan a kind of Casaubon, who, in George Eliot's *Middlemarch* (1872), 'found himself suddenly on the dark river-brink and heard the plash of the oncoming oar' when contemplating his fatal illness (Chapter 42).

If the journal is to be believed, the Baroness arrives in Venice a few days later. Luxulyan feels reconciled to her love, and lies in bed in a 'queer fever' for 'some Venetian chill has got into my very bones' (p. 311). He reads Balzac's 'Catherine of the Médicis' (1830–42) and identifies with its portrait of a Calvinist martyr recovering after torture. 'The world, ideas, sensations, all are fluid, and I flow through them, like a gondola carried along by the current; no, like a weed adrift on it' (p. 311), he concludes. His writing is 'faint and unsteady' just like his hold on life.

Despite the evident overlaps and intersections between Symons and Luxulyan, it would be a mistake to read the story from a naively biographical standpoint. Symons was a cunning and conscious artist who mixed his palette with great care, blending material from his own life with his wide and eclectic reading. Luxulyan, like Trevalga, is the name of a Cornish village, in this case, one renowned for its production of china clay and granite, and one might wonder if these symbolise the contrasting elements of the men's character. The portrait of Luxulyan as a clever but otherworldly boy who shuns sport in favour of solitary dreams of fame chimes with the quasi-Symons of 'A Prelude to Life', but the repetition is suggestive rather than conclusively 'fixing' their identification. The collapse of the Argonaut Building Society is modelled on the ruin brought by that of Jabez Balfour's Liberator Building Society in the mid-1890s, a rare allusion to current affairs in Symons's work, while the vitriol attack on the Baroness augments Symons's encounter with Bertha with a story familiar from works such as Maupassant's 'Jadis' (1880) and Gissing's *The Nether World* (1889), not to mention popular papers such as the *Illustrated Police News*. The Baron's viciousness draws on the *conte cruel*; indeed, as Matthew Creasy discusses in this volume (Chapter 5), Symons would rework the story in 'The Sinister Guest' (1919), his loose adaptation of Villiers de l'Isle-Adam. His use of the journal form draws attention to absences, elisions, gaps, and silences, not least in the ways in which the text is edited by an old friend of Luxulyan, who changes names, and makes 'omissions' which are apparently minor but not indicated. 'It seems to me a genuine document', he says (p. 244), a comment which, as Max Saunders cynically observes, is guaranteed to arouse 'our scepticism about its authenticity'.[48]

Luxulyan's struggles with Clare and the Baroness are a crucial aspect of the story, and derive considerable force from Venice's traditionally feminine associations such as 'The Queen of the Adriatic' and 'La Serenissima'. Symons wrote about Venetian women at some length in *Cities of Italy*, but his pose as a connoisseur, a man who, like Roserra, regards women as 'a delightful luxury, to be taken with discretion' (p. 178) concealed a profoundly troubled outlook. On his first visit, the twenty-nine-year-old Symons had, according to an amused Herbert Horne, 'spent the whole of that April in the search of a real Venetian tart' but had 'left Venice without having succeeded in getting hold of one'.[49] Fourteen years later and now married, Symons watched a woman with 'golden and inquisitive eyes' — another Balzac allusion — at the opera. 'Her eyes haunted me, I admit', he wrote, 'and I followed her out of the theatre until she went suddenly into the night'.[50] In a city renowned for its decadent licentiousness, Symons's failed sexual pursuits may be laughable and pathetic, as Horne believed, but they may indicate a more complex failure to achieve a coherent, or as Block has it, 'integrated' self. 'I have never understood myself', Luxulyan confesses, 'and just now the brain in me seems to sit aside and reserve judgment, while all manner of feelings, instincts, sensations, chatter among themselves' (pp. 294–95).

Luxulyan's inability to acknowledge properly or act upon his feelings leaves him angry and bewildered. If Symons used the story to explore his complicated attitudes towards women, sex, love, marriage, and artistic failure or unfulfillment, its Venetian setting takes on particular relevance. The editor regards the journal as a revelation of 'the real subterranean being whom I had known, during his life-time, only by a few, scarcely perceptible outlines on the surface' (p. 244). This distinction between surface and true though buried selves invites the story to be interpreted psychoanalytically, as Block does, though to see it in isolation, rather than in dialogue with Symons's other writings on Venice, is misleading. It is more fruitful to apply such ideas to the story's setting, drawing on Donald Friedman's discussion of the representation of Bruges, the so-called 'Venice of the north', by Belgian Symbolists, writers and artists whose work Symons knew well. Being 'remote from the rapid shift and flow of the commercial metropolis', Friedman writes, Bruges and Ghent became 'canal cities of mirage that call stability into question [...] hovering in a half state both aqueous and terrestrial'. Writers and artists 'found in the canal city a landscape profoundly suggestive of visionary experience', with the 'watery depths and blindly meandering passageways' providing 'a structural metaphor for the unconscious mind'. A 'voyage in the canal city' was thus 'a severance from the world, a symbolic disincarnation and descent into the underworld'.[51]

All of these elements are present in Symons's version of Venice; the city shows Symons/Luxulyan in its glassy waters just as it does its bell-towers and palazzi. It is precisely this reflective quality which makes it so suited to the brooding self-analysis in which the two men indulge. With his interest in astrology and magic, Yeats may well have seen Venice's attraction for Symons as an inevitable consequence of his being born under the water sign of Pisces, and figured the city as a scrying mirror in which the most hidden secrets of the self might be perceived and made manifest. Symons did not share these occult enthusiasms, but nevertheless, by staring repeatedly into the lagoon and the canals and, by extension, into himself, he did perhaps call up something his art was no longer able to banish.

Interpreting the events of 1908 in this way may seem fanciful, but there is no doubt that Symons was increasingly overwrought in the year or so before his breakdown: he admits as much in the early pages of *Confessions*. The second edition of *The*

Symbolist Movement in Literature, a book much concerned with madness, mysticism, and visionary experience, had appeared in March, his marriage was under strain, and he was maintaining a punishing schedule of writing and reviewing. The pressures on him that September were intense and seemingly intractable, and he may well have broken down if he had been in London or Paris. Perhaps, however, Venice itself was partially responsible for what happened to him. The heat and humidity of the late summer, the layers of personal association and reminiscence that the city inspired, and the acute sense of isolation it evoked all contributed to the catastrophe. Maybe, in his heightened state, Symons was drawn to Venice in order to confront himself in ways that were not possible elsewhere, but found that, as William James argued, the mystical state was ineffable and noetic, 'providing insight into the depths of truth unplumbed by the discursive intellect' and, though inarticulable, carrying with it 'a curious sense of authority for after-time'.[52] In his madness, Symons recalled, 'wild imaginings [...] kept me warily awake and intensely alive; I lived a kind of double life, inward and outward, both jumbled together in an inextricable confusion'.[53] This he documented to some extent in his memoirs, but though he admitted the role Venice played in his collapse, he ultimately refused to enumerate what it might have been. 'I have no intention of giving many details of the month I spent in Venice in September 1908', he wrote, 'nor of the adventures that happened to me'.[54]

Notes to Chapter 8

1. Arthur Symons, 'Venice', in *Cities of Italy* (London: J. M. Dent, 1907), pp. 71–114 (p. 99).
2. Arthur Symons, 'A Prelude to Life', in *Spiritual Adventures* (1905), p. 49.
3. Robert Browning, 'Rhyme for a Child Viewing a Naked Venus in a Painting of "The Judgement of Paris"' [c. 1872], in *The New Oxford Book of Victorian Verse*, ed. by Christopher Ricks (Oxford: Oxford University Press, 1987), p. 158.
4. Arthur Symons, 'An Autumn City', in *Spiritual Adventures* (1905), pp. 177–200 (p. 178).
5. Symons, 'Venice', p. 73.
6. Ibid., p. 76.
7. Arthur Symons, 'Venetian Nights V: Alle Zattere', in *London Nights*, p. 58.
8. Arthur Symons to James Dykes Campbell, 6 May 1894, in *Arthur Symons: Selected Letters*, ed. by Beckson and Munro, p. 106.
9. Pater, 'Conclusion', in *The Renaissance*, pp. 186–90 (p. 189).
10. Beckson, *Arthur Symons*, p. 105.
11. Walter Pater, 'Preface', in *The Renaissance*, pp. xix–xxv (p. xx).
12. Arthur Symons, 'Venice in Easter: Impressions and Sensations', *Harper's New Monthly Magazine*, 90 (April 1895), 738–51.
13. Arthur Symons, 'To Madame la Comtesse de la Tour', in *Cities* (London: J. M. Dent, 1903), pp. v–vii (p. v).
14. Ibid., pp. v–vi.
15. Symons, 'Venice', p. 77.
16. Arthur Symons, 'Siena', in *Cities of Italy*, pp. 209–26 (p. 210).
17. *Harper's New Monthly Magazine* had published Symons's most influential single essay, 'The Decadent Movement in Literature', in November 1893.
18. See, for example, his poem 'Venice', dated 6 August 1907, first printed in the *Atlantic Monthly* (February 1909) and included in *Knave of Hearts* (1913), and the essays 'Venice: On the Giudecca' (*Land and Water*, 15 November 1917), and 'A Masque of Kings in Venice', written in 1894, used

in part in 'Venice' in *Cities of Italy*, and printed in full in his late collection *Wanderings* (1931).
19. Symons, 'Venice', p. 73.
20. Ibid., pp. 99–100.
21. Ibid., p. 100.
22. Arthur Symons, 'London: A Book of Aspects', in *Cities and Sea-Coasts and Islands* (London: W. Collins, 1918), pp. 159–226 (p. 171). The essay was written in the winter of 1906–07.
23. Symons, 'Venice', p. 103.
24. Arthur Symons, 'Venetian Glamour', *Saturday Review*, 88 (14 October 1899), 480.
25. Ibid., p. 480.
26. Catherine Maxwell, 'Whistlerian Impressionism and the Venetian Variations of Vernon Lee, John Addington Symonds, and Arthur Symons', *Yearbook of English Studies*, 40 (2010), 217–45 (p. 243).
27. Symons, 'Venice', p. 76.
28. Arthur Symons to Edward Hutton, undated letter, quoted by Beckson, *Arthur Symons*, p. 254. Beckson also notes that the letter reveals a worrying deterioration of Symons's handwriting.
29. Arthur Symons, 'Music in Venice', *Saturday Review*, 106 (17 October 1908), 480–81. Lhombreaud suggests that the article was 'composed on the spot', *Arthur Symons*, p. 234.
30. The poem was collected in *Knave of Hearts*, in Arthur Symons, *Collected Works*, 9 vols (London: Secker, 1924), III, 43.
31. Arthur Symons to Florence Kahn, undated letter, in Beckson, *Arthur Symons*, p. 255. He reiterated the claim in *Confessions: A Study in Pathology* (London: Jonathan Cape, 1930), p. 7, which reprints a lengthy extract from 'Music in Venice' (pp. 7–8).
32. Hélène Cixous, *Insister of Jacques Derrida*, trans. by Peggy Kamuf (Edinburgh: Edinburgh University Press, 2007), p. 15.
33. [Anon.], 'Cities. By Arthur Symons', *Athenæum*, 3968 (14 November 1903), 641–42.
34. Lhombreaud, *Arthur Symons*, p. 236.
35. Andrew Mangravite, 'Arthur Symons' Travel Writing: The Decadent Abroad' (2000), <www.victorianweb.org/authors/symons/am1.html> [accessed 16 August 2015].
36. Edwin F. Block, Jr., *Rituals of Dis-Integration: Romance and Madness in the Victorian Psychomythic Tale* (New York: Garland, 1993), p. 164.
37. Christopher Isherwood, *All the Conspirators* (London: Jonathan Cape, 1928), p. 115.
38. Symons, 'Venice', p. 71.
39. 'The Genesis of Spiritual Adventures' is an unpublished, undated, and unpaginated forty-three-page typescript held at Princeton University, Arthur Symons Papers, C0182, Box 9, Folder 7. Obviously typed by the elderly Symons rather than a professional typist, it is filled with typographical errors, hand-written corrections and additions, and material cut and pasted from Symons's other essays.
40. The couple lived together for three years. Block assumes Clare and Luxulyan were married (*Rituals of Dis-Integration*, p. 175), but the story itself is inconclusive on this point.
41. Arthur Symons, 'Extracts from the Journal of Henry Luxulyan', in *Spiritual Adventures* (1905), pp. 241–314 (pp. 300–01). Further references are given in the text.
42. [Symons], 'Bertha at the Fair', p. 88.
43. The Harry Ransom Center, Austin, Texas, holds Symons's diaries for 1907 and 1921 (MS-4141, Container 3.1).
44. Henry James, *The Art of the Novel: Critical Prefaces* (New York: Charles Scribner's Sons, 1934), pp. 59, 61.
45. Symons, 'Venice', p. 111.
46. Richard Whittington-Egan, *Lionel Johnson: Victorian Dark Angel* (Great Malvern: Cappella Archive, 2012), p. 187.
47. Symons, *Confessions* (1930), p. 6.
48. Max Saunders, *Self Impression: Life-Writing, Autobiografiction, and the Forms of Modern Literature* (Oxford: Oxford University Press, 2010), p. 254.
49. Herbert Horne to Edgar Jepson, 22 January 1897, in Beckson, *Arthur Symons*, p. 163.
50. Symons, 'Music in Venice', p. 481.

51. Donald Friedman, 'Belgian Symbolism and a Poetics of Place', in *Les XX and the Belgian Avant Garde: Prints, Drawings and Books ca. 1890*, ed. by Stephen H. Goddard (Lawrence: University of Kansas/Spencer Museum of Art, 1992), pp. 126–38 (p. 129).
52. William James, *The Varieties of Religious Experience: A Study in Human Nature* [1902] (London: Longmans, Green, and Co. 1915), pp. 380–81.
53. Symons, *Confessions* (1930), p. 81.
54. Ibid., p. 6.

CHAPTER 9

Symons on Italy and the Metamorphoses of Aesthetic Travel Writing

Elisa Bizzotto

Italy is a significant presence in Symons's travel writing: it is the main subject of his first volume on places, *Cities* (1903), while his second, *Cities of Italy* (1907), takes the country as its exclusive focus. Composed from 1894 and all through the following decade, Symons's Italian pieces collected in the two books not only set forth the features of his subsequent travel writing, but also offered clues to the literary influences and borrowings in his later works.[1] In particular, the Italian essays proclaimed Symons's adherence to the Symbolist principles that urged him to capture the essence of things and find analogies between them in reality. As he argued in the introduction to *Cities*, and repeated verbatim in the next collection, his essays are based on the belief that 'cities are like people, with souls and temperaments of their own'.[2] The essays also show that he only trusted his perceptions and impressions in visiting the cities whose 'souls and temperaments' were congenial to him; thus, as he explains in the introduction, he devoted himself to urban travelling, one of his 'chief pleasures'. This is further elucidated in a passage from the autobiographical imaginary portrait 'A Prelude to Life' (1905), reprinted in Symons's posthumous *Memoirs* (1977), in which the narrator confesses to having perceived a huge difference between the theoretical study and direct sensual experience of places, ever since his schooldays:

> I have never been able to make out why geography was so completely beyond my power. I have travelled since then over most of Europe, and I have learned geography with the sight of my eyes. But with all my passion for places I have never been able to find my way in them until I have come to find it instinctively, and I suppose that is why the names in the book or on the map said nothing to me.[3]

In addition to containing Symbolist and Impressionist influences, Symons's travel writing relied on the aesthetic principles of describing places as works of art, mainly evoking their spirit through representative artists and masterpieces.[4] His adherence to Aestheticism is also conveyed through his focus on small towns and minor artistic personalities; this selective search for the unusual and unpopular distanced him from the standards set by travel guides, those unavoidable tools of nineteenth-century mainstream tourism.[5] Symons's dislike of guidebooks was expressed as early as his first travel essay, 'Venice', where guides were labelled 'a necessary evil', unable to convey those 'lasting impressions' that could be elicited by sensory reactions and discriminating judgement.[6]

The immediate antecedent for Symons's dependence on individual responses to beauty can be identified in Walter Pater, whose famous 'Conclusion' to *The Renaissance* (1873) both praised 'the elect' for possessing a superior aesthetic understanding and urged them to depend on ephemeral sensations, not analytical practices, in their perception of reality. But Pater never tried his hand at travel writing and only described travel experiences in his fiction. Instead, John Addington Symonds offered a more direct model for Symons's writings on places, when it came both to his themes and methods; the two writers entertained an intellectual dialogue since as early as 1886, when Symons sent Symonds a copy of his edition of *Titus Andronicus*. A correspondence ensued in which the older writer often recognised the value of Symons's work — especially his poetry — and acted as a kind of literary counsellor. The two met in person only three years later in London.[7] The encounter was described by Symons himself in 'A Study of John Addington Symonds' (1924), where he also recorded their eager conversation about the cities they had seen, their travels, and sensations.[8]

Symons's recollections suggest that he shared his approach to places, based on highly personal responses, with his interlocutor. Like Symons, moreover, Symonds predominantly focused on Italy and its off-the-beaten-track attractions, as evidenced in his travelogues *Sketches in Italy and Greece* (1874), *Sketches and Studies in Italy* (1879), *Italian Byways* (1883), and the posthumous *New Italian Sketches* (1894). By doing so, as Manfred Pfister has noted, Symonds and Symons were united in 'both the esthete's need to dissociate himself from the touristic canon and the decadent's fascination with the curious'.[9] Nevertheless, the themes and approaches in Symons's Italian essays reveal the most striking similarities to yet another author's work: Vernon Lee was seriously committed to the same genre, had strong links to the Aesthetic Movement, and joined Symonds and Symons in both her penchant for literary Impressionism and love for Italy.[10] Lee published her first volume on places in 1897, but had begun to write on the subject in the previous decade, and would compile seven travel books, mostly devoted to Italy, by 1925.[11] Lee's career as a travel writer was roughly contemporaneous with that of Symons, whose last collection of travel sketches, *Wanderings*, was issued in 1931 though completed about ten years before.[12] Prior to this, he had produced *London: A Book of Aspects* (1908) and *Cities and Sea-Coasts and Islands* (1918), *Cities*, and *Cities of Italy*. In their works on travelling, both Lee and Symons displayed an ambition to create finely-crafted pieces meant for fastidious connoisseurs who shunned the standardised impersonality of guidebooks; in doing so, they prefigured the traveller-versus-tourist debate, which is still ongoing.[13] They also revealed a willingness to grasp the soul of places based on their subjective responses to reality.

As is well known, Lee and Symons had strong links with Pater and shared relevant connections with some of the leading international voices of Aestheticism and Decadence: Symonds, Oscar Wilde, Gabriele D'Annunzio, Henry James, and Paul

Bourget, among others. More peculiarly, they were both familiar with important Italian literary circles at the *fin de siècle*. One of Lee's closest literary associates in Florence, Enrico Nencioni, was considered by Symons 'the best Italian critic' and wrote a review of Symons's first book, *An Introduction to the Study of Browning* (1886) for the Florentine quarterly *Nuova antologia* in 1887.[14] These Italian connections were still alive ten years later, in 1896–97, when Symons spent time in Rome in the company of such friends of Lee as the photographer and collector Giuseppe Primoli and salon hostess Laura Minghetti.[15] Even more significantly, Symons had a certain familiarity with the poet A. Mary F. Robinson, who was Lee's companion in the early-to-mid 1880s. He attended Robinson's salon during his 1890 visit to Paris, where she was living after her marriage to French Orientalist James Darmesteter; in the following year, he wrote an appreciative 'Introduction' to a selection of her verse in Alfred H. Miles's ponderous twelve-volume anthology, *The Poets and the Poetry of the Nineteenth Century*. Here Symons argued that Robinson had reached her most mature poetic voice with *An Italian Garden: A Book of Songs* (1886), a collection whose composition was affected not simply by Lee's presence, as Robinson herself recognised, but also by Lee's peculiar response to Italy, so keenly expressed in her travel books.[16] It is therefore likely that Robinson's poems on the Italian countryside and urbanscapes, some of which appear in the Miles series ('Florentine May' and 'Venetian Nocturne' are cases in point), represented an indirect channel for Lee's influence on Symons's travel literature.[17]

As Lawrence W. Markert has contended, there were other ways in which Lee's work reached Symons. Indeed, he first became aware of her *oeuvre* in the early 1880s, through some of her essays on Italian culture in the *Westminster Gazette* and *Cornhill Magazine*.[18] In the latter periodical in particular, Lee published pieces such as 'Botticelli at the Villa Lemmi' (reprinted in *Juvenilia* in 1887) and 'The Portrait Art of the Renaissance' (reprinted in *Euphorion* in 1884), which Markert views as crucial influences on Symons's approach to travel writing and his focus on Italy.[19]

Whatever the origins of his knowledge of Lee's work, there is substantial evidence of Symons's enthusiasm for it; this establishes Lee as a fundamental presence in his early career, especially in the context of his emerging commitment to travel writing and interest in Italy. In the mid 1880s, as a precocious young author, Symons admitted to imitating Lee's style and to admiring her 'vastly'.[20] He was, therefore, impressed by her perspective on Italian culture. As Karl Beckson reports, it is not surprising that when Charles Churchill Osborne, Symons's teacher and mentor, read *An Introduction to the Study of Browning*, he 'detected the influence of Vernon Lee [...], whose *Euphorion* [...] depicted [...] the evils of life during the Italian Renaissance as well as the idealism and purity of its art'.[21] Another of Symons's early champions, the scholar Frederick James Furnivall, identified *Euphorion* as a model for Symons's debut work. Worried about his pupil's lack of originality, Furnivall 'damned heartily Vernon Lee for writing her book a year too soon'.[22] Symons confirmed his reliance on Lee's authority by quoting her *Studies of the Eighteenth Century in Italy* (1880) as a key source of information for his Browning volume — namely, on details relating to the Venetian composer Baldassare Galuppi.[23] He also published two annotations, 'Galuppi — Vernon Lee' and 'Vernon Lee on "The Ring and the Book"', in the proceedings of the Browning Society (1884–85).[24]

Lee's Italian pieces show clear points of intersection with those of Symons. Both authors concentrate on lesser-known sites and cities — mainly Tuscan villages, for her; Tivoli and the *castelli romani*, Brescia, and Bergamo, for him — and show an inclination for Impressionist descriptions. This is not to say that they were entirely aligned: in Lee, more than in Symons, these descriptions stem from Pater's theories on perception in *The Renaissance*, rather than from an endorsement of contemporary artistic, especially French, trends. As Stefano Evangelista has demonstrated, Lee had been under the spell of Paterian ideas since the early 1880s, when she published *Belcaro* (1881), her volume on aesthetics, and *Euphorion*, appearing later in the decade and so influential for Symons.[25] Likewise indebted to Pater and his belief in the subjectivity of artistic reception is the theory of the *genius loci*: the original and characteristic, if elusive, guiding principle of Lee's travel writing, employed to designate the divine presence or deep character of a place. It is probable that the idea of *genius loci* in Lee's late nineteenth-century Italian essays was a similarly appealing and enduring principle for Symons. He adapted it to articulate the aesthetic concerns that were central, though not necessarily exclusive, to his Italian travel pieces.

Lee first uses the expression *genius loci* — the spirit of a place in classical Roman culture — apropos of Rome and Verona in her 1899 collection *Genius Loci*; yet the concept, still unnamed but defined in its essence, had already pervaded both her miscellaneous volume *Limbo*, from two years before, and the Italian writings of the early 1880s that so excited Symons. As Lee makes clear in the introduction to the 1899 volume, *genius loci* is a 'spiritual reality' only perceived by 'certain among us' whenever visiting localities that 'become objects of intense and most intimate feeling' and 'touch us like living creatures'.[26] It is, she adds, 'of the substance of our heart and mind' and its 'visible embodiment [...] is the place itself'.[27] In subsequent passages she compares 'the feelings we can have for places with the feelings awakened in us by certain of our friends'; this is a remarkable anticipation of Symons's own analogy between cities and people, which lies at the heart of his travel writing.[28]

Starting from these thoughts, it is easy to see that Lee's theory of the *genius loci* overlaps with the professed 'ultimate aim' of Symons's travel literature, articulated in both *Cities* and *Cities of Italy*: that is to say, the ideal of *la vraie vérité*. Like *genius loci*, *la vraie vérité* is a complex and fluid principle with a somewhat tortuous genealogy. As John J. Conlon suggests, Symons derived it from Pater, who in his turn appears to have taken it from the French critic Charles Augustin Sainte-Beuve, possibly via Matthew Arnold.[29] More specifically, in Sainte-Beuve's words, *la vérité vraie* emerges as a supreme ideal in both art and life, which is very difficult to recognise and pursue, and has a value only few can understand:

> Pauvre vérité, vérité vraie, vérité nue, que de peine on a à te faire sortir de ton puits, et quand on est parvenu à t'en tirer à demi et à mi-corps, que de gens accourus de toutes parts, qui ont hâte de t'y renfoncer![30]
>
> [Poor truth, truth itself, naked truth — to what lengths must one go to bring

you out of your well, and when one does manage to pull you half-way out, how many people come rushing from all directions, hastening to push you back in.]

Arnold was among the select few who could gauge the importance of *la vraie vérité*. In a letter of 13 January 1864 to Sainte-Beuve, he confessed his own indebtedness to the French writer as far as the principle was concerned: 'si la nature m'a donné un certain goût pour la modération et pour la *vraie vérité*, c'est de vous, uniquement de vous, que j'ai un peu appris la manière de m'en servir et den [*sic*] tirer parti' [If nature has given me a certain taste for moderation and for the *vraie vérité*, it is from you, and from you alone, that I have learned something of the way to use it and to take advantage of it].[31] Arnold leaves little doubt about the origins of his longing for *la vraie vérité*, or what he calls the 'vital truth [of things]', and presents it as a typically French concept in his *National Review* essay on Joseph Joubert, first published in the same month he wrote his letter.[32]

It is therefore not a coincidence that Symons relates the concept of *la vraie vérité* to French culture in his essay 'The Goncourts' (1894), in which '*la vie vécue, la vraie vérité*' becomes 'the only thing worth representing' and the final artistic pursuit of the two brother writers.[33] He had already offered a version of it and alluded to its French roots in 'The Decadent Movement in Literature' (1893); here, it was identified as the common quality and aim of Impressionism and Symbolism, two fundamental influences in his art that sought '*la vérité vraie*, the very essence of truth — the truth of appearances to the senses, of the visible world to the eyes that see it; and the truth of spiritual things to the spiritual vision'.[34] However, only in his essay on Pater does Symons most seriously ponder the potential of *la vraie vérité* and offer his ultimate interpretation of it.

In order to contextualise Symons's use of the concept more fully, it is important to consider his primary source. Pater mentions *la vraie vérité* on three occasions and in each of them he communicates aesthetic principles, progressively adding and modifying details from previous definitions. He first discusses *la vraie vérité* in 'The School of Giorgione' — written in 1877, just a year after Sainte-Beuve's appeal to *la vraie vérité* was published in the posthumous *Les Cahiers de Sainte-Beuve* — in a long and complicated formula. It is eventually summarised as corresponding to:

> Those more liberal and durable impressions which, in respect of any really considerable person or subject, anything that has at all intricately occupied men's attention, lie beyond, and must supplement, the narrower range of the strictly ascertained facts about it.[35]

Pater returns to *la vraie vérité* in the essay on 'Style' (1889), where it is more straightforwardly identified as 'truth [...] as accuracy, truth [...] as expression, the finest and most intimate form of truth'; it is 'that absolute accordance of expression to idea' characteristic of 'the highest [...] literature'.[36] Finally, in 'Plato and the Sophists' (1893) he sees *la vraie vérité* as conveying one of the fundamentals of Western thought: that is to say, 'the essential function of the Socratic method', which consists in making 'men interested in themselves as being the very ground of all reality for them'.[37]

What emerges from comparing these accounts is that *la vraie vérité* relies on both individual judgement and 'impressions', Pater's own word in the Giorgione essay, and the need to transform them accurately into either artistic forms or philosophical beliefs. Whether it has to do with literature (as he argues in 'Style'), or more broadly with human life and experiences (as in 'The School of Giorgione' and 'Plato and the Sophists'), *la vraie vérité* is, for Pater, a guiding principle and the supreme goal of the highest spirits. In the Giorgione essay, particularly, Pater associates the principle not only with impressions, but also with subjectivity and individualism. This is exactly what he does in his famous definition of 'aesthetic criticism' in the 'Preface' to *The Renaissance*, emphasising the significance of *la vraie vérité* to his critical method:

> In aesthetic criticism the first step towards seeing one's object as it really is, is to know one's own impression as it really is, to discriminate it, to realise it distinctly. [...] What is this song or picture, this engaging personality presented in life or in a book, to me? What effect does it really produce on me? Does it give me pleasure? and if so, what sort or degree of pleasure? How is my nature modified by its presence, and under its influence? The answers to these questions are the original facts with which the aesthetic critic has to do.[38]

Not surprisingly, similar features come to light in Symons's own analysis of Pater's *vraie vérité*, but Symons's focus shifts towards art. In his interpretation of 'The School of Giorgione', Pater's 'impressions', which 'lie beyond facts', are equated to the 'earthly beauty' that Pater can recognise in the world and transform into art. Pater is, after all, a real artist; the same implicitly applies to Symons himself:

> Pater seemed to draw up into himself every form of earthly beauty, or of the beauty made by men [...]; and his work was the giving out of all this again, with a certain labour to give it wholly. It is all, the criticism, and the stories, and the writing about pictures and places, a confession, the *vraie vérité* (as he was fond of saying) about the world in which he lived.[39]

In this extract, and even more in Pater's descriptions of *la vraie vérité*, the thorough response to beauty in his experience of reality, along with the relentless endeavour to pursue that beauty and transfer it into his work, delineate a situation comparable to Lee's quest for and reaction to the *genius loci*. Like Pater's search for *la vraie vérité* — which Symons in fact sees as a confessional process in the passage just cited — Lee's search is extremely personal, bringing to light what is most intimate in the subject and revealing some truth that is important to the critic. Lee's *genius loci* is thus 'a spiritual reality', whose 'visible embodiment' is different for each of us and may be identified with those places in which we discern some superior reality valid for ourselves. As Lee explains, for 'each individual' the *genius loci* lies just in 'one or two places [...] where he may live habitually, yet never lose the sense of delight, wonder, and gratitude': in her case it is represented by 'the Tuscan valleys and stony hillsides', although the supreme example is Rome.[40] The *genius loci*, in other words, can be described as a subjective and innermost truth perceived by sensitive spirits in certain places; its recognition presupposes a highly personal and painstaking quest for the ideal. The main object of Lee's travel writings, then, is to find such essential truth; she seems to borrow the Paterian theory of *la vraie vérité*, apply it exclusively to the places she visits, and call it *genius loci*. Accordingly, the notion became very influential for Symons, who adopted Pater's phraseology to articulate what were Lee's ideas as well as those of Pater.

The conflation of Pater's and Lee's principles in Symons's version of *la vraie vérité* is evident in the introduction to *Cities* and *Cities of Italy*, where the concept explicitly refers to travel literature. Loyal to Pater's stylistic and intellectual rigour, Symons on the one hand defines *la vraie vérité* as an attempt to render as faithfully as possible the beauty discovered in his travel experiences; on the other hand, following Lee's *genius loci*, *la vraie vérité* signifies a certain respect for his sensations when he delves into the secrets of places. Espousing the theories of both, finally, Symons sees *la vraie vérité* as expressing the laborious quest for representation, which becomes 'a difficult kind of truth' and the critic's 'ultimate attainment':

> I have respected the sight of my eyes and the judgment of my senses, and I have tried to evoke my cities in these pages exactly as they appeared to me to be in themselves. It is part of my constant challenge to myself, in everything I write, to be content with nothing short of that *vraie vérité* which one imagines to exist somewhere on this side of ultimate attainment. It is so much easier to put oneself into things than to persuade things to give up their own secrets; and I like to aim at this difficult kind of truth.[41]

Once we recognise that Symons's formulation of *la vraie vérité* merges his debts to Pater and Lee, it is also possible to find it in *London: A Book of Aspects*, the extreme metamorphosis of Symons's travel writing, though not his last endeavour in the genre. *London* is in fact much more oriented toward modernity than the rest of Symons's volumes on travel, both in its setting — no longer provincial Italy or other peripheral areas, but one of the world's greatest metropolises — and for its fragmentary, nonlinear structure. Accentuating the Impressionist tendencies of Symons's previous essays, *London* is made up of loosely related paragraphs that tell of solipsistic wanderings and of the mental associations they elicit; as Nicholas Freeman has argued, the writing moves swiftly 'from description of the scene to reflection, and then to a comparison with life in a Cornish village without having to integrate the account into a wider narrative scheme'.[42] These two aspects — a disconnected narrative structure, a focus on cityscapes — appear to anticipate metropolitan scenes in avant-garde and Modernist literature.

In support of this argument, it should be noted that *London* was conceived as a markedly experimental work, the fruit of Symons's collaboration with the American photographer Alvin Langdon Coburn, whom he met in 1906. Symons's prose sketches and Coburn's pictures complemented one another in the volume. It marked a fulfilment for Symons, bringing together ideas contained in the other book he was writing at the time, the aesthetic treatise *Studies in Seven Arts* (1906), as well as *The Symbolist Movement in Literature* (1899) and *Plays, Acting, and Music* (1903), both written earlier. In the introductory remarks to *Plays, Acting, and Music*, Symons testified to his long-standing ambition to create 'the concrete expression of a theory, or system of aesthetics, of all the arts':

> In my book on 'The Symbolist Movement in Literature' I made a first attempt

to deal in this way with literature [...]. The present volume deals mainly with the stage, and, secondarily, with music; it is to be followed by a volume called 'Studies in the Seven Arts,' in which music will be dealt with in greater detail, side by side with painting, sculpture, architecture, handicraft, dancing, and the various arts of the stage.[43]

His overarching aesthetic project included travel writing, for in his view 'life too is a form of art, and the visible world the chief storehouse of beauty'.[44]

Firmly grounded in his own aesthetic system, the book Symons planned with Coburn ultimately followed theories that dated back to Pater's 'The School of Giorgione', which Symons recognised as the founding text for interart hybridisations in British Aestheticism. At the very beginning of *Studies in Seven Arts*, he explained that Pater's essay was crucial to his own ambition to study 'the special qualities, the special limits, of the various arts', with the final aim of mastering 'the universal science of beauty'.[45] The effects of these theories are apparent in *London*, which is the result of a compelling artistic interchange, in which Symons's prose sketches are matched with Coburn's photographs and offer a complex, complete Impressionist-Symbolist representation of the modern metropolis. Indeed, the book was so unconventional, and potentially high-cost, that it was too risky a venture for publishers; in the end, only two copies were privately printed in 1914 by the American Edmund D. Brooks. Brooks had already published Symons's prose contributions, without Coburn's illustrations, in another private edition of twelve copies in 1908.[46] Reissued the following year, this earlier version was finally included in *Cities, Sea-Coasts and Islands*.

Despite the metropolitan setting, experimental approach, and stress on the artificiality and alienation of modernity of the London sketches, their inclusion in *Cities, Sea-Coasts and Islands* implies they were not entirely discordant with Symons's more traditional travel writings and somehow belonged to the same genre. Indeed, *Cities, Sea-Coasts and Islands* reproduces pieces written between 1892 and 1908 that contained typical features of Symons's previous writings on places. Moreover, it is not accidental that, in *London*, Symons points to a significant thematic continuum within his own corpus when he first sets London apart from other capitals — Vienna, Paris, Prague, or Constantinople — in the opening pages, but soon afterwards contradicts his statement by finding similarities between London and Venice, the subject of his first travel essay and inspiration for those that followed:

> A London sunset, seen through vistas of narrow streets, has a colour of smoky rose which can be seen in no other city, and it weaves strange splendours, often enough, on its edges and gulfs of sky, not less marvellous than Venice can lift over the Giudecca.[47]

Still, the main *trait d'union* between *London* and Symons's earlier travel writing is his aspiration to grasp the essential quality of places: what he once called *la vraie vérité* and now does not define with a precise formula, but by using a variety of terms that may indicate new influences in his work. A recurring and interesting example among these terms is 'atmosphere'. Atmosphere is, for Symons, what 'makes and unmakes' London and represents its distinctiveness and superiority, so that 'in

[...] the magic of atmosphere, London is not to be excelled'.[48] Atmosphere is the city's constitutive feature, associated to an oxymoronic 'natural magic', and hence tantamount to a supernatural power or presence:

> But for the most part the appeal of London is made by no beauty or effect in things themselves, but [...] by the atmosphere which makes and unmakes this vast and solid city every morning and every evening with a natural magic peculiar to it.[49]

Presented in such a light, Symons's atmosphere seems conceptually very close to the essence of a place, being both transcendent and inherent to it — a kind of *genius loci* or *vraie vérité*. It is not altogether surprising, therefore, that Symons already used the term in his Italian travel essays when he wanted to evoke certain features of places and transpose them into written form: he described, for instance, 'that atmosphere of positive, unspiritual things which I had breathed in St. Peter's, and which seemed to me so typical of Rome'.[50]

Despite showing a certain continuity with previous travel pieces, the term 'atmosphere' is given greater relevance in *London*, where it also establishes a more evident connection with visuality. As a matter of fact, Symons could have borrowed the word from pictorial Impressionism, which generally employed it with a literal meaning — to refer to the weather. This followed contemporary scientific research on the topic, which was mostly conducted in France: among the several studies on atmosphere there was, for example, the volume *Atmospheric Actinometry and the Actinic Constitution of the Atmosphere* (1896) by Émile Duclaux, a renowned scientist and pupil of Pasteur who became A. Mary F. Robinson's second husband in 1901.

Given this connection to current debates and to discourses on the visual in particular, it does not seem strange that Symons used the term more frequently in *London*, where for the first time in his travel writing, and in fact in his writings *tout court*, he was engaged in a sustained interchange with photographic material. He had only used a photograph once before, in his *Cities* essay on Naples: this was an anonymous picture taken from the Florentine Alinari Archive, included for decorative and illustrative reasons and with no claim to interart poetics. In order to approach the new photographic subject in *London*, Symons needed to appropriate a vocabulary more specific to visuality and to photographic modalities and techniques of representation. Atmosphere was perfect for this purpose: it was closely related not only to Impressionist painting but also photography, whose existence obviously depends on the conditions of the air, as explained in Symons's time by the photography scientist Josef Maria Eder.[51] Besides, the word was often used in photographic discourse in an aesthetic sense, to express the general mood of a picture, with occasional Impressionist connotations. Both aspects were considered by photographer Alfred Stieglitz, who was, incidentally, Coburn's main mentor:

> Atmosphere is the medium through which we see all things. In order, therefore, to see them in their true value on a photograph, as we do in Nature, atmosphere must be there. Atmosphere softens all lines; it graduates the transition from light to shade; it is essential to the reproduction of the sense of distance. That dimness of outline which is characteristic for distant objects is due to atmosphere. Now, what atmosphere is to Nature, tone is to a picture.[52]

In his book on London, Symons gave atmosphere a significance that was close to Stieglitz's interpretation. However, he also emphasised the psychological implications of atmosphere as connected to places, and consequently to people. This was becoming typical of early twentieth-century art and culture: as Steven Connor explains, Modernism testifies to an enduring interest in weather phenomena and 'the atmosphere', which 'became the name for that which broke in from the outside'.[53] At the time, he adds:

> Atmospherics became the sphere in which a new conception of mixed and mutually pervasive bodies was worked out. The fortunes of the word 'atmosphere' itself express this. On the one hand, the word 'atmosphere' came to be used more and more to express the qualities of specific places or environments, according to the logic of the aura whereby a figure might be thought to exhale or extrude its own niche. But 'atmospherics' in general came more and more to mean the effects of interference, suggesting the confusions, interpenetrations, unpredictable mutations and compoundings of those places.[54]

This more metaphorical use of the term has been seen to characterise, for example, the travel writings of Hugo von Hofmannsthal — an author familiar to Symons, who translated his *Electra* in 1908 — as well as Virginia Woolf's description of urbanscapes in *Mrs Dalloway*, where atmosphere emerges as the 'sense of the infused energy of London'.[55] It is also important for Walter Benjamin, who often applies it to his depiction of cities; indeed, it has been compared to his more famous notion of 'aura', which is in turn associated with the concepts of authenticity and quintessentiality.[56] These two attributes, needless to say, are constitutive of *la vraie vérité*, so that by evoking London's atmosphere Symons hints at an aesthetic and methodological persistence in his past and present writings on places.

Indeed, the parallel between London and Venice suggests that the intratextual continuum between Symons's essays on Italy and his later book encompasses critical approaches, themes, and techniques. Solipsistic momentary responses and enjoyments, so crucial in his Italian pieces, are still necessary to Symons's perception of metropolitan landscapes: he confesses, for instance, that 'London was for a long time my supreme sensation, and to roam in the streets, especially after the lamps were lighted, my chief pleasure'.[57] While describing London, moreover, Symons still searches for the atmosphere — or *vraie vérité* or *genius loci* — in the things, places, and people that reflect his own sensitivity, and whose peculiar beauty appeals to his senses; he establishes idiosyncratic connections with them. Even more radically than in his Italian travel writings, he focuses on marginal locations, personalities, and art forms. Accordingly, he lays emphasis on London's music halls and their performers, such as the *diseuse* Yvette Guilbert, whom he compares to Sarah Bernhardt and whose art he describes as 'always classic; it has restraint, form, dignity, in its wildest licence'.[58] His taste for the untouristic brings him to engage in solitary ramblings along the most sordid parts of the Edgware Road, the East End, and the Docks — an area of London he does not know well, and possibly makes him feel like a tourist in his own city. In perceiving London as foreign and alienating, he displays an attitude that prefigures famous urban Modernist writing. To guide him there is no Baedeker of sorts, but the insider Josiah Flynt (the pseudonym of Frank Willard), a wanderer of urban spaces whose gusto for the extraordinary leads him to live up to the central dogma of Pater's Aestheticism. As Symons states:

> It seems to me that few men have realized, as this man has realized, that 'not the fruit of experience, but experience itself, is the end.' He has chosen his life for himself, and he has lived it, regardless of anything else in the world. He has desired strange, almost inaccessible things, and he has attained whatever he has desired.[59]

Josiah Flynt was a remarkable character. The brother of Katherine Willard, Symons's one-time romantic interest, he was educated in the United States, where he was born, and in Germany, building up a cosmopolitan background until he later became a sociologist. After spending several years of his youth as a vagabond in his home country and Europe, he recounted his experiences in *Tramping with Tramps: Studies and Sketches of Vagabond Life* (1899). Partly Symons's *alter ego*, Flynt also becomes his ontological model. In *London*, Symons delineates a fine portrait of Flynt as the perfect vagabond-aesthete:

> To desire so much, and what is so human, to make one's life out of the very fact of living it as one chooses; to create a unique personal satisfaction out of discontent and curiosity; to be so much oneself in learning so much from other people: is not this, in its way, an ideal, and has not my friend achieved it? What I like in him so much is that he is a vagabond without an object.[60]

Using another Paterian phrase, Symons believes that Flynt has reached 'success in life', or what may otherwise be termed *la vraie vérité* — for Pater, the supreme goal of the highest spirits.[61]

Highly personal as it was, Symons's re-elaboration of specific concepts from Pater and Lee in his travel writings did contribute to create what Freeman has called 'a language of metropolitan representation during the fin de siècle'.[62] In fact, this language reaches forward to Modernism and, in doing so, exposes a strong continuity between the two centuries. Symons's 'language of metropolitan representation' manages to accomplish an essential mediation between past and present expressions of the genre. In his portrayals of Italy, Symons set the coordinates for the travel writing of the Aesthetic Movement, alongside Vernon Lee and Symonds; eventually, however, he employed the Impressionist and Symbolist features of his travel poetics and the aesthetic faithfulness to *la vraie vérité* and *genius loci* in a modern(ist) metropolitan setting. He transformed the genre by steering away from Italian provincial and rural settings, and towards English cosmopolitan urbanscapes. He also abandoned *fin-de-siècle* vocabulary for the aesthetic travel experience in favour of a more contemporary poetics, which described physical and psychological places in new and challenging ways.

Notes to Chapter 9

1. *Cities* includes 'Venice' (1894, 1897, 1903), 'Rome' (1896, 1903), 'Naples' (1897, 1903), 'Seville' (1898), 'Prague' (1897, 1899), 'Moscow' (1897), 'Budapest, Belgrade, and Sophia' (1901), and 'Constantinople' (1901). *Cities of Italy* reprints the essays on Venice, Rome, and Naples from the previous collection and adds 'Florence: An Interpretation' [n. d.], 'Ravenna' (1903), 'Pisa' (1904),

'Siena' [n. d.], 'Verona' (1903), 'Bologna' (1897), 'Bergamo and Lorenzo Lotto' (1903), 'Brescia and Romanino' (1903), and 'On a Rembrandt in Milan' (1903).

2. Arthur Symons, 'To Madame la Comtesse de la Tour', in *Cities*, pp. v–vii (p. v).
3. Arthur Symons, 'A Prelude to Life', in *Spiritual Adventures* (1905), pp. 3–50 (p. 9).
4. *The Fatal Gift of Beauty: The Italies of British Travellers, An Annotated Anthology*, ed. by Manfred Pfister (Amsterdam and Atlanta: Rodopi, 1996), p. 518.
5. The growing late-Victorian and Edwardian denigration of guidebooks — a phenomenon that continued well into Modernism — is discussed by James Buzard, *The Beaten Track: European Tourism, Literature, and the Ways to 'Culture' 1800–1918* (Oxford: Oxford University Press, 1993), pp. 285–92.
6. Symons, 'Venice', p. 63.
7. *Arthur Symons: Selected Letters*, ed. by Beckson and Munro, p. 20, n. 2.
8. Arthur Symons, 'A Study of John Addington Symonds', *Fortnightly Review*, 115 (February 1924), 228–39. The essay was reprinted in *The Memoirs of Arthur Symons*, ed. by Beckson, pp. 115–21. Beckson and Munro maintain that the encounter took place in 1889 (see previous note); in his *Fortnightly Review* article Symons wrongly dates it to 1892.
9. *The Fatal Gift of Beauty*, ed. by Pfister, pp. 518–19. Symonds's passion for small Italian towns, their history and art, is also considered by Kenneth Churchill, *Italy and English Literature 1764–1930* (London: Macmillan, 1980), pp. 118–20.
10. For a fine analysis of Impressionistic writing in Lee, Symonds, and Symons, see Maxwell, 'Whistlerian Impressionism and the Venetian Variations of Vernon Lee, John Addington Symonds, and Arthur Symons'.
11. *Limbo and Other Essays* (1897), *Genius Loci: Notes on Places* (1899), *The Enchanted Woods, and Other Essays on the Genius of Places* (1905), *The Spirit of Rome: Leaves From a Diary* (1906), *The Sentimental Traveller: Notes on Places* (1908), *The Tower of the Mirrors, and Other Essays on the Spirit of Places* (1914), and *The Golden Keys and Other Essays on the Genius Loci* (1925).
12. In a 1921 letter to his American patron John Quinn, Symons expressed disappointment in finding no publisher for the volume, which Brentano had kept for two years but finally rejected; see *Arthur Symons: Selected Letters*, ed. by Beckson and Munro, pp. 248–49.
13. Besides Buzard's study mentioned above, significant references to this topic occur in Graham Dann, 'Writing out the Tourist in Space and Time', *Annals of Tourism Research*, 26 (1999), 159–87; Vasiliki Galani-Moutafi, 'The Self and the Other: Traveler, Ethnographer, Tourist', *Annals of Tourism Research*, 27 (2000), 203–24; Adrian Franklin and Mike Crang, 'The Trouble with Tourism and Travel Theory', *Tourist Studies*, 1 (2001), 5–22; and Camille C. O'Reilly, 'Tourist or Traveller? Narrating Backpacker Identity', in *Discourse, Communication and Tourism*, ed. by Adam Jaworski and Annette Pritchard (Cleveland: Channel View Publications, 2005), pp. 150–69.
14. *Arthur Symons: Selected Letters*, ed. by Beckson and Munro, p. 22.
15. Ibid., pp. 113–14.
16. Vineta Colby, *Vernon Lee: A Literary Biography* (Charlottesville & London: University of Virginia Press, 2003), pp. 120–21, and Ana Parejo Vadillo, 'Immaterial Poetics: A. Mary F. Robinson and the Fin-de-Siècle Poem', in *The Fin-de-siècle Poem: English Literary Culture and the 1890s*, ed. by Joseph Bristow (Athens: Ohio University Press, 2005), pp. 231–60 (p. 260, n. 57). As Vadillo notes, Lee shared Symons's enthusiasm for *An Italian Garden* (pp. 251–52).
17. Arthur Symons, 'A. Mary F. Darmesteter', in *The Poets and the Poetry of the Nineteenth Century*, ed. by Alfred H. Miles, 12 vols (London: Routledge; New York: Dutton, 1907), XI, 359–64.
18. Markert, *Arthur Symons*, p. 74. Lee collaborated with these magazines from 1878, and most frequently between 1881 and 1883. See also Peter Gunn, *Vernon Lee: Violet Paget, 1856–1935* (London: Oxford University Press, 1964), p. 66; and Colby, *Vernon Lee*, p. 79.
19. Vernon Lee, 'Botticelli at the Villa Lemmi', *Cornhill Magazine*, 46 (July-December 1882), 159–73; and 'The Portrait Art of the Renaissance', *Cornhill Magazine*, 47 (January-June 1883), 564–81.
20. Arthur Symons to James Dykes Campbell, 4 October 1886, in *Arthur Symons: Selected Letters*, ed. by Beckson and Munro, p. 42, n. 5.
21. Beckson, *Arthur Symons*, pp. 24–25.

22. Ibid., pp. 24–25.
23. Arthur Symons, *An Introduction to the Study of Browning* (London: Cassell, 1886), p. 100, n.
24. Markert, *Arthur Symons*, p. 74.
25. Stefano Evangelista, 'Vernon Lee and the Gender of Aestheticism', in *Vernon Lee: Decadence, Ethics, Aesthetics*, ed. by Catherine Maxwell and Patricia Pulham (Basingstoke: Palgrave Macmillan, 2006), pp. 91–111 (pp. 92–95).
26. Vernon Lee, *Genius Loci: Notes on Places* (London: Richards, 1899), p. 3.
27. Ibid., p. 5.
28. Ibid., p. 6.
29. John J. Conlon, *Walter Pater and the French Tradition* (Lewisburg, PA: Bucknell University Press, 1982), pp. 104, 125.
30. Charles Augustin Sainte-Beuve, *Les Cahiers de Sainte-Beuve* (Paris: Lemerre, 1876), p. 139. All translations are the author's own unless otherwise stated. See also Lander McClintock, *Sainte-Beuve's Critical Theory and Practice After 1849* (Chicago: University of Chicago Press, 1920), pp. 8–10, 99.
31. Quoted in Matthew Arnold, *Lectures and Essays in Criticism*, ed. by R. H. Super, 2nd edn (Ann Arbor: University of Michigan Press, 1962), p. 457. For a general description of the relationship between the two writers, see Arnold Whitridge, 'Matthew Arnold and Sainte-Beuve', *PMLA*, 53 (1938), 303–13; and F. J. W. Harding, *Matthew Arnold: The Critic and France* (Geneva: Librairie Droz, 1964), pp. 79–95.
32. Arnold, 'Joubert', in *Lectures and Essays in Criticism*, pp. 183–211 (p. 210).
33. Arthur Symons, 'The Goncourts', in *Figures of Several Centuries* (New York: Dutton, 1916), pp. 336–50 (p. 338).
34. Symons, 'The Decadent Movement in Literature', *Harper's New Monthly Magazine* (November 1893), repr. in *The Symbolist Movement in Literature*, p. 170.
35. Walter Pater, 'The School of Giorgione', in *The Renaissance*, pp. 102–22 (p. 121).
36. Walter Pater, 'Style', in *The Library Edition of the Works of Walter Pater*, 10 vols (London: Macmillan, 1910), V, 5–38 (p. 34).
37. Walter Pater, 'Plato and the Sophists', in *The Library Edition of the Works of Walter Pater*, VI, 99–123 (p. 120).
38. Pater, 'Preface', in *The Renaissance*, pp. xix–xxv (pp. xix–xx).
39. Arthur Symons, 'Walter Pater' [1906], in *Figures of Several Centuries*, pp. 316–35 (p. 319). The passage was reprinted in Symons's 'Introduction' to his edition of Pater's *Renaissance* (New York: The Modern Library, [1919]).
40. Lee, *Genius Loci*, p. 7.
41. Symons, 'To Madame la Comtesse de la Tour', pp. vi–vii.
42. Nicholas Freeman, *Conceiving the City: London, Literature, and Art, 1870–1914* (Oxford: Oxford University Press, 2007), p. 143.
43. Symons, *Plays, Acting, and Music* (1903), n. p.
44. Ibid.
45. Arthur Symons, 'To Rhoda', in *Studies in Seven Arts*, pp. v–vi (p. vi).
46. One of these two copies was presented by Coburn to Reading University in 1966, shortly before his death, and is still housed there. It seems that Symons never saw the edition. Thorough details on the volume's publishing history are found in Nicholas Freeman, 'Literary Representations of London, 1905–1909: A Study of Ford Madox Ford, Arthur Symons, John Davidson, and Henry James' (unpublished PhD dissertation University of Bristol, 1999). I am grateful to the author for allowing me to consult this work.
47. Symons, *London*, pp. 1–2, 5
48. Ibid., p. 8.
49. Ibid., p. 2.
50. Arthur Symons, 'Rome', in *Cities of Italy*, pp. 3–67 (p. 12).
51. See Josef Maria Eder, *History of Photography* [1932] (New York: Dover Publications, 1945).
52. Alfred Stieglitz, 'A Plea for Art Photography in America', *Photographic Mosaics* (1892), 135–37 (p. 137).

53. Steven Connor, *The Matter of Air: Science and Art of the Ethereal* (London: Reaktion, 2010), p. 38.
54. Ibid., p. 194.
55. For Hofmannsthal, see Jennifer Anna Gosetti-Ferencei, *Exotic Spaces in German Modernism* (Oxford: Oxford University Press, 2011), pp. 21–23. Gosetti-Ferencei defines atmosphere in Hofmannsthal as 'the quality of place as felt and lived' (p. 21). For Woolf, see Kristy Martin, *Modernism and the Rhythms of Sympathy: Vernon Lee, Virginia Woolf, and D. H. Lawrence* (Oxford: Oxford University Press, 2013), pp. 104–07.
56. See, for instance, 'Marseilles' (1929) and 'A Berlin Chronicle' (1932) in Walter Benjamin, *Reflections: Essays, Aphorisms, Autobiographical Writings*, ed. by Peter Demetz, trans. by Edmund Jephcott (New York: Shocken, 1978). See also Gernot Böhme, 'Atmosphere as the Fundamental Concept of a New Aesthetics', *Thesis Eleven*, 36 (1993), 113–26 (pp. 116–18).
57. Symons, *London*, p. 30.
58. Ibid., p. 58.
59. Ibid., p. 41.
60. Ibid., p. 42.
61. Ibid., p. 42.
62. Freeman, *Conceiving the City*, p. v.

CHAPTER 10

'Against Civilisation': Symons, the Gypsy Lore, and Politicised Aestheticism

Katharina Herold

> I want gradually to get together a collection of Romani literature. [...] I have an idea. I want to reach more readers than a society can possibly reach.
> ARTHUR SYMONS to Robert Andrew Scott Macfie, 19 March 1908[1]

In a 1919 letter to John Quinn, Arthur Symons recounts a sojourn in Oxford, using language suggestive of an exotic adventure:

> I have spent a week here — an absolute enchantment — these marvellous gardens, the ancient colleges: I saw Brasenose where Pater lived, right on the Bodleian. I spent yesterday with Robin de la Condamine; spent several hours with Robert Bridges in his house and on a bench under the sun — where I write now — Worcester Garden. A wild Arab boy has taken me over Oxford — we boated down the river.[2]

Symons's sensualised description of Oxford's lush gardens, historic sites, and prominent figures is laden with references to his cosmopolitan taste for travelling, and demonstrates his central role as theorist and facilitator of literary Decadence in England. The prologue to his first collection of poems, *Days and Nights* (1889), advocates borderless art that draws inspiration from life: art must be quintessentially mobile and transgressive in the literal sense, Symons argues, going 'beyond the boundaries' with a keen interest to explore 'strange lands'.[3] This fascination with the Other, embodied in his letter by 'a wild Arab boy', shows Symons's distinct interest in foreign, particularly Eastern cultures. He travelled extensively within Europe, reaching as far as Constantinople in 1903. Yet a predilection for travelling also manifested itself early in his life in his 'gypsylorism': the romanticisation and longing for a nomadic way of life as practised by the traveller communities. Beyond pursuing an anthropological interest in Romani culture, he elevated the figure of the gypsy, using him (or her) as a metaphor for the generic mobility of the Aesthetic text. As a Romantic longing for the foreign Other, gypsylorism encapsulates Symons's curiosity in strange and exotic sensuality. Pervading the whole of his career, this fascination for the gypsies generated an inclusive image of the East, both for him and for many of his fellow 'gypsylorists': 'I realised that there were other people in the world besides the conventional people I knew [...]. And I realised that there was another escape from these people besides a solitary flight in books'.[4] This passion for live encounter with other cultures, which sets 'the blood [...] on fire for wandering', not merely mediated by literature and mind travel, makes Symons stand out as an active, if not activist, aesthete.[5] For Symons, it was not enough to stylise the East in the way that Oscar Wilde had, conceptualising Japan as 'pure invention'.[6] Instead, he politicised the tensions between enchantment and repulsion evoked by the East; these tensions had decisively shaped Decadent canonical texts, including Gustave Flaubert's *Salammbô* (1862) and Wilde's *Salomé* (1891). Moreover, he experimented with definitions of exoticism and East-West binaries, the rigidity of which Edward Said and later postcolonialists criticised in their studies of nineteenth-century Orientalism. Whilst seemingly neglecting literary developments after his often-discussed breakdown in 1908, Symons used his Orientalised, post-Decadent writings to generate a journalistic interaction between Aestheticism and political agendas long seen as programmatically in opposition.[7] Symons now writes not 'against nature' but 'against civilisation'.[8]

Considered as a minor figure of European Decadence, Symons was in many respects a unique transistor and creator of networks, bridging different national literatures in his many translations from French, Spanish, Italian, and even Romani. He was a mediator between Decadence and early Modernism; for example, his influence was crucial in James Joyce's early career. Similarly, his friendship with Joseph Conrad and W. B. Yeats helped fashion these authors' literary reputations. As part of the inner circle of the 1890s avant-garde, Symons was acquainted with and corresponded with key Decadent figures such as Wilde, Verlaine, Mallarmé, and Beardsley. Despite his undoubted status as one of the most influential English critics of Decadence and author of 'The Decadent Movement in Literature' (1893), our impression of his literary achievements is all too often limited to his collections of dance-hall poetry. As a result, his life-long fascination for the East's promising mysteries of 'Oriental heat' and travelling communities, 'the wandering, wise, outcast sons | Of Pharaoh', remains unexplored.[9]

The mobile and mobilising qualities of Aesthetic texts in Symons's post-1895 writings, viewed in a larger context, enabled a transformation of Théophile Gautier's concept of 'art for art's sake'. Symons's activities as gypsylorist can thus provide a lens through which to analyse this shift towards a politicised Aestheticism. How does Aesthetic literature employ Orientalist tropes to build imagined and real communities with the political aim of promoting cultural exchange, instead of cultural classification? To answer this question, I consider Symons's membership of the Gypsy Lore Society and his controversial article 'In Praise of Gypsies' written for the *Journal of the Gypsy Lore Society* (hereafter *JGLS*) in 1908.

The generic clash of journalism and highly stylised prose in Symons's work re-defines the dynamics of response between author, text, and reader. The article makes the reader a 'passionate spectator' rather than a passive consumer, who is torn between extremes of aesthetic sensual enjoyment and political responsibility.[10] One thereby oscillates like the Decadents themselves between borders of inclusivity and exclusivity. Much like Matthew Arnold's scholar-gypsy, introduced in the eponymous poem in 1853, the Decadents simultaneously formed part of the bourgeois establishment whilst taking the role of self-fashioned outcasts, affiliating themselves with a 'counter-culture'.

Symons's depictions of the East reinvent the post-Romantic notions of Orientalism formulated by Gautier, Gustave Flaubert, and Charles Baudelaire; Gautier's travelogue, *Constantinople* (1854), and Baudelaire's work became Symons's trusted travel companions.[11] Symons detects 'something Oriental in Baudelaire's genius; a nostalgia that never left him after he had seen the East: there where one finds hot midnights, feverish days, strange sensations; for only the East, when one has lived in it, can excite one's vision to a point of ardent ecstasy'; this recalls his own youthful urge to undertake 'some ecstatic pilgrimage'.[12] Symons projects this ecstasy onto the gypsy as an extreme version of Baudelaire's *flâneur*. As such the gypsy is 'the wanderer whom all of us who are poets, or love the wind, are summed up in. He does what we dream. He is the last romance left in the world'.[13] The gypsy's Oriental otherness is thus associated with the Decadent's otherness in modernity, as described by Baudelaire in *Peintre de la vie moderne* (1863). Baudelaire defines the *flâneur* as an 'observer, philosopher [...] he is the painter of the passing moment and of all suggestions of eternity that it contains'.[14] The *flâneur* is 'not precisely an *artist*, but rather a *man of the world*': a judgement to which Symons himself was often subjected.[15]

In contrast to the passive 'opposition and revolt' found in the dandy's indifference, the perfect *flâneur* in the Baudelairean sense is the 'passionate spectator'.[16] Marked by 'an immense joy to set up house in the heart of the multitude', it is his innate disposition 'to be away from home and yet to feel [himself] everywhere at home; to see the world, to be at the centre of the world, and yet to remain hidden from the world'.[17] Symons's gypsy-*flâneur* crucially differs from Baudelaire's concept in that the gypsy for Symons serves as both a tool of literary creation and an object of study.

Symons's textual *flânerie* epitomises Impressionism as defined in 'The Decadent Movement in Literature'. Even though Symons distanced himself from the Decadent movement after the Wilde trials in 1895, he persisted in revising fundamental ideals of Decadence and Decadent writing. Symons's travel writings and gypsylorism are driven by 'a restless curiosity in research' exploring 'whatever corner of the visible world has to be realized'.[18] As Deborah Epstein Nord notes, English renderings of gypsylorism contrast with the French Bohemian-gypsy who generically represents 'an urban type who leans toward, rather than away from, the modernity of the metropolis'.[19] Similarly, Lisa Tickner classifies this *flânerie* of the urban bohemian as analogue to rural 'tramping' and the affiliations with caravan camps which the 'amateur gypsies' frequently sought.[20] In that respect Symons again must be considered a hybrid of the French and English traditions. In developing Baudelaire's proto-Modernist ideas, he introduces a political momentum into Aesthetic principles. In *Studies in Seven Arts* (1906), he writes:

> Beauty and the modern world are in open and inevitable war; life is a thing to be escaped from, not turned to one's purpose; [...] the modern world is a thing to struggle with, to conquer in fair fight, to compel to one's purpose, no matter at what cost.[21]

As Patricia Clements observes, this struggle with modernity is both his 'subject and method'.[22] By exploring 'strangeness' in its double meaning of unfamiliarity and abnormality, Symons encapsulates the East in the figure of the gypsy. In that way the gypsy acts as a vital catalyst for the innovation of Symons's post-Decadent style mediated by Baudelaire, Pater, and Wilde. The author, as well as the reader, becomes a *flâneur*, a 'decoder of experience', as Symons demonstrates both in his Constantinople travelogue and in his many gypsy poems.[23]

Very early on, he cast himself as a gypsy-lover and admirer of the Romani culture in his life writings, poetry, and fiction alike. In an 1888 letter to James Dykes Campbell, he declared himself to be a 'fervent Borrovian'; he was referring to the poet-scholar George Henry Borrow (1803–81), who disseminated Romantic notions of gypsylorism far and wide.[24] Through Borrow's influential publications, most famously *Lavengro: The Scholar, the Gypsy, the Priest* (1851) and its sequel *The Romani Rye* (1857), the gypsy was firmly established as an artistic metaphor. During the second half of the nineteenth century, these works acquired the status of a breviary for the gypsylorists, inspiring Symons to take up the study of Romani.[25] By 1893 and 1900 Theodore Watts-Dunton, another successful gypsy-writer with whom Symons corresponded, had edited both of Borrow's works.[26] Watts-Dunton's own gypsy-novel *Aylwin* (1898) sparked a literary sensation, selling over a hundred thousand copies by 1914.

In Symons's own writings, the gypsy turns into the ultimate symbol of transgressive liberty, perpetuating the notion of a dynamic internationalisation of Aesthetic and Decadent ideas. Symons's memoir, *Mes souvenirs* (1929), explicates his Orientalist conceptualisation of the gypsies:

> A race I have always admired beyond all other races, and which I have often come into contact with almost all over Europe: they are the Eternal Wanderers, and they are our only link with the East with Magic, and with Mystery.[27]

The gypsy as 'the only link' thus functions as connection not only to the East, but also bygone civilisations. Symons's emotional attachment to this interpretation of Romani culture is based on Romantic preconceptions. According to his portrayal, the gypsy is in touch with sensual and mystic inclinations rather than with the intellectual endeavours we might associate with modernity.[28] In Symons's case, the conceptual kinship between Orientalism and gypsylorism constructs European Romani cultures as 'the Orientals within', as Regenia Gagnier puts it.[29] Gypsies are poeticised, in that they represent 'the last picturesque relics of another age in today's prosaic epoch of steam and iron'; they are deliberately upheld as figures 'against Progress'.[30] Consequently, Symons's cultural philanthropy hovers between the idealisation of the gypsy's exotic charisma and his or her Orientalist exploitation.

Symons glamorises gypsies in his many gypsy-themed poems such as 'White Magic' (1894), 'The Tarot Cards' (1908), and 'The Gypsy's Song' (1917), all of which

FIG. 10.1. Photograph of Arthur Symons (second from right) posing with his Romani friends, ('Snapshots of Arthur Symons, with wife Rhoda, & with Gs.', possibly in Dora Yates's hand), University of Liverpool, Gypsy Lore Society Archive, GLS C1/13 [19]. By courtesy of the University of Liverpool.

are saturated with Decadent Orientalist tropes and regressive images of female sexuality. These texts replicate clichés such as 'the legend of Egyptian origin, the palm reading, the claim of magic powers, [...] flamboyant dance, the improvised violin music, the physical beauty and sexual allure'.[31] And yet, Symons's prose writings speak a different language from his poetry. Here he styles the gypsies' Edenic existence as an exemplary *Naturvolk* [primitive people]. In his semi-autobiographical record, 'A Prelude to Life' (1905), he reassesses his reading of Borrow as a quasi-spiritual experience:

> I got my first taste of a sort of gipsy element in literature, which was to become a passion, when later on, 'Lavengro' fell into my hands. The reading of 'Lavengro' did many things for me. It absorbed me from the first page. [...] 'Lavengro' [meaning: master of words in Romany] took my thoughts into the open air, and gave me my first conscious desire to wander. I learned a little Romany [*sic*], and was always on the lookout for gipsies. [...] Humanity began to exist for me.[32]

Following these early beginnings, Symons's enthusiasm came to the forefront in the later phase of his life, when he compiled a 'Gypsy portfolio, where [he kept] notes and letters and all scraps relating to the subject'.[33] As a natural consequence of his interest in the Romani culture, in November 1907 he joined the Gypsy Lore Society (hereafter GLS).

FIG. 10.2. Photograph of Arthur Symons (left) posing with his Romani friends ('Snapshots of Arthur Symons, with wife Rhoda, & with Gs.', possibly in Dora Yates's hand), University of Liverpool, Gypsy Lore Society Archive, GLS C1/13 [18].
By courtesy of the University of Liverpool.

Together with his fellow 'gypsyologists', as members referred to themselves, Symons undertook field trips to socialise with Romani travellers in Wales and Cornwall (Figs. 10.1–10.2). Symons's rich correspondence with fellow gypsyologists John Sampson and Robert Andrew Scott Macfie, archived in the GLS collections at the University of Liverpool, documents the society's zealous endeavour both to fathom Romani culture intellectually and experience it through live encounter. Symons signed a postcard sent to Sampson, reporting a chance meeting with two gypsy girls, simply with 'Love the Romani!!'.[34] In a letter to Sampson, he declares his admiration for the Romani once again: 'It has always been one of my desires to go with you amongst the Gypsies in Wales. It would not only be magnificent, but transcedent [sic].'[35] In a letter to Macfie he reiterates his temptation to become part of the travelling community:

> I was coming up from London the other day and just before Orpington I saw a big encampment, in a lane and two fishers' tents up, cooking utensils on the van, men, women, and children cowering and lying about. I was very much minded to jump out at the station, but should have lost my last train home, and so I refrained.[36]

His fervent interest in the transliteration and documentation of Romani dialects (he claimed to possess over 'a hundred books on this subject') and his childlike fascination for the people conflicts with his dandified pose as a Romani Ray (also 'Rye' or 'Rai').[37] The relationship between such 'Gypsy gentlemen' and the travelling communities was marked by an Orientalist belief in privileged dependency; denominating themselves as friends and benefactors of the local Romani community, this unbalanced 'friendship' model was not always reciprocated or appreciated.[38]

By the end of the nineteenth century, societies conducting scientific studies of the gypsies were flourishing. As Deborah Epstein Nord argues, the declared goal of these societies was to explore and record racial, linguistic, and cultural differences, yet also to draw out inter-cultural similarities in a 'mix of serious scholarship and nostalgia'.[39] The GLS, as one such group, grew from a mere collection of enthusiasts to an internationally recognised institution and self-declared authority on 'Romany matters'.[40] Founded in 1888, its members counted among them Edward Henry Palmer, Professor of Arabic at Cambridge, the 'Gipsy Archduke' Karl of Austria,[41] and Sir Richard Burton, whom Symons admired. Symons's circle of correspondents included Watts-Dunton, who acted as president of the society in 1909–10; painter Augustus John, president from 1937 to 1961; and Townley Searle, a bibliophile and bookseller, who in 1912 set up an artistic sub-group of the GLS called the 'Gypsy Salon'.[42] Searle's 'Salon', renamed the 'Gypsy and Folklore Club' in 1912, provided the platform for the editors and contributors of the magazine *The Gypsy* (1915–16) to meet. Symons was one of the contributors (Fig. 10.3).

Macfie's record of news clippings concerning gypsies, compiled throughout the year 1908, provides unparalleled insight into the workings of the GLS. On the one hand the compilation is witness to an exploitative fascination and sensationalism; yet it also documents the society's political engagement with the Romanis' civil rights. Looking through the newspaper clippings it becomes clear that the gypsies were regarded as a domestic security risk by many European nations. As a statement by the linguist Henry T. Crofton suggests — 'Gypsies are the Arabs of Pastoral England' — the Romani were demonised as a potential danger lurking in the midst of society.[43] They were associated with crime and illegal activities such as theft and fortune-telling. Headlines about elopements and unorthodox family affairs caused sensationalist outcries not only within England but also in Switzerland ('gypsi banditti'), France, Germany, Austria-Hungary ('Poisoning Gypsies — Appalling Acts of Revenge by Croatian Peasants'), and even New York ('Shall We Abolish Gypsies? — How Can You Catch the Children?').[44]

The now questionable nineteenth-century attempts to define the gypsies, or even to establish them as the Darwinian 'missing link', resulted in waves of literary and non-literary publications by self-declared gypsy-anthropologists.[45] These publications contributed to the stigmatisation of the Romani as a community of outsiders who were unfit for civilisation. Nord observes that the Romani suffered from 'persistent efforts to outlaw and destroy their way of life'.[46] Ironically, then, the GLS's aim was to prevent the decline of a culture that was directly identified as

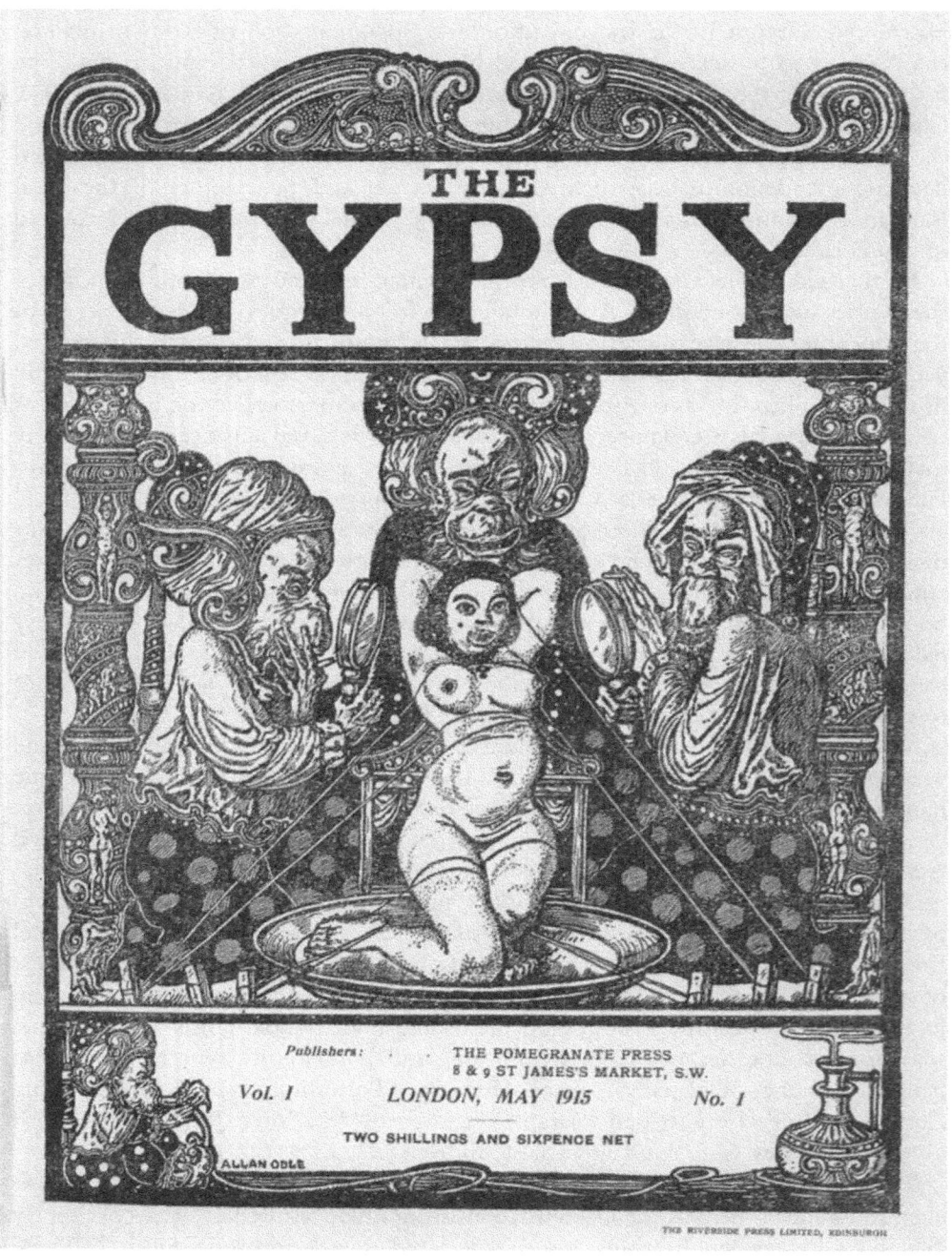

FIG. 10.3. Alan Odle, frontispiece for *The Gypsy*, 1.1 (May 1915), Oxford, Bodleian Libraries, Per. 2705 d.316 (1/2(1915/1916)). By permission of The Marsh Agency Ltd on behalf of the Estate of Alan Odle and the Bodleian Library, Oxford.

a threat to English society. Indeed, as Nord points out, the gypsylorists and gypsyologists were concerned to 'preserve the "purity" of Gypsy culture and to protect the pure-blooded Gypsies who best exemplified it' whilst undercutting their intention by embarking on first-hand 'field research' and mingling with travelling communities.[47] The interest in the Romani people was comparable to the hype of Egyptomania in the 1880s and 1890s, expanding into a pan-European sport of researching the 'gypsy' as a cultural phenomenon. This anthropological exploitation conflates, as Katie Trumpener remarks, 'literary traditions with living people'; this reached its climax during the Holocaust, with lasting tension felt up to the present day.[48]

At the turn of the century, these political controversies and the results of gypsyologist research were published in the *JGLS*. The journal's distribution was ensured by the society's affiliation with a number of universities, public libraries, and other anthropological societies. After its brief publication success from 1888 to 1892, the GLS and its journal folded. From 1906 Sampson and Macfie became the driving force behind the research work and publication of the *JGLS*. David MacRitchie, president of the GLS and the journal's chief editor from 1907 to 1908, resumed the society's activities until its second decline, around the outset of the First World War in 1914. From 1922 to 1974 the GLS was once more revived and thrived under its Honorary Secretary Dora Yates. Whilst fading out in the UK, an American branch of the association continues to grow today and twice yearly publishes the *JGLS* under its revised name *Romani Studies*.[49]

In 1908, the *JGLS* printed Symons's controversial article 'In Praise of Gypsies'. In the same year governmental measures to solve the so-called 'Gypsy Question' intensified, bringing about an extensive series of legislative actions against travelling communities. Reacting to the Moveable Dwellings Act and Children's Act passed in 1908, Symons took initiative for his Romani friends. In doing so, he abandoned his existence as one of the 'hothouse' Aesthetes and set out into the wildernesses of anthropological politics. His article, written in one evening 'with great heat', as he recalls, transfigures the gypsy into a symbol of transcendence and a means by which to recover sensual experience in modernity.[50] The article is important because it is Decadent in its hyperbolic representation of the gypsies, yet simultaneously relates to the contemporary political world. Symons argues against a sterile modernity ('civilisation') by glorifying the 'gypsy way of living' as the alternative. In contrast to the antithetical narratological strategies in his travelogues, the tone applied here is didactical rather than dialectical. Despite the attempt to root his argument in historical and linguistic scholarly detachment, the fast-paced opening of the article reflects the hot-headedness in which it was conceived. This suggests that the article is not only a political outcry, but also a defence of Symons's personal artistic agenda. As such, it represents an aestheticised political intervention against the decay of post-Victorian Aesthetic culture.

Opening the article is a shower of indefinite pronouns — 'these' and 'them' — which introduces a polemical tone; at times, this makes the opposed parties, the establishment and the travellers, indistinguishable. Symons opens the debate by pitting the 'reproving voice' of pamphleteer Samuel Roberts, an individualist and the spokesman of 'all wise men', against the nameless voice of the 'hateful' mass of technocrats:

> The people who hate *them* [the gypsies], and would control *them* and banish them [...]. The lawgivers hate *them*, the stationary powers hate *them*, the people who wear uniform and take wages hate *them*. *Those* who do not understand *them*, that is to say the main part of the civilised world, hate *them*.[51]

This generalisation becomes full-fledged hyperbole: 'From the *first* entry of the Gypsies into Europe, the hand of *every* man has been against them' (p. 298, my emphasis). Though this does not necessarily make Symons's argument persuasive, the text rightly questions the generic boundaries of criticism it has just tried to establish.

As if looking for the right word to express his agitation, Symons lists in quick succession the assumed enemies: 'the officials, the prose people, the mechanical minds' (p. 294). Noteworthy here is the poeticisation of political content through alliteration. Drawing on his observations from his visit to Constantinople, he now deems England, not the land of the 'Turks', 'our barbarous land' (p. 295). Not the East but Western capitalism acts as the state enemy:

> There has been great talk of late of degeneracy, decadence, and what are supposed to be perversities: such as religion, art, genius, individuality. But it is the millionaire, the merchant, the money-maker, the sweater, who are the degenerates of civilisation, and as the power comes into their hands all noble and beautiful things are being crushed out one after another. (p. 298)

While Symons suggests that recovering the 'gypsy way of living' may be a remedy against such decay, his argument simultaneously discriminates against it. As Janet Lyon contends, all categories of postcolonial critique apply here. The gypsies are made an 'object' of study; Symons's portrait is clearly racist and degrading despite his best efforts to elevate their cause. Nord argues that 'Symons's vision [...] amounts ultimately to a defence of his own social and cultural stance as a man prominently associated with the Decadent movement and French symbolism'.[52] While Lyon regards Symons's 'agitated essay' as 'deficient as a piece of activist journalism' and as a 'romanticized example of racist practices', I want to draw attention to the ambivalence of such representations in post-Decadent texts.[53]

By rendering the gypsy as a meta-national 'link with the East' (p. 296), Symons inverts imperial binaries. As he understands it, the East is, in its primitivist culture, closer to humanist progress than the West, which is degenerating into 'the likeness of a vast machine' (p. 298). By inverting the common associations between technology and progress, Symons plays with the reader's preconceptions of modernity. If Symons had engineered a Swiftian trapdoor of satirical and intentionally grotesque argument, heralded by Wilde's 'The Soul of Man under Socialism' (1891) some years earlier, this would be an excellent piece of criticism. However, despite neglecting a conscious commitment to satire, the text still manages to challenge the actual meaning of words: it raises questions of who are 'they'? What is meant by 'progress' and 'degeneration'? Who are the 'barbarians'? Is this text written from the perspective of an outsider or by a member of the establishment?

Equally, the analogy that suggests gypsies are 'nearer to the animals than any race known to us in Europe' (p. 296) is laden with racist discrimination. Yet this can be read as a pamphlet against the decay of Decadent culture, since civilisation, for Symons, can only be preserved by a radical return to nature. Through primitive ways of living far removed from the cult of artifice, the post-Decadents and gypsies alike act as pioneers; their ambition must be to rediscover one's instincts. This does not happen through an over-stimulation of the nerves, à la Des Esseintes or Dorian Gray, who are representative of 'a civilisation grown over-luxurious'.[54] Instead, a reconnection to the animalistic senses is required in order to protect 'nature before civilisation' (p. 296). This re-naturalisation was a prominent subject of contemporary research conducted by sociologists and philosophers such as Georg Simmel, whose essay 'Die Großstädte und das Geistesleben' [The Metropolis and Mental Life] was published in 1903 in Dresden. Like Symons, Simmel is concerned about the increase of mechanisation and the onslaught of urban sensations on the human psyche. A restoration of natural instincts is called for, if man is to preserve his or her individuality from the 'sovereign powers' of modern society.[55]

At the peripeteia of Symons's article, the use of anaphora positions the gypsy as a focal point at which the two narratives of art and politics meet:

> The Gypsy represents nature before civilisation. [...] His is the only free race, and the tyranny of law and progress would suppress his liberty. That is the curse of all civilisation, it is a tyranny, it is the force of repression. To try to repress the Gypsies is to fight against instinct, to try to cut out of humanity its rarest impulse. (p. 296)

Symons's concept of 'humanity's rarest impulse' reinterprets Pater's 'gem-like flame'.[56] Once the source of Decadent sensual inquisitiveness, Symons now sees it turning to cinders, at risk of being stifled by modernity. In an apologetic tone Symons adds in defence of the gypsies and poets that 'their secrecy is a fine art'; lying is 'a sign of what is imaginative in them' (p. 297). Wilde playfully teased his readers in 'The Decay of Lying' (1891), but Symons's defence of lying as the art of gypsies and poets alike leaves the reader to feel the uneasiness of the text as it tries to situate itself between political and artistic manifesto. Indeed, that is where the article's true political potential lies: in discomfiting, and creating conflicts within, its reader.

In comparison to Wilde's ambiguous aphorisms, Symons leaves no room for speculation about the unsettling analogies between literary and political reality. Like the gypsies, the Decadents are a travelling community:

> Here to-day and there to-morrow; you cannot follow them, for all the leafy tracks that they leave for each other on the ground. They are distinguishable from the people of every land which they inhabit; there is something in them finer, stranger, more primitive, something baffling to all who do not understand them through a natural sympathy. [They] are to be found wherever one travels, east or west. (p. 297)

In this passage Symons once more conflates the gypsies and the Decadent artists as 'extreme *flâneurs*' seeking sensations in a modern sterile environment. He quotes Pater: '"Like one on a secret errand," as Walter Pater said of the mysterious Leonardo, they pass through the world' (p. 296). Symons equates Pater's Leonardo, a symbol of Western artistic ingenuity who, in Pater's description, drew inspiration for his *Gioconda* from Eastern and Western mythologies, with the gypsy. As post-Renaissance men, the Decadent artists also need to resort to the East — to take inspiration from gypsy culture — in order for Aestheticism to survive in modernity: 'It is eastward that one must go to find their least touched beauty, their original splendour' (p. 297). The ambiguity of the text is also apparent in Symons's self-plagiarism from passages already used in *Cities*; he recycles material from his travels, during which he 'saw the beauty of the Gypsies in its most exact form' (p. 297). Read in this way, the perspectives of argument are manifold; artistic and political discourses are palimpsestically superimposed.

The article addresses the global significance of 'the Gypsy Question'. In line with Orientalist practice, Symons aggrandises the East and admonishes the Western world's ignorance of a:

> Civilisation, as it was thousands of years ago, in China, in India, [which] was an art of living, beside whose lofty beauty *we* are like street urchins scrambling in a gutter. *We* live to pick up scraps; *they* lived a tranquil and rational existence. The secret is lost to all the nations of Europe, squabbling about trade, prattling about precedence. (p. 298–99, my emphasis)

Moreover, the *JGLS*'s editorial note establishes the 'Gypsy Question' as a pan-European concern. The nineteenth-century aficionados of gypsydom lobbied for the protection of the gypsy 'species', threatened by industrial progress and the institutionalisation of culture. Symons, the advocate of 'The Decadent Movement in Literature', now ironically argues against 'Decadent internalism and separation'.[57] Symons's article thus demonstrates the fluidity of the word 'Decadent'. The reader is left wondering which process is signified as Decadent. Does Symons refer to the impending disappearance of gypsy culture, which in his eyes is a decaying culture? Or is the article to be understood as testimony to Symons's own career in decline, a statement on the future of Decadent writing made by a writer who represents a nostalgic remnant of the 1890s set? How can Symons's appeal for a progressive liberalism appear conservative and even anti-modern in tone and style?

Symons transmutes the gypsy into an aesthetic concept as well as a political agenda. He casts the gypsy as an extreme *flâneur*, experiencing reality through art, diving in and out of society *ad libitum*, embodying the 'in-between' of landlessness. His gypsylorism is therefore an expression of an artistic conviction but equally a manifestation of his political awareness. For Symons and many of his fellow writers, late nineteenth-century and early-Modernist notions of gypsylorism served to connect past and present, establishment and counter-culture; they also facilitated cosmopolitan exchange.

Starting from an anthropological examination in *Cities*, Symons styles the gypsy as an abstract, post-Romantic, immaterial, and immortal concept. Despite its politicising thrust, Symons's 'In Praise of Gypsies' is conspicuously Decadent in style. While still championing Decadent notions of transience and (im)mortality through his depiction of the gypsies as the 'eternal wanderers', Symons writes a modern manifesto. The result therefore is a very pressing, immediate, and political force. His defence of what he regarded as the gypsy philosophy voices strong anti-Modernist tendencies, while also trying to alert the reader to take action and intervene in current affairs.

Symons's engagement with the gypsies must be read as a political manifesto for an Aestheticism based on principles of cosmopolitan exchange and freedom of expression. Moreover, the gypsy comes to represent 'unfettered communicative interaction'.[58] The conceptualisation of the gypsy in the text as the alter ego of Decadence thus emphasises the importance of co-operation between its writers and readers: the text wanders in a Paterian sense between aesthetics and criticism, bordering on extremes of social inclusivity and exclusivity. The gypsy assumes the role of communicator between not only Aestheticism and modernity, but also the imagined Orient and Europe, thus complicating the conception of the Other.

Finally, Symons's post-Decadent text successfully calls into question the conditions of cosmopolitanism and Decadent tendencies toward an auto-exoticism through the identification with figures such as the gypsy. His treatment of the gypsy as a mediator of post-Decadent self-production between art and politics shows him to be a visionary critic. During the First World War, Britain and its colony Egypt were pitted against Wilhelmine Germany and its Ottoman alliance in Turkey; the exaltation of art above domestic and even global politics engendered a radically politicised Aestheticism at the beginning of the new century. Attempting a re-positioning of Decadence in Modernism, the Aesthetic magazine entitled *The Gypsy* appeared in two volumes from 1915 to 1916. It featured Symons's poems 'Nini Patte-en-l'air', originally published in the *Star* in 1894. *The Gypsy*'s decisive appeal to resurrect the 'art of knowing how to be | Part lewd, aesthetical in part, | And *fin de siècle* essentially', stresses the vital importance of artistic and political interaction — something which Symons had already fostered in his engagement with gypsylorism.

Notes to Chapter 10

1. University of Liverpool, Gypsy Lore Society, MS GLS A4, 535.
2. Arthur Symons to John Quinn, September 1919, in *Arthur Symons: Selected Letters*, ed. by Beckson and Munro, pp. 244–45. Robin de la Condamine was a Spanish actor, who used the name 'Robert Farquharson' on the English stage. In 1918 Symons wrote that Farquharson's performance showed 'a kind of rare and wandering genius, sinister, sombre, perverse and passionate' (*Selected Letters*, p. 245).
3. Symons, 'Prologue of *Days and Nights*', in *Days and Nights*, pp. 1–4 (p. 1).
4. Symons, *Spiritual Adventures* (1905), pp. 32–33.
5. Arthur Symons, 'The Gypsy's Song', in *Lesbia and other Poems* (New York: Dutton, 1920), pp. 66–67 (p. 67).
6. Oscar Wilde, 'The Decay of Lying', in *Complete Works of Oscar Wilde*, ed. by Ian Small and others (Oxford: Oxford University Press, 2000–), IV (2007), 72–103 (p. 98).
7. *Arthur Symons: Selected Letters*, ed. by Beckson and Munro, p. xi.
8. Arthur Symons, 'In Praise of Gypsies', *Journal of the Gypsy Lore Society*, n.s. 1:4 (April 1908), 294–99 (p. 298).

9. Arthur Symons, 'Alvisi Contarini', in *Love's Cruelty* (London: Martin Secker, 1923), p. 13; 'Perfect Grief', in *Images of Good and Evil* (London: W. Heinemann, 1899), p. 168.
10. Charles Baudelaire, 'The Painter of Modern Life', in *The Painter of Modern Life and Other Essays*, ed. and trans. by Jonathan Mayne (London: Phaidon, 1995), pp. 1–42 (p. 9).
11. Patricia Clements, *Baudelaire and the English Tradition* (Princeton, NJ: Princeton University Press, 1985), p. 214.
12. Arthur Symons, 'Mundi victima', in *Amoris victima* (London: Smithers, 1897), pp. 55–72 (p. 66); *Charles Baudelaire: A Study* (London: Elkin Mathews, 1920), p. 39.
13. Symons, 'In Praise of Gypsies', p. 296.
14. Baudelaire, 'The Painter of Modern Life', pp. 4–5.
15. Ibid., p. 7.
16. Ibid., pp. 28, 9.
17. Ibid., p. 9.
18. Symons, 'The Decadent Movement in Literature', in *The Symbolist Movement in Literature*, pp. 169–84 (pp. 169–70).
19. Deborah Epstein Nord, *Gypsies and the British Imagination, 1807–1930* (New York: Columbia University Press, 2006), pp. 131–32.
20. Lisa Tickner, *Modern Life and Modern Subjects: British Art in the Early Twentieth Century* (New Haven, CT: Yale University Press, 2000), pp. 53–54.
21. Symons, *Studies in Seven Arts*, p. 108.
22. Clements, *Baudelaire and the English Tradition*, p. 187.
23. Ibid., p. 197.
24. Arthur Symons to James Dykes Campbell, 2 January 1888, British Library, Add. MS 49522.
25. Beckson, *Arthur Symons*, p. 13.
26. Catherine Maxwell, *Second Sight: The Visionary Imagination in Late Victorian Literature* (Manchester & New York: Manchester University Press, 2007), p. 170.
27. Arthur Symons, *Mes souvenirs* (Chapelle-Réanville: Hours, 1929), p. 38.
28. Nicholas Saul, *Gypsies and Orientalism in German Literature and Anthropology of the Long Nineteenth Century* (Oxford: Legenda, 2007), p. 6.
29. Regenia Gagnier, *Individualism, Decadence and Globalization: On the Relationship of Part to Whole, 1859–1920* (Basingstoke: Palgrave Macmillan, 2010), p. 126. For a thorough discussion of the parallels between Orientalism and gypsylorism see Ken Lee, 'Orientalism and Gypsylorism', *Social Analysis*, 2 (2000), 129–56 (p. 130).
30. Gagnier, *Individualism, Decadence and Globalization*, pp. 8, 127.
31. Saul, *Gypsies and Orientalism in German Literature and Anthropology of the Long Nineteenth Century*, p. 3.
32. Symons, *Spiritual Adventures* (1905), pp. 32–33.
33. Arthur Symons to Robert Andrew Scott Macfie, 1 April 1908, MS GLS A4 537.
34. Arthur Symons to John Sampson 16 August 1911, MS GLS C1/13 (10).
35. Arthur Symons to John Sampson, 27 August 1910, MS GLS C1/13 (11).
36. Arthur Symons to Robert Andrew Scott Macfie, 1 July 1908, MS GLS A6 (736).
37. Arthur Symons to Dora Yates, undated, MS GLS C1/13 (14).
38. Lee, 'Orientalism and Gypsylorism', p. 139.
39. Nord, *Gypsies and the British Imagination, 1807–1930*, p. 126.
40. Theodore Watts-Dunton to John Sampson, 5 May 1908, MS GLS B15 (59). For a more detailed history of the GLS see Angus Fraser, 'A Rum Lot', in *100 Years of Gypsy Studies*, ed. by Matt T. Salo (Cheverly, MD: Gypsy Lore Society, 1990), pp. 1–15.
41. Theodore Watts-Dunton to John Sampson, 8 May 1908, MS GLS, B15 (60).
42. See <http://www.liv.ac.uk/library/sca/colldescs/gypsy/index.html> [accessed 6 March 2015].
43. B. C. Smart and Henry T. Crofton, *The Dialect of the English Gypsies* (London: Asher, 1875), p. xvi.
44. [Anon.], 'Poisoning Gypsies — Appalling Acts of Revenge by Croatian peasants', *Morning Reader* (26 February 1908); and [Anon.], 'Shall We Abolish Gypsies? — How Can You Catch the Children?', *Public Opinion* (10 April 1908), cuttings albums (1907–1913), Liverpool University, Scott Macfie Gypsy Collections, SMGC 5/2.

45. Saul, *Gypsies and Orientalism in German Literature and Anthropology of the Long Nineteenth Century*, p. 9.
46. Nord, *Gypsies and the British Imagination, 1807–1930*, p. 3.
47. Ibid., p. 150.
48. Katie Trumpener, 'The Time of the Gypsies: A "People Without History"', in *Identities*, ed. by Anthony Appiah and Henry Louis Gates, Jr. (Chicago: University of Chicago Press, 1995), pp. 338–80 (p. 344).
49. See <http://www.gypsyloresociety.org> [accessed 15 March 2017].
50. Arthur Symons to Edward Hutton, 16 April 1908, cited by Beckson, *Arthur Symons*, p. 251.
51. Symons, 'In Praise of Gypsies', pp. 294–95, my emphasis. Further references to this article are given in the main body of the text.
52. Nord, *Gypsies and the British Imagination, 1807–1930*, p. 137.
53. Janet Lyon, 'Gadže Modernism', *Modernism/Modernity*, 11:3 (2004), 517–38 (p. 520).
54. Symons, 'The Decadent Movement in Literature', p. 170.
55. Georg Simmel, 'The Metropolis and Mental Life', in *The Sociology of Georg Simmel*, ed. and trans. by Kurt H. Wolff (London: Macmillan, 1950), pp. 409–24 (p. 409).
56. Pater, *The Renaissance*, p. 189.
57. Gagnier, *Individualism, Decadence and Globalization*, p. 129.
58. Ibid., p. 126.

CHAPTER 11

❖

'Serious in the Reality of his Devotion to Art': The Genealogy of Symons's Assessment in *A Study of Oscar Wilde*

Laura Giovannelli

Before analysing the structure and content of *A Study of Oscar Wilde*, a slim, largely neglected volume first published in a limited luxury edition in December 1930, it will be useful to consider Arthur Symons's assessments of Oscar Wilde's personality and artistic career from the late 1880s to the age of Modernism.[1] This approach is justified not only by Symons's well-known post-1908 propensity to assemble, revise, and tamper with previously published material, but by the admittedly shifting and strained relation between him and the Irish author;[2] though Wilde was less influential in Symons's cultural growth than, say, Robert Browning, Walter Pater, or W. B. Yeats, his presence and impact were nonetheless significant.

The young Symons — a sensitive interpreter of Pater, subtle critic, and spokesman for the 'Parisian lesson' — appears, in fact, to have initially dismissed Wilde. In an 1887 letter, he dryly confessed to having 'never looked upon him as anything but a flighty-brained enthusiast and *poseur*'.[3] Wilde, however, during his editorship of the *Woman's World*, published Symons's poem 'Charity' in September 1888 and commissioned the article that would eventually appear as 'Villiers de l'Isle-Adam' in October 1889, by which time Wilde no longer held his editorial position. After an early phase of desultory correspondence, they probably met for the first time in October 1890, although in Symons's blurred reminiscences the date would be postponed to 1894.[4] Symons paid further visits to Wilde's home in Tite Street, Chelsea, and they occasionally encountered one another at the Rhymers' Club and the Café Royal. Their relationship and interactions were complex and, though their artistic paths crossed several times, they often operated at cross-purposes.

Wilde seems to have first appreciated Symons's perceptive understanding of French literature and art alongside Pater's seminal writings. After this fleeting enthusiasm, however, he cooled down when faced with Symons's overwhelming stream of publications, assuming a 'jokingly contemptuous attitude' towards him at least until 1898, when Symons wrote an approving review of *The Ballad of Reading Gaol*.[5] Wilde seemed to paint Symons as a weak man with no sense of self; his was the disconsolate, coreless profile of 'an Egoist who had no Ego'.[6] As critics have often underlined, this oscillating and ambiguous attitude was vividly captured by Vincent O'Sullivan, an Irish-American novelist, poet, and friend of Wilde, especially in his post-prison days. In O'Sullivan's relatively reliable reconstruction, which Joseph Bristow regards as 'one of the first steps in the direction of a more dependable biographical study' of Wilde,[7] we find that:

> [Wilde] did not like the writings of Arthur Symons, but as Symons wrote the best article that appeared on the publication of the *Ballad,* he felt obliged to rectify his attitude towards the poet of *London Nights*. He advanced the theory that there was a syndicate which produced a mass of printed matter under the corporate name of Arthur Symons. 'I have written to my solicitor to inquire about shares in Symons Ltd.' He added, 'Naturally in mass productions of that kind you can never be certain of the quality. But I think one might risk some shares in Symons'.[8]

Symons's feelings about Wilde took a different course. At the beginning, Wilde's personality did nothing but pique the curiosity of the restrained Symons, who was later to experience a fitful surge of interest in Wilde in the 1890s. During and after the 1895 trials, he chose instead to keep aloof, until he finally moved towards a downright condemnation in a number of pieces written in the first half of the twentieth century. As we shall see, however, *A Study of Oscar Wilde* might be considered something of an exception within this trend.

Besides these fluctuating and overlapping perspectives, it is worth drawing attention to the fact that, as is well-known, his 1908 breakdown marked a watershed in Symons's life, morals, and mental attitude. His decision eventually to take an open stand against Wilde's 'sins' and supposed depravity is, of course, bound up with the long-lasting consequences of the event, which impaired his analytical capacity, plunged him into solitude and estrangement, and revived the old religious fears that he had introjected as a child. Symons did not totally lose touch with Wildean subjects — the idea of the egotist and quintessential Decadent artist, his mastery as a stylist and brilliant talker — but he was arguably driven by renewed recollections of his Methodist background and obsession with evil and damnation. Thus, he played the worn card of the corrupting/corrupted Oscar going against nature, and forgot the fine intellectual qualities and engaging dialectic he had once praised so insightfully in the author of *Intentions*.

When unencumbered by this strait-laced, puritanical morality, or worse, a depressive state, Symons did however see through Wilde's achievements. As Karl Beckson has noticed, he even managed to pave the way for Wilde's modern reception. At the end of the nineteenth century, Wilde was often hastily accused of plagiarism, affectation, lawless extravagance, mediocrity, and, needless to say, sickly Decadence. Symons realised that there was much more than this, pointing to 'the alchemy involved in the creative process' that informed Wilde's borrowings.[9] This view characterises his 1891 unsigned review of *Intentions* in the *Speaker*, which also appeared, in a slightly revised form, as Chapter 2 ('*Intentions*') in *A Study of Oscar Wilde*:

> Mr. Wilde is much too brilliant to be ever believed; he is much too witty to be ever taken seriously. A passion for caprice, a whimsical Irish temperament,

> a love of art for art's sake — it is in qualities such as these that we find the origin of the beautiful farce of æstheticism, the exquisite echoes of the *Poems*, the subtle decadence of *Dorian Gray*, and the paradoxical truths, the perverted common sense, of the *Intentions*. Mr. Wilde, with a most reasonable hatred of the *bourgeois* seriousness of dull people, has always taken refuge from the commonplace in irony. Intentionally or not — scarcely without intention — he has gained a reputation for frivolity which does injustice to a writer who has at least always been serious in the reality of his devotion to art. The better part of his new book is simply a plea for the dignity, an argument for the supremacy, of imaginative art.[10]

This idea of Wilde's consciousness as an artist — the awareness that he did anything but underestimate his aesthetic covenant, and was often earnest about questions relating to composition, imagery, and style — confirms Symons's foresight. In his observations about Wilde's professionalism and the complexity of such works as *The Picture of Dorian Gray* (1890, 1891), he anticipates evaluations that only became mainstream in the twentieth century. In its thin but glittering discursive texture, Symons's review encourages the reader to move to a higher hermeneutic plane, pondering the standards of Wilde's *oeuvre* and appreciating how, as Merlin Holland remarked with reference to Wilde's letters a hundred years after his death:

> The perception of Wilde as the lightweight author of society comedies, a few memorable poems and some fairy stories must finally make room for Wilde as a hard-working professional writer, deeply interested by the issues of his day and carrying in his intellectual baggage something that we all too frequently overlook, a quite extraordinary classical, literary and philosophical education.[11]

In Symons's observations, with their faint echoes of Pater's 'Conclusion' to *The Renaissance* (1873), we might find a sense of sympathy with Wilde's critical principles — the hints and flashes of the 'sensitive examination', that brushing aside of the 'final vestiges of Victorianism and provincialism in British criticism', which Arnold B. Sklare singled out as some of Symons's distinguishing traits as an anti-*bourgeois* literary critic. It is as if Wilde's example helped him further incorporate Pater's influence, although 'Symons conscientiously endeavoured to be a creative critic; Wilde merely talked about the idea'.[12]

In 1891, the year he reviewed *Intentions*, Symons had already come into contact with such influential figures as Pater (the dedicatee of *Days and Nights*, his 1889 volume of poems), Stéphane Mallarmé, J.-K. Huysmans, and Paul Verlaine; when he joined the Rhymers' Club, he would meet W. B. Yeats and forge yet another crucial bond. To this coterie he seems to have granted Wilde an oblique, intermittent access through the years. In 'The Decadent Movement in Literature' (1893), he confines himself to citing the 'most beautiful' and 'perfectly finished' prose of Pater and the verse of W. E. Henley as the two significant English landmarks in the rise of Decadence.[13] The fact that Wilde's name kept being glossed over in the various chapters of *The Symbolist Movement in Literature* (1899) indicates, once again, a discontinuous and problematic alliance. Yet we can assume that, before he openly emerged in 1893 as 'the spokesman for the English Decadence', Symons was more willing to take unbeaten paths and explore unconventional ideas freely — even proudly.[14] Moreover, his praise of Wilde's lucid mind is in tune with both his own self-consciousness as a polished craftsman and his reflections on Browning's intellectual vigour in *An Introduction to the Study of Browning* (1886). In a piece from *Days and Nights* — the melodramatic interlude entitled 'An Episode Under the Nihilists' — it is tempting to see Wilde's *Vera; or, The Nihilists* as a likely source of inspiration for Symons's bathos and wooden characterisation of Dmitri and Vera.[15]

These are, then, a few deeper connections which may help better to contextualise the *Speaker* review, written during Symons's fervid and experimental Decadent phase. While giving the elements of wit, flamboyant performing, and sparkling Irishness their due — what James Joyce would figuratively gloss via the image of Wilde playing 'court jester to the English' — in that article he proceeds to place greater emphasis on Wilde's substantial commitment to art than on his frivolity.[16] Though the words 'serious' and 'reality' might clash with the image of the self-indulgent dandy, luxuriating in both popular and media attention, they are, in fact, instrumental: they aim to mark out what is really important and vital in the aesthetic/spiritual dimension from the shallow and inexpressive composure of philistinism ('the *bourgeois* seriousness of dull people'). In strengthening the case for recognising a seriousness behind Wilde's irony, masks, and anti-pedagogical bent — as opposed to the pseudo-gravity of middle-class morality — Symons also adumbrates future theoretical approaches, e.g. by Michel Foucault, to the conflicts between dominant ideologies and cultural counter-currents, bourgeois power structures and the potentially disruptive standpoint. Far from being light-heartedly dégagé, the author of a challenging book like *Intentions* ought thus to be understood as engaged both in the intellectual and political arenas: Wilde is participating in a discussion about the agency and domain of the artist and critic, about the effects of dramatic representation and the opportunities it offers, and about the unstable nature of truth. Symons clearly discerned something that lay at the heart of Wilde's writing: the way that art's fascinating lies might push against the constraints of verisimilitude, referentiality, action, or ethical responsibility.

Rooted in ancient traditions, this Wildean discourse could hardly be considered vain or absurd. Instead, it had an essential, if disguised, rationality, and was a kind of mainstay for Symons. After quoting some powerful and now largely familiar maxims from 'The Decay of Lying' (such as 'Life imitates art far more than art imitates life' and 'Art never expresses anything but itself'), Symons asserts:

> All this, startling as it sounds, needs only to be properly apprehended, to be properly analysed, and we get an old doctrine, indeed, but a doctrine in which there is a great deal of sanity and a perfectly reasonable view of things. The two long dialogues called 'The Critic as Artist' present a theory of criticism which might certainly be justified by the practice of some of the most perfect among critical writers.[17]

Finally, this positive commentary illuminates another facet of Wilde's praxis besides his paradoxes and epigrams: namely, his recourse to what we could now call a kaleidoscopic intertextual method, crucial to both Modernism and Postmodernism:

> At his best, to our thinking, when he is most himself — an artist in epigram — he can be admirable even when his eloquence reminds us of the eloquent writing of others. He is conscious of the charm of graceful echoes, and is always original in his quotations.[18]

Being original in one's own quotations — a paradox applied to a master of paradoxes — might, of course, simply mean that Wilde liked to sift out passages with which the reading public was unfamiliar. But that phrase also carries us forward to T. S. Eliot's idea of a 'simultaneous order', or even to Harold Bloom's 'map of misreading': all things considered, Wilde's method of critical revisiting, manipulation, and conflation of sources provides the groundwork for a host of textual practices ranging from deconstructive contamination to creative misquotation.[19] Instead of accusing Wilde of theft, Symons reinforces the belief that such a polyphonic mode could conceal a clever dialogic strategy.

Symons was also sympathetic to Wilde's ostracism by the philistine public in the wake of his suffering. Although he did not attend the trials and was wary of mentioning Wilde in his post-1895 correspondence, he was only too aware of the anxiety fuelled by the gross indecency scandal. It is probably no coincidence that his turning away from hedonistic unrest and fleshly Decadence towards Symbolism should date back to the years 1895–96, when he was struggling with depression and came to find his beliefs more consonant with Yeats's transcendent vision. Interestingly, too, the first plans for *The Savoy* (the magazine which he was to edit in 1896 as an outlet for Aestheticism, after Aubrey Beardsley's dismissal as art editor of the 'purged' *Yellow Book*) were conceived in Dieppe, 'where Beardsley and Symons had fled after Wilde's disgrace, not because they were in any way connected with the scandal, but simply because it was sufficient to have been distantly associated with Wilde to incur public censure'.[20]

This is also when Leonard Smithers, the Sheffield solicitor and notorious publisher of erotica, enters the picture in relation to both *The Savoy* and Wilde. Smithers joined Symons and Beardsley, who had produced the sensuous illustrations for *Salomé* (1894), in the establishment of the new London periodical, and he would soon endeavour to publish *The Ballad of Reading Gaol*. While he distanced himself during the trials (when he led a sort of secluded, circumspect and quiet life), in 1898 Symons got in touch with Smithers and offered help: 'I see by your advertisement in the *Athenaeum* that you are publishing Wilde's poem. I need scarcely say that if I could do anything that would be of service to Wilde, now that he is making his first attempt to return to literature, I should be only too glad to do it'.[21] And here is Wilde's response, again via the publisher: 'Pray thank Arthur Symons from me for his kind offer, and say how gratified I should be to be reviewed by him. I hope the *Saturday* will have an article by him'.[22]

This article was the 1898 signed review of *The Ballad of Reading Gaol* in the *Saturday Review*, partly reprinted in Chapter 3 of *A Study of Oscar Wilde*. Symons's appraisal was so warm that Wilde himself was touched by the 'sensitive and intellectual appreciation' in this 'admirably written' piece, and expressed his gratitude to Frank Harris, then editor of the *Saturday Review*, Leonard Smithers, the publisher of the poem, and Robert Ross.[23] In spite of its conventional form and pragmatic aim of urging prison reform, Symons read the *Ballad* as a turning-point in Wilde's career: it was the moment when 'a romantic artist' found himself 'working on realistic material', coming to grips with 'genuine human emotion' and raw facts. Symons describes Wilde as:

> A great spectacular intellect, to which, at last, pity and terror have come in their own person, and no longer as puppets in a play. In its sight, human life has always been something acted on the stage; a comedy in which it is the wise man's part to sit aside and laugh, but in which he may also disdainfully take part, as in a carnival, under any mask. The unbiassed, scornful intellect, to which humanity has never been a burden, comes now to be unable to sit aside and laugh [...]. And now [...] it has gone, not unnaturally, to an extreme, and taken, on the one hand, humanitarianism, on the other realism, at more than their just valuation in matters of art.[24]

The 'artist in epigram' toying with intellectual abstractions now appears incapable of overlooking morality. Instead, he dissects and problematises it, having endured tragic experiences. Here, then, is a piece of work originating from both head and heart; it has an obvious literary status, is a testament to lived experience, and takes the reader to a place of sinister, gloomy reverie. When compared to other contemporary reviews of the poem, Symons's contribution reads like the most carefully meditated and offers the 'greatest praise'.[25]

After Wilde's death, though, the energy and conviction that informed Symons's observations lost intensity. In *A Study of Oscar Wilde*, he appended a note explaining that a number of passages had appeared in literary journals but were 'thoroughly revised so as to exclude ephemeral allusions from an original and more fully considered appreciation of Wilde' (p. 89). These amendments gave way to some sad afterthoughts. In the twenty-eight-page third chapter of the volume, the original paragraphs of the *Saturday Review* piece are re-assembled and supplemented with a deeper focus on the *Ballad*'s stages of composition, including some updated references to the controversy involving Lord Alfred Douglas and his bitterly polemical *Oscar Wilde and Myself* (1914). Douglas claimed, among other things, to have helped Wilde write the poem while in Naples. Quotations from Douglas (which Symons acknowledges but refrains from judging) are complemented by a selection of more humane comments by Frank Harris, by a sort of muddled survey of Wilde's literary models, and by what admittedly sounds like an uncalled-for outline of the development of the ballad form throughout the decades (from the ancient ballade, a dance-song, to the writings of François Villon, Thomas Hood, D. G. Rossetti, and Tennyson). The remaining sections of the chapter consist of borrowings from Symons's own 'An Artist in Attitudes: Oscar Wilde', a 1901 piece that would appear in *Studies in Prose and Verse* and be translated into French; these passages criticised the Irish author for his excessive posturing, 'primarily for his lack of sincerity, or what Yeats would have called his "lack of intensity"'.[26] In resuming the logical thread of his 1898 considerations, Symons eventually comes to Wilde's artistic decline after the prison years:

> When *The Ballad of Reading Gaol* was published, it seemed to some people that such a return to, or so startling a first acquaintance with, real things was precisely what was most required to bring into relation, both with life and art, an extraordinary talent, so little in relation with matters of common experience, so fantastically alone in a region of intellectual abstractions. [...] Nothing followed. Wit remained, to the very end, the least personal form of speech, and thus the kindest refuge for one who had never loved facts in themselves. [...] His intellect was dramatic, and the whole man was not so much a personality as an attitude. Without being a sage, he maintained the attitude of a sage; without being a poet, he maintained the attitude of a poet; without being an artist, he maintained the attitude of an artist. And it was precisely in his attitudes that he was most sincere. (*A Study of Oscar Wilde*, pp. 44, 46–47)[27]

Much of the 1930 book highlights the motif of attitudes and posturing: Symons builds an image of Wilde where the brilliant intellectual component is set against the artist's ultimate failure to go deeper — to show his human face, the 'unrealised part of himself' — behind the parade of masks (p. 47). The same argument ran through Symons's unsigned review of Robert Ross's *First Collected Edition of the Works of Oscar Wilde* (1908) published in the *Athenaeum*. Here, Symons cast Wilde as a wit and 'prodigious entertainer' who stretched himself in different directions without committing to any of them; he was an author of verse and prose 'spoken by carefully directed marionettes', a kind of orchestrator who presided over 'paradox-puppets turn[ing] somersaults like agile acrobats'.[28]

In the early twentieth century, therefore, and following the author's death, Symons's bright portrayal of Wilde as the enemy of orthodoxies and forerunner of multi-perspectivism became darker. He went even further in a couple of unpublished items from the 1920s and 1930s, describing the self-conscious Irish 'showman's' traits as bestial:

> If ever any man of my generation indulged in unreal passions, and to excess, and with a kind of Asiatic luxury — passions, to begin with for women; these passions, utterly extinguished, passion for men and boys; these, to the end, unextinguished, these leading him to an open proclamation of his peculiar and sinister Vice, to an obvious and evident, however carefully or carelessly concealed, advertisement of his Male Prostitution; who trailed with him, or after him, a series of painted boys, and with these was as shameless as Nero or Tiberius — it was Oscar Wilde.[29]
>
> Wilde's vices were not simply intellectual perversions, they were physiological. This miserable man had always been under the influence of one of those sexual inversions which turned him into a kind of Hermaphroditus. [...] Lautrec saw him in Paris, and in the appalling portrait of him he shows Wilde, swollen, puffed out, bloated and sinister. The form of the mouth which he gave him is more than any thing exceptional; no such mouth ought ever to have existed: it is a woman's that no man who is normal could ever have had. The face is bestial.[30]

In these excerpts from a miscellaneous collection to be entitled *Memoirs* — unsuccessfully submitted to Jonathan Cape in 1932, then re-arranged and edited by Karl Beckson in 1977 — the convoluted syntax and hyperbolic and harsh tone scarcely need emphasising. While he could never bring himself to dwell on Wilde's 'degeneracy' publicly when the artist was alive, Symons, who was once a close friend of the pioneering sexologist Havelock Ellis, now pathologised Wilde's 'sexual inversion': he stigmatised him through a phobic language of vice and physical corruption, particularly evident in the description of his supposedly feminine mouth.

Given that Symons was at a breaking-point — caught between spirit and flesh, repressing amoral drives and urges — it is little wonder that he reacted with the harshness of, in Sklare's colourful language, 'a hopeless puritan who sipped *vin rouge* with the guilt of one sinning against his Methodist upbringing in Cornwall'.[31] What seems surprising, however, is his decision to strike a generally fairer balance in *A Study of Oscar Wilde*, which, as it happens, came out in the same year as his incoherent and at times unreadable *Confessions: A Study in Pathology*. If in the rancorous asides from *Memoirs* we might detect a deep emotional and psychic turmoil, combining guilt, sex, and an over-sensitive imagination, in the book concerning Wilde his judgements are more considered, with some reassuringly basic principles laid down.

Made up of six chapters, the study opens with the introductory section 'Art and the English Public': a short literary survey which, if now and then wandering from the subject or overstating the case, argues for Wilde's important contribution to the aesthetic field.[32] Symons castigates the English public for its alleged narrow-mindedness and shrinking sense of propriety — 'the least artistic and the least liberal public in the world', locked in a vicious circle by the forces of Puritanism and imperialism (p. 5). He then begins to elucidate his assessment of Wilde, which purports not to depend too heavily on the tragedy of his fall — a misguided approach unfortunately privileged by readers, supplanting 'essence' with 'accidents' (p. 15) — but rather to do justice to the transcendent quality of his output, striving to take 'a work of art as a work of art' (p. 16).

Chapters 2 and 3 offer a commentary on Wilde's oeuvre, implicitly charting the distance between *Intentions* and *The Ballad of Reading Gaol,* and are followed by another three chapters centred on, respectively, *The Picture of Dorian Gray*, the plays, and *De Profundis* (1897). In Chapter 4 Symons does not exactly champion the novel; he speaks of it in impressionistic tones, redolent of the language of Decadence, and draws on Pater, Arthur Ransome, André Gide, and of course himself.[33] He also takes pains to ground Wilde's flair for blatant intertextual contaminations in a reactive, rather than creative, temperament, his effectiveness resembling that of 'an actor when he makes parade of his part' (p. 62); hence the stress on the 'brilliant sudden gymnastic, with words in which the phrase itself was always worth more than what it said' (p. 64).[34] Unfortunately, though, only half of the chapter actually pertains to *The Picture of Dorian Gray*; the rest gives way to the carelessness and rambling thoughts of post-1908 Symons at his worst, and touches upon Poe, Baudelaire, Whistler, and Swinburne.

The foundations on which Symons's analysis of the plays rests are much less shaky, based as they are on his review of Ross's *Collected Edition*, from which he expunged a handful of acerbic passages — for example, those relating to the 'paradox-puppets' and puppeteer's wires. From *Vera; or, The Nihilists* to the final works, he offers evaluations of plot construction, action, and register; *Vera* and *A Florentine Tragedy* are at the bottom of the pile, *Salomé* also fares rather badly, but both *Lady Windermere's Fan* and *The Importance of Being Earnest* stand out for their wit.

A terse analytical imprint finally characterises the closing chapter. Here, Symons succeeds in making a concluding statement on Wilde's writings. *De Profundis* (in an expurgated version, since the unabridged text was only to come out in England in 1949) is appraised as a work of 'psychological interest' (p. 77), a record of the devastating effect of prison solitude as well as the rhetorically crafted testament of 'an architect of style in art'. Symons also believes that the book should be read aloud: its eloquence is calculated for the voice and the beauty of its phrases, which can scarcely be perceived as one reads them silently, comes into them as they are spoken (p. 87).

It is then, again, the darting nature of Wilde's intellect, his flights from reality, his parade of moods ('to him everything was drama', p. 84), his spiralling logic, and his capacity to build a new palace of art out of sorrow that both mesmerised and provoked Symons, prompting him to make a space for Wilde in literary history. This ultimately redemptive approach invites one to look back at what Eric Warner and Graham Hough have called 'the third and arguably greatest phase' of Symons's career (1899–1907), where 'the ideal of artifice, of a non-natural nature more significant and expressive for man, becomes dominant, and Symons becomes obsessed with puppets, make-up, pantomime — anything which moves away from the local and unique to the abstract and universal'.[35] Moreover, in a wider British perspective Symons's relatively balanced account of Wilde is at a significant crossroads between the first attempts to rehabilitate him in the 1910s — through the endeavours of Robert Ross, Stuart Mason (Christopher Millard), Arthur Ransome, John Cowper Powys, and Holbrook Jackson — and the bolder undertakings of the 1930s by Charles Ricketts, Walford Graham Robertson, and Vincent O'Sullivan. In the 1940s, these would be followed by Hesketh Pearson's pathbreaking *Life of Oscar Wilde* (1946) and H. Montgomery Hyde's *Trials of Oscar Wilde* (1948).[36] Taken collectively, these studies give us a taste of what would gradually emerge in terms of Wilde research, moving away from malicious gossip, sensationalism, or anecdotal misrepresentation and towards ever more corroborated methods of reconstruction and analysis. Symons's foray is noteworthy in light of the fact that, for several years after his death, 'Wilde certainly did have a reputation, but it was that of an infamous homosexual rather than a figure worthy of intellectual or academic attention'.[37] Furthermore, it marked a change in direction in 1930s Wilde scholarship and anticipated O'Sullivan's commendable biography of 1936.

All in all, *A Study of Oscar Wilde* remains a rare example of Wilde's serious reception in the age of Modernism. It is a plea to recognise his artistic commitment in a period when most of the published reminiscences were met with indifference among academics. It is also an important testimony of Symons's role in historicising the *fin de siècle* in the twentieth century — similar in this way to Max Beerbohm's metaphorical exhumation of the spectres of the Nineties in *Ghosts*, an exhibition held at the Leicester Galleries just two years before the publication of *A Study of Oscar Wilde*. As Kristin Mahoney has recently argued in her study of a resurgent political undercurrent of Decadence in the context of British modernity, 'meditating on the late-Victorian period, bringing the period's practices to bear on the present' provided 'an illuminating point of comparison, and critical detachment from the contemporary' for a circle of artists and intellectuals disappointed with the new avant-garde. Here, the 'critical function of Decadence was, it seems, multiplied and reinforced in the twentieth century'.[38] There is little doubt that Symons's excursions into the near past achieved a similar end.

Notes to Chapter 11

1. See Arthur Symons, *A Study of Oscar Wilde: With a Portrait* (London: Sawyer, 1930). Further references to this edition appear in the text. When not totally overlooked, this book has had a mixed reception; reviewers pointed to its cannibalised sections, discrepancies, and supposed ambivalence towards its subject. One reviewer, however, praised Symons's sensitive and sympathetic approach, and the book's 'absence of the besetting sin of intellectualistic critics, dogmatism'; see David Leslie Murray, 'Oscar Wilde', *Times Literary Supplement* (8 January 1931), p. 25, quoted in *Arthur Symons, Critic Among Critics: An Annotated Bibliography*, ed. by C. Jay Fox, Carol Simpson Stern, and Robert S. Means (Greensboro, NC: ELT Press, 2007), p. 194.
2. John M. Munro makes this point very clearly and goes even further, claiming that '[w]ith only one or two exceptions, Symons' writings after 1908 add nothing favorable to his reputation. If they have any significance at all, it must be for the light they throw on his temperament rather than for their qualities as literature', see Munro, *Arthur Symons*, p. 113. Munro stresses Symons's habit of using pre-existing sources 'sometimes in collections of essays reprinting whole articles without revision, sometimes revising them before reprinting, sometimes running two or more previously published pieces together, sometimes stringing together paragraphs from a number of different articles and interspersing them with additional comments and personal reminiscence' (p. 163).
3. Arthur Symons to Churchill Osborne, 4 October 1887, quoted in Lhombreaud, *Arthur Symons*, p. 46. Lhombreaud himself contends that, in spite of their common interest in French art, 'the two men never held each other in much esteem', although he claims Symons 'did justice to the artist' in *A Study of Oscar Wilde* (p. 111). Karl Beckson implicitly confirms this view, see *Arthur Symons*, pp. 114–15.
4. See 'Frank Harris and Oscar Wilde', in *The Memoirs of Arthur Symons*, ed. by Beckson, pp. 134–36 (p. 135). It is difficult to determine who approached whom in the first place, but we do know that Wilde's earliest surviving letter to Symons is postmarked 1 October 1890 and that three weeks later it was followed by an invitation: 'Dear Mr Symons [...] I hope you will come and dine with us some night. It was a great pleasure meeting you, as I had admired your work for a long time', see *The Complete Letters of Oscar Wilde*, ed. by Merlin Holland and Rupert Hart-Davis (London: Fourth Estate, 2000), p. 455.
5. These are Holland and Hart-Davis's words regarding a letter in which Symons was subjected to some nasty innuendo; see Wilde to Leonard Smithers, 4 August 1897, in *The Complete Letters of Oscar Wilde*, ed. by Holland and Hart-Davis, p. 922, n.
6. Frank Harris recalled Wilde's comment in *Oscar Wilde, His Life and Confessions* (New York: Covici, Friede, 1930), p. 330 (quoted in *Arthur Symons, Critic Among Critics*, ed. by Fox and others, p. 125).
7. Joseph Bristow, 'Picturing His Exact Decadence: The British Reception of Oscar Wilde', in *The Reception of Oscar Wilde in Europe*, ed. by Stefano Evangelista (London & New York: Continuum, 2010), pp. 20–50 (p. 43).

8. Vincent O'Sullivan, *Aspects of Wilde* (London: Constable and Company, 1936), pp. 76–77 (quoted by Lhombreaud, *Arthur Symons*, pp. 111–12).
9. Karl Beckson, 'Introduction', in *Oscar Wilde: The Critical Heritage*, ed. by Karl Beckson (London: Routledge & Kegan Paul, 1970), pp. 1–32 (p. 2).
10. Arthur Symons, 'Arthur Symons on *Intentions*' (1891), in *Oscar Wilde: The Critical Heritage*, ed. by Beckson, pp. 94–96 (p. 94). If *Intentions*, with its provocatively subtle and stimulating essays, was more favourably received than *Vera; or, The Nihilists* and *The Picture of Dorian Gray*, Beckson claims that Symons's was nevertheless 'a comment about Wilde rarely seen in the literary reviews' (p. 12). See also Symons, *A Study of Oscar Wilde*, pp. 18–19.
11. Merlin Holland, 'Introduction', in *The Complete Letters of Oscar Wilde*, ed. by Holland and Hart-Davis, pp. xiii–xxi (p. xiv).
12. Arnold B. Sklare, 'Arthur Symons: An Appreciation of the Critic of Literature', *Journal of Aesthetics & Art Criticism*, 9 (1951), 316–22 (pp. 318–19).
13. See Symons, 'The Decadent Movement in Literature' (1893), in *The Symbolist Movement in Literature*, pp. 182–83.
14. Munro, *Arthur Symons*, p. 15.
15. Ibid., pp. 23–24.
16. James Joyce, 'Oscar Wilde: The Poet of *Salome*', in *Oscar Wilde: A Collection of Critical Essays*, ed. by Richard Ellmann (Englewood Cliffs, NJ: Prentice-Hall, 1969), pp. 56–60 (p. 58).
17. Symons, 'Arthur Symons on *Intentions*', p. 95; see also *A Study of Oscar Wilde*, pp. 20–21.
18. Symons, 'Arthur Symons on *Intentions*', p. 96; see also *A Study of Oscar Wilde*, pp. 22–23.
19. T. S. Eliot, 'Tradition and the Individual Talent', in *Selected Essays*, 3rd edn (London: Faber & Faber, 1963), pp. 13–22 (p. 14). Consider another of Eliot's well-known statements: 'Immature poets imitate; mature poets steal; bad poets deface what they take, and good poets make it into something better, or at least something different', 'Philip Massinger', in *The Sacred Wood: Essays on Poetry and Criticism* (London: Methuen, 1960), pp. 123–43 (p. 125). See also Harold Bloom's speculations in *A Map of Misreading* (New York: Oxford University Press, 1975) on the post-Miltonic process of literary creation as a rewriting of the 'Father': a deliberate act of misreading and misinterpreting earlier works.
20. Munro, *Arthur Symons*, p. 48.
21. *The Oscar Wilde Collection of John B. Stetson, Jr* (New York: Anderson Galleries, 1920), sale catalogue, lot 408, quoted in *Arthur Symons: Selected Letters*, ed. by Beckson and Munro, p. 116.
22. Oscar Wilde to Leonard Smithers, 18 February 1898, in *The Complete Letters of Oscar Wilde*, ed. by Holland and Hart-Davis, p. 1018.
23. See respectively Oscar Wilde to Frank Harris, c. 15 March 1898, to Leonard Smithers, 15 March 1898, and to Robert Ross, 17 March 1898, in *The Complete Letters of Oscar Wilde*, ed. by Holland and Hart-Davis, pp. 1036, 1037, 1038.
24. Arthur Symons, 'Arthur Symons on *The Ballad of Reading Gaol*' (1898), in *Oscar Wilde: The Critical Heritage*, ed. by Beckson, pp. 218–21 (p. 219); see also *A Study of Oscar Wilde*, pp. 44–46.
25. Beckson, 'Introduction', p. 25.
26. Munro, *Arthur Symons*, p. 72.
27. See also Arthur Symons, 'An Artist in Attitudes: Oscar Wilde', in *Studies in Prose and Verse*, pp. 124–28 (pp. 124–25).
28. Arthur Symons, 'Arthur Symons on Wilde as "a prodigious entertainer"' (1908), in *Oscar Wilde: The Critical Heritage*, ed. by Beckson, pp. 294–301 (p. 294). In this review, written four months before his illness took a turn for the worse, Symons sounded newly sceptical of *Intentions* and attacked Wilde's Irish origins: 'From the first, one of Wilde's limitations had been his egoism, his self-absorption, his self-admiration. This is one of the qualities which have marred the delightful genius of the Irish nation' (p. 298).
29. Arthur Symons, 'Lillie Langtry and Oscar Wilde', in *The Memoirs of Arthur Symons*, ed. by Beckson, pp. 131–33 (pp. 132–33).
30. Arthur Symons, 'Sex and Aversion', in *The Memoirs of Arthur Symons*, ed. by Beckson, pp. 137–40 (pp. 138–39).
31. Sklare, 'Arthur Symons', p. 318.

32. See, for instance, the following passage: '[The English] have no body of ideas, no general principles of art, no schools, no groups, only individuals. Words like "Symbolism", "Naturalism", even "Romanticism", are foreign to our soil, and when they reach it are handed about like curiosities. We have good writers and bad writers: that is all' (Symons, *A Study of Oscar Wilde*, p. 7). In this sentence, however, Symons at the same time establishes a pattern of ideological alliance with Wilde, as suggested by his clear echo of the aphorism 'There is no such thing as a moral or an immoral book. Books are well written, or badly written. That is all.' See Oscar Wilde, 'The Preface' to *The Picture of Dorian Gray*, in *Complete Works of Oscar Wilde*, ed. by Small and others, III (2005), 167–68 (p. 167). Symons divides his study into chapters devoted, respectively, to 'Art and the English Public', pp. 5–17; '*Intentions*', pp. 18–24; '*The Ballad of Reading Gaol*', pp. 25–52; '*Dorian Gray*', pp. 53–66; 'The Plays', pp. 67–76; '*De Profundis*', pp. 77–88. The following is a list of Symons's self-borrowings: review in the *Speaker* (4 July 1891), as the basis for Chapter 2; review in the *Saturday Review*, 85 (12 March 1898), and 'An Artist in Attitudes', incorporated in Chapter 3; review in the *Athenaeum*, 4203 (16 May 1908), partly reprinted with the 1898 review as 'A Jester with Genius', *Bookman*, 51 (April 1920), 129–34, and incorporated in Chapters 5 and 6; 'A Jester without Genius', *London Quarterly Review*, 129 (April 1918), 253–56, incorporated in Chapter 6. The 1891, 1898, and 1908 pieces also informed Symons's introduction to a 1923 American edition of *The Complete Works of Oscar Wilde*. For a general overview of Symons's writings on Wilde, see *Arthur Symons: A Bibliography*, ed. by Beckson and others.
33. On pp. 55 and 56 we come across a few sentences that have already appeared on pp. 18–19 and 23.
34. This passage can also be found in 'Frank Harris and Oscar Wilde' (p. 136), one of the typescripts which was to be included in the *Memoirs*.
35. Eric Warner and Graham Hough, 'Arthur Symons (1865–1945)', in *Strangeness and Beauty*, ed. by Warner and Hough, II, 210–72 (p. 214).
36. For a detailed and updated account of these contributions, see Bristow, 'Picturing His Exact Decadence'.
37. Ian Small, 'The Myth of Wilde', in *Oscar Wilde Revalued: An Essay on New Materials & Methods of Research* (Greensboro, NC: ELT Press, 1993), pp. 1–9 (p. 2).
38. Mahoney, *Literature and the Politics of Post-Victorian Decadence*, p. 3.

BIBLIOGRAPHY

Works by Arthur Symons

'A. Mary F- Darmesteter', in *The Poets and the Poetry of the Nineteenth Century*, ed. by Alfred H. Miles, 12 vols (London: Routledge; New York: Dutton, 1907), XI, 359–64
Amoris victima (London: Smithers, 1897)
'An Apology for Puppets', *Saturday Review*, 84 (17 July 1897), 55–56
'Are the English People Musical?', Letter to the Editor, *Pall Mall Gazette*, 15 December 1890, 2
'Arles', *Saturday Review*, 86 (22 October 1898), 528–29
Arthur Symons: Selected Letters, 1880–1935, ed. by Karl Beckson and John M. Munro (Basingstoke: Macmillan, 1989)
'Un artiste dans ses attitudes: Oscar Wilde', *La Plume*, 371 (1 May 1905), 397–400
'Aubrey Beardsley', *Fortnightly Review*, 63 (May 1898), 752–61
Aubrey Beardsley, trans. by Jack Cohen, Édouard and Louis Thomas (Paris: Floury, 1906)
'Aubrey Beardsley', trans. by Michèle Duclos, *Temporel* (25 April 2009), <http://temporel.fr/Arthur-Symons-version-francaise> [accessed 21 April 2016]
Aventures spirituelles, trans. by Pierre Leyris (Paris: Mercure de France, 1964)
'Ballet, Pantomime, and Poetic Drama', *Dome*, 1, n.s. (1898), 65
'Ballet, Pantomime, and Poetic Drama', *Mask*, 4 (1912), 188–89
'Barbara Roscorla's Child', *Little Review*, 4 (October 1917), 25–36
'A Belgian Poet', *Saturday Review*, 86 (20 August 1898), 243
'Belgium. Literature', in *The New Volumes of the Encyclopædia Britannica*, 10th edn (Edinburgh & London: A. & C. Black, 1902), XXVI, 203–04
'Bertha at the Fair: An Encounter', *The Savoy*, 3 (July 1896), 86–88
'A Book of French Masks', *Saturday Review*, 82 (21 November 1896), 550–51
'Bruges', *Nation*, 2791 (28 December 1918), 796–97
'Casanova à Dux: un chapitre d'histoire inédit', *Mercure de France*, 48:166 (October 1903), 60–88
'Le Chant du vagabond', trans. by Edouard and Louis Thomas, *Vers et prose*, 3 (1905), 97
Charles Baudelaire: A Study (London: Elkin Mathews, 1920)
'Chopin', trans. by Édouard and Louis Thomas, *Mercure musical*, 3:1 (January 1907), 323
'Christian Trevalga', *Société nouvelle*, 2nd series, 13:7–8 (January-February 1908), 145–57
Cities (London: Dent, 1903)
Cities and Sea-Coasts and Islands (London: Collins, 1918)
Cities of Italy (London: Dent, 1907)
Collected Works, 9 vols (London: Secker, 1924)
Colour Studies in Paris (London: Chapman & Hall, 1918)
Confessions: A Study in Pathology (London: Cape, 1930; New York: Haskell House, 1972)
'D'Annunzio in English', *Saturday Review*, 85 (29 January 1898), 52–53
Days and Nights (London: Macmillan, 1889)
'The Decadent Movement in Literature', *Harper's New Monthly Magazine*, 88 (November 1893), 858–67

'Les Demoiselles de Bienfilâtre', *Two Worlds*, 1.1 (September 1925), 97–104
'Les Dessins de Rodin', *La Plume*, 12 (June 1900), 383–84
'Les Dessins de Rodin', trad. by Henry D.-Davray, in *Auguste Rodin et son œuvre*, (Paris: Éditions de 'La Plume', 1900), pp. 47–48
'Dieu à Londres: l'art et le public anglais', *L'Antée*, 5 (October 1906), 471–80
Dramatis Personae (Indianapolis, IN: Bobbs-Merrill, 1923)
Eleonora Duse (London: Elkin Mathews, 1926)
'Émile Verhaeren', *English Review* (March 1918), 234–39
'English Literature in 1893', *The Athenaeum*, 3454 (6 January 1894), 17–19
Figures of Several Centuries (New York: Dutton, 1916)
The Fool of the World and Other Poems (London: Heinemann, 1906)
'Frédéri Mistral', *National Review*, 8 (December 1886), 659–70
'A French Blake: Odilon Redon', *Art Review*, 7 (July 1890), 206–07
From Toulouse-Lautrec to Rodin with Some Personal Impressions (London: John Lane, 1929)
'Gérard de Nerval', *Fortnightly Review*, 63 (January 1898), 81–91
'Henrik Ibsen', *Quarterly Review*, 405 (October 1906), 375–97
'Hymn to Earth', *Weekly Critical Review*, 53 (22 January 1904), 15
Images of Good and Evil (London: Heinemann, 1899)
'The Improvements of Rome', *Weekly Critical Review*, 61 (18 March 1904), 229–30
'In Praise of Gypsies', *Journal of the Gypsy Lore Society*, n.s. 1:4 (April 1908), 294–99
'Introduction', in Gabriele D'Annunzio, *The Child of Pleasure*, trans. by Georgina Harding and Arthur Symons (London: Heinemann, 1898), pp. v–xii
'Introduction', in Gabriele D'Annunzio, *Francesca da Rimini*, trans. by Arthur Symons (London: Heinemann, 1902), pp. vii–xiv
'Introduction', in Émile Verhaeren, *The Dawn*, trans. by Arthur Symons (London: Duckworth, 1898)
An Introduction to the Study of Browning (London: Cassell, 1886)
'J.-K. Huysmans', *Fortnightly Review*, 51 (March 1892), 402–04
Journal de Henry Luxulyan, trans. by Frédéric Roger-Cornaz (Paris: Kra, Coll. Carnets littéraires, Série cosmopolite, 1928)
Knave of Hearts, 1894–1908 (London: Heinemann, 1913)
Lesbia and Other Poems (New York: Dutton, 1920)
'La Littérature anglaise', *Mercure de France*, 10:50 (February 1894), 105–11
London: A Book of Aspects (London & Minneapolis, MN: Privately Printed, 1909)
London Nights (London: Smithers, 1895)
Love's Cruelty (London: Secker, 1923)
'Maeterlinck as a Mystic', *Contemporary Review*, 72 (1897), 349–54
'Le Mauvais-Riche', *Antée*, 13 (June 1907), 1269–74
The Memoirs of Arthur Symons: Life and Art in the 1890s, ed. by Karl Beckson (University Park & London: Pennsylvania State University Press, 1977)
Mes souvenirs (Chapelle-Réanville: Hours Press, 1929)
'"Monna Vanna"', *The Academy*, 63 (5 July 1902), 45
'"More Natural than Nature, more Artificial than Art": The Dance Criticism of Arthur Symons, introduced and annotated by Jane Pritchard', *Dance Research*, 21:2 (Winter 2003), 36–89
'Le Mouvement symboliste: introduction' and 'Stéphane Mallarmé', trans. by Bénédicte Coste, in *Les grands mouvements littéraires anglo-saxons*, ed. by Christine Reynier (Paris: Houdiard, 2009), 72–85
'Mr. Gordon Craig and the Painters in Tempera', *Outlook*, 15 (24 June 1905), 906
'Music in Venice', *Saturday Review*, 106 (17 October 1908), 480–81

'A New Art of the Stage', *Monthly Review*, 7 (1902), 157
'A New French Quarterly', *Outlook*, 15:383 (3 June 1905), 797
'Nini Patte-en-l'air', *The Gypsy*, 1:1 (May 1915), 11
'A Note on George Meredith', *Fortnightly Review*, 62 (November 1897), 673–78
'Notes on Toulouse Lautrec and his Lithographs', *Two Worlds*, 1.2 (December 1925), 162–69
'Notes on Verlaine's Adventures and Sensations', *Two Worlds*, 1.3 (March 1926), 267–79
'Odilon Redon', *Revue indépendante*, 18 (March 1891), 390–96
'Paul Verlaine', *National Review*, 19 (June 1892), 501–15
'Paul Verlaine', *New Review*, 9:55 (December 1893), 609–17
'Philip Massinger', trans. by Georges Darondeau, *Revue politique et littéraire*, 15 (5 August 1933), 472–76
'La Place de William Blake', trans. by Georges Luciani, *Navire d'argent*, 4 (September 1925), 371–82
Plays, Acting, and Music (London: Duckworth, 1903; London: Constable, 1909)
'Poèmes', *Société nouvelle*, 2nd series, 13:2 (August 1907), 245–51
Poésies (Bruges: Herbert, 1907)
Portraits anglais, trans. by Jack Cohen and others (Bruges: Herbert, 1907)
'Preface', in Charles Baudelaire, *Poems in Prose*, trans. by Arthur Symons (London: Elkin Mathews, 1905), p. 5
'Preface', in Charles Baudelaire, *Baudelaire: Prose and Poetry*, trans. by Arthur Symons (New York: Boni, 1926), pp. v–ix
'Preface', in Jean-Marie-Mathias-Philippe-Auguste Villiers de l'Isle-Adam, *Claire Lenoir*, trans. by Arthur Symons (New York: Boni, 1925), pp. vii–x
'*The Princess Maleine* and *The Intruder*', *The Athenaeum* (23 April 1892), 525–26
'Purcell and Ellen Terry', *Star*, 26 March 1901, 1
'Quatre poèmes', trans. by Paul Verlaine, *Vers et prose*, 4 (1906), 10
'Qu'est-ce que la poésie', trans. by Edouard and Louis Thomas, *Vers et prose*, 3 (1905), 29–33
'The Question of Censorship', *The Academy*, 63 (28 June 1902), 21–22
'Remy de Gourmont', *Saturday Review*, 96 (18 November 1903), 675–76
'Reviews' [review of Van Lerberghe's *La Chanson d'Ève*], *Saturday Review*, 98 (1 October 1904), 432
'Review' [review of Van Lerberghe's *Pan*], *Saturday Review*, 102 (7 July 1906), 16–17
'Robert Buchanan', *L'Antée*, 7 (December 1906), 648–52
Selected Early Poems, ed. by Jane Desmarais and Chris Baldwick, MHRA Critical Texts: Jewelled Tortoise, 2 (Cambridge: Modern Humanities Research Association, 2017)
'Should Translators Improve Their Authors?', *Bookman's Journal and Print Collector*, 5:4 (January 1922), 109–12
Silhouettes (London: Mathews & Lane, 1892; London: Smithers, 1896)
'The Sinister Guest', *English Review*, 129 (August 1919), 105–19
'Some French Verse', *Saturday Review*, 84 (24 July 1897), 94–95
Spiritual Adventures (London: Constable, 1905)
Spiritual Adventures, ed. by Nicholas Freeman, MHRA Critical Texts: Jewelled Tortoise, 3 (Cambridge: Modern Humanities Research Association, 2017)
Studies in Prose and Verse (London: Dent, 1904)
Studies in Seven Arts (London: Constable, 1906)
Studies in Two Literatures (London: Smithers, 1897)
'A Study of John Addington Symonds', *Fortnightly Review*, 115 (February 1924), 228–39
A Study of Oscar Wilde: With a Portrait (London: Sawyer, 1930)

'A Study of Toledo', *Monthly Review*, 2 (March 1901), 144–54
'Sur un air de Rameau', *Antée*, 2 (July 1906), 111
The Symbolist Movement in Literature (London: Heinemann, 1899)
The Symbolist Movement in Literature, ed. by Matthew Creasy (Manchester: Fyfield-Carcanet, 2014)
'Tears in my Heart', *The Academy*, 38 (12 July 1890), 31
'Venetian Glamour', *Saturday Review*, 88 (14 October 1899), 480
'Venice in Easter: Impressions and Sensations', *Harper's New Monthly Magazine*, 90 (April 1895), 738–51
'Verlaine in London', *Star*, 22 November 1893, 2
'Villiers de l'Isle Adam', *The Athenaeum*, 3229 (14 September 1889), 354
'Villiers de l'Isle-Adam', *Woman's World*, 24 (October 1889), 657–60
'Villiers de l'Isle Adam', *Illustrated London News*, 98 (2701) (24 January 1891), 118
'Villiers de l'Isle Adam', *Fortnightly Review*, 66 (August 1899), 197–204
'Walter Pater: "Imaginary Portraits"', *Time*, 6 (August 1887), 157–62
'Walter Pater', *Mercure de France* (February 1898), 450–62
Wanderings (London: Dent, 1931)
'Whistler', *Weekly Critical Review*, 28 (30 July 1903), 36–37; 29 (6 August 1903), 49–50; 30 (13 August 1903), 81–82
'William Morris', trans. by Édouard and Louis Thomas, *Mercure de France* (15 December 1896), 221–32
'William Morris's Prose', *Saturday Review*, 84 (11 December 1897), 669–70

Archival and Manuscript Sources

Austin, Texas, The Harry Ransom Center
  MS 414 B51 8.6, Arthur Symons, 'The Sinister Guest'
  MS 4141, Container 3.1, Arthur Symons's diaries for 1907 and 1921
Brussels, Archives et Musée de la littérature
  MS ML 770/2, postcard from Arthur Symons to Charles Van Lerberghe, 2 June 1906
  MS ML 7065/182, letter from Arthur Symons to Stuart Merrill, 26 April 1907
  MS FS XVI 148/1190, letter from Arthur Symons to Émile Verhaeren, 12 February 1902
  MS FS XVI 148/1191, letter from Arthur Symons to Émile Verhaeren, 19 March 1907
  MS FS XVI 148/1192, letter from Arthur Symons to Émile Verhaeren, 22 March 1907
  MS FS XVI 148/1193, letter from Arthur Symons to Émile Verhaeren, [early 1898]
  MS FS XVI 148/1194, letter from Arthur Symons to Émile Verhaeren, [early 1898]
Gardone Riviera, Fondazione Il Vittoriale degli Italiani, Archivi del Vittoriale
  AG XLIX, 2, Putnam & Co. to Mondadori, 24 July 1935, AG XLIX, 2
  AG XLIX, 2, reader's report for Putnam & Co. on *Il libro segreto*, AG XLIX, 2
Liverpool, University of Liverpool, Gypsy Lore Society Archive
  MS GLS A4 535, letter from Arthur Symons to Robert Andrew Scott Macfie, 19 March 1908
  MS GLS A4 537, letter from Arthur Symons to Robert Andrew Scott Macfie, 1 April 1908
  MS GLS A6 (736), letter from Arthur Symons to Robert Andrew Scott Macfie, 1 July 1908
  MS GLS C1 13 (10), letter from Arthur Symons to John Sampson, 16 August 1911
  MS GLS C1 13 (11), letter from Arthur Symons to John Sampson, 27 August 1910
  MS GLS C1 13 (14), letter from Arthur Symons to Dora Yates, undated
  MS GLS B15 59, letter from Theodore Watts-Dunton to John Sampson, 5 May 1908

MS GLS B15 60, letter from Theodore Watts-Dunton to John Sampson, 8 May 1908
Liverpool, University of Liverpool, Scott Macfie Gypsy Collections
  SMGC 5/2, cuttings album 1907–1913 (microfilm)
London, British Library
  Add. MS 49522, letter from Arthur Symons to James Dykes Campbell, 2 January 1888
Princeton, Princeton University
  Arthur Symons Papers, C0182, Box 9, Folder 7, 'The Genesis of Spiritual Adventures'
  Arthur Symons Papers, C0182, Box 24, Folder 16, letter to Ernest Rhys, 8 March 1890

Secondary Sources

[Anon.], '"And Yet — He is a Master"', *The Academy*, 58 (2 June 1900), 464–65
[Anon.], 'An Atmospheric Tragedy', *Academy and Literature*, 64 (12 January 1903), 48
[Anon.], 'Bibliographie. La Littérature anglaise traduite en français. VI Les Derniers Victoriens, les Edwardiens et les Georgiens', *Navire d'argent*, 6 (1 November 1925), 22
[Anon.], 'Books of the Week', *Manchester Guardian*, 6 December 1898, p. 4
[Anon.], 'Books of the Week', *Manchester Guardian*, 26 August 1902, 7
[Anon.], '*The Child of Pleasure* by Gabriele D'Annunzio', *Academy*, 55 (26 November 1898), 333
[Anon.], 'Chit Chat', *The Stage*, 920 (3 November 1898), 14
[Anon.], '*Cities*. By Arthur Symons', *The Athenaeum*, 3968 (14 November 1903), 641–42
[Anon.], 'D'Annunzio in English', *The Academy*, 53 (5 February 1898), 141–42
[Anon.], 'Mr. Arthur Symons as Translator', *The Academy*, 55 (3 December 1898), 370–71
[Anon.], 'New Books', *The Scotsman*, 24 October 1898, p. 3
[Anon.], 'Recent Poetry and Verse', *Speaker: A Review of Politics, Letters, Science and the Arts*, 19 (7 January 1899), 26
[Anon.], 'Translations', *The Athenæum*, 3725 (18 March 1899), 336
Ando, Tomoko, 'Rodin's Reputation in Great Britain: The Neglected Role of Alphonse Legros', *Nineteenth-Century Art Worldwide: A Journal of Nineteenth-Century Visual Culture*, 15:3 (Autumn 2016), <http://www.19thc-artworldwide.org/index.php/autumn16/ando-on-rodin-reputation-in-great-britain-neglected-role-of-alphonse-legros> [accessed 18 April 2017]
Archer, William, 'A Pessimist Playwright', *Fortnightly Review*, 50 (September 1891), 346–54
Arnold, Matthew, *Lectures and Essays in Criticism*, ed. by R. H. Super, 2nd edn (Ann Arbor: University of Michigan Press, 1962)
Baudelaire, Charles, *Baudelaire: Prose and Poetry*, trans. by Arthur Symons (New York: Boni, 1926)
—— 'The Painter of Modern Life', in *The Painter of Modern Life and Other Essays* [1964], ed. and trans. by Jonathan Mayne (London: Phaidon, 1995), pp. 1–42
—— *Poems in Prose from Charles Baudelaire*, trans. by Arthur Symons (London: Elkin Mathews, 1905)
Beckson, Karl, *Arthur Symons: A Life* (Oxford: Clarendon Press, 1987)
—— 'Symons' "A Prelude to Life," Joyce's "A Portrait," and the Religion of Art', *James Joyce Quarterly*, 15: 3 (Spring 1978), 222–28
Beckson, Karl, ed., *Oscar Wilde: The Critical Heritage* (London: Routledge & Kegan Paul, 1970)
Beckson, Karl, and others, eds, *Arthur Symons: A Bibliography* (Greensboro, NC: ELT Press, 1990)
Bellow, Juliet, 'Beyond Movement: Auguste Rodin and the Dancers of his Time', in

Rodin and Dance: The Essence of Movement, ed. by Alexandra Gerstein, Courtauld Gallery and Musée Rodin (London: Holberton, 2016), pp. 41–59

BENJAMIN, WALTER, *Reflections: Essays, Aphorisms, Autobiographical Writings*, ed. by Peter Demetz, trans. by Edmund Jephcott (New York: Shocken, 1978)

BERNHEIMER, CHARLES, *Decadent Subjects*, ed. by T. Jefferson Kline and Naomi Schor (Baltimore: Johns Hopkins Press, 1996)

BLAIKIE MURDOCH, W. G., *The Renaissance of the Nineties* (London: Moring, 1911)

BLANCHE, JACQUES-ÉMILE, 'Aubrey Beardsley', *Antée*, 11 (April 1907), 1103–22

BLOCK, EDWIN F. JR, *Rituals of Dis-Integration: Romance and Madness in the Victorian Psychomythic Tale* (New York: Garland, 1993)

BLOOM, HAROLD, *A Map of Misreading* (New York: Oxford University Press, 1975)

BÖHME, GERNOT, 'Atmosphere as the Fundamental Concept of a New Aesthetics', *Thesis Eleven*, 36 (1993), 113–26

BOURDIEU, PIERRE, *The Rules of Art*, trans. by Susan Emanuel (Stanford, CA: Stanford University Press, 1995)

BOYIOPOULOS, KOSTAS, *The Decadent Image: The Poetry of Wilde, Symons, and Dowson* (Edinburgh: Edinburgh University Press, 2015)

BRAKE, LAUREL, *Subjugated Knowledges: Journalism, Gender and Literature in the Nineteenth Century* (Basingstoke: Palgrave Macmillan, 1994; New York: New York University Press, 1994)

BRANDES, GEORG, 'Verdensliteratur' [1899], in *Samlede Skrifter*, 18 vols (Copenhagen: Gyldendal, 1899–1910), XII, 23–28, <http://adl.dk/adl_pub/pg/cv/ShowPgImg.xsql?nnoc=adl_pub&p_udg_id=20&p_sidenr=23> [accessed 18 April 2017]

BRISTOW, JOSEPH, 'Picturing His Exact Decadence: The British Reception of Oscar Wilde', in *The Reception of Oscar Wilde in Europe*, ed. by Stefano Evangelista (London & New York: Continuum, 2010), pp. 20–50

BROGNIEZ, LAURENCE, 'Charles Van Lerberghe, préraphaélite flamand? Tradition anglophile et héritage flamand', *Textyles*, 22 (2003), 94–108

―― *Préraphaélisme et symbolisme: peinture littéraire et image poétique* (Paris: Champion, 2003)

BROPHY, BRIGID, *Black and White* (London: Cape, 1968)

BROWNING, ROBERT, 'Rhyme for a Child Viewing a Naked Venus in a Painting of "The Judgement of Paris"' [c. 1872], in *The New Oxford Book of Victorian Verse*, ed. by Christopher Ricks (Oxford: Oxford University Press, 1987), p. 158

BRULÉ, ANDRÉ, 'Review of *From Toulouse-Lautrec to Rodin* by Arthur Symons', *Revue anglo-américaine*, 8:1 (1930), 185–86

BULLEN, J. B., 'Introduction', in Clive Bell, *Art* (Oxford: Oxford University Press, 1987), pp. xxi–l

BUZARD, JAMES, *The Beaten Track: European Tourism, Literature, and the Ways to 'Culture' 1800–1918* (Oxford: Oxford University Press, 1993)

CALIARO, ILVANO, *Da Bisanzio a Roma: studi su Gabriele D'Annunzio* (Verona: Fiorini, 2004)

CARRIÈRE, Eugène, *L'Œuvre de Rodin: exposition Rodin*, Pavillon de Hanovre (Paris: Société d'Édition Artistique, Imprimerie D. Dumoulin, 1900)

CASANOVA, PASCALE, *The World Republic of Letters*, trans. by M. B. DeBevoise (Cambridge, MA, & London: Harvard University Press, 2004)

CAZAMIAN, MADELEINE, *Le Roman et les idées en Angleterre: l'anti-intellectualisme et l'esthétisme (1880–1900)* (Paris: Champion, 1935)

[CHILD, HAROLD HANNYNGTON], 'Arthur Symons', *Times Literary Supplement* (3 February 1945), 55

CHURCHILL, KENNETH, *Italy and English Literature 1764–1930* (London: Macmillan, 1980)

CIMINI, MARIO, ed., *Carteggio D'Annunzio-Hérelle (1891–1931)* (Lanciano: Carabba, 2004)
CIXOUS, HÉLÈNE, *Insister of Jacques Derrida*, trans. by Peggy Kamuf (Edinburgh: Edinburgh University Press, 2007)
CLEMENTS, PATRICIA, *Baudelaire and the English Tradition* (Princeton, NJ: Princeton University Press, 1985)
CNUDDE-KNOWLAND, ANNE, 'Maurice Maeterlinck and English and Anglo-Irish Literature: A Study of Parallels and Influences' (unpublished doctoral thesis, University of Oxford, 1984)
COLBY, VINETA, *Vernon Lee: A Literary Biography* (Charlottesville & London: University of Virginia Press, 2003)
COLENBRANDER, JOANNA, *A Portrait of Fryn: A Biography of F. Tennyson Jesse* (London: Deutsch, 1984)
COLLINS, SARAH, 'Absolute Music and Ideal Content: Autonomy, Sensation and Experience in Arthur Symons's "Theory of Musical Aesthetics"', *Australasian Journal of Victorian Studies*, 19 (2014), 45–66
CONLON, JOHN J., *Walter Pater and the French Tradition* (Lewisburg, PA: Bucknell University Press, 1982)
CONNOR, STEVEN, *The Matter of Air: Science and Art of the Ethereal* (London: Reaktion, 2010)
CONSTABLE, LIZ, DENNIS DENISOFF, and MATTHEW POTOLSKY, eds, *Perennial Decay: On the Aesthetics and Politics of Decadence* (Philadelphia: University of Pennsylvania Press, 1999)
CRAIG, EDWARD GORDON, 'The Actor and the Über-Marionette', *Mask*, 1 (1908), 3–15
—— *The Art of the Theatre* (Edinburgh and London: Foulis, 1905)
—— *On the Art of the Theatre* (London: Heinemann, 1911)
CUMMINS, ANTHONY, 'Émile Zola's Cheap English Dress: The Vizetelly Translations, Late-Victorian Print Culture and the Crisis of Literary Value', *Review of English Studies*, 60:243 (2008), 108–32
DANN, GRAHAM, 'Writing out the Tourist in Space and Time', *Annals of Tourism Research*, 26 (1999), 159–87
D'ANNUNZIO, GABRIELE, *The Child of Pleasure*, trans. by Georgina Harding and Arthur Symons (London: Heinemann, 1898)
—— *The Dead City*, trans. by Arthur Symons (London: Heinemann, 1900)
—— *Francesca da Rimini*, trans. by Arthur Symons (London: Heinemann, 1902)
DAVRAY, HENRY-D., 'Lettres anglaises', *Mercure de France*, 19:80 (August 1896), 373
—— 'Lettres anglaises', *Mercure de France*, 34:125 (May 1900), 553–59
—— 'Lettres anglaises', *Mercure de France*, 64:228 (15 November 1906), 298–302
—— 'Revue de la quinzaine', *Mercure de France*, 107:400 (16 February 1914), 862–66
—— 'Revues et journaux', *Mercure de France*, 17:75 (March 1896), 438
DELATTRE, FLORIS, 'Review of Albert Farmer, *Le Mouvement esthétique et décadent en Angleterre (1873–1900)*', *Revue belge de philologie et d'histoire*, 13 (1934), 273
DEMOOR, MARYSA, and FREDERICK MOREL, 'Laurence Binyon and the Belgian Artistic Scene: Unearthing Unknown Brotherhoods', *Victorian Periodicals Review*, 44:2 (2011), 184–97
DENIS, BENOÎT, and JEAN-MARIE KLINKENBERG, *La Littérature belge: précis d'histoire sociale* (Brussels: Labor, 2005)
DESMARAIS, JANE, *The Beardsley Industry: The Critical Reception in England and France, 1893–1914* (Aldershot: Ashgate, 1998)
—— 'The Musical Analogy in Beardsley Criticism 1898–1914', *Journal of Pre-Raphaelite Studies*, 6 (Spring 1997), 64–90
DESSY, CLÉMENT, 'Les Vies britanniques d'Émile Verhaeren', *Textyles*, 50–51 (2016), 119–36

DETEMMERMAN, JACQUES, 'Van Lerberghe et la pédagogie: rêveries et velléités', in *Littératures en contact: mélanges offerts à Vic Nachtergaele*, ed. by Jan Herman, Steven Engels, and Alex Demeulenaere (Leuven: Presses universitaires de Louvain, 2003), pp. 75–88

DOWLING, LINDA, *Language and Decadence in the Victorian Fin de Siècle* (Princeton, NJ: Princeton University Press, 1986)

DOWSON, ERNEST, *The Letters of Ernest Dowson*, ed. by Desmond Flower and Henry Maas (Rutherford, NJ: Fairleigh Dickinson University Press, 1967)

—— *The Poems of Ernest Dowson*, with a memoir by Arthur Symons (London: Bodley Head, 1922)

DUBOIS, JACQUES, and PIERRE BOURDIEU, 'Champ littéraire et rapports de domination', *Textyles*, 15 (1999), 12–16

DUCREY, GUY, 'Le Passeur du symbolisme français: Arthur Symons', in *'Curious about France': visions littéraires victoriennes*, ed. by Ignacio Ramos Gay (Bern: Peter Lang, 2014), pp. 137–52

DUNCAN, ISADORA, *My Life* (London: Gollancz, 1928)

EDER, JOSEF MARIA, *History of Photography* [1932] (New York: Dover Publications, 1945)

EDWARDS, OSMAN, 'Émile Verhaeren', *Daily Chronicle*, 16 May 1895, 3

—— 'Émile Verhaeren', *The Savoy*, 7 (November 1896), 65–78

ELIOT, T. S., 'Baudelaire in our Time', in *The Complete Prose of T. S. Eliot*, ed. by Ronald Schuchard and others, 8 vols (Baltimore, MD: Johns Hopkins University Press, 2014–), III (2015), 71–82

—— 'The Perfect Critic', in *The Complete Prose of T. S. Eliot*, ed. by Ronald Schuchard and others, 8 vols (Baltimore, MD: Johns Hopkins University Press, 2014–), II (2014), 262–72

—— 'Philip Massinger', in *The Sacred Wood: Essays on Poetry and Criticism* (London: Methuen, 1960), pp. 123–43

—— 'Tradition and the Individual Talent', in *Selected Essays*, 3rd edn (London: Faber & Faber, 1963), pp. 13–22

ELLMANN, RICHARD, ed., *The Artist as Critic: Critical Writings of Oscar Wilde* (Chicago: University of Chicago Press, 1969)

—— 'Dangerous Acquaintances', *New York Review of Books*, 4:12 (15 July 1965), <http://www.nybooks.com/articles/1965/07/15/dangerous-acquaintances/> [accessed 14 April 2016]

—— *James Joyce*, 2nd edn (Oxford: Oxford University Press, 1984)

EMMANUEL, MAURICE, *La Danse grecque antique* (Paris: Librairie Hachette et Cie, 1896)

EVANGELISTA, STEFANO, 'Vernon Lee and the Gender of Aestheticism', in *Vernon Lee Decadence, Ethics, Aesthetics*, ed. by Catherine Maxwell and Patricia Pulham (Basingstoke Palgrave Macmillan, 2006), pp. 91–111

FARMER, ALBERT, *Le Mouvement esthétique et 'décadent' en Angleterre (1873–1900)* (Paris Champion, 1931)

FENAILLE, MAURICE, ed., *Les Dessins de Auguste Rodin reproduits en fac-similé par la Maison Goupil* (Paris: Boussod, Manzi, Joyant et Cie, 1897)

FERGONZI, FLAVIO, and MARIA LAMBERTI, *Rodin and Michelangelo: A Study in Artistic Inspiration* (Philadelphia: Philadelphia Museum of Art, 1997)

FORD, FORD MADOX, *Letters of Ford Madox Ford*, ed. by Richard Ludwig (Princeton, NJ: Princeton University Press, 1965)

FOX, C. JAY, CAROL SIMPSON STERN, and ROBERT S. MEANS, eds, *Arthur Symons, Critic Among Critics: An Annotated Bibliography* (Greensboro, NC: ELT Press, 2007)

FRANKLIN, ADRIAN, and MIKE CRANG, 'The Trouble with Tourism and Travel Theory', *Tourist Studies*, 1 (2001), 5–22

FRASER, ANGUS, 'A Rum Lot', in *100 Years of Gypsy Studies*, ed. by Matt T. Salo (Cheverly, MD: Gypsy Lore Society, 1990), pp. 1–14

FREEMAN, NICHOLAS, *Conceiving the City: London, Literature, and Art, 1870–1914* (Oxford: Oxford University Press, 2007)

—— '"The Harem of Words": Attenuation and Excess in Decadent Poetry', in *Decadent Poetics: Literature and Form at the British Fin de Siècle*, ed. by Jason David Hall and Alex Murray (London: Palgrave Macmillan, 2013), pp. 83–99

—— 'Literary Representations of London, 1905–1909: A Study of Ford Madox Ford, Arthur Symons, John Davidson, and Henry James' (unpublished PhD dissertation, University of Bristol, 1999)

—— '"Mad Music Rising": Chopin, Sex, and Secret Language in Arthur Symons's *Christian Trevalga*', *Victoriographies*, 1 (2011), 157–76

FRIEDMAN, DONALD, 'Belgian Symbolism and a Poetics of Place', in *Les XX and the Belgian Avant Garde: Prints, Drawings and Books ca. 1890*, ed. by Stephen H. Goddard (Lawrence: University of Kansas/Spencer Museum of Art, 1992), pp. 126–38

FRY, ROGER, 'Aubrey Beardsley's Drawings', *The Athenaeum*, 4019 (5 November 1904), 627–28

—— 'An Essay in Aesthetics', *New Quarterly*, 2 (April 1909), 171–90

—— 'Post Impressionism', *Fortnightly Review*, 89 (May 1911), 856–67

GAGNIER, REGENIA, *Individualism, Decadence and Globalization: On the Relationship of Part to Whole, 1859–1920* (Basingstoke: Palgrave Macmillan, 2010)

GALANI-MOUTAFI, VASILIKI, 'The Self and the Other: Traveler, Ethnographer, Tourist', *Annals of Tourism Research*, 27 (2000), 203–24

GARELICK, RHONDA K., *Electric Salome: Loie Fuller's Performance of Modernism* (Princeton, NJ: Princeton University Press, 2007)

GERTZMAN, JAY A., *Samuel Roth, Infamous Modernist* (Gainesville: University Press of Florida, 2013)

GOSETTI-FERENCEI, JENNIFER ANNA, *Exotic Spaces in German Modernism* (Oxford: Oxford University Press, 2011)

GOSSE, EDMUND, 'M. Verhaeren's New Poem', *Saturday Review*, 85 (23 April 1898), 560

GOURMONT, REMY DE, *Correspondance*, ed. by Vincent Gogibu, 3 vols (Paris: Éditions du Sandre, 2010)

—— 'Journaux et revues', *Mercure de France*, 5:29 (May 1892), 82–85

—— 'Journaux et revues', *Mercure de France*, 5:31 (July 1892), 276–77

—— 'Littérature anglaise', *Mercure de France*, 1:6 (June 1890), 219–20

—— 'Les Livres', *Mercure de France*, 5:31 (July 1892), 274–75

—— 'Livres', *Mercure de France*, 15:68 (August 1895), 243

—— *Promenades littéraires*, 7 vols (Paris: Mercure de France, 1929)

GROSS, KENNETH, *Puppet: An Essay on Uncanny Life* (Chicago: University of Chicago Press, 2011)

GUIETTE, ROBERT, 'Un cas de symbiose dans la Symbolisme en France', *Comparative Literature Studies*, 4 (1967), 103–07

GULLACE, GIOVANNI, *Gabriele D'Annunzio in France: A Study in Cultural Relations* (Syracuse, NY: Syracuse University Press, 1966)

GUNN, PETER, *Vernon Lee: Violet Paget, 1856–1935* (London: Oxford University Press, 1964)

HALL, JASON DAVID, and ALEX MURRAY, 'Introduction', in *Decadent Poetics: Literature and Form at the British Fin de Siècle*, ed. by Jason David Hall and Alex Murray (London: Palgrave Macmillan, 2013), pp. 1–25

HAMERTON, P. G., *Contemporary French Painters* (London: Seeley, Jackson and Halliday, 1868)

HARDING, F. J. W., *Matthew Arnold: The Critic and France* (Geneva: Librairie Droz, 1964)
HARRIS, FRANK, *Oscar Wilde, His Life and Confessions* (New York: Covici, Friede, 1930)
HAYES, SEBASTIAN, *Arthur Symons: Leading Poet of the English Decadence* (Shaftesbury: Brimstone Press, 2007)
HEGEL, GEORG WILHELM FRIEDRICH, *Aesthetics: Lectures on Fine Art (1835–8)*, trans. by T. M. Knox, 2 vols (Oxford: Clarendon Press, 1975)
HEROLD, KATHARINA, 'Dancing the Image: Sensoriality and Kinaesthetics in the Poetry of Stéphane Mallarmé and Arthur Symons', in *Decadence and the Senses*, ed. by Jane Desmarais and Alice Condé (Oxford: Legenda, 2017), pp. 141–61
HERZOG, PATRICIA, '"The Condition to Which All Art Aspires": Reflections on Pater on Music', *British Journal of Aesthetics*, 36 (April 1996), 122–34
HUXLEY, MICHAEL, and NOEL WITTS, eds, *The Twentieth-Century Performance Reader* (London: Routledge, 2002)
HUYSMANS, J. K., *Against Nature*, trans. by Robert Baldick (London: Penguin, 1959)
INNES, CHRISTOPHER, *Edward Gordon Craig* (Cambridge: Cambridge University Press, 1983)
IRONSIDE, ROBIN, 'Aubrey Beardsley'. *Horizon*, 14 (September 1946), 190–202
ISHERWOOD, CHRISTOPHER, *All the Conspirators* (London: Jonathan Cape, 1928)
JAMES, HENRY, *The Art of the Novel. Critical Prefaces* (New York: Charles Scribner's Sons, 1934)
JAMES, WILLIAM, *The Varieties of Religious Experience: A Study in Human Nature* [1902] (London: Longmans, Green, and Co. 1915)
JAMES, W. P., 'The Literary World', *St. James's Gazette*, 5 November 1898, 12
JAULME, ANDRÉ, and HENRI MONCEL, eds, *Cinquantenaire du symbolisme; exposition de manuscrits autographes, estampes, peintures, sculptures, éditions rares, portraits, objets d'art* (Paris Éditions des Bibliothèques nationales, 1936)
JEAN-AUBRY, GEORGES, 'Paul Verlaine et l'Angleterre: 1872–1892', *Revue de Paris*, 6 (1 December 1918), 600–20
JESSE, F. TENNYSON, *Secret Bread* (London: Heinemann, 1917)
JONES, SUSAN, '"Une écriture corporelle": The Dancer in the Text of Mallarmé and Yeats', in *The Body and the Arts*, ed. by Corinne Saunders, Ulrika Maude, and Jane Macnaughton (Basingstoke: Palgrave Macmillan. 2009), pp. 237–53
JOYCE, JAMES, 'Oscar Wilde: The Poet of *Salome*', in *Oscar Wilde: A Collection of Critical Essays*, ed. by Richard Ellmann (Englewood Cliffs, NJ: Prentice-Hall, 1969), pp. 56–60
JOYCE, STANISLAUS, *My Brother's Keeper*, ed. by Richard Ellmann (London: Faber & Faber, 1958)
JUDRIN, CLAUDIE, 'Dessins: l'obscur et le clair', in *Rodin en 1900: l'exposition de l'Alma*, Musée du Luxembourg, ed. by Antoinette Le Normand-Romain (Paris: Réunion des Musées Nationaux, 2001), pp. 344–51
KEATS, JOHN, *The Poems of John Keats*, ed. by Jack Stillinger (London: Heinemann, 1978)
KERMODE, FRANK, *Romantic Image* (London: Routledge and Kegan Paul, 1957)
KOSZUL, ANDRÉ, 'Review of *Arthur Symons, A Critical Study* by T. Earle Welby', *Revue anglo-américaine* (December 1925), 255–56
KURTH, PETER, *Isadora: A Sensational Life* (New York & London: Little, Brown, 2001)
LACLOS, CHODERLOS DE, *Poésies de Choderlos de Laclos*, ed. by Arthur Symons and Louis Thomas (Paris: chez Dorbon l'Ainé, 1908)
LAOUREUX, DENIS, 'Maurice Maeterlinck et l'invention d'un théâtre de l'image', in *Les Arts de la scène à l'épreuve de l'histoire: les objets et les méthodes de l'historiographie des spectacles produits sur la scène française (1635–1906)*, ed. by Roxane Martin and Marina Nordera (Paris: Champion, 2011), pp. 113–21

LAURENT, FRANÇOIS, and BÉATRICE MOUSLI, *Les Éditions du Sagittaire, 1919–1979* (Paris: Éditions de l'IMEC, 2003)
LAVERS, ANNETTE, 'Aubrey Beardsley: Man of Letters', in *Romantic Mythologies*, ed. by Ian Fletcher (London: Routledge, 1967), pp. 243–70
LEE, KEN, 'Orientalism and Gypsylorism', *Social Analysis*, 2:44 (November 2000), 129–56
LEE, VERNON, 'Botticelli at the Villa Lemmi', *Cornhill Magazine*, 46 (July-December 1882), 159–73
—— *Genius Loci: Notes on Places* (London: Richards, 1899)
—— 'The Nature of Literature, II', *Contemporary Review*, 86 (1 July 1904), 645–61
—— 'The Portrait Art of the Renaissance', *Cornhill Magazine*, 47 (January-June 1883), 564–81
LE NORMAND-ROMAIN, ANTOINETTE, '"When I Consider the Honours that Have Been Bestowed Upon Me in England"', in *Rodin*, ed. by Catherine Lampert, exhibition catalogue (London: Royal Academy of Arts, 2006), pp. 118–31
LE NORMAND-ROMAIN, ANTOINETTE, ed., *Rodin en 1900: l'exposition de l'Alma*, Musée du Luxembourg (Paris: Réunion des Musées Nationaux, 2001)
LEYRIS, PIERRE, *La Chambre du traducteur* (Paris: José Corti, 2007)
—— 'Pour Arthur Symons: à propos d'une biographie', *Mercure de France* (January 1964), 3–10
—— *Pour mémoire: ruminations d'un petit clerc à l'usage de ses frères humains et des vers légataires* (Paris: Corti, 2002)
LHOMBREAUD, ROGER, *Arthur Symons: A Critical Biography* (London: Unicorn Press, 1963)
LOMBARDO, AGOSTINO, *La poesia inglese dall'estetismo al simbolismo* (Rome: Edizioni di storia e letteratura, 1950)
LYON, JANET, 'Gadže Modernism', *Modernism/Modernity*, 11:3 (2004), 517–38
MABIRE, JEAN-CHRISTOPHE, *L'Esposition Universelle de 1900* (Paris: l'Harmattan, 2000)
MCCARREN, FELICIA M., *Dance Pathologies: Performance, Poetics, Medicine* (Stanford, CA: Stanford University Press, 1998)
MCCLINTOCK, LANDER, *Sainte-Beuve's Critical Theory and Practice After 1849* (Chicago: University of Chicago Press, 1920)
MACDONELL, AGNES, 'The Symbolist Movement in Literature', *Bookman*, 18:105 (June 1900), 94
MACFALL, HALDANE, *Aubrey Beardsley: The Man and His Work* (London: Lane, 1928)
MACINTOSH, FIONA, 'Dancing Maenads in Early Twentieth-Century Britain', in *The Ancient Dancer in the Modern World: Responses to Greek and Roman Dance*, ed. by Fiona Macintosh (Oxford: Oxford University Press, 2010), pp. 188–208
MACLEOD, KIRSTEN, *Fictions of British Decadence: High Art, Popular Writing and the Fin de Siècle* (Basingstoke: Palgrave Macmillan, 2008)
MAHONEY, KRISTIN, *Literature and the Politics of Post-Victorian Decadence* (Cambridge: Cambridge University Press, 2015)
MALLARMÉ, STÉPHANE, *Correspondance*, ed. by Henri Mondor and Lloyd James Austin, 11 vols (Paris: Gallimard, 1983)
—— *Igitur, Divagations, Un coup de dés*, ed. by Bertrand Marchal (Paris: Gallimard, 2003)
MANGRAVITE, ANDREW, 'Arthur Symons' Travel Writing: The Decadent Abroad' (2000), <www.victorianweb.org/authors/symons/am1.html> [accessed 18 April 2017]
MARCOVITCH, HEATHER, 'Dance, Ritual, and Arthur Symons's *London Nights*', *English Literature in Transition, 1880–1920*, 56:4 (2013), 462–82
MARKERT, LAWRENCE W., *Arthur Symons: Critic of the Seven Arts* (Ann Arbor: University of Michigan Research Press, 1988)
MARRAUD, HÉLÈNE, *Rodin: Revealing Hands* (Paris: Éditions du Musée Rodin, 2005)

MARTIN, KRISTY, *Modernism and the Rhythms of Sympathy: Vernon Lee, Virginia Woolf, and D. H. Lawrence* (Oxford: Oxford University Press, 2013)
MARTIN, STODDARD, *Wagner to 'The Waste Land': A Study of the Relationship of Wagner to English Literature* (London: Macmillan, 1982)
MARX, JACQUES, 'Verhaeren et ses traducteurs anglais', *Revue de littérature comparée*, 299:3 (2001), 443–54
MAXWELL, CATHERINE, *Second Sight: The Visionary Imagination in Late Victorian Literature* (Manchester & New York: Manchester University Press, 2007)
—— 'Whistlerian Impressionism and the Venetian Variations of Vernon Lee, John Addington Symonds, and Arthur Symons', *Yearbook of English Studies*, 40 (2010), 217–45
MERCIER, PASCAL, 'André Gide stratège ou tacticien?', in *La Belle Époque des revues, 1880– 1914*, ed. by Jacqueline Pluet-Despatin, Michel Leymarie, and Jean-Yves Mollier (Paris: Éditions de l'IMEC, 2002), pp. 93–100
MEREDITH, GEORGE, *Essai sur la comédie: de l'idée de comédie et des exemples de l'esprit comique, précédé d'une introduction par Arthur Symons*, trans. by Henry-D. Davray (Paris: Société du Mercure de France, 1898)
MERRILL, STUART, 'Arthur Symons', *L'Aube*, 2 (January 1897), 151–53
—— 'L'Œuvre poétique d'Arthur Symons', *Antée*, 13 (June 1907), 66–82
MIRBEAU, OCTAVE, 'La Princess Maleine de M. Maerterlinck', *Le Figaro*, 24 August 1890, 1
MIRBEAU, OCTAVE, and OTHERS, *Auguste Rodin et son œuvre*, trans. by Henry-D. Davray (Paris: Éditions de la Plume, 1900)
MONTESQUIOU-FEZENSAC, ROBERT DE, 'Beardsley en Raccourci', *Assemblée de Notables* (Paris, 1909), 17–27
MUNRO, JOHN M., *Arthur Symons* (New York: Twayne, 1969)
MURAT, LAURE, *Passage de l'Odéon: Sylvia Beach, Adrienne Monnier et la vie littéraire à Paris dans l'entre-deux-guerres* (Paris: Gallimard/Folio, 2005)
MURRAY, DAVID LESLIE, 'Oscar Wilde', *Times Literary Supplement* (8 January 1931), 25
NENCIONI, ENRICO, *Nuovi saggi critici di letterature straniere e altri scritti* (Florence: Le Monnier, 1909)
NEWMAN, ERNEST, 'Mr. Arthur Symons on Richard Strauss', *Speaker: The Liberal Review*, 8 (11 April 1903), 35–36
NORD, DEBORAH EPSTEIN *Gypsies and the British Imagination, 1807–1930* (New York Columbia University Press, 2006)
O'REILLY, CAMILLE C., 'Tourist or Traveller? Narrating Backpacker Identity', in *Discourse Communication and Tourism*, ed. by Adam Jaworski and Annette Pritchard (Cleveland Channel View Publications, 2005), pp. 150–69
O'SULLIVAN, VINCENT, *Aspects of Wilde* (London: Constable and Company, 1936)
OUIDA, 'The Genius of D'Annunzio', *Fortnightly Review*, 61 (March 1897), 349–73
PAREJO VADILLO, ANA, 'Immaterial Poetics: A. Mary F. Robinson and the Fin-de-Siècle Poem', in *The Fin-de-siècle Poem: English Literary Culture and the 1890s*, ed. by Joseph Bristow (Athens: Ohio University Press, 2005), pp. 231–60
PARKES, KINETON, 'The Decadence' [review of *From Toulouse-Lautrec to Rodin* by Arthur Symons], *The Bookman*, 77.459 (December 1929), 226
PATER, WALTER, *Imaginary Portraits*, ed. by Lene Østermark-Johansen, Jewelled Tortoise, 2 (London: Modern Humanities Research Association, 2014)
—— *Portraits imaginaires*, trans. by George Khnopff (Paris: Éditions de la Société du Mercure de France, 1898)
—— *The Library Edition of the Works of Walter Pater*, 10 vols (London: Macmillan, 1910)
—— *The Renaissance: Studies in Art and Poetry*, ed. by Donald L. Hill (Berkeley: University of California Press, 1980)

Pfister, Manfred, ed., *The Fatal Gift of Beauty: The Italies of British Travellers, An Annotated Anthology* (Amsterdam and Atlanta: Rodopi, 1996)

Picard, Edmond, 'L'Âme belge', *Revue encyclopédique*, 7:207 (24 July 1897), 595–99

Pieri, Giuliana, *The Influence of Pre-Raphaelitism on Fin de Siècle Italy: Art, Beauty, and Culture* (London: Modern Humanities Research Association, 2007)

'The Pilgrim', pseud., 'Un manifeste littéraire anglais', *Mercure de France*, 4:27 (March 1892), 200

Pinet, Hélène, 'Loïe Fuller and Auguste Rodin: Dancer and Impresario', in *Body Stages: The Metamorphosis of Loïe Fuller*, ed. by Emma Cavazzini and Doriana Comerlati (Milan: Skira, 2014), pp. 55–63

Pointner, Petra, *A Prelude to Modernism: Studies in the Urban and Erotic Poetry of Arthur Symons* (Heidelberg: Universitätsverlag Winter, 2004)

Porterfield, Susan Azar, 'Symons as Critic of the Visual Arts', *English Literature in Transition, 1880–1920*, 44:3 (2001), 260–74

Potolsky, Matthew, *The Decadent Republic of Letters: Taste, Politics and Cosmopolitan Community from Baudelaire to Beardsley* (Philadelphia: University of Pennsylvania Press, 2013)

Praz, Mario, *The Romantic Agony*, trans. by Angus Davidson, 2nd edn (London: Oxford University Press, 1951)

—— *Storia della letteratura inglese* (Florence: Sansoni, 1937)

Prins, Yopie, 'Greek Maenads, Victorian Spinsters', in *Victorian Sexual Dissidence*, ed. by Richard Dellamora (Chicago: University of Chicago Press, 1999), pp. 43–82

Ribeyrol, Charlotte, 'Poetic Podophilia: Gautier, Baudelaire, Swinburne, and Classical Foot-Fetishism', *Journal of Victorian Culture*, 20:2 (2015), 212–29

Ricks, Christopher, *Allusion to the Poets* (Oxford: Oxford University Press, 2002)

Rilke, Rainer Maria, *Auguste Rodin*, trans. by Jessie Lemont and Hans Trausil (London: Pallas Athene, 2006)

Rodin, Auguste, *Cathedrals of France*, trans. by Elisabeth Chase Geissbuhler (London & New York: Country Life, 1965)

Rosenblatt, Louise, *L'Idée de l'art pour l'art dans la littérature anglaise pendant la période victorienne* (Paris: Champion, 1931)

Ross, Robert, 'Aubrey Beardsley', *The Academy*, 70 (27 January 1906), 95–96

Rossetti, Dante Gabriel, *The Early Italian Poets* (London: Smith, Elder & Co, 1861)

Roth, Samuel, 'Adrift in London: An Extract from *Count Me Among the Missing*', *Journal of Modern Literature*, 3:4 (April 1974), 922–27

Rothenstein, William, *Men and Memories: Recollections of William Rothenstein 1872–1900*, 2 vols (London: Faber & Faber, 1931)

—— *Since Fifty: Men and Memories, 1922–1938: Recollections of William Rothenstein* (London: Faber, 1939)

Ruyters, André, 'La Critique d'Arthur Symons', *Antée*, 11 (April 1907), 1153–58

Sainte-Beuve, Charles Augustin, *Les Cahiers de Sainte-Beuve* (Paris: Lemerre, 1876)

Sargeant-Quittanson, Régine, 'Arthur Symons et les mouvements décadents des années 1890' (unpublished doctoral thesis, University of Rheims, 1981)

Saul, Nicholas, *Gypsies and Orientalism in German Literature and Anthropology of the Long Nineteenth Century* (Oxford: Legenda, 2007)

Saunders, Max, *Ford Madox Ford: A Dual Life. Volume II — The After-War World* (Oxford: Oxford University Press, 1996)

—— *Self Impression: Life-Writing, Autobiografiction, and the Forms of Modern Literature* (Oxford: Oxford University Press, 2010)

Seiler, R. M., ed., *Walter Pater: The Critical Heritage* (London: Routledge & Kegan Paul, 1980)

Sharp, William, 'La Jeune Belgique', *Nineteenth Century*, 34 (September 1893), 416–36

SHERRY, VINCENT, *Modernism and the Reinvention of Decadence* (Cambridge: Cambridge University Press, 2014)
SIMMEL GEORG, 'The Metropolis and Mental Life', in *The Sociology of Georg Simmel*, ed. and trans. by Kurt H. Wolff (London: Macmillan, 1950), pp. 409–24
SKLARE, ARNOLD B., 'Arthur Symons: An Appreciation of the Critic of Literature', *Journal of Aesthetics & Art Criticism*, 9 (1951), 316–22
SMALL, IAN, *Oscar Wilde Revalued: An Essay on New Materials & Methods of Research* (Greensboro, NC: ELT Press, 1993)
SMART, B. C., and HENRY T. CROFTON, *The Dialect of the English Gypsies* (London: Asher, 1875)
SPOO, ROBERT, *Without Copyrights: Piracy, Publishing and the Public Domain* (Oxford: Oxford University Press, 2013)
STIEGLITZ, ALFRED, 'A Plea for Art Photography in America', *Photographic Mosaics* (1892), 135–37
SUTTON, EMMA, *Aubrey Beardsley and British Wagnerism in the 1890s* (New York: Oxford University Press, 2002)
—— '"The Music Spoke for Us": Music and Sexuality in Fin-de-Siècle Poetry', in *The Figure of Music in Nineteenth-Century British Poetry*, ed. by Phyllis Weliver (Aldershot: Ashgate, 2005), pp. 213–29
SWINBURNE, A. C., 'King Lear', *Harper's Monthly Magazine*, 106 (December 1902), 3–8
—— 'Othello', *Harper's Monthly Magazine*, 109 (October 1904), 660–67
—— *Three Plays of Shakespeare* (New York: Harper and Brothers, 1909)
SYMINGTON, MICÉALA, *Écrire le tableau: l'approche poétique de la critique d'art à l'époque symboliste* (Bern: Lang, 2006)
SYMONS, A. J. A., ed., *An Anthology of 'Nineties Verse'* (London: Elkin Mathews and Marrot, 1928)
THOMAS, LOUIS, *Les Dernières Leçons de Marcel Schwob sur François Villon* (Paris: Éditions de Psyché, 1906)
THOMSON, CLIVE, ed., *Georges Hérelle: archéologie de l'inversion sexuelle 'fin de siècle'* (Paris: Éditions du Félin, 2014)
TICKNER, LISA, *Modern Life and Modern Subjects: British Art in the Early Twentieth Century* (New Haven, CT: Yale University Press, 2000)
TOSI, GUY, ed., *Gabriele D'Annunzio à Georges Hérelle: correspondance accompagné de douze sonnets cisalpines* (Paris: Éditions Denoël, 1946)
TREVOR, JOHN, *French Art and English Morals* (London: Sonnenschein, 1886)
TRUMPENER, KATIE, 'The Time of the Gypsies: A "People Without History" in the Narratives of the West', in *Identities*, ed. by Anthony Appiah and Henry Louis Gates Jr (Chicago: University of Chicago Press, 1995), pp. 338–80
VAN DEN ABEELE, ANDRIES, 'Une maison d'édition brugeoise: Arthur Herbert (1906–1907)', *Textyles*, 23 (2003), 95–101
VAN GENNEP, ARNOLD, 'Revue de la quinzaine', *Mercure de France*, 74:268 (August 1908), 697
VAN LERBERGHE, CHARLES, 'The Night-Comers (Englished by William Sharp)', *Evergreen, The Northern Seasonal*, 2 (Autumn 1895), 59–71
VAN PUYMBROECK, BIRGIT, 'Anglo-French Relations in the *Anglo-French Review*: "Bien en Advienne"', *English Literature in Transition, 1880–1920*, 55:1 (2012), 69–93
VERHAEREN, ÉMILE, *The Dawn*, trans. by Arthur Symons (London: Duckworth, 1898)
VERLAINE, PAUL, 'Deux poètes anglais', *Revue encyclopédique*, 114 (July 1895), 325–26
VILLIERS DE L'ISLE-ADAM, JEAN-MARIE-MATHIAS-PHILIPPE-AUGUSTE, *Claire Lenoir by Villiers de l'Isle-Adam*, trans. by Arthur Symons (New York: Boni, 1925)
—— *Oeuvres complètes*, ed. by Alan Raitt and Pierre-Georges Castex, 2 vols (Paris: Gallimard/Pléiade, 1986)

VOGELER, MARTHA S., *Austin Harrison and the English Review* (Columbia: University of Missouri Press, 2008)

VOGÜÉ, EUGÈNE-MELCHIOR DE, 'La Renaissance latine: Gabriel D'Annunzio, poèmes et romans', *Revue des deux mondes* (1 January 1895), 187–206, <http://rddm.revuedesdeuxmondes.fr/archive/article.php?code=66236> [accessed 10 January 2017]

WADE, ALLAN, 'Arthur Symons', *Times Literary Supplement* (10 March 1945), 115

WALKER, R. A., ed., *A Beardsley Miscellany* (London: Bodley Head, 1949)

WARNER, ERIC, and GRAHAM HOUGH, 'Arthur Symons (1865–1945)', in *Strangeness and Beauty: An Anthology of Aesthetic Criticism 1840–1910*, ed. by Eric Warner and Graham Hough, 2 vols (Cambridge: Cambridge University Press, 2009), II, 210–72

WAUGH, ARTHUR, 'London Letter', *The Critic*, 20 (9 December 1893), 383

WEIR, DAVID, *Decadence and the Making of Modernism* (Amherst: University of Massachusetts Press, 1995)

WELIVER, PHYLLIS, *The Musical Crowd in English Fiction, 1840–1910: Class, Culture, and Nation* (Basingstoke: Palgrave Macmillan, 2006)

—— *Women Musicians in Victorian Fiction, 1860–1900: Representations of Music, Science and Gender in the Leisured Home* (London: Routledge, 2016)

WHITRIDGE, ARNOLD, 'Matthew Arnold and Sainte-Beuve', *PMLA*, 53 (1938), 303–13

WHITTINGTON-EGAN, RICHARD, *Lionel Johnson: Victorian Dark Angel* (Great Malvern: Cappella Archive, 2012)

WILDE, OSCAR, *The Complete Letters of Oscar Wilde*, ed. by Merlin Holland and Rupert Hart-Davis (London: Fourth Estate, 2000)

—— *Complete Works of Oscar Wilde*, ed. by Ian Small and others (Oxford: Oxford University Press, 2000–)

WILSON, SIMON, *Beardsley* (Oxford: Phaidon, 1983)

WOODHOUSE, JOHN, *Gabriele D'Annunzio: Defiant Archangel* (Oxford: Clarendon Press, 1998)

—— 'Il *Trionfo della Morte*: traduzioni, reazioni e interpretazioni anglosassoni', in *Trionfo della Morte: atti del III convegno internazionale di studi dannunziani*, ed. by Edoardo Tiboni and Luigia Abrugiati (Pescara: Centro nazionale di studi dannunziani, 1981), pp. 239–58

YEATS, W. B., *Uncollected Prose, Volume II: Later Reviews, Articles and Other Miscellaneous Prose 1897–1939*, ed. by John P. Frayne and Colton Johnson (London: Macmillan, 1975)

—— *Yeats's Poems*, ed. and annotated by A. Norman Jeffares (London: Macmillan, 1989)

ZIMMERN, HELEN, 'D'Annunzio's *La Figlia di Iorio*', *North American Review*, 41 (1 January 1905), 41–47

Electronic Resources

<http://www.andriesvandenabeele.net/index.htm> [accessed 1 October 2016]
<http://www.gypsyloresociety.org> [accessed 6 March 2015]
<http://irhis.recherche.univ-lille3.fr/00-SiteUniversite/htdocs/koszul-andre.html> [accessed 16 April 2017]
<http://www.liv.ac.uk/library/sca/colldescs/gypsy/index.html> [accessed 6 March 2015]
<http://www.mercuredefrance.fr/unepage-historique-historique-1-1-0-1.html> [accessed 14 May 2016]
<https://textyles.revues.org/796> [accessed 16 April 2017]

INDEX

Abrugiati, Luigia 67 n. 13
Alighieri, Dante 55, 58
Alma-Tadema, Laurence 90
Anderson, Benedict 72
Ando, Tomoko 27 n. 27
Appia, Adolphe 44
Appiah, Anthony 159 n. 48
Aquinas, Thomas 36
Archer, William 84, 90–91, 100 n. 20, 100 n. 22
Aretino, Pietro 65
Arnold, Matthew 5, 74, 134–35, 143 n. 31, 143 n. 32, 147
Artaud, Antonin 42, 51
Austin, Lloyd James 112 n. 3
Aznavour, Charles 118

Bakunin, Michail 99
Baldick, Robert 67 n. 20
Baldwick, Chris 6, 9 n. 4
Balfour, Jabez Spencer 126
Balzac, Honoré de 72, 124, 126, 127
Balzagette, Léon 108
Barnes, Djuna 111
Baron Corvo 75
Barrès, Maurice 99
Baudelaire, Charles 2, 3, 4, 5, 7, 9 n. 4, 15, 16, 19, 29 n. 58, 54, 70, 71, 74, 82 n. 8, 82 n. 15, 86, 89, 91, 98, 111, 147–48, 158 n. 10, 158 n. 14, 167
Beach, Sylvia 76, 109
Beardsley, Aubrey 7, 31, 35–39, 40–41 n. 50, 75, 104, 108, 115 n. 47, 146, 164
Beck, Christian, *see* Bossi, Joseph
Beckett, Samuel 51
Beckson, Karl 4, 9 n. 2, 9 n. 7, 10 n. 11, 10 n. 16, 10 n. 17, 10 n. 18, 27 n. 7, 27 n. 10, 27 n. 15, 27 n. 18, 27 n. 20, 38, 41 n. 57, 44, 51 n. 5, 51 n. 6, 66 n. 1, 74, 76, 79, 82 n. 20, 82 n. 21, 82 n. 32, 82 n. 39, 83 n. 41, 83 n. 45, 83 n. 58, 83 n. 60, 100 n. 3, 100 n. 17, 101 n. 56, 111 n. 63, 114 n. 34, 119, 122, 128 n. 8, 128 n. 10, 129 n. 28, 129 n. 31, 129 n. 49, 133, 142 n. 7, 142 n. 8, 142 n. 12, 142 n. 14, 142 n. 20, 142 n. 21, 157 n. 2, 157 n. 7, 158 n. 25, 159 n. 50, 161, 166, 169 n. 3, 169 n. 4, 170 n. 9, 170 n. 10, 170 n. 21, 170 n. 24, 170 n. 25, 170 n. 28, 170 n. 29, 170 n. 30, 171 n. 17, 171 n. 32
Beerbohm, Max 75, 122, 168

Beethoven, Ludwig van 33, 36, 43
Bell, Clive 7, 31, 39, 41 n. 52
Bellow, Juliet 29 n. 52
Benjamin, Walter 140, 144 n. 56
Berenson, Bernard 37
Bergson, Henri 110
Bernhardt, Sarah 42, 64, 140
Bever, Adolphe van 76
Binyon, Laurence 94
Bizzotto, Elisa 8
Blake, William 4, 108, 111
Blanche, Jacques-Émile 37, 40 n. 48, 115 n. 47
Blès, Arthur 107
Block, Edwin F. Jr. 123, 127, 129 n. 36
Bloom, Harold 164, 170 n. 19
Boccaccio, Giovanni 58, 71
Böcklin, Arnold 121
Böhme, Gernot 144 n. 56
Borrow, George Henry 148–49
Bossi, Joseph 98
Boudin, Philomène 76
Bourdieu, Pierre 100 n. 9, 100 n. 12
Bourget, Paul, 72, 132–33
Boyiopoulos, Kostas 10 n. 19
Brake, Laurel 5, 10 n. 23, 83 n. 53
Brandes, Georg 54, 67 n. 3
Brecht, Bertold, 42
Breuer, Joseph, 122
Bridges, Robert, 145
Brieux, Eugène, 97
Brion, Marcel 115 n. 53
Bristow, Joseph 142 n. 16, 161, 169 n. 7, 171 n. 36
Brogniez, Laurence 100 n. 16, 101 n. 45
Brook, Peter 42, 51
Brooks, Edmund D. 138
Brophy, Brigid 41 n. 50
Browning, Robert 2, 3, 108, 118, 119, 128 n. 3, 133–34, 160, 163
Brulé, André 110, 116 n. 58
Bullen, J. B. 37, 41 n. 52
Bunyan, John 36
Buonarroti, Michelangelo 16, 27 n. 22
Burton, Sir Richard 151
Buzard, James 142 n. 5, 142 n. 13

Caliaro, Ilvano 67 n. 20

Campbell, James Dykes 75, 82 n. 32, 119, 121, 128 n. 8, 142 n. 20, 148, 158 n. 24
Campbell, Mrs Patrick 101 n. 42
Capus, Alfred 107
Carrière, Eugène 17, 27 n. 25
Casanova, Giacomo 106
Casanova, Pascale 56, 67 n. 9, 90, 100 n. 15
Castex, Pierre-Georges 81 n. 2
Cavazzini, Emma 28 n. 48
Cazamian, Louis 110, 111
Cazamian, Madeleine 111, 113 n. 5, 116 n. 65
Cestre, Charles 110
Chateaubriand, François-René de 114 n. 28
Chevrillon, André 110
Child, Harold Hannyngton 9 n. 10
Choderlos de Laclos, Pierre-Ambroise-François 65
Chopin, Frédéric 33, 38, 124
Churchill, Kenneth 142 n. 9
Cimini, Mario 67 n. 4, 68 n. 35, 68 n. 36, 68 n. 37, 68 n. 38, 68 n. 39, 68 n. 41
Cixous, Hélène 122, 129 n. 32
Cladel, Judith 18
Cladel, Léon 99
Clarétie, Jules 107
Claudel, Paul 109
Cnudde-Knowland, Anne 101 n. 39
Coburn, Alvin Langdon 137–39, 143 n. 46
Cocteau, Jean 22, 24, 28 n. 47
Cohen, Jack 106, 114 n. 30, 114 n. 32
Colby, Vineta 142 n. 16, 142 n. 18
Colenbrander, Joanna 83 n. 67
Collins, Sarah 33, 39 n. 3, 39 n. 19
Comerlati, Doriana 28 n. 48
Condamine, Robin de la, *see* Farquharson, Robert
Condé, Alice 40 n. 29
Conlon, John J. 134, 143 n. 29
Connor, Steven 140, 144 n. 53
Conrad, Joseph 109, 146
Constable, Liz 10 n. 22
Constance, Olive 4
Coote, William Alexander 75
Coste, Bénédicte 8
Courson, Comtesse Roger de 107
Crang, Mike 142 n. 13
Creasy, Matthew 6, 7, 10 n. 27, 82 n. 23, 100 n. 35, 103, 126
Crofton, Henry T. 151, 158 n. 43
cummings, e. e. 109
Cummins, Anthony 82 n. 34
Cunard, Nancy 109–10

Dann, Graham 142 n. 13
D'Annunzio, Gabriele 3, 4, 6, 7, 54–68, 92, 95, 132
Dantine, Marie 80
Da Ponte, Lorenzo 69
Darondeau, Georges 115 n. 56

Davray, Henry-D. 27 n. 19, 104, 105, 106, 107, 108, 113 n. 19, 113 n. 21, 113 n. 25, 114 n. 26, 114 n. 27, 115 n. 49
De Coster, Charles 89
Delattre, Floris 116 n. 64
Dellamora, Richard 29 n. 58
Delteil, Joseph 109
Deman, Edmond 89, 96
Demetz, Peter 144 n. 56
Demeulenaere, Alex 101 n. 46
Demoor, Marysa 101 n. 47
Denis, Benoît 100 p. 10
Denisoff, Dennis 10 n. 22
De Quincey, Thomas 111
Deschamps, Léon 114 n. 26
Desmarais, Jane 6, 7, 9 n. 4, 40 n. 29, 40 n. 35, 41 n. 50
Dessy, Clément 8, 61, 101 n. 42, 107
Destrée, Olivier-Georges 94
Detemmerman, Jacques 101 n. 46
Dickens, Charles 119
Donne, John 4
Doubleday, Herbert Arthur 98, 108
Douglas, Alfred Lord 165
Dovzhy, Sasha 81 n. 1
Dowling, Linda 78, 83 n. 56
Dowson, Ernest 4, 5, 12, 14, 74, 86, 88, 100 n. 7, 108
Druet, Eugène 19, 22
Dubois, Jacques 100 n. 12
Duclaux, Émile 139
Duclaux, Mary, *see* Robinson, Agnes Mary Frances
Duclos, Michèle 116 n. 76
Ducrey, Guy 100 n. 8, 112 n. 4, 116 n. 76
Du Maurier, Daphne 121
Duncan, Isadora 7, 13, 23–26, 29 n. 53, 29 n. 54, 29 n. 56, 52 n. 9
Duncan, Raymond 23
Duse, Eleonora 42, 43, 49, 61, 64–65

Eder, Josef Maria 139, 143 n. 51
Edward VII, King of England 17
Edwards, Osman 84, 95, 98, 101 n. 54, 101 n. 55
Eekhoud, Georges 89, 99
Egan, Beresford 75
Eliot, George 126
Eliot, Thomas Stearns 2–3, 5, 7, 9, 9 n. 6, 9 n. 8, 10 n. 25, 38, 74–75, 76, 79, 82 n. 22, 82 n. 23, 82 n. 24, 82 n. 27, 109, 164, 170 n. 19
Ellis, Havelock 3, 29 n. 58, 35, 123, 167
Ellmann, Richard 82 n. 35, 83 n. 53, 111, 116 n. 68, 170 n. 16
Emanuel, Susan 100 n. 9
Emerson, Ralph Waldo 99
Emmanuel, Maurice 23, 29 n. 55
Engels, Steven 101 n. 46
Euclid 32

Evangelista, Stefano 7, 95, 99 n. 1, 134, 143 n. 25, 169 n. 7

Farmer, Albert 110–11, 112, 116 n. 63
Farquharson, Robert 145, 157 n. 2
Fell, Jill 99 n. 1
Fenaille, Maurice 28 n. 37
Fergonzi, Flavio 27 n. 22
Fernandez, Ramon 109
Field, Michael 24
Flaubert, Gustave 146, 147
Fletcher, Ian 41 n. 50
Flower, Desmond 100 n. 7
Flynt, Josiah 8, 123, 140–41
Fontainas, André 104
Forster, Edward Morgan 38
Fox, C. Jay 169 n. 1, 169 n. 6
Franklin, Adrian 142 n. 13
Frayne, John P. 40 n. 27
Fredericq, Paul 91
Freeman, Nicholas 6, 8, 9 n. 1, 10 n. 20, 31, 39 n. 9, 40 n. 24, 40 n. 46, 137, 141, 143 n. 42, 143 n. 46, 144 n. 62
Freud, Sigmund 51, 122
Friedman, Donald 127, 130 n. 51
Fry, Roger 7, 31, 37–39, 41 n. 51, 41 n. 53, 41 n. 54
Fuller, Loïe 7, 13, 20–26, 28 n. 49
Furnivall, Frederick James 133

Gagnier, Regenia 148, 158 n. 29, 158 n. 30, 159 n. 57
Galani-Moutafi, Vasiliki 142 n. 13
Gallimard, Gaston 109
Galuppi, Baldassare 133
Garelick, Rhonda K. 20, 28 n. 42, 28 n. 47, 28 n. 49, 28 n. 50
Gates, Henry Louis, Jr. 159 n. 48
Gauricus, Pomponius 18
Gautier, Théophile 7, 32, 39 n. 13, 84, 146, 147
Geissbuhler, Elisabeth Chase 28 n. 34
Gerstein, Alexandra 29 n. 52
Gertzman, Jay A. 82 n. 37
Gide, André 108, 109, 167
Giovannelli, Laura 9
Gissing, George 126
Goddard, Stephen H. 130 n. 51
Gogibu, Vincent 112 n. 2
Goldoni, Carlo 119
Goncourt, Edmond de 88, 89
Goncourt, Jules de 88, 89
Gordine, Dora 13
Gosetti-Ferencei, Jennifer Anna 144 n. 55
Gosse, Edmund 3, 9 n. 7, 89, 97, 101 n. 68, 105, 110
Gourmont, Jean de 114 n. 29
Gourmont, Remy de 6, 103, 104–05, 107, 108, 109, 111, 112 n. 2, 113 n. 6, 113 n. 7, 113 n. 11, 113 n. 14, 113 n. 18, 114 n. 40, 115 n. 43

Gray, John 4
Gross, Kenneth 51, 52 n. 21
Guiette, Robert 116 n. 75
Guilbert, Yvette 110, 140
Gullace, Giovanni 55, 67 n. 5
Gunn, Peter 142 n. 18
Gurdon, John 107

Hall, Jason David 4, 10 n. 20
Hamerton, Philip Gilbert 36, 40 n. 36
Handel, George Frideric 45
Harding, F. J. W. 143 n. 31
Harding, Georgina 56–57, 59, 62, 67 n. 18
Hardy, Thomas 89, 90
Harris, Frank 106, 120, 164, 165, 169 n. 6, 170 n. 23
Harrison, Jane 24
Hart-Davis, Rupert 169 n. 4, 169 n. 5, 170 n. 11, 170 n. 22, 170 n. 23
Hawthorne, Nathaniel 112
Hayes, Sebastian 10 n. 19
Hegel, Georg Wilhelm Friedrich 31, 38, 39 n. 10
Heinemann, William 56, 67 n. 16
Hemingway, Ernest 109
Henley, William Ernest 17, 54, 162
Herbert, Arthur, see Doubleday, Herbert Arthur
Hérelle, Georges 55, 56, 57, 60, 63, 64, 68 n. 25, 68 n. 35, 68 n. 36, 68 n. 37, 68 n. 38, 68 n. 39, 68 n. 41
Herman, Jan 101 n. 46
Herold, Katharina 8, 34, 40 n. 29, 105
Hervieu, Anne 115 n. 53
Herzog, Patricia 39 n. 13, 39 n. 16
Hewlett, Maurice 106
Hill, Donald L. 39 n. 12
Hofmannsthal, Hugo von 7, 95, 140, 144 n. 55
Hogg, James 112
Holland, Merlin 162, 169 n. 4, 169 n. 5, 170 n. 11, 170 n. 22, 170 n. 23
Hood, Thomas 165
Horne, Herbert 127, 129 n. 49
Hough, Graham 10 n. 18, 168, 171 n. 35
Housman, Alfred Edward 107
Housman, Laurence 106
Hughes, Agatha 67 n. 16
Hugo, Victor 104
Hutton, Edward 129 n. 28, 159 n. 50
Huxley, Michael 29 n. 59
Huysmans, Joris-Karl 6, 58, 67 n. 20, 72, 86, 99, 105, 107, 162
Hyde, Harford Montgomery 168

Ibsen, Henrik 46, 55, 62, 97, 114 n. 27
Innes, Christopher 52 n. 8
Ironside, Robin 41 n. 50
Isherwood, Christopher 123, 129 n. 37

James, Henry 18, 125, 129 n. 44, 132
James, William 128, 130 n. 52
James, W. P. 101 n. 59
Jarry, Alfred 43, 48
Jaulme, André 116 n. 67
Jaworski, Adam 142 n. 13
Jean-Aubry, Georges 109, 115 n. 51
Jeffares, A. Norman 26 n. 5
Jephcott, Edmund 144 n. 56
Jepson, Edgar 83 n. 40, 129 n. 49
Jesse, F. Tennyson 80, 83 n. 65, 83 n. 66
John, Augustus 27 n. 15, 151
Johnson, Colton 40 n. 27
Johnson, Lionel 4, 12, 14, 108
Jones, Susan 28 n. 45
Joseph Karl, Archduke of Austria 151
Joubert, Joseph 135
Joyce, James 3, 9 n. 2, 76, 109, 146, 163, 170 n. 16
Joyce, Stanislaus 83 n. 53
Judrin, Claudie 28 n. 38

Kahn, Florence 129 n. 31
Kahn, Gustave 99, 114 n. 26
Kamuf, Peggy 129 n. 32
Keats, John 13, 26 n. 4
Kermode, Frank 4, 10 n. 15, 13, 27 n. 6
Khnopff, Georges 106, 133 n. 24
Kipling, Rudyard 54, 66 n. 3, 67 n. 3, 110
Klingsor, Tristan 104
Klinkenberg, Jean-Marie 100 n. 10
Klossowski, Pierre 111
Knox, T. M. 39 n. 10
Koszul, André 110, 116 n. 57
Kra, Simon 115 n. 55
Kurth, Peter 29 n. 56, 29 n. 57, 29 n. 60

Lacomblez, Paul 89
Lamb, Charles 43
Lamberti, Maria 27 n. 22
Lanson, Gustave 110
Laoureux, Denis 100 n. 27
Larbaud, Valéry 109
La Tour, Mathilde de (Comtesse Victor Sallier de La Tour) 107, 108, 123
Laurent, François 115 n. 55
Lavers, Annette 41 n. 50
Lawrence, David Herbert 38
Leconte de Lisle, Charles Marie René 84
Lecoq, Jacques 51
Lee, Ken 158 n. 29, 158 n. 38
Lee, Vernon 3, 8, 59, 60, 68 n. 24, 75, 129 n. 26, 132–34, 136–37, 141, 142 n. 10, 142 n. 16, 142 n. 18, 142 n. 19, 143 n. 26
Le Gallienne, Richard 4
Legros, Alphonse 17, 27 n. 27
Leighton, Frederic 17

Lemonnier, Camille 89, 99
Lemont, Jessie 28 n. 32
Le Normand-Romain, Antoinette 27 n. 24, 28 n. 28, 28 n. 38
Lessing, Gotthold Ephraim 43
Leymarie, Michel 115 n. 50
Leyris, Pierre 104, 111–12, 116 n. 68, 116 n. 69, 116 n. 70, 116 n. 74
Lhombreaud, Roger 4, 10 n. 11, 10 n. 16, 111, 112, 122, 129 n. 29, 129 n. 34, 169 n. 3, 170 n. 8
Liszt, Franz 121
Lombardo, Agostino 4, 10 n. 14
Louÿs, Pierre 3, 54
Luciani, Georges 109, 115 n. 53
Ludwig, Richard 83 n. 40
Lugné-Poe, Aurélien 91
Lydia 120
Lyon, Janet 154, 159 n. 53

Maas, Henry 100 n. 7
Mabire, Jean-Christophe 28 n. 41
Macdonell, Agnes 101 n. 37
MacFall, Haldane 37, 39, 40 n. 50, 41 n. 58
Macfie, Robert Andrew Scott 145, 150, 151, 153, 158 n. 33, 158 n. 36, 158 n. 44
Macintosh, Fiona 29 n. 58
MacLeod, Kirsten 77, 83 n. 52
Macnaughton, Jane 28 n. 45
MacRitchie, David 153
Maeterlinck, Maurice 4, 6, 8, 42, 46, 48, 49, 50, 62, 63, 65, 84, 89, 90–94, 97, 99, 101 n. 42, 105
Mahaut, see La Tour, Mathilde de
Mahoney, Kristin 5, 10 n. 24, 71, 75–76, 78, 81, 81 n. 7, 82 n. 29, 82 n. 30, 83 n. 68, 169, 171 n. 38
Mallarmé, Stéphane 3, 6, 16, 20–22, 28 n. 45, 34, 37, 40 n. 29, 44, 54, 63, 88, 89, 103, 111, 112, 112 n. 3, 146, 162
Mangravite, Andrew 122, 129 n. 35
Marchal, Bertrand 28 n. 45
Marcovitch, Heather 14, 27 n. 12, 29 n. 58
Markert, Lawrence W. 4, 10 n. 18, 27 n. 8, 51 n. 1, 133, 142 n. 18, 143 n. 24
Marraud, Hélène 29 n. 51
Martin, Kristy 144 n. 55
Martin, Roxane 100 n. 27
Martin, Stoddard 39 n. 17
Marx, Jacques 101 n. 53
Mason, Stuart 168
Mathews, Elkin 70, 74
Matisse, Henri 24
Mauclair, Camille 114 n. 26
Maude, Ulrika 28 n. 45
Maupassant, Guy de 126
Maxwell, Catherine 121, 129 n. 26, 142 n. 10, 143 n. 25, 158 n. 26

May, James Lewis 107
Mayne, Jonathan 158 n. 10
McBurney, Simon 51
McCarren, Felicia M. 21, 28 n. 46
McClintock, Lander 143 n. 30
McEwan, Ian 121
Means, Robert S. 169 n. 2
Mendelssohn-Bartholdy, Jakob Ludwig Felix 33
Mendès, Catulle 107
Mercier, Pascal 115 n. 50
Meredith, George 79, 90, 106, 113 n. 25
Merrill, Stuart 98, 99, 102 n. 75, 102 n. 78, 105–06, 108, 112, 113 n. 22, 114 n. 26, 115 n. 48
Métra, Jean-Louis-Olivier 81 n. 6
Meyerhold, Vsevolod 42
Miles, Alfred H. 133, 142 n. 17
Millard, Christopher Sclater, *see* Mason, Stuart
Minghetti, Laura 133
Miomandre, Francis de 98
Mirbeau, Octave 91, 100 n. 21, 114 n. 26
Mollier, Jean-Yves 115 n. 50
Moncel, Henri 116 n. 67
Mondor, Henri 112 n. 3
Montesquiou, Robert de 37, 40 n. 48
Montfort, Eugène 98, 109
Monticelli, Adolphe 37
Morel, Auguste 115 n. 53
Morel, Frederick 101 n. 47
Morris, William 99
Mourey, Gabriel 63
Mousli, Béatrice 115 n. 55
Munro, John M. 4, 9 n. 7, 10 n. 11, 10 n. 16, 10 n. 17, 27 n. 15, 40 n. 44, 82 n. 32, 100 n. 3, 100 n. 17, 101 n. 56, 101 n. 63, 128 n. 8, 142 n. 7, 142 n. 8, 142 n. 12, 142 n. 14, 142 n. 20, 157 n. 2, 157 n. 7, 169 n. 2, 170 n. 14, 170 n. 20, 170 n. 21, 170 n. 26
Murat, Laure 115 n. 52
Murdoch, W. G. Blaikie 37, 40 n. 49
Murray, Alex 4, 10 n. 20
Murray, David Leslie 169 n. 1
Musset, Alfred de 91, 119
Mussolini, Benito 65, 68 n. 43

Nancy, Jean-Luc 72
Nencioni, Enrico 59, 67 n. 22, 133
Nero 166
Nerval, Gérard de 79
Newman, Ernest 30, 39 n. 9, 107
Newton, Isaac 43
Nietzsche, Friedrich 24, 29 n. 58, 49, 55, 57, 61, 99, 115 n. 47
Nord, Deborah Epstein 147, 151, 153, 154, 158 n. 19, 158 n. 39, 159 n. 46, 159 n. 52
Nordera, Marina 100 n. 27

Odle, Alan 152,
O'Reilly, Camille C. 142 n. 13
Osborne, Charles Churchill 133, 169 n. 3
Østermark-Johansen, Lene 7, 68 n. 27
Ostrovsky, Alexander Nikolayevich 97
O'Sullivan, Vincent 108, 161, 168, 170 n. 8
Ouida 56, 57, 58, 67 n. 10

Pachmann, Vladimir de 33–34
Paget, Violet, *see* Lee, Vernon
Palmer, Edward 151
Parejo Vadillo, Ana 142 n. 16
Parkes, Kineton 116 n. 61
Pater, Walter 2, 3, 4, 5, 6, 7, 9 n. 4, 9 n. 6, 32, 36, 39 n. 12, 39 n. 13, 39 n. 16, 43–44, 51 n. 4, 54, 58–61, 67 n. 21, 68 n. 27, 72, 74, 82 n. 27, 109, 119, 128 n. 9, 128 n. 11, 132, 134, 135–38, 141, 143 n. 35, 143 n. 36, 143 n. 37, 143 n. 38, 143 n. 39, 145, 148, 155, 156, 159 n. 56
Pearson, Hesketh 168
Péladan, Joséphin 67 n. 18
Petrarch 58
Pfister, Manfred 132, 142 n. 4, 142 n. 9
Picard, Edmond 90, 100 n. 13
Piérard, Louis 98
Pieri, Giuliana 67 n. 17
The Pilgrim 104, 113 n. 13
Pinet, Hélène 28 n. 48
Pluet-Despatin, Jacqueline 115 n. 50
Poe, Edgar Allan 63, 70, 91, 167
Pointner, Petra 10 n. 19
Pound, Ezra 76, 111
Powell, Fredrick York 17
Powys, John Cowper 168
Praz, Mario 4, 10 n. 12, 10 n. 13
Primoli, Giuseppe 133
Prins, Yopie 29 n. 58
Pritchard, Annette 142 n. 13
Pulham, Patricia 143 n. 25
Purcell, Henry 44

Querlon, Pierre de 114 n. 40
Quinn, John 76, 86, 100 n. 3, 142 n. 12, 145, 157 n. 2

Raine, Kathleen 111
Raitt, Alan 81 n. 2
Ramée, Marie Louise de la, *see* Ouida
Ramos Gay, Ignacio 100 n. 8
Ransome, Arthur 167, 168
Redon, Odilon 104
Renoir, Auguste 37
Reynier, Christine 116 n. 76
Rhys, Ernst 70, 81 n. 4
Rhys, Jean 111
Ribeyrol, Charlotte 29 n. 58
Ricketts, Charles 168

Ricks, Christopher 79, 83 n. 61, 128 n. 3
Rilke, Rainer Maria 18, 24, 28 n. 32
Roberts, Samuel 153
Robertson, Walford Graham 168
Robinson, Agnes Mary Frances 24, 110, 133, 139
Roche, Pierre 20
Rodenbach, Georges Raymond Constantin 89, 98, 99
Rodin, Auguste 7, 12–13, 15–20, 22–26, 27 n. 15,
    27 n. 22, 27 n. 25, 27 n. 27, 28 n. 31, 28 n. 34, 43,
    106, 107
Rolfe, Frederick, *see* Baron Corvo
Roger-Cornaz, Frédéric 109, 115 n. 55
Rops, Félicien 84–87, 88
Rosenblatt, Louise 112, 116 n. 75
Rosny, J. H. 107
Ross, Robert 36, 40 n. 38, 165, 166, 167, 168,
    170 n. 23
Rossetti, Dante Gabriel 71, 82 n. 11, 106, 165
Roth, Samuel 76–77, 82 n. 36
Rothenstein, William 17–18, 27 n. 26, 27 n. 27,
    28 n. 30, 28 n. 31, 110, 113 n. 8, 116 n. 62
Rubens, Pieter Paul 88
Ruskin, John 119
Ruysbroeck, Jan van 91, 92
Ruyters, André 98, 108, 115 n. 47

Sainte-Beuve, Charles Augustin de 134–35, 143 n. 30
Saint-Georges de Bouhélier (Stéphane-Georges
    Lepelletier de Bouhélier) 98
Sampson, John 150, 153, 158 n. 34, 158 n. 35,
    158 n. 40, 158 n. 41
Sargeant-Quittanson, Régine 116 n. 76
Saunders, Corinne 28 n. 45
Saunders, Max 82 n. 40, 126, 129 n. 48
Sauvage, Henri 20
Searle, Townley 151
Shakespeare, William 46, 47, 91, 93, 97, 116 n. 57
Sharp, William 94, 101 n. 44
Shaw, Peter 79
Shelley, Mary 116 n. 57
Shelley, Percy Bysshe 57, 116 n. 57
Sherry, Vincent 4, 5, 10 n. 21, 10 n. 24, 77, 83 n. 47
Sienkiewicz, Henryk 97
Silhouette, *see* Symons, Arthur, life
Simmel, George 155, 159 n. 55
Sindici, Magda, *see* Vivaria, Kassandra
Sklare, Arnold B. 162, 167, 170 n. 12, 170 n. 31
Small, Ian 157 n. 6, 171 n. 32, 171 n. 37
Smart, B. C. 158 n. 43
Smithers, Leonard 2, 88, 104; 105, 164, 169 n. 5,
    170 n. 22, 170 n. 23
Spaak, Paul 98
Spoo, Robert 82 n. 38
Stepniak, Sergius (Sergey Mikhaylovich Stepnyak-
    Kravchinsky) 97
Stern, Carol Simpson 169 n. 1

Stieglitz, Alfred 139–40, 143 n. 52
Stillinger, Jack 26 n. 4
Stokes, John 7, 90
Strauss, Richard 33, 43, 69
Strettell, Alma 95
Strindberg, Johan August 97
Super, R. H. 143 n. 31
Sutton, Emma 39 n. 17, 40 n. 47
Swinburne, Algernon Charles 3, 6, 7, 9 n. 6, 29 n. 58,
    36, 63, 80, 83 n. 63, 83 n. 64, 90, 115 n. 53, 167
Symington, Miceala 112, 112 n. 3, 116 n. 76
Symonds, John Addington 8, 132, 141, 142 n. 9,
    142 n. 10
Symons, A. J. A. 75, 116 n. 66
Symons, Arthur:
  works, editions, translations and unpublished
    materials:
    'A. Mary F. Darmesteter' 142 n. 17
    Amoris Victima 120
      'Mundi Victima' 158 n. 12
      'Venice 1897' 120
    'An Apology for Masks' 74
    'Un artiste dans ses attitudes: Oscar Wilde'
      114 n. 31
    'Are the English People Musical?' 33, 39 n. 20
    'Arles' 68 n. 32
    'Arthur Symons on *Intentions*' 170 n. 10,
      170 n. 17, 170 n. 18
    'Arthur Symons on The Ballad of Reading Gaol'
      170 n. 24
    'Arthur Symons on Wilde as "a prodigious
      entertainer"' 170 n. 28
    Arthur Symons Papers 81 n. 4, 81 n. 5, 129 n. 39
    'Aubrey Beardsley' 39 n. 6, 40 n. 41, 116 n. 76
    Aubrey Beardsley 106, 111, 114 n. 32
    'Les Aventures intellectuelles' 115 n. 44
    Aventures spirituelles 112, 116 n. 74
    'Ballet, Pantomime, and Poetic Drama' 48,
      52 n. 10
    'Barbara Roscorla's Child' 92, 95, 101 n. 38,
      101 n. 40
    Baudelaire: Prose and Poetry 5, 74, 82 n. 15
      'Preface' 82 n. 15
    'A Belgian Poet' 94, 101 n. 48
    'Belgium. Literature' 100 n. 11, 100 n. 14
    'Bertha at the Fair: An Encounter' 88, 100 n. 6,
      124, 129 n. 42
    'Bruges' 100 n. 5, 102 n. 76
    'Casanova à Dux: un chapitre d'histoire inédit'
      114 n. 27
    'Le Chant du vagabond' 115 n. 46
    'Charity' 160
    Charles Baudelaire: A Study 158 n. 12
    The Child of Pleasure 57, 60, 67 n. 18, 95
      'Introduction' 60, 67 n. 18
    'Chopin' 106, 114 n. 33

'The Chopin Player' 33
Cities 123, 131, 132, 134, 137, 141 n. 1, 156
    'To Madame la Comtesse de la Tour'
        128 n. 13, 142 n. 2, 143 n. 41
Cities and Sea-Coasts and Islands 132, 138
    'London: A Book of Aspects' 119, 129 n. 22
Cities of Italy 125, 126, 131, 132, 134, 137, 141 n. 1
    'Rome' 143 n. 50
    'Siena' 128 n. 16
    'Venice' 120, 128 n. 1, 129 n. 18
Cleopatra in Judea 108
Claire Lenoir 70, 71
    'Preface' 71, 82 n. 11, 82 n. 12, 82 n. 28
Colour Studies in Paris:
    'Notes on Paris and Paul Verlaine' 40 n. 33
Complete Works 110
'Confessions' 77
Confessions: A Study in Pathology 32, 39 n. 18, 112,
    118, 129 n. 31, 167
'D'Annunzio in English' 67 n. 15
Dante Gabriel Rossetti by Arthur Symons 106
The Daughter of Ioris 61
The Dawn 61, 68 n. 30, 95, 97, 98
    'Introduction' 95, 101 p. 60
Days and Nights 2, 6, 84, 103, 104, 113 n. 14, 145,
    162, 163
    'L'Aveu' 104
    'An Episode Under the Nihilists' 163
    'Prologue of Days and Nights' 157 n. 3
    'The Temptation of Saint Anthony (After a
        Design by Félicien Rops)' 84, 100 n. 2
Dead City 61, 62, 63, 68 n. 31, 95
'The Decadent Movement in Literature' 3, 54,
    55, 60, 66 n. 2, 91, 100 n. 29, 128 n 17, 135,
    143 n. 34, 146, 147, 156, 158 n. 18, 159 n. 54,
    162, 170 n. 13
'Les Demoiselles de Bienfilâtre' 76, 78, 83 n. 54
'Les Dessins de Rodin' 27 n. 19, 28 n. 39,
    28 n. 40, 114 n. 26
'Dieu à Londres' 102 n. 74
Dramatis Personae:
    'Impressionistic Writing' 40 n. 45
The Drunkard 95
Electra 95, 140
Eleonora Duse 65, 66 n. 1, 68 n. 42
'Émile Verhaeren' 102 n. 72
'English Literature in 1893' 105, 113 n. 17
Figures of Several Centuries:
    'The Goncourts' 143 n. 33
    'Walter Pater' 143 n. 39
The Flame of Life 61, 67 n. 16
The Fool of the World and Other Poems 40 n. 25
Francesca da Rimini 61, 63, 64, 65, 95
    'Introduction' 68 n. 40
'Frédéri Mistral' 113 n. 9
'A French Blake: Odilon Redon' 113 n. 9

From Toulouse-Lautrec to Rodin with Some Personal
    Impressions 15, 27 n. 14, 110
'Galuppi — Vernon Lee' 134
'The Genesis of Spiritual Adventures' 123,
    129 n. 39
'George Meredith' 115
'Gérard de Nerval' 83 n. 59
Gioconda 61, 95
'Henrik Ibsen' 114 n. 27
'Hymn to Earth' 107, 114 n. 38
Images of Good and Evil 111
    'Perfect Grief' 158 n. 9
    'Venetian Night' 120
'The Improvements of Rome' 114 n. 36
'In Praise of Gypsies' 105, 146, 153, 156, 157 n. 8,
    158 n. 13, 159 n. 51
An Introduction to the Study of Browning 133,
    143 n. 23, 163
'J.-K. Huysmans' 113 n. 14
Journal de Henry Luxulyan 115 n. 55
Knave of Hearts 82 n. 17, 128 n. 18, 129 n. 30
    'Venice' 121
Lesbia and Other Poems:
    'The Gypsy's Song' 157 n. 5
'La Littérature anglaise' 105, 113 n. 16
London: A Book of Aspects 8, 73, 82 n. 18, 132, 137
London Nights 105, 106, 161
    'At the Stage Door' 40 n. 30
    'Intermezzo: Venetian Nights' 120
    'La Mélinite: Moulin Rouge' 40 n. 28
    'Preface' to the second edition 2, 9 n. 5, 106
    'Prologue' 14, 27 n. 13
    'Stella Maris' 106
    'Venetian Nights V: Alle Zattere' 128 n. 7
    'White Magic' 148
Love's Cruelty:
    'Alvisi Contarini' 158 n. 9
'Maeterlinck as a Mystic' 84, 92, 100 n. 32
'Mains' 108
'Le Mauvais-Riche' 115 n. 47
The Memoirs of Arthur Symons 10 n. 17, 142
    'Bohemian Years in London' 83 n. 45,
    'Frank Harris and Oscar Wilde' 169 n. 4
    'Lillie Langtry and Oscar Wilde' 170 n. 29
    'Mental Collapse in Italy' 83 n. 60
    'Sex and Aversion' 170 n. 30
Mes souvenirs 109, 148, 158 n. 27
'"Monna Vanna"' 90, 100 n. 18
'Le Mouvement symboliste dans la littérature'
    115 n. 44
'Le Mouvement symboliste: introduction'
    116 n. 76
'Music in Venice' 121, 129 n. 29, 129 n. 31,
    129 n. 50
'A New French Quarterly' 115 n. 46
'Nini Patte-en-l'air' 157

'A Note on George Meredith' 113 n. 25
'Notes on Toulouse Lautrec and his Lithographs'
    83 n. 42
'Notes on Verlaine's Adventures and Sensations'
    83 n. 43
'Odilon Redon' 113 n. 9
'Paris' 108
'Paul Verlaine' (in *National Review*) 113 n. 14
'Paul Verlaine' (in *New Review*) 113 n. 8
'Philip Massinger' 115 n. 56
'La Place de William Blake' 115 n. 53
Plays, Acting, and Music 6, 10 n. 28, 32, 33, 42, 52,
    90, 100 n. 19, 137, 143 n. 43
    'An Apology for Puppets' 49, 73, 82 n. 19,
        90
    'Mozart in the Mirabell-Garten' 33, 40 n. 22
    'On Writing about Music' 39 n. 11, 39 n. 14
    'Pachmann and the Piano' 30, 33, 39 n. 1,
        40 n. 25, 40 n. 26
    'Preface' 30, 39 n. 2, 44
    'Technique and the Artist' 40 n. 23
'Poèmes' 102 n. 77
Poems in Prose from Charles Baudelaire 74
    'Preface' 82 n. 8
Poésies 102 n. 80, 108, 115 n. 45
Poésies de Choderlos de Laclos 114 n. 29
    'Appendice: une édition perdue des Liaisons
        dangereuses' 106
Portraits anglais 98, 108, 114 n. 30
'*The Princess Maleine* and *The Intruder*' 91,
    100 n. 24, 100 n. 28, 101 n. 43
'Purcell and Ellen Terry' 51 n. 7
'Quatre poèmes' 115 n. 46
'Qu'est-ce que la poésie' 115 n. 46
'The Question of Censorship' 90, 100 n. 18
'Remy de Gourmont' 114 n. 40
The Renaissance:
    'Introduction' 143 n. 39
'Reviews' 101 n. 50
'Robert Buchanan' 102 n. 74
'The Secret of Ancient Music' 70
'Should Translators Improve Their Authors?'
    82 n. 9
Silhouettes:
    'Javanese Dancers' 13–14, 19, 27 n. 9,
    'Music and Memory' 35, 40 n. 32, 105
'The Sinister Guest' 70–75, 78–81, 81 n. 6, 126
'Some French Verse' 113 n. 10
'The Soul of Venice' 120
Spiritual Adventures 6, 7, 10 n. 27, 33, 104, 111,
    112, 123, 124, 157 n. 4, 158 n. 32
    'An Autumn City' 118, 124, 125, 128 n. 4
    'Christian Trevalga' 32, 38, 40 n. 25, 41 n. 56,
        102 n. 77, 124
    'The Death of Peter Waydelin' 109
    'Esther Kahn' 124

'Extracts from the Journal of Henry Luxulyan'
    73, 82 n. 16, 109, 123, 129 n. 41
'A Prelude to Life' 1, 5, 9, 9 n. 1, 9 n. 2,
    9 n. 3, 40 n. 21, 122, 124, 126, 128 n. 2,
    131, 142 n. 3, 149
'Seaward Lackland' 112
'Stéphane Mallarmé' 116 n. 76
Studies in the Elizabethan Drama:
    'Philip Massinger' 110
Studies in Prose and Verse 6, 54, 114 n. 30,
    115 n. 43
    'An Artist in Attitudes: Oscar Wilde' 165,
        170 n. 27, 171 n. 32
    'Gabriele D'Annunzio' 60, 68 n. 26, 68 n. 27
    'What is Poetry?' 39 n. 4
Studies in Seven Arts 6, 7, 12, 15, 16, 18, 26,
    32, 42, 43, 44, 45, 46, 48, 49, 50, 51 n. 2,
    51 n. 3, 52 n. 9, 52 n. 13, 137, 138, 147,
    158 n. 21
    'Beethoven' 39 n. 15, 40 n. 31
    'A New Art of the Stage' 43, 44, 45, 46, 47, 48
    'Pantomime and the Poetic Drama' 48
    'Rodin' (in *Studies in Seven Arts*) 12, 15–16,
        19, 26 n. 1, 26 n. 2, 26 n. 3, 27 n. 22,
        27 n. 23, 43
    'Rodin' (in *From Toulouse-Lautrec to Rodin with
        Some Personal Impressions*) 15, 18, 19,
        27 n. 21
    'A Symbolist Farce' 47
    'To Rhoda' 143 n. 45
    'The World as Ballet' 12, 25, 48–49
Studies in the Elizabethan Drama:
    'Philip Massinger' 110
Studies in Two Literatures 6, 54, 108
'A Study of John Addington Symonds' 132,
    142 n. 8
A Study of Oscar Wilde 9, 160–62, 164–71
'A Study of Toledo' 68 n. 32
'Sur un air de Rameau' 102 n. 74
The Symbolist Movement in Literature 3, 6, 10 n. 27,
    32, 52 n. 19, 54, 66 n. 2, 82 n. 23, 83 n. 49,
    84, 92, 100 n. 29, 100 n. 33, 100 n. 35,
    108, 111, 137–38, 143 n. 34, 158 n. 18, 162,
    170 n. 13
'The Tarot Cards' 148
'Tears in my Heart' 113 n. 8
Titus Andronicus 132
The Torch under the Bushel 61
Tristan and Iseult 32
'Venetian Glamour' 120, 121, 129 n. 24
'Venetian Sensations' 120, 124, 125
'Venice in Easter: Impressions and Sensations'
    120, 121, 128 n. 12
'Venice: on the Giudecca' 128 n. 18
'Venice. Minuet: The Masque of the Ghosts' 121
'Verlaine in London' 113 n. 8

'Vernon Lee on "The Ring and the Book"' 134
The Victim 57
'Villiers de l'Isle-Adam' (in *Athenaeum*) 81 n. 3, 82 n. 33
'Villiers de l'Isle-Adam' (in *Woman's World*) 113 n. 6, 160
'Villiers de l'Isle-Adam' (in *Illustrated London*) 83 n. 48
'Villiers de l'Isle-Adam' (in *Fortnightly Review*) 83 n. 49, 83 n. 50, 83 n. 57
Wanderings 129 n. 18, 132
    'A Masque of Kings in Venice' 122, 128 n. 18
'Whistler' 107, 114 n. 35
William Blake 111
    'Preface' 109
'William Morris' 106
'William Morris's Prose' 114 n. 30
collaborations with, and mentions in, periodicals:
    L'Antée 93, 98, 101 n. 42, 102 n. 74, 102 n. 75, 107–08, 115 n. 43, 115 n. 44, 115 n. 47, 115 n. 48
    Academy 59, 62, 90, 97, 100 n. 18, 101 n. 58, 106, 113 n. 8
    Art Review 113 n. 9
    Athenaeum 6, 70, 81 n. 3, 82 n. 33, 91, 92, 97, 100 n. 24, 105, 133 n. 10, 113 n. 17, 122, 129 n. 33, 164, 166, 171 n. 32
    Black and White 70
    Bookman's Journal and Print Collector 71, 82 n. 9
    Dance Research 27 n. 11
    Dome 48
    English Review 70, 75, 80, 81, 81 n. 6, 98, 102 n. 72
    Fortnightly Review 15, 31, 36, 39 n. 6, 70, 77, 78, 79, 83 n. 49, 83 n. 50, 83 n. 51, 83 n. 57, 83 n. 59, 105, 113 n. 14, 113 n. 25, 142 n. 8
    Gypsy 157
    Harper's New Monthly Magazine 66 n. 1, 100 n. 29, 120, 128 n. 12, 128 n. 17, 143 n. 34
    Illustrated London News 70, 77, 83 n. 48
    Imperial and Colonial Magazine Review 68 n. 26
    Journal of the Gypsy Lore Society 105, 146, 157 n. 8
    Little Review 92, 101 n. 38
    Mask 49, 52 n. 10
    Mercure de France 95, 103, 104–08, 111, 112, 113 n. 7, 113 n. 11, 113 n. 13, 113 n. 14, 113 n. 16, 113 n. 21, 113 n. 24, 114 n. 26, 114 n. 27, 114 n. 29, 114 n. 30, 116 n. 68
    Mercure musical 106, 114 n. 33
    Monthly Review 45, 68 n. 32
    Nation 100 n. 5
    National Review 105, 113 n. 9, 113 n. 14
    Navire d'argent 104, 109, 115 n. 53
    New Review 113 n. 8
    Outlook 45, 114 n. 29, 115 n. 46

    Pall Mall Gazette 9 n. 4, 33, 39 n. 20
    La Plume 27 n. 19, 106, 114 n. 26, 114 n. 31
    Quarterly Review 114 n. 27, 171 n. 32
    Revue européenne 109
    La Revue franco-anglaise 107
    Revue indépendante 113 n. 9
    Revue politique et littéraire 110, 115 n. 56
    Saturday Review 33, 37, 67 n. 15, 68 n. 32, 74, 82 n. 19, 94, 98, 101 n. 48, 101 n. 50, 107, 113 n. 10, 114 n. 30, 114 n. 40, 120, 129 n. 24, 129 n. 25, 129 n. 29, 164, 165, 171 n. 32
    Savoy 2, 37, 54, 95, 100 n. 6, 104, 105, 110, 112, 124, 164
    La Société nouvelle 99, 102 n. 77
    Speaker 161, 163, 171 n. 32
    Star 6, 14, 42, 45, 51 n. 7, 113 n. 8, 157
    Temporel 116 n. 76
    Time 9 n. 4
    The Times 90
    Times Literary Supplement 3, 9 n. 9, 9 n. 10
    Two Worlds 76, 77, 83 n. 42, 83 n. 43, 83 n. 54
    Two Worlds Monthly 76, 83 n. 46
    Vers et prose 108, 115 n. 46
    Weekly Critical Review 107, 114 n. 35, 114 n. 36, 114 n. 38
    Woman's World 9, 70, 113 n. 6, 160
subjects:
    Aestheticism 2, 3–4, 6, 25, 32–33, 56–60, 66, 74, 111, 131–33, 135–36, 138, 141, 145–46, 147, 148, 153, 156–57, 162, 164
    Arts and Crafts 43
    Austrian culture 7
    avant-garde 2, 3, 12, 26, 38, 62, 104, 105, 106, 108, 137, 146, 169
    ballet and dance 1, 2, 7, 12–15, 20–26, 27 n. 11, 34, 42–43, 47, 48–49, 52 n. 9, 72–73, 119, 138, 149
    Belgian culture 6, 8, 54, 84–100
    Bloomsbury Group 38
    the city 8, 62, 89, 107, 119, 131–32, 134, 137, 141–42 n. 1
        London 1, 13–14, 74, 119, 121, 124, 128, 137–41
        Paris 2, 13–14, 76, 120, 128, 138
        Venice 2, 3, 8, 32, 118–29, 132, 138, 140, 141 n. 1, 142 n. 6
    cosmopolitanism 1–2, 6, 8, 33, 36, 38, 57, 95, 99, 103–05, 106–07, 109, 112, 141, 145, 156–57
    critic 1–8, 9 n. 6, 12–15, 17, 26, 27 n. 11, 30–33, 35–36, 38–39, 42–43, 54, 61, 70, 75, 77, 78–79, 82 n. 23, 84, 91, 93, 94, 95, 98, 103, 104, 108, 111, 112, 114 n. 27, 122, 125, 133, 136–37, 140, 146, 154, 157, 160, 162, 163, 169, 159 n. 1
    cultural mediator 2, 6, 7–8, 9, 54–68, 84–102, 103–15, 141, 146, 148, 157

Decadence 2–5, 7, 9, 54–62, 64, 66, 71–78, 81, 90–93, 104, 110–11, 132–33, 135, 145, 146–49, 153–57, 161–63, 164, 167, 169
flâneur/flânerie 1, 140–41, 147–48, 155–56
French culture 2–3, 4, 5–6, 7–8, 12, 15–20, 26, 35–37, 54, 55–56, 57–58, 70–81, 84, 88, 89–90, 97, 98, 99, 103–16, 134–35, 139
German culture 17, 90
Gesamtkunstwerk and the 'Seven Arts' 4, 7, 12–16, 18, 19–26, 30–32, 38–39, 42–52, 108, 137, 138, 139
Gypsilorism and the gypsy 1, 9, 105, 145–59
Impressionism 2, 3, 8, 35, 37, 89, 94, 131, 120, 123, 131, 132, 134, 135, 137, 138, 139, 141, 142 n. 10, 147
Italian culture 3, 4, 6, 7, 8, 32, 54–68, 73, 120–22, 131–34, 137, 139, 140, 141
life 1–2, 3, 5, 8, 15–16, 19, 27 n. 15, 32, 35, 74, 76–77, 79, 86, 99, 104, 108, 111–14, 118–19, 120–21, 122, 124–28, 131, 133–34, 145–46, 149, 161, 167
'Silhouette' (pseudonym) 6, 14, 51 n. 7
Modernism 2, 3, 4–5, 7, 8, 9, 20, 59, 66, 71, 74, 81, 104, 109–10, 111, 137, 140, 141, 142 n. 5, 146, 147, 156, 157, 160, 163, 168
music 1, 2, 4, 6, 7, 12, 21, 23, 30–41, 42–44, 46, 48, 50, 107, 120, 138
music-hall 1, 6, 14–15, 42, 105, 140
Naturalism 97
nervous breakdown, *see* life
Orientalism 146–49, 151, 156, 158 n. 29
painting 12, 13, 15, 16, 43, 76, 104, 138, 139
photography 19, 22–23, 133, 137–39
poet 1, 2, 3–4, 5, 6, 7, 10 n. 19, 12, 13–17, 22, 25, 26, 31, 34–35, 36, 43, 48, 63, 64, 74, 84, 103, 104–06, 107, 108, 109, 110, 111, 112, 122, 132, 146, 148, 149, 161
Primitivism 149, 154–55
progress 154–55, 156
the puppet/(Über-)marionette 7, 19, 22, 43, 49–51, 73, 91–92, 166, 168
racism 154–55
religion 1, 47, 50–51, 74, 111, 118, 154, 161
Romani culture 145–46, 148–52, 153
Rhymers' Club 2, 12, 14, 104–05, 160, 162
sculpture 6, 7, 12–13, 15–20, 22–26, 43, 50, 138
Symbolism 3, 4, 7,12, 25, 34, 42, 48–51, 61–62, 65, 77, 78, 84–99, 103, 104, 106, 108, 111, 112, 131, 135, 138, 141, 154, 164
theatre 2, 4, 6, 7, 12, 13, 32, 42–52, 61–65, 77, 90–93, 94, 95–98, 101 n. 42, 105–06, 108, 110, 124, 140, 157 n. 2, 163, 167–68
translator and translated 3, 4, 5, 6, 7–8, 54–68, 70–77, 78, 81, 81 n. 6, 84, 90, 91, 92, 95–99, 103–12, 122, 140, 146, 165

travel writing 4, 6, 8, 62, 107, 118–28, 131–44, 145, 147–48, 153, 156
vagabond 1–2, 5, 8, 9, 141
Yellow Nineties 105, 111
Symons, Rhoda 15, 19, 27 n. 15, 43, 120, 123, 149, 150

Tennyson, Alfred Lord 165
Thomas, Édouard 106, 108, 114 n. 30, 114 n. 32, 114 n. 33, 115 n. 46
Thomas, Louis 98, 99, 106, 108, 114 n. 28, 114 n. 29, 114 n. 30, 114 n. 32, 114 n. 33, 115 n. 46
Thompson, Francis 107
Thomson, Clive 68 n. 25
Tiberius 166
Tiboni, Edoardo 67 n. 13
Tickner, Lisa 147, 158 n. 20
Tintoretto (Jacopo Robusti) 119
Tolstoy, Leo 37
Tosi, Guy 67 n. 4, 67 n. 18
Toulouse-Lautrec, Henri de 76, 81 n. 6
Tourneur, Cyril 91
Trausil, Hans 28 n. 32
Trevor, John 40 n. 34
Trumpener, Katie 153, 159 n. 48

Umberto I of Savoy, King of Italy 122

Valéry, Paul 109
Valette, Alfred 104
Van den Abeele, Andries 102 n. 73, 114 n. 28, 115 n. 42
Vandeputte, Henri 98
Van Gennep, Arnold 105, 113 n. 15
Van Lerberghe, Charles 8, 84, 93–94, 101 n. 44, 101 n. 51
Van Puymbroeck, Birgit 115 n. 41
Van Rysselberghe, Théo 96
Van Vechten, Carl 75
Vasari, Giorgio 18
Verbeke, Édouard 98
Verhaeren, Émile 3, 6, 8, 54, 61, 68 n. 30, 84, 89, 92, 95–98, 99, 101 n. 57, 101 n. 60, 101 n. 63, 102 n. 70, 102 n. 79
Verlaine, Paul 2, 3, 6, 12, 34, 35, 37, 54, 65, 73, 76–77, 88, 89, 91, 104, 105, 108, 109, 112, 113 n. 8, 113 n. 18, 114 n. 26, 115 n. 46, 146, 162
Villiers de l'Isle-Adam, Philippe de 7, 54, 70–81, 81 n. 2, 82 n. 12, 82 n. 28, 84, 89, 97, 103, 104, 113 n. 6, 126
Villon, François 165
Vivaria, Kassandra 67 n. 16
Vizetelly, Henry 75
Vogüé, Eugène-Melchior de 55–56, 57, 58, 67 n. 7, 67 n. 19, 107

Wade, Allen 3, 9 n. 9
Wagner, Richard 32, 33, 43, 44, 46, 48, 119
Warner, Eric 10 n. 18, 168, 171 n. 35
Watson, Jon 81 n. 1
Watts-Dunton, Theodore 107, 148, 151, 158 n. 42, 158 n. 41
Waugh, Arthur 113 n. 8
Webster, John 91
Weir, David 10 n. 24
Welby, Thomas Earle 110
Weliver, Phyllis 40 n. 47
Wells, Herbert George 106
Whistler, James Abbott McNeill 17, 32, 36, 37, 107, 167
Whitman, Walt 91
Whitridge, Arnold 143 n. 31
Whittington-Egan, Richard 129 n. 46
Wilde, Oscar 2, 3, 5, 9, 60, 74, 89, 98, 106, 111, 121, 132, 146, 147, 148, 154, 155, 157 n. 6, 160–69, 169 n. 4, 169 n. 5, 169 n. 6, 170 n. 10, 170 n. 22, 170 n. 23, 170 n. 28, 171 n. 32

Wilhelm II, German Emperor and King of Prussia 122
Willard, Frank, *see* Flynt, Josiah
Willard, Katherine 35, 141
Wilson, Simon 41 n. 50
Witts, Noel 29 n. 59
Wolff, Kurt H. 159 n. 55
Woodhouse, John 67 n. 13, 68 n. 29, 68 n. 43
Woolf, Virginia 3, 38, 140, 144 n. 55
Wratislaw, Theodore 4

Yates, Dora 149, 150, 153, 158 n. 37
Yeats, William Butler 3, 12, 13, 14, 26 n. 5, 34, 40 n. 27, 44, 47, 78, 90, 107, 108, 109, 111, 125, 127, 146, 160, 162, 164, 165
Ysaÿe, Eugène 33

Zimmern, Helen 68 n. 28
Zola, Émile 3, 54, 56, 75, 88, 89, 95

www.ingramcontent.com/pod-product-compliance
Lightning Source LLC
LaVergne TN
LVHW061251060426
835507LV00017B/2011